Poetry By Heart

Poetry By Heart

Poems for Learning and Reciting

Edited by
Julie Blake, Mike Dixon,
Andrew Motion and Jean Sprackland

VIKING
an imprint of
PENGUIN BOOKS

VIKING

Published by the Penguin Group
Penguin Books Ltd, 80 Strand, London WC2R ORL, England
Penguin Group (USA) Inc., 375 Hudson Street, New York, New York 10014, USA
Penguin Group (Canada), 90 Eglinton Avenue East, Suite 700, Toronto, Ontario, Canada M4P 2Y3
(a division of Pearson Penguin Canada Inc.)
Penguin Ireland, 25 St Stephen's Green, Dublin 2, Ireland (a division of Penguin Books Ltd)
Penguin Group (Australia), 707 Collins Street, Melbourne, Victoria 3008, Australia
(a division of Pearson Australia Group Pty Ltd)
Penguin Books India Pvt Ltd, 11 Community Centre, Panchsheel Park, New Delhi – 110 017, India
Penguin Group (NZ), 67 Apollo Drive, Rosedale, Auckland 0632, New Zealand
(a division of Pearson New Zealand Ltd)
Penguin Books (South Africa) (Pty) Ltd, Block D, Rosebank Office Park,
181 Jan Smuts Avenue, Parktown North, Gauteng 2193, South Africa

Penguin Books Ltd, Registered Offices: 80 Strand, London WC2R ORL, England

www.penguin.com

First published 2014
001

Set in Sabon LT Std 10.5/14 pt
Typeset by Palimpsest Book Production Limited, Falkirk, Stirlingshire
Printed in Great Britain by Clays Ltd, St Ives plc

A CIP catalogue record for this book is available from the British Library

ISBN: 978-0-241-18554-4

www.greenpenguin.co.uk

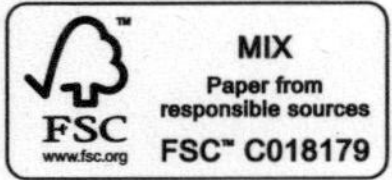

Contents

Introduction

In its deepest traditions, poetry is an acoustic form. Praise-songs and battle-songs, history-narratives, love-chants and spells, ceremonial hymns: in the mead hall and thereabouts, all these things were delivered to their audiences with an assumption that the sound of words spoken aloud was an essential part of their meaning.

When printed books were invented, and as more eyes were able to see words on a page than ever before, this sound world modified. Gradually, it became more and more involved with the page world – with the arrangement and look of words, and with the idea that the 'meaning' of a poem depended on the understandings generated through the eye as much as it did on those received through the ear. Or perhaps depended more on the eye than it did on the ear. In fact, as generation upon generation of silent readers followed, the ear became increasingly like a sleeping partner in the appreciation of poetry. Its appetites were fed by conversations about metre and rhyme but its hunger to hear things out loud was generally ignored or left unsatisfied.

As things have turned out, the Internet, that very new-fangled thing, has been able to restore the very old-fangled truths about poetry's deep nature. About breath and noise. About acoustic. The Poetry Archive proves this. It was launched in 2005 to host recordings of poets reading their own work, and now has a large audience. At the time of writing, around 200,000 people use the site every month, and every month they listen to over a million pages of poetry: English-language poetry, ranging from the earliest recordings (Tennyson and Browning) to brand-new contemporaries; and all wrapped around with editorial material that gives useful information and opinion.

The Poetry Archive celebrates what Robert Frost called 'the sound of sense', as it is exemplified by poets themselves. And, in 2013, this celebration was elaborated into Poetry By Heart – an annual competition for secondary schools in England which asks contestants to learn two or three poems and be judged on their recitations. This seems to have awoken a half-forgotten pleasure. In the first year alone, many hundreds of schools registered for the competition; in the second, the number of competing schools increased by 20 per cent.

Until now, students entering Poetry By Heart have been invited to choose which poems to recite from the competition's website (poetrybyheart.org.uk). This year, to coincide with the third year of the competition, we are publishing the anthology as a book as well. This book. Partly because it allows the collection to have a different sort of permanence. Partly because it allows the old alliance of page and ear to be reaffirmed. And also because we feel the collection deserves an audience beyond that of the competition and the website.

So what were our guiding principles as we put the anthology together? Our starting point was a wish to give as much collateral benefit to the competition as possible – in particular, by encouraging students to read more widely than any curriculum easily allows. For this reason, we ask them to choose one poem written before 1914 and one written after, which is why we have ordered the anthology chronologically, as far as is possible, by date of publication or composition. We have in most cases regularized the spelling of older poems to make them more immediately accessible for recitation purposes, though we recognize that something of the historical authenticity of our changing language may be obscured in that way. We have tried to bring as much variety into our selection as possible: almost unknown poems and familiar poems from the mainstream; love poems and war poems; funny poems and heartbroken poems; poems that re-create the world we know and poems written on the dark side of the moon.

And all have been chosen with a view to their being recited out loud. Not booming poems, necessarily (though there are a few of them), but poems that in striking, fascinating and subtle ways rely as much on sound as they do on sense to communicate their meaning. Poems that allow for no separation between these activities, that live in our ears just as resoundingly as they do in our eyes.

We hope poetry recitation is recovered as an enjoyable way to learn about poetry in schools. And we hope the sound waves of this anthology will dilate beyond the confines of the competition and into all lives everywhere, reminding us about the time-honoured qualities of poetry in new ways.

Enjoy it.

Julie Blake
Mike Dixon
Andrew Motion
Jean Sprackland

Editors' Note

Poetry By Heart is a poetry recitation competition for schools and colleges in England that was launched in 2013. Young people aged fourteen to eighteen learn two or three poems by heart from the collection originally published on our website, poetrybyheart.org.uk, and now in this volume. They compete in a school or college competition from which a winner progresses to a county contest; county contest winners take part in regional semi-finals, and the last eight students compete in a national final judged by contemporary poets and poetry experts. Our winners to date have been Kaiti Soultana of Bilborough College, Nottingham, and Matilda Neill of Whitley Bay High School, Tyne and Wear.

Poetry By Heart is an educational initiative of the Poetry Archive (poetryarchive.org, the premier online collection of recordings of poets reading their own work), which was developed in association with The Full English (thefullenglish.org.uk, a research-informed curriculum workshop). It is currently supported financially by the Department for Education.

We have enjoyed collaborating with a host of people and organizations to make Poetry By Heart happen: the many inspiring teachers and students who had the courage and imagination to get involved from the beginning; Sandy Nairne and his Learning Team colleagues at the National Portrait Gallery; Paul Munden and his colleagues at the National Association of Writers in Education, the Poetry Society and Writing West Midlands; the National Association for the Teaching of English and colleagues running PGCE and Teach First programmes; Michael Proffitt and his colleagues at Oxford University Press; the Principal and Fellows of Homerton College, Cambridge; the team at the First World War Digital Poetry Archive; Steve Young at the Poetry Foundation, who gave us so much help getting started, and our colleagues running related competitions in Ireland and Canada; Professor Catherine Robson of New York University, whose history of poetry recitation is one of our intellectual touchstones, and David Whitley and Debbie Pullinger at the Faculty of Education, Cambridge University, whose Poetry and Memory research project will help to theorize further what we are doing in practical terms.

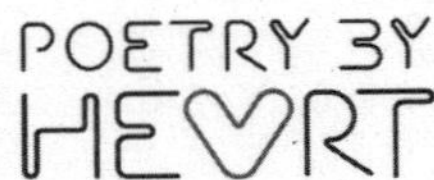

Acknowledgements

The editors would like to thank all of the people associated with Poetry By Heart who have contributed to the development of this anthology, in both its print and website versions. Special thanks are due to Richard Carrington and Kate Dent of the Poetry Archive for their work in producing the audio recordings that exist on the website and link to the QR codes here; to Tim Shortis of The Full English for his work on the conceptual design of the anthology as an interactive digital timeline; and to our colleagues at Howoco, who made such a beautiful job of creating it; to our colleagues at Oxford University Press for their support in adding free links to valuable digital reference content in the *Oxford English Dictionary* and the *Oxford Dictionary of National Biography*; to the National Portrait Gallery for its support in adding so many wonderful poet portraits to the website; and to Lucy Drury for researching and negotiating all the image permissions; to Peter Osborn and Tom Osborn for creating the video recordings of student recitations which accompany the poems on the website; to Alison Powell, Lorna Smith and Neil Bowen, who researched and drafted additional poem and poet introductions; to Tom Boughen, project assistant at Poetry By Heart, for indefatigable fact-checking, text updating and chasing of copyright permissions; and to Kirstie Orpen, Mike Shortis and Jack Miller, former project assistants, for creating the first version of the website anthology in seven weeks flat; to Kath Lee, Poetry By Heart project coordinator, for keeping track of all the data about student poem choices to inform our decisions about changes to the anthology; and to all our colleagues at Penguin, who saw the value of this anthology and have been such a delight to work with.

About the Poem and Poet Notes

Mike Dixon, co-editor of this book, was commissioned to create the poet and poem notes for the original website, and substantially revised and edited them for this book. These were never designed to say 'This is what you should think about the poem.' On the contrary, we wanted them to anticipate questions readers might have about the poems and to ask a few of our own to stimulate further thought. We intended the commentaries to be self-effacing but not tentative; confident but not dogmatic. Our aim was to prompt and suggest; to explain historical and social context where appropriate but to avoid it where it seemed not to help a reader's appreciation of a poem.

We did not, however, want to be suggest that 'a poem can mean anything you want it to mean'. Instead, our intention was to draw attention to the craft of writing, to the shapes and sounds of language and, most certainly, we wanted to encourage enjoyment in wrestling with ambiguity. The Poetry By Heart commentaries are designed to stimulate awareness of ambiguity and to foster debate about the realities individuals may find in their responses to poems in the anthology. In dealing with these two hundred poems, we set out to be respectful but not reverential; to initiate conversation and dialogue. To put it simply, we were aiming to allow a reader to respond to a poem without putting ourselves in the way.

About the QR Codes

In the notes, you will find QR codes which either link to recordings of older poems read by contemporary poets, or to recordings of the poet reading their own poem. This is part of the Poetry Archive's ongoing recording programme and not all poems and poets have yet been recorded. To use these QR codes, you need to download a QR code scanner on to your smartphone or tablet. Scan the code in this book with the scanner, and the poem page on the Poetry Archive website will open (as long as you have Internet access). Click the play button to listen. These recordings are also available to buy in the Poetry Archive downloads store, if you would like to save them and listen to them offline.

About the Sequence of the Poems

The Poetry By Heart competition anthology was always conceived as a timeline. The idea was to help students and teachers to 'see' poetry as a conversation across time, with influences, connections and arguments mapped over a thousand years, with changes in literary language and poetic convention flowing through it. We selected one poem by each poet to help give the broadest view possible within a modestly sized collection.

To make the poems appear on the digital timeline on the website, we had to 'pin' each poem to a specific year. This is no mean feat, as there is rarely any such thing as *the* poem: early versions appearing in magazines and small press publications are not necessarily the same as versions in later collections or anthologies. What is counted as the publication date depends on which version is chosen. Our default has been to select the first printed collection in which the poem appeared, not the first publication in a magazine or a pamphlet.

Then there is the difficulty that, sometimes, a poet's work is published only posthumously, such as happened in the case of Gerard Manley Hopkins. If we had fixed the poem to the publication date in this case, there would have been some strange chronological effects. His poem 'Inversnaid' was first published in 1918, although it was written in 1881 and Hopkins died in 1889. This would have been confusing on our timeline website, where the dates of the poet's birth and death appear alongside the date of the poem. Our default has therefore been to use publication dates where these exist within the lifespan of the poet, and to use composition dates where the poems were published after the poet's death.

In preparing the publication of the anthology in this printed volume, we retained this chronological sequence. We hope you will enjoy the time travelling, forwards and back, which it involves.

Anonymous

Beowulf (ll. 736–90)

Modern English version by Seamus Heaney

Mighty and canny,
Hygelac's kinsman was keenly watching
for the first move the monster would make.
Nor did the creature keep him waiting
but struck suddenly and started in;
he grabbed and mauled a man on his bench,
bit into his bone-lappings, bolted down his blood
and gorged on him in lumps, leaving the body
utterly lifeless, eaten up
hand and foot. Venturing closer,
his talon was raised to attack Beowulf
where he lay on the bed, he was bearing in
with open claw when the alert hero's
comeback and armlock forestalled him utterly.
The captain of evil discovered himself
in a handgrip harder than anything
he had ever encountered in any man
on the face of the earth. Every bone in his body
quailed and recoiled, but he could not escape.
He was desperate to flee to his den and hide
with the devil's litter, for in all his days
he had never been clamped or cornered like this.
Then Hygelac's trusty retainer recalled
his bedtime speech, sprang to his feet
and got a firm hold. Fingers were bursting,
the monster back-tracking, the man overpowering.
The dread of the land was desperate to escape,
to take a roundabout road and flee
to his lair in the fens. The latching power
in his fingers weakened; it was the worst trip

the terror-monger had taken to Heorot.
And now the timbers trembled and sang,
a hall-session that harrowed every Dane
inside the stockade: stumbling in fury,
the two contenders crashed through the building.
The hall clattered and hammered, but somehow
survived the onslaught and kept standing:
it was handsomely structured, a sturdy frame
braced with the best of blacksmith's work
inside and out. The story goes
that as the pair struggled, mead-benches were smashed
and sprung off the floor, gold fittings and all.
Before then, no Shielding elder would believe
there was any power or person upon earth
capable of wrecking their horn-rigged hall
unless the burning embrace of a fire
engulf it in flame. Then an extraordinary
wail arose, and bewildering fear
came over the Danes. Everyone felt it
who heard that cry as it echoed off the wall,
a God-cursed scream and strain of catastrophe,
the howl of the loser, the lament of the hell-serf
keening his wound. He was overwhelmed,
manacled tight by the man who of all men
was foremost and strongest in the days of this life.

The Gawain Poet

Sir Gawain and the Green Knight (ll. 713–39)

Mony klyf he ouerclambe in contrayez straunge,
Fer floten fro his frendez fremedly he rydez.
At vche warþe oþer water þer þe wyȝe passed
He fonde a foo hym byfore bot ferly hit were,
And þat so foule and so felle þat feȝt hym byhode.
So mony meruayl bi mount þer þe mon fyndez,
Hit were to tore for to telle of þe tenþe dole.
Sumwhyle wyth wormez he werrez and with wolues als,
Sumwhyle wyth wodwos þat woned in þe knarrez,
Boþe wyth bullez and berez and borez oþerquyle,
And etaynez þat hym anelede of þe heȝe felle;
Nade he ben duȝty and dryȝe and dryȝtyn had serued,
Douteles he hade ben ded and dreped ful ofte.
For werre wrathed hym not so much þat wynter was wors,
When þe colde cler water fro þe cloudez schadden,
And fres er hit falle myȝt to þe fale erþe;
Ner slayn wyth þe slete he sleped in his yrnes
Mo nyȝtez þen innoghe in naked rokkez,
Þer as claterande fro þe crest þe colde borne rennez,
And henged heȝe ouer his hede in hard ysse ikkles.
Þus in peryl and payne and plytes ful harde
Bi contray cayrez þis knyȝt tyl krystmasse euen,
    Al one;
    Be knyȝt wel þat tyde
    To mary made his mone,
    Þat ho hym red to ryde
    And wysse hym to sum wone.

Modern English version by Simon Armitage

In a strange region he scales steep slopes;
far from his friends he cuts a lonely figure.
Where he bridges a brook or wades through a waterway
ill fortune brings him face to face with a foe
so foul or fierce he is bound to use force.
So momentous are his travels among the mountains
to tell just a tenth would be a tall order.
Here he scraps with serpents and snarling wolves,
here he tangles with wodwos causing trouble in the crags,
or with bulls and bears and the odd wild boar.
Hard on his heels through the highlands come giants.
Only diligence and faith in the face of death
will keep him from becoming a corpse or carrion.
And the wars were one thing, but winter was worse:
clouds shed their cargo of crystallized rain
which froze as it fell to the frost-glazed earth.
With nerves frozen numb he napped in his armour,
bivouacked in the blackness amongst bare rocks
where melt-water streamed from the snow-capped summits
and high overhead hung chandeliers of ice.
So in peril and pain Sir Gawain made progress,
criss-crossing the countryside until Christmas
Eve. Then
at that time of tiding,
he prayed to highest heaven.
Let Mother Mary guide him
towards some house or haven.

Geoffrey Chaucer

The Wife of Bath (ll. 445–76)

(from The General Prologue)

A GOOD WIF was ther of biside BATHE,
But she was somdel deef and that was scathe.
Of clooth-makyng she hadde swich an haunt,
She passed hem of Ypres and of Gaunt.
In al the parisshe wif ne was ther noon
That to the offrynge bifore hire sholde goon,
And if ther dide, certeyn so wrooth was she,
That she was out of alle charitee.
Hir coverchiefs ful fyne weren of ground, –
I dorste swere they weyeden ten pound, –
That on a Sonday weren upon hir heed.
Hir hosen weren of fyn scarlet reed
Ful streite yteyd, and shoes ful moyste and newe.
Boold was hir face, and fair, and reed of hewe.
She was a worthy womman al hir lyve:
Housbondes at chirche dore she hadde fyve,
Withouten oother compaignye in youthe, –
But therof nedeth nat to speke as nowthe.
And thries hadde she been at Jerusalem;
She hadde passed many a straunge strem;
At Rome she hadde been, and at Boloigne,
In Galice at Seint-Jame, and at Coloigne,
She koude muchel of wandrynge by the weye.
Gat-tothed was she, soothly for to seye.
Upon an amblere esily she sat,
Y-wympled wel, and on hir heed an hat
As brood as is a bokeler or a targe;
A foot-mantel aboute hir hipes large,
And on hir feet a paire of spores sharpe.
In felaweshipe wel koude she laughe and carpe.
Of remedies of love she knew per chaunce,
For she koude of that art the olde daunce.

Anonymous

'I syng of a mayden'

I syng of a mayden
That is makeles:
King of alle kinges
to here sone che chees.

He cam also stille
Ther his moder was
As dew in Aprylle,
That fallyt on the gras.

He cam also stille
To his modres bowr
As dew in Aprylle,
That falleth on the flowr.

He cam also stille
Ther his moder lay
As dew in Aprylle,
That falleth on the spray.

Moder and mayden
Was nevere noon but she:
Well may swich a lady
Godes moder be.

Modern English version by David Breeden

I sing of a maiden
That is matchless,
King of all kings
For her son she chose.

He came as still
Where his mother was
As dew in April
That falls on the grass.

He came as still
To his mother's bower
As dew in April
That falls on the flower.

He came as still
Where his mother lay
As dew in April
That falls on the spray.

Mother and maiden
There was never, ever one but she;
Well may such a lady
God's mother be.

Thomas Wyatt

'They flee from me that sometime did me seek'

They flee from me that sometime did me seek
With naked foot, stalking in my chamber.
I have seen them gentle, tame, and meek,
That now are wild and do not remember
That sometime they put themselves in danger
To take bread at my hand; and now they range,
Busily seeking with a continual change.

Thanked be fortune it hath been otherwise
Twenty times better; but once in special,
In thin array after a pleasant guise,
When her loose gown from her shoulders did fall,
And she me caught in her arms long and small;
Therewithall sweetly did me kiss,
And softly said, 'Dear heart, how like you this?'

It was no dream: I lay broad waking.
But all is turned thorough my gentleness
Into a strange fashion of forsaking;
And I have leave to go of her goodness,
And she also to use newfangleness.
But since that I so kindly am served,
I would fain know what she hath deserved.

Philip Sidney

Song from Arcadia

My true-love hath my heart and I have his,
   By just exchange one for the other given:
I hold his dear, and mine he cannot miss;
   There never was a better bargain driven.

His heart in me keeps me and him in one;
   My heart in him his thoughts and senses guides:
He loves my heart, for once it was his own;
   I cherish his because in me it bides.

His heart his wound received from my sight;
   My heart was wounded with his wounded heart;
For as from me on him his hurt did light,
   So still, methought, in me his hurt did smart:

      Both equal hurt, in this change sought our bliss,
      My true-love hath my heart and I have his.

Christopher Marlowe

'In summer's heat, and mid-time of the day'

(after Ovid, *Amores*, Book 1, Poem 5)

In summer's heat, and mid-time of the day,
To rest my limbs, upon a bed I lay,
One window shut the other open stood,
Which gave such light as twinkles in a wood,
Like twilight glimpse at setting of the sun,
Or night being past, and yet not day begun.
Such light to shamefaced maidens must be shown,
Where they may sport, and seem to be unknown.
Then came Corinna in a long loose gown,
Her white neck hid with tresses hanging down:
Resembling fair Semiramis going to bed
Or Laïs of a thousand wooers sped.
I snatched her gown, being thin, the harm was small,
Yet strived she to be covered therewithal.
And striving thus as one that would be cast,
Betrayed herself, and yielded at the last.
Stark naked as she stood before mine eye,
Not one wen in her body could I spy.
What arms and shoulders did I touch and see,
How apt her breasts were to be pressed by me?
How smooth a belly, under her waist saw I?
How large a leg, and what a lusty thigh?
To leave the rest, all liked me passing well,
I clinged her naked body, down she fell,
Judge you the rest: being tired she bade me kiss.
Jove send me more such afternoons as this.

Chidiock Tichborne

Elegy

My prime of youth is but a frost of cares;
My feast of joy is but a dish of pain,
My crop of corn is but a field of tares,
And all my good is but vain hope of gain:
The day is past, and yet I saw no sun,
And now I live, and now my life is done.

My tale was heard, and yet it was not told,
My fruit is fallen, and yet my leaves are green,
My youth is spent, and yet I am not old,
I saw the world, and yet I was not seen;
My thread is cut, and yet it is not spun,
And now I live, and now my life is done.

I sought my death, and found it in my womb,
I looked for life, and saw it was a shade,
I trod the earth, and knew it was my tomb,
And now I die, and now I was but made;
The glass is full, and now my glass is run,
And now I live, and now my life is done.

John Donne

The Good Morrow

I wonder by my troth, what thou and I
  Did, till we loved? Were we not weaned till then?
But sucked on country pleasures, childishly?
  Or snorted we in the Seven Sleepers' den?
'Twas so; but this, all pleasures fancies be.
If ever any beauty I did see,
Which I desired, and got, 'twas but a dream of thee.

And now good morrow to our waking souls,
  Which watch not one another out of fear;
For love, all love of other sights controls,
  And makes one little room an everywhere.
Let sea discoverers to new worlds have gone,
Let maps to others, worlds on worlds have shown,
Let us possess one world; each hath one, and is one.

My face in thine eye, thine in mine appears,
  And true plain hearts do in the faces rest;
Where can we find two better hemispheres
  Without sharp North, without declining West?
Whatever dies was not mixed equally;
If our two loves be one, or, thou and I
Love so alike that none do slacken, none can die.

Walter Ralegh

Walsingham

'As you came from the holy land
   Of Walsingham,
Met you not with my true love
   By the way as you came?'

'How shall I know your true love,
   That have met many a one,
As I went to the holy land,
   That have come, that have gone?'

'She is neither white nor brown,
   But as the heavens fair;
There is none hath a form so divine
   In the earth or the air.'

'Such an one did I meet, good sir,
   Such an angelic face,
Who like a queen, like a nymph, did appear
   By her gait, by her grace.'

'She hath left me here all alone,
   All alone, as unknown,
Who sometimes did me lead with herself,
   And me loved as her own.'

'What's the cause that she leaves you alone,
   And a new way doth take,
Who loved you once as her own,
   And her joy did you make?'

'I have loved her all my youth,
   But now old, as you see,
Love likes not the falling fruit
   From the withered tree.

'Know that Love is a careless child,
   And forgets promise past;
He is blind, he is deaf when he list,
   And in faith never fast.

'His desire is a dureless content
   And a trustless joy;
He is won with a world of despair
   And is lost with a toy.

'Of womenkind such indeed is the love
   Or the word love abused,
Under which many childish desires
   And conceits are excused.

'But true love is a durable fire,
   In the mind ever burning;
Never sick, never old, never dead,
   From itself never turning.'

Mary Sidney Herbert

O

Oh, what a lantern, what a lamp of light
  Is thy pure word to me
    To clear my paths and guide my goings right!
I swore and swear again,
  I of the statutes will observer be,
    Thou justly dost ordain.

The heavy weights of grief oppress me sore:
  Lord, raise me by the word,
    As thou to me didst promise heretofore.
And this unforced praise
  I for an offering bring, accept, O Lord,
    And show to me thy ways.

What if my life lie naked in my hand,
  To every chance exposed!
    Should I forget what thou dost me command?
No, no, I will not stray
  From thy edicts though round about enclosed
    With snares the wicked lay.

Thy testimonies as mine heritage,
  I have retained still:
    And unto them my heart's delight engage,
My heart which still doth bend,
  And only bend to do what thou dost will,
    And do it to the end.

Robert Southwell

The Burning Babe

As I in hoary winter's night stood shivering in the snow,
Surprised I was with sudden heat which made my heart to glow;
And lifting up a fearful eye to view what fire was near,
A pretty Babe all burning bright did in the air appear;
Who, scorched with excessive heat, such floods of tears did shed
As though his floods should quench his flames which with his
  tears were fed.
'Alas!' quoth he, 'but newly born, in fiery heats I fry,
Yet none approach to warm their hearts or feel my fire but I.
My faultless breast the furnace is, the fuel wounding thorns,
Love is the fire, and sighs the smoke, the ashes shame and scorns;
The fuel Justice layeth on, and Mercy blows the coals,
The metal in this furnace wrought are men's defiled souls,
For which, as now on fire I am to work them to their good,
So will I melt into a bath, to wash them in my blood.'
With this he vanished out of sight, and swiftly shrunk away,
And straight I callèd unto mind that it was Christmas day.

Edmund Spenser

'So oft as I her beauty do behold'

(*Amoretti*, LV)

So oft as I her beauty do behold,
And therewith do her cruelty compare,
I marvel of what substance was the mould
The which her made at once so cruel-fair.
Not earth; for her high thoughts more heavenly are:
Not water; for her love doth burn like fire:
Not air; for she is not so light or rare:
Not fire; for she doth freeze with faint desire.

Then needs another element inquire
Whereof she might be made; that is, the sky.
For to the heaven her haughty looks aspire,
And eke her mind is pure immortal high.
  Then, sith to heaven ye likened are the best,
  Be like in mercy as in all the rest.

William Shakespeare

'When that I was and a little tiny boy'

(from *Twelfth Night*)

When that I was and a little tiny boy,
  With hey, ho, the wind and the rain,
A foolish thing was but a toy,
  For the rain it raineth every day.

But when I came to man's estate,
  With hey, ho, the wind and the rain,
'Gainst knaves and thieves men shut their gate,
  For the rain it raineth every day.

But when I came, alas! to wive,
  With hey, ho, the wind and the rain;
By swaggering could I never thrive,
  For the rain it raineth every day.

But when I came unto my beds,
  With hey, ho, the wind and the rain,
With toss-pots still had drunken heads,
  For the rain it raineth every day.

A great while ago the world begun,
  With hey, ho, the wind and the rain,
But that's all one, our play is done,
  And we'll strive to please you every day.

Ben Jonson

To Celia

Drink to me only with thine eyes,
   And I will pledge with mine;
Or leave a kiss but in the cup,
   And I'll not look for wine.
The thirst that from the soul doth rise
   Doth ask a drink divine;
But might I of Jove's nectar sup,
   I would not change for thine.

I sent thee late a rosy wreath,
   Not so much honouring thee
As giving it a hope that there
   It could not withered be.
But thou thereon didst only breathe,
   And sent'st it back to me;
Since when it grows, and smells, I swear,
   Not of itself but thee!

George Herbert

Love

Love bade me welcome. Yet my soul drew back
Guilty of dust and sin.
But quick-eyed Love, observing me grow slack
From my first entrance in,
Drew nearer to me, sweetly questioning,
If I lacked anything.

'A guest,' I answered, 'worthy to be here.'
Love said, 'You shall be he.'
'I the unkind, ungrateful? Ah my dear,
I cannot look on thee.'
Love took my hand, and smiling did reply,
'Who made the eyes but I?'

'Truth Lord, but I have marred them: let my shame
Go where it doth deserve.'
'And know you not,' says Love, 'who bore the blame?'
'My dear, then I will serve.'
'You must sit down,' says Love, 'and taste my meat:'
So I did sit and eat.

Richard Lovelace

To Althea from Prison

When Love with unconfined wings
  Hovers within my gates,
And my divine Althea brings
  To whisper at the grates;
When I lie tangled in her hair,
  And fettered to her eye,
The Gods that wanton in the air
  Know no such liberty.

When flowing cups run swiftly round
  With no allaying Thames,
Our careless heads with roses bound,
  Our hearts with loyal flames;
When thirsty grief in wine we steep,
  When healths and draughts go free,
Fishes that tipple in the deep
  Know no such liberty.

When like committed linnets, I
  With shriller throat shall sing
The sweetness, mercy, majesty,
  And glories of my King;
When I shall voice aloud how good
  He is, how great should be,
Enlarged winds that curl the flood
  Know no such liberty.

Stone walls do not a prison make,
  Nor iron bars a cage;
Minds innocent and quiet take
  That for an hermitage;

If I have freedom in my love,
  And in my soul am free,
Angels alone, that soar above
  Enjoy such liberty.

Robert Herrick

To the Virgins, to Make Much of Time

Gather ye rosebuds while ye may,
   Old Time is still a-flying;
And this same flower that smiles today
   Tomorrow will be dying.

The glorious lamp of heaven, the sun,
   The higher he's a-getting,
The sooner will his race be run,
   And nearer he's to setting.

That age is best which is the first,
   When youth and blood are warmer;
But being spent, the worse, and worst
   Times still succeed the former.

Then be not coy, but use your time,
   And while ye may, go marry;
For having lost but once your prime,
   You may for ever tarry.

Andrew Marvell

Bermudas

Where the remote Bermudas ride
In the ocean's bosom unespied,
From a small boat that rowed along,
The listening winds received this song:
'What should we do but sing His praise
That led us through the watery maze
Unto an isle so long unknown,
And yet far kinder than our own?
Where He the huge sea monsters wracks,
That lift the deep upon their backs.
He lands us on a grassy stage,
Safe from the storms and prelate's rage.
He gave us this eternal Spring
Which here enamels every thing,
And sends the fowls to us in care,
On daily visits through the air.
He hangs in shades the orange bright,
Like golden lamps in a green night;
And does in the pomegranates close
Jewels more rich than Ormus shows.
He makes the figs our mouths to meet
And throws the melons at our feet;
But apples plants of such a price,
No tree could ever bear them twice.
With cedars, chosen by His hand,
From Lebanon, He stores the land,
And makes the hollow seas that roar
Proclaim the ambergris on shore.
He cast (of which we rather boast)
The Gospel's pearl upon our coast,
And in these rocks for us did frame

A temple, where to sound His name.
Oh let our voice His praise exalt,
Till it arrive at Heaven's vault;
Which thence (perhaps) rebounding, may
Echo beyond the Mexique Bay.'
  Thus sung they in the English boat
An holy and a cheerful note,
And all the way, to guide their chime,
With falling oars they kept the time.

Katherine Philips

Epitaph

(*On her son H.P. at St Syth's Church where her body also lies interred.*)

What on Earth deserves our trust?
Youth and beauty both are dust.
Long we gathering are with pain,
What one moment calls again.
Seven years childless marriage past,
A son, a son is born at last:
So exactly limbed and fair,
Full of good spirits, mien, and air,
As a long life promised,
Yet, in less than six weeks dead.
Too promising, too great a mind
In so small room to be confined:
Therefore, as fit in Heaven to dwell,
He quickly broke the prison shell.
So the subtle alchemist,
Can't with Hermes Seal resist
The powerful spirit's subtler flight,
But t'will bid him long good night.
And so the sun if it arise
Half so glorious as his eyes,
Like this infant, takes a shroud,
Buried in a morning cloud.

Henry King

An Exequy to His Matchless Never to be Forgotten Friend (ll. 81–120)

Sleep on, my love, in thy cold bed,
Never to be disquieted!
My last goodnight! Thou wilt not wake
Till I thy fate shall overtake;
Till age, or grief, or sickness must
Marry my body to that dust
It so much loves, and fill the room
My heart keeps empty in thy tomb.
Stay for me there, I will not fail
To meet thee in that hollow vale.
And think not much of my delay;
I am already on the way,
And follow thee with all the speed
Desire can make, or sorrows breed.
Each minute is a short degree,
And every hour a step towards thee.
At night when I betake to rest,
Next morn I rise nearer my west
Of life, almost by eight hours' sail,
Than when sleep breathed his drowsy gale.
Thus from the sun my bottom steers,
And my day's compass downward bears;
Nor labour I to stem the tide
Through which to thee I swiftly glide.
'Tis true, with shame and grief I yield,
Thou like the van first took'st the field,
And gotten hast the victory
In thus adventuring to die
Before me, whose more years might crave

A just precedence in the grave.
But hark! my pulse like a soft drum
Beats my approach, tells thee I come;
And slow howe'er my marches be,
I shall at last sit down by thee.
  The thought of this bids me go on,
And wait my dissolution
With hope and comfort. Dear (forgive
The crime) I am content to live
Divided, with but half a heart,
Till we shall meet and never part.

Anne Bradstreet

Verses upon the Burning of Our House

In silent night when rest I took,
For sorrow near I did not look,
I wakened was with thundering noise
And piteous shrieks of dreadful voice.
That fearful sound of 'fire' and 'fire,'
Let no man know is my desire.
I, starting up, the light did spy,
And to my God my heart did cry
To strengthen me in my distress
And not to leave me succourless.
Then, coming out, behold a space
The flame consume my dwelling place.
And when I could no longer look,
I blest His grace that gave and took,
That laid my goods now in the dust.
Yea, so it was, and so 'twas just.
It was his own; it was not mine.
Far be it that I should repine,
He might of all justly bereft
But yet sufficient for us left.
When by the ruins oft I past
My sorrowing eyes aside did cast
And here and there the places spy
Where oft I sat and long did lie.
Here stood that trunk, and there that chest,
There lay that store I counted best,
My pleasant things in ashes lie
And them behold no more shall I.
Under thy roof no guest shall sit,
Nor at thy table eat a bit.
No pleasant tale shall 'ere be told

Nor things recounted done of old.
No candle e'er shall shine in thee,
Nor bridegroom's voice e'er heard shall be.
In silence ever shalt thou lie.
Adieu, adieu, all's vanity.
Then straight I 'gin my heart to chide:
And did thy wealth on earth abide,
Didst fix thy hope on mouldering dust,
The arm of flesh didst make thy trust?
Raise up thy thoughts above the sky
That dunghill mists away may fly.
Thou hast an house on high erect
Framed by that mighty architect,
With glory richly furnished
Stands permanent, though this be fled.
It's purchased and paid for too
By Him who hath enough to do.
A price so vast as is unknown,
Yet by His gift is made thine own.
There's wealth enough; I need no more.
Farewell, my pelf, farewell, my store.
The world no longer let me love;
My hope and treasure lies above.

John Milton

Paradise Lost (Book 1, ll. 242–70)

'Is this the region, this the soil, the clime,'
Said then the lost archangel, 'this the seat
That we must change for Heaven, this mournful gloom
For that celestial light? Be it so, since he
Who now is sovereign can dispose and bid
What shall be right: furthest from him is best
Whom reason hath equalled, force hath made supreme
Above his equals. Farewell happy fields
Where joy for ever dwells: hail horrors, hail
Infernal world, and thou profoundest hell
Receive thy new possessor: one who brings
A mind not to be changed by place or time.
The mind is its own place, and in itself
Can make a heaven of Hell, a Hell of Heaven.
What matter where, if I be still the same,
And what I should be, all but less than he
Whom thunder hath made greater? Here at least
We shall be free; the almighty hath not built
Here for his envy, will not drive us hence:
Here we may reign secure, and in my choice
To reign is worth ambition though in Hell:
Better to reign in Hell, than serve in Heaven.
But wherefore let we then our faithful friends,
The associates and copartners of our loss
Lie thus astonished on the oblivious pool,
And call them not to share with us their part
In this unhappy mansion, or once more
With rallied arms to try what may be yet
Regained in Heaven, or what more lost in Hell?'

John Dryden

A Song for St Cecilia's Day (ll. 1–54)

From harmony, from heavenly harmony
  This universal frame began;
  When nature underneath a heap
    Of jarring atoms lay,
  And could not heave her head,
The tuneful voice was heard from high,
    'Arise, ye more than dead!'
Then cold, and hot, and moist, and dry,
In order to their stations leap,
    And Music's power obey.
From harmony, from heavenly harmony
  This universal frame began:
  From harmony to harmony
Through all the compass of the notes it ran,
The diapason closing full in man.

What passion cannot Music raise and quell?
    When Jubal struck the chorded shell,
  His listening brethren stood around,
    And, wondering, on their faces fell
  To worship that celestial sound:
Less than a God they thought there could not dwell
    Within the hollow of that shell
    That spoke so sweetly, and so well.
What passion cannot Music raise and quell?

  The trumpet's loud clangour
    Excites us to arms,
  With shrill notes of anger
    And mortal alarms,
  The double double double beat

Of the thundering drum
Cries, 'Hark, the foes come;
Charge, charge, 'tis too late to retreat!'

The soft complaining flute
In dying notes, discovers
The woes of hopeless lovers,
Whose dirge is whispered by the warbling lute.

Sharp violins proclaim
Their jealous pangs and desperation,
Fury, frantic indignation,
Depth of pains, and height of passion,
For the fair, disdainful dame.

But O, what art can teach,
What human voice can reach,
The sacred organ's praise?
Notes inspiring holy love,
Notes that wing their heavenly ways
To mend the choirs above.

Orpheus could lead the savage race;
And trees unrooted left their place,
Sequacious of the lyre;
But bright Cecilia raised the wonder higher:
When to her organ vocal breath was given,
An angel heard, and straight appeared
Mistaking Earth for heaven.

Aphra Behn

A Thousand Martyrs

A thousand martyrs I have made,
    All sacrificed to my desire;
A thousand beauties have betrayed,
    That languish in resistless fire.
The untamed heart to hand I brought,
And fixed the wild and wandering thought.

I never vowed nor sighed in vain
    But both, though false, were well received.
The fair are pleased to give us pain,
    And what they wish is soon believed.
And though I talked of wounds and smart,
Love's pleasures only touched my heart.

Alone the glory and the spoil
    I always laughing bore away;
The triumphs, without pain or toil,
    Without the hell, the heaven of joy.
And while I thus at random rove
Despise the fools that whine for love.

John Wilmot, Earl of Rochester

The Mistress

An age in her embraces passed,
  Would seem a winter's day;
Where life and light, with envious haste
  Are torn and snatched away.

But oh, how slowly minutes roll
  When absent from her eyes,
That feed my love, which is my soul:
  It languishes and dies.

For then no more a soul, but shade,
  It mournfully does move
And haunts my breast, by absence made
  The living tomb of love.

You wiser men, despise me not
  Whose love-sick fancy raves
On shades of souls, and heaven knows what:
  Short ages live in graves.

Whene'er those wounding eyes, so full
  Of sweetness, you did see,
Had you not been profoundly dull,
  You had gone mad like me.

Nor censure us, you who perceive
  My best beloved and me
Sigh and lament, complain and grieve:
  You think we disagree.

Alas! 'tis sacred jealousy,
   Love raised to an extreme;
The only proof 'twixt her and me,
   We love, and do not dream.

Fantastic fancies fondly move
   And in frail joys believe,
Taking false pleasure for true love;
   But pain can ne'er deceive.

Kind jealous doubts, tormenting fears,
   And anxious cares, when past,
Prove our hearts' treasure fixed and dear,
   And make us blest at last.

Anne Finch

The Hog, the Sheep and Goat, Carrying to a Fair

Who does not wish ever to judge aright,
  And, in the course of life's affairs,
To have a quick, and far-extended sight,
  Though it too often multiplies his cares?
And who has greater sense, but greater sorrow shares?

This felt the swine, now carrying to the knife;
  And whilst the lamb and silent goat
In the same fatal cart lay void of strife,
  He widely stretches his foreboding throat,
Deafening the easy crew with his outrageous note.

The angry driver chides the unruly beast,
  And bids him all this noise forbear;
Nor be more loud nor clamorous than the rest,
  Who with him travelled to the neighbouring fair,
And quickly should arrive and be unfettered there.

'This,' quoth the swine, 'I do believe is true,
  And see we're very near the town;
Whilst these poor fools, of short and bounded view,
  Think 'twill be well, when you have set them down,
And eased one of her milk, the other of her gown.

'But all the dreadful butchers in a row,
  To my far-searching thoughts appear,
Who know indeed we to the shambles go,
  Whilst I, whom none but Beelzebub would shear,
Nor but his dam would milk, must for my carcase fear.'

'But tell me then, will it prevent thy fate?'
  The rude, unpitying farmer cries;
'If not, the wretch who tastes his sufferings late,
  Not he, who through the unhappy future pries,
Must of the two be held most fortunate and wise.'

Alexander Pope

Epistle to Miss Blount

(*On her leaving the town, after the coronation*)

As some fond virgin, whom her mother's care
Drags from the town to wholesome country air,
Just when she learns to roll a melting eye,
And hear a spark, yet think no danger nigh;
From the dear man unwilling she must sever,
Yet takes one kiss before she parts forever:
Thus from the world fair Zephalinda flew,
Saw others happy, and with sighs withdrew;
Not that their pleasures caused her discontent;
She sighed not that they stayed, but that she went.
She went to plain-work, and to purling brooks,
Old-fashioned halls, dull aunts, and croaking rooks;
She went from opera, park, assembly, play,
To morning walks, and prayers three hours a day;
To part her time 'twixt reading and bohea,
To muse, and spill her solitary tea,
Or o'er cold coffee trifle with the spoon,
Count the slow clock, and dine exact at noon;
Divert her eyes with pictures in the fire,
Hum half a tune, tell stories to the squire;
Up to her godly garret after seven,
There starve and pray, for that's the way to heaven.
Some squire, perhaps, you take delight to rack,
Whose game is whisk, whose treat a toast in sack;
Who visits with a gun, presents you birds,
Then gives a smacking buss, and cries – 'No words!'
Or with his hounds comes hollowing from the stable,
Makes love with nods and knees beneath a table;
Whose laughs are hearty, though his jests are coarse,
And loves you best of all things – but his horse.

In some fair evening, on your elbow laid,
You dream of triumphs in the rural shade;
In pensive thought recall the fancied scene,
See coronations rise on every green;
Before you pass the imaginary sights
Of lords and earls and dukes and gartered knights,
While the spread fan o'ershades your closing eyes;
Then give one flirt, and all the vision flies.
Thus vanish sceptres, coronets, and balls,
And leave you in lone woods, or empty walls.
So when your slave, at some dear idle time
(Not plagued with headaches or the want of rhyme)
Stands in the streets, abstracted from the crew,
And while he seems to study, thinks of you:
Just when his fancy points your sprightly eyes,
Or sees the blush of soft Parthenia rise,
Gay pats my shoulder, and you vanish quite;
Streets, chairs, and coxcombs rush upon my sight;
Vexed to be still in town, I knit my brow,
Look sour, and hum a tune – as you may now.

Jonathan Swift

A Satirical Elegy on the Death of a Late Famous General

His Grace! impossible! what dead!
Of old age too, and in his bed!
And could that mighty warrior fall?
And so inglorious, after all!
Well, since he's gone, no matter how,
The last loud trump must wake him now:
And, trust me, as the noise grows stronger,
He'd wish to sleep a little longer.
And could he be indeed so old
As by the newspapers we're told?
Threescore, I think, is pretty high;
'Twas time in conscience he should die.
This world he cumbered long enough;
He burnt his candle to the snuff;
And that's the reason, some folks think,
He left behind so great a stink.
Behold his funeral appears,
Nor widow's sighs, nor orphan's tears,
Wont at such times each heart to pierce,
Attend the progress of his hearse.
But what of that, his friends may say,
He had those honours in his day.
True to his profit and his pride,
He made them weep before he died.
  Come hither, all ye empty things,
Ye bubbles raised by breath of kings;
Who float upon the tide of state,
Come hither, and behold your fate.
Let pride be taught by this rebuke,

How very mean a thing's a duke;
From all his ill-got honours flung,
Turned to that dirt from whence he sprung.

Mary Leapor

The Visit

With walking sick, with curtseys lame,
And frighted by the scolding dame,
Poor Mira once again is seen
Within the bounds of Goslin-Green.
O Artemisia! dear to me
As to the lawyer golden fee;
Whose name dwells pleasant on my tongue,
And first and last shall grace my song;
Receive within your friendly door
A wretch that vows to rove no more.
In some close corner let me hide,
Remote from compliments and pride;
Where morals grave, or sonnets gay,
Delude the guiltless, cheerful day;
Where we a sprightly dame may find,
Besides enquiring where's the wind,
Or whispering who and who's together,
And criticizing on the weather;
Where careless creatures such as I,
May 'scape the penetrating eye
Of students in physiognomy;
Who read your want of wit and grace
Not from your manners, but your face;
Whose tongues are for a week supplied
From one poor mouth that's stretched too wide;
Who greatly blame a freckled hand,
A skinny arm, full shoulders; and,
Without a microscope, can spy
A nose that's placed an inch awry.
In vain to gloomy shades you flee,
Like mice, in darkness they can see;

In vain to glaring lights you run,
Their eyes can face a midday sun:
You'll find no safety in retreat,
Like sharks they never mince their meat;
Their dreadful jaws they open throw,
And, if they catch you, down you go.

Mary Wortley Montagu

A Receipt to Cure the Vapours

I

Why will Delia thus retire,
And idly languish life away?
While the sighing crowd admire,
'Tis too soon for hartshorn tea.

II

All those dismal looks and fretting
Cannot Damon's life restore;
Long ago the worms have ate him,
You can never see him more.

III

Once again consult your toilette,
In the glass your face review:
So much weeping soon will spoil it,
And no Spring your charms renew.

IV

I, like you, was born a woman,
Well I know what vapours mean:
The disease, alas! is common;
Single, we have all the spleen.

V

All the morals that they tell us,
Never cured the sorrow yet:
Choose, among the pretty fellows,
One of honour, youth, and wit.

VI

Prithee hear him every morning
  At least an hour or two;
Once again at night returning –
  I believe the dose will do.

Thomas Gray

Elegy Written in a Country Churchyard (ll. 1–80)

The curfew tolls the knell of parting day,
The lowing herd wind slowly o'er the lea,
The ploughman homeward plods his weary way,
And leaves the world to darkness and to me.

Now fades the glimmering landscape on the sight,
And all the air a solemn stillness holds,
Save where the beetle wheels his droning flight,
And drowsy tinklings lull the distant folds;

Save that from yonder ivy-mantled tower
The moping owl does to the moon complain
Of such, as wandering near her secret bower,
Molest her ancient solitary reign.

Beneath those rugged elms, that yew tree's shade,
Where heaves the turf in many a mouldering heap,
Each in his narrow cell forever laid,
The rude forefathers of the hamlet sleep.

The breezy call of incense-breathing morn,
The swallow twittering from the straw-built shed,
The cock's shrill clarion, or the echoing horn,
No more shall rouse them from their lowly bed.

For them no more the blazing hearth shall burn,
Or busy housewife ply her evening care;
No children run to lisp their sire's return,
Or climb his knees the envied kiss to share.

Oft did the harvest to their sickle yield,
Their furrow oft the stubborn glebe has broke;
How jocund did they drive their team afield!
How bowed the woods beneath their sturdy stroke!

Let not Ambition mock their useful toil,
Their homely joys and destiny obscure;
Nor Grandeur hear, with a disdainful smile,
The short and simple annals of the poor.

The boast of heraldry, the pomp of power,
And all that beauty, all that wealth e'er gave,
Awaits alike the inevitable hour.
The paths of glory lead but to the grave.

Nor you, ye proud, impute to these the fault,
If Memory o'er their tomb no trophies raise,
Where through the long-drawn aisle and fretted vault
The pealing anthem swells the note of praise.

Can storied urn or animated bust
Back to its mansion call the fleeting breath?
Can Honour's voice provoke the silent dust,
Or Flattery soothe the dull cold ear of Death?

Perhaps in this neglected spot is laid
Some heart once pregnant with celestial fire;
Hands that the rod of empire might have swayed,
Or waked to ecstasy the living lyre.

But Knowledge to their eyes her ample page
Rich with the spoils of time did ne'er unroll;
Chill Penury repressed their noble rage,
And froze the genial current of the soul.

Full many a gem of purest ray serene
The dark unfathomed caves of ocean bear:

Full many a flower is born to blush unseen,
And waste its sweetness on the desert air.

Some village Hampden that with dauntless breast
The little tyrant of his fields withstood;
Some mute inglorious Milton here may rest,
Some Cromwell guiltless of his country's blood.

Th' applause of listening senates to command,
The threats of pain and ruin to despise,
To scatter plenty o'er a smiling land,
And read their history in a nation's eyes,

Their lot forbade: nor circumscribed alone
Their growing virtues, but their crimes confined;
Forbade to wade through slaughter to a throne,
And shut the gates of mercy on mankind,

The struggling pangs of conscious truth to hide,
To quench the blushes of ingenuous shame,
Or heap the shrine of Luxury and Pride
With incense kindled at the Muse's flame.

Far from the madding crowd's ignoble strife
Their sober wishes never learned to stray;
Along the cool sequestered vale of life
They kept the noiseless tenor of their way.

Yet even these bones from insult to protect
Some frail memorial still erected nigh,
With uncouth rhymes and shapeless sculpture decked,
Implores the passing tribute of a sigh.

Christopher Smart

'For I will consider my Cat Jeoffry'

(from *Jubilate Agno*)

For I will consider my Cat Jeoffry.
For he is the servant of the Living God, duly and daily serving him.
For at the first glance of the glory of God in the East he worships in
  his way.
For is this done by wreathing his body seven times round with
  elegant quickness.
For then he leaps up to catch the musk, which is the blessing of God
  upon his prayer.
For he rolls upon prank to work it in.
For having done duty and received blessing he begins to consider
  himself.
For this he performs in ten degrees.
For first he looks upon his forepaws to see if they are clean.
For secondly he kicks up behind to clear away there.
For thirdly he works it upon stretch with the forepaws extended.
For fourthly he sharpens his paws by wood.
For fifthly he washes himself.
For sixthly he rolls upon wash.
For seventhly he fleas himself, that he may not be interrupted upon
  the beat.
For eighthly he rubs himself against a post.
For ninthly he looks up for his instructions.
For tenthly he goes in quest of food.
For having considered God and himself he will consider his
  neighbour.
For if he meets another cat he will kiss her in kindness.
For when he takes his prey he plays with it to give it a
  chance.
For one mouse in seven escapes by his dallying.
For when his day's work is done his business more properly begins.

For he keeps the Lord's watch in the night against the adversary.
For he counteracts the powers of darkness by his electrical skin and glaring eyes.
For he counteracts the Devil, who is death, by brisking about the life.
For in his morning orisons he loves the sun and the sun loves him.
For he is of the tribe of Tiger.
For the Cherub Cat is a term of the Angel Tiger.
For he has the subtlety and hissing of a serpent, which in goodness he suppresses.
For he will not do destruction if he is well-fed, neither will he spit without provocation.
For he purrs in thankfulness when God tells him he's a good Cat.
For he is an instrument for the children to learn benevolence upon.
For every house is incomplete without him, and a blessing is lacking in the spirit.
For the Lord commanded Moses concerning the cats at the departure of the Children of Israel from Egypt.
For every family had one cat at least in the bag.
For the English Cats are the best in Europe.
For he is the cleanest in the use of his forepaws of any quadruped.
For the dexterity of his defence is an instance of the love of God to him exceedingly.
For he is the quickest to his mark of any creature.
For he is tenacious of his point.
For he is a mixture of gravity and waggery.
For he knows that God is his Saviour.
For there is nothing sweeter than his peace when at rest.
For there is nothing brisker than his life when in motion.
For he is of the Lord's poor, and so indeed is he called by benevolence perpetually – Poor Jeoffry! poor Jeoffry! the rat has bit thy throat.
For I bless the name of the Lord Jesus that Jeoffry is better.
For the divine spirit comes about his body to sustain it in complete cat.
For his tongue is exceeding pure so that it has in purity what it wants in music.

For he is docile and can learn certain things.
For he can sit up with gravity, which is patience upon approbation.
For he can fetch and carry, which is patience in employment.
For he can jump over a stick, which is patience upon proof positive.
For he can spraggle upon waggle at the word of command.
For he can jump from an eminence into his master's bosom.
For he can catch the cork and toss it again.
For he is hated by the hypocrite and miser.
For the former is afraid of detection.
For the latter refuses the charge.
For he camels his back to bear the first notion of business.
For he is good to think on, if a man would express himself neatly.
For he made a great figure in Egypt for his signal services.
For he killed the Icneumon rat, very pernicious by land.
For his ears are so acute that they sting again.
For from this proceeds the passing quickness of his attention.
For by stroking of him I have found out electricity.
For I perceived God's light about him both wax and fire.
For the electrical fire is the spiritual substance which God sends
  from heaven to sustain the bodies both of man and beast.
For God has blessed him in the variety of his movements.
For, though he cannot fly, he is an excellent clamberer.
For his motions upon the face of the earth are more than any
  other quadruped.
For he can tread to all the measures upon the music.
For he can swim for life.
For he can creep.

Samuel Johnson

On the Death of Dr Robert Levet

Condemned to Hope's delusive mine,
   As on we toil from day to day,
By sudden blasts, or slow decline,
   Our social comforts drop away.

Well tried through many a varying year,
   See Levet to the grave descend;
Officious, innocent, sincere,
   Of every friendless name the friend.

Yet still he fills Affection's eye,
   Obscurely wise, and coarsely kind;
Nor, lettered Arrogance, deny
   Thy praise to merit unrefined.

When fainting Nature called for aid,
   And hovering Death prepared the blow,
His vigorous remedy displayed
   The power of art without the show.

In Misery's darkest cavern known,
   His useful care was ever nigh,
Where hopeless Anguish poured his groan,
   And lonely want retired to die.

No summons mocked by chill delay,
   No petty gain disdained by pride,
The modest Wants of every day
   The toil of every day supplied.

His virtues walked their narrow round,
   Nor made a pause, nor left a void;
And sure the Eternal Master found
   The single talent well employed.

The busy day, the peaceful night,
   Unfelt, uncounted, glided by;
His frame was firm, his powers were bright,
   Though now his eightieth year was nigh.

Then with no throbbing fiery pain,
   No cold gradations of decay,
Death broke at once the vital chain,
   And freed his soul the nearest way.

Charlotte Smith

On being Cautioned against Walking on a Headland Overlooking the Sea, because It was Frequented by a Lunatic

Is there a solitary wretch who hies
To the tall cliff, with starting pace or slow,
And, measuring, views with wild and hollow eyes
Its distance from the waves that chide below;
Who, as the sea-born gale with frequent sighs
Chills his cold bed upon the mountain turf,
With hoarse, half-uttered lamentation, lies
Murmuring responses to the dashing surf?
In moody sadness, on the giddy brink,
I see him more with envy than with fear;
He has no *nice felicities* that shrink
From giant horrors; wildly wandering here,
He seems (uncursed with reason) not to know
The depth or the duration of his woe.

William Cowper

Epitaph on a Hare

Here lies, whom hound did ne'er pursue,
   Nor swifter greyhound follow,
Whose foot ne'er tainted morning dew,
   Nor ear heard huntsman's halloo,

Old Tiney, surliest of his kind,
   Who, nursed with tender care,
And to domestic bounds confined,
   Was still a wild jack-hare.

Though duly from my hand he took
   His pittance every night,
He did it with a jealous look,
   And, when he could, would bite.

His diet was of wheaten bread,
   And milk, and oats, and straw,
Thistles, or lettuces instead,
   With sand to scour his maw.

On twigs of hawthorn he regaled,
   On pippins' russet peel;
And, when his juicy salads failed,
   Sliced carrot pleased him well.

A Turkey carpet was his lawn,
   Whereon he loved to bound,
To skip and gambol like a fawn,
   And swing his rump around.

His frisking was at evening hours,
   For then he lost his fear;
But most before approaching showers,
   Or when a storm drew near.

Eight years and five round-rolling moons
   He thus saw steal away,
Dozing out his idle noons,
   And every night at play.

I kept him for his humour's sake,
   For he would oft beguile
My heart of thoughts that made it ache,
   And force me to a smile.

But now, beneath this walnut-shade
   He finds his long, last home,
And waits in snug concealment laid,
   'Till gentler Puss shall come.

He, still more aged, feels the shocks
   From which no care can save,
And, partner once of Tiney's box,
   Must soon partake his grave.

Hannah More

Slavery: A Poem (ll. 69–98)

For no fictitious ills these numbers flow,
But living anguish, and substantial woe;
No individual griefs my bosom melt,
For millions feel what Oroonoko felt:
Fired by no single wrongs, the countless host
I mourn, by rapine dragged from Afric's coast.
   Perish the illiberal thought which would debase
The native genius of the sable race!
Perish the proud philosophy, which sought
To rob them of the powers of equal thought!
Does then the immortal principle within
Change with the casual colour of a skin?
Does matter govern spirit? or is mind
Degraded by the form to which 'tis joined?
   No: they have heads to think, and hearts to feel,
And souls to act, with firm, though erring, zeal;
For they have keen affections, kind desires,
Love strong as death, and active patriot fires;
All the rude energy, the fervid flame,
Of high-souled passion, and ingenuous shame:
Strong, but luxuriant virtues boldly shoot
From the wild vigour of a savage root.
   Nor weak their sense of honour's proud control,
For pride is virtue in a pagan soul;
A sense of worth, a conscience of desert,
A high, unbroken haughtiness of heart:
That self-same stuff which erst proud empires swayed,
Of which the conquerers of the world were made.
Capricious fate of man! that very pride
In Afric scourged, in Rome was deified.

William Blake

The Chimney Sweeper

When my mother died I was very young,
And my father sold me while yet my tongue
Could scarcely cry "'weep! 'weep! 'weep! 'weep!'
So your chimneys I sweep and in soot I sleep.

There's little Tom Dacre, who cried when his head
That curled like a lamb's back, was shaved, so I said,
'Hush, Tom! never mind it, for when your head's bare,
You know that the soot cannot spoil your white hair.'

And so he was quiet, and that very night,
As Tom was a-sleeping, he had such a sight!
That thousands of sweepers, Dick, Joe, Ned, and Jack,
Were all of them locked up in coffins of black;

And by came an Angel who had a bright key,
And he opened the coffins and set them all free;
Then down a green plain, leaping, laughing, they run,
And wash in a river and shine in the Sun.

Then naked and white, all their bags left behind,
They rise upon clouds, and sport in the wind.
And the Angel told Tom, if he'd be a good boy,
He'd have God for his father and never want joy.

And so Tom awoke; and we rose in the dark
And got with our bags and our brushes to work.
Though the morning was cold, Tom was happy and
  warm;
So if all do their duty, they need not fear harm.

Joanna Baillie

A Mother to Her Waking Infant

Now in thy dazzling half-oped eye,
Thy curled nose and lip awry,
Thy up-hoist arms and noddling head,
And little chin with crystal spread,
Poor helpless thing! what do I see,
  That I should sing of thee?

From thy poor tongue no accents come,
Which can but rub thy toothless gum:
Small understanding boasts thy face,
Thy shapeless limbs nor step nor grace:
A few short words thy feats may tell,
  And yet I love thee well.

When sudden wakes the bitter shriek,
And redder swells thy little cheek;
When rattled keys thy woe beguile,
And through the wet eye gleams the smile,
Still for thy weakly self is spent
  Thy little silly plaint.

But when thy friends are in distress,
Thou'lt laugh and chuckle ne'er the less;
Nor e'en with sympathy be smitten,
Tho' all are sad but thee and kitten;
Yet little varlet that thou art,
  Thou twitchest at the heart.

Thy rosy cheek so soft and warm;
Thy pinky hand and dimpled arm;
Thy silken locks that scantly peep,

With gold-tipped ends, where circles deep
Around thy neck in harmless grace,
So soft and sleekly hold their place,
Might harder hearts with kindness fill,
  And gain our right good will.

Each passing clown bestows his blessing,
Thy mouth is worn with old wives' kissing:
E'en lighter looks the gloomy eye
Of surly sense, when thou art by;
And yet I think whoe'er they be,
  They love thee not like me.

Perhaps when time shall add a few
Short years to thee, thou'lt love me too;
And after that, through life's weary way
Become my sure and cheering stay;
Wilt care for me and be my hold,
  When I am weak and old.

Thou'lt listen to my lengthened tale,
And pity me when I am frail –
But see, the sweepy spinning fly
Upon the window takes thine eye.
Go to thy little senseless play;
  Thou dost not heed my lay.

Robert Burns

Song ('Ae fond kiss, and then we sever')

Ae fond kiss, and then we sever;
Ae fareweel, alas, for ever!
Deep in heart-wrung tears I'll pledge thee,
Warring sighs and groans I'll wage thee.
Who shall say that Fortune grieves him,
While the star of hope she leaves him?
Me, nae cheerful twinkle lights me;
Dark despair around benights me.

I'll ne'er blame my partial fancy,
Naething could resist my Nancy;
But to see her was to love her;
Love but her, and love for ever.
Had we never loved sae kindly,
Had we never loved sae blindly,
Never met – or never parted –
We had ne'er been broken-hearted.

Fare-thee-weel, thou first and fairest!
Fare-thee-weel, thou best and dearest!
Thine be ilka joy and treasure,
Peace, enjoyment, love and pleasure!
Ae fond kiss, and then we sever!
Ae fareweel, alas, for ever!
Deep in heart-wrung tears I'll pledge thee,
Warring sighs and groans I'll wage thee.

Anna Laetitia Barbauld

The Rights of Woman

Yes, injured Woman! rise, assert thy right!
Woman! too long degraded, scorned, oppressed;
O born to rule in partial Law's despite,
Resume thy native empire o'er the breast!

Go forth arrayed in panoply divine,
That angel pureness which admits no stain;
Go, bid proud Man his boasted rule resign,
And kiss the golden sceptre of thy reign.

Go, gird thyself with grace; collect thy store
Of bright artillery glancing from afar;
Soft melting tones thy thundering cannon's roar,
Blushes and fears thy magazine of war.

Thy rights are empire: urge no meaner claim –
Felt, not defined, and if debated, lost;
Like sacred mysteries, which withheld from fame,
Shunning discussion, are revered the most.

Try all that wit and art suggest to bend
Of thy imperial foe the stubborn knee;
Make treacherous Man thy subject, not thy friend;
Thou mayst command, but never canst be free.

Awe the licentious, and restrain the rude;
Soften the sullen, clear the cloudy brow:
Be, more than princes' gifts, thy favours sued –
She hazards all, who will the least allow.

But hope not, courted idol of mankind,
On this proud eminence secure to stay;
Subduing and subdued; thou soon shalt find
Thy coldness soften, and thy pride give way.

Then, then, abandon each ambitious thought;
Conquest or rule thy heart shall feebly move,
In Nature's school, by her soft maxims taught,
That separate rights are lost in mutual love.

Robert Southey

After Blenheim

It was a summer evening,
   Old Kaspar's work was done,
And he before his cottage door
   Was sitting in the sun,
And by him sported on the green
His little grandchild Wilhelmine.

She saw her brother Peterkin
   Roll something large and round,
Which he beside the rivulet
   In playing there had found;
He came to ask what he had found,
That was so large, and smooth, and round.

Old Kaspar took it from the boy,
   Who stood expectant by;
And then the old man shook his head,
   And, with a natural sigh –
''Tis some poor fellow's skull,' said he,
'Who fell in the great victory.

'I find them in the garden,
   For there's many here about;
And often when I go to plough,
   The ploughshare turns them out.
For many thousand men,' said he,
'Were slain in that great victory.'

'Now tell us what 'twas all about,'
   Young Peterkin, he cries;
And little Wilhelmine looks up

With wonder-waiting eyes;
'Now tell us all about the war,
And what they killed each other for.'

'It was the English,' Kaspar cried,
'Who put the French to rout;
But what they killed each other for,
I could not well make out;
But everybody said,' quoth he,
'That 'twas a famous victory.

'My father lived at Blenheim then,
Yon little stream hard by;
They burnt his dwelling to the ground,
And he was forced to fly;
So with his wife and child he fled,
Nor had he where to rest his head.

'With fire and sword the country round
Was wasted far and wide,
And many a childing mother then,
And new-born baby died;
But things like that, you know, must be
At every famous victory.

'They say it was a shocking sight
After the field was won;
For many thousand bodies here
Lay rotting in the sun;
But things like that, you know, must be
After a famous victory.

'Great praise the Duke of Marlbro' won
And our good Prince Eugene.'
'Why, 'twas a very wicked thing!'
Said little Wilhelmine.

‘Nay – nay, my little girl,’ quoth he,
‘It was a famous victory.

‘And everybody praised the Duke
  Who this great fight did win.’
‘But what good came of it at last?’
  Quoth little Peterkin.
‘Why that I cannot tell,’ said he,
‘But ’twas a famous victory.’

Mary Robinson

Female Fashions for 1799

A FORM, as any taper, fine;
	A head like half-pint bason;
Where golden cords, and bands entwine,
	As rich as fleece of JASON.

A pair of shoulders strong and wide,
	Like *country clown* enlisting;
Bare arms long dangling by the side,
	And shoes of ragged listing!

Cravats like towels, thick and broad,
	Long tippets made of bear-skin,
Muffs that a RUSSIAN might applaud,
	And *rouge* to spoil a fair skin.

Long petticoats to *hide* the feet,
	Silk hose with clocks of scarlet;
A load of perfume, sickening sweet,
	Bought of PARISIAN VARLET.

A bush of hair, the brow to shade,
	Sometimes the eyes to cover;
A necklace that might be displayed
	By OTAHEITEAN lover!

A bowl of straw to deck the head,
	Like porringer unmeaning;
A bunch of POPPIES flaming red,
	With motly ribands streaming.

Bare ears on either side the head,
  Like wood-wild savage SATYR;
Tinted with deep vermilion red,
  To shame the blush of nature.

Red elbows, gauzy gloves, that add
  An icy covering merely;
A wadded coat, the shape to pad,
  Like Dutch-women – or nearly.

Such is CAPRICE! but, lovely kind!
  Oh! let each mental feature
Proclaim the labour of the *mind*,
  And leave your charms to NATURE.

Anonymous

Lord Randal

'O where ha' you been, Lord Randal my son?
And where ha' you been, my handsome young man?'
'I ha' been at the greenwood; mother, mak my bed soon,
For I'm wearied wi' hunting and fain wad lie down.'

'An wha met ye there, Lord Randal my son?
An wha met you there, my handsome young man?'
'O I met wi my true-love; mother, mak my bed soon,
For I'm wearied wi' hunting and fain wad lie down.'

'And what did she give you, Lord Randal my son?
And what did she give you, my handsome young man?'
'Eels fried in a pan; mother, mak my bed soon,
For I'm wearied wi' hunting and fain wad lie down.'

'And wha gat your leavins, Lord Randal my son?
And wha gat your leavins, my handsome young man?'
'My hawks and my hounds; mother, mak my bed soon,
For I'm wearied wi' hunting, and fain wad lie down.'

'And what becam of them, Lord Randal my son?
What becam of them, my handsome young man?'
'They stretched their legs out and died; mother, mak my bed soon,
For I'm wearied wi huntin, and fain wad lie down.'

'O I fear you are poisoned, Lord Randal my son!
I fear you are poisoned, my handsome young man!'
'O yes, I am poisoned; mother, mak my bed soon,
For I'm sick at the heart, and I fain wad lie down.'

'What d'ye leave to your mother, Lord Randal my son?
What d'ye leave to your mother, my handsome young man?'
'Four and twenty milk kye; mother, mak my bed soon,
For I'm sick at the heart and I fain wad lie down.'

'What d'ye leave to your sister, Lord Randal my son?
What d'ye leave to your sister, my handsome young man?'
'My gold and my silver; mother, mak my bed soon,
For I'm sick at the heart and I fain would lie down.'

'What d'ye leave to your brother, Lord Randal my son?
What d'ye leave to your brother, my handsome young man?'
'My house and my lands; mother, mak my bed soon,
For I'm sick at the heart and I fain wad lie down.'

'What d'ye leave to your true-love, Lord Randal my son?
What d'ye leave to your true-love, my handsome young man?'
'I leave her hell and fire; mother, mak my bed soon,
For I'm sick at the heart and I fain wad lie down.'

Anonymous

The Wife of Usher's Well

There lived a wife at Usher's Well,
  And a wealthy wife was she;
She had three stout and stalwart sons,
  And sent them o'er the sea.

They hadna been a week from her,
  A week but barely ane,
Whan word came to the carlin wife
  That her three sons were gane.

They hadna been a week from her,
  A week but barely three,
Whan word came to the carlin wife
  That her sons she'd never see.

'I wish the wind may never cease,
  Nor fashes in the flood,
Till my three sons come hame to me,
  In earthly flesh and blood.'

It fell about the Martinmass,
  When nights are lang and mirk,
The carlin wife's three sons came hame,
  And their hats were o' the birk.

It neither grew in skye nor ditch,
  Nor yet in ony sheugh;
But at the gates o' Paradise,
  That birk grew fair eneugh.

‘Blow up the fire, my maidens,
  Bring water from the well;
For a’ my house shall feast this night,
  Since my three sons are well.’

And she has made to them a bed,
  She’s made it large and wide,
And she’s ta’en her mantle her about,
  Sat down at the bedside.

Up then crew the red, red cock,
  And up and crew the gray;
The eldest to the youngest said,
  ‘’Tis time we were away.’

The cock he hadna crawed but once,
  And clapped his wings at a’,
When the youngest to the eldest said,
  ‘Brother, we must awa’.

‘The cock doth craw, the day doth daw,
  The channerin’ worm doth chide;
Gin we be mist out o’ our place,
  A sair pain we maun bide.

‘Fare ye weel, my mother dear!
  Fareweel to barn and byre!
And fare ye weel, the bonny lass
  That kindles my mother’s fire!’

William Wordsworth

The Solitary Reaper

Behold her, single in the field,
   Yon solitary Highland Lass!
Reaping and singing by herself;
   Stop here, or gently pass!
Alone she cuts and binds the grain,
And sings a melancholy strain;
O listen! for the vale profound
Is overflowing with the sound.

No nightingale did ever chant
   More welcome notes to weary bands
Of travellers in some shady haunt,
   Among Arabian sands:
A voice so thrilling ne'er was heard
In springtime from the cuckoo-bird,
Breaking the silence of the seas
Among the farthest Hebrides.

Will no one tell me what she sings? –
   Perhaps the plaintive numbers flow
For old, unhappy, far-off things,
   And battles long ago:
Or is it some more humble lay,
Familiar matter of today?
Some natural sorrow, loss, or pain,
That has been, and may be again?

Whate'er the theme, the maiden sang
   As if her song could have no ending;
I saw her singing at her work,
   And o'er the sickle bending; –

I listened, motionless and still;
And, as I mounted up the hill,
The music in my heart I bore,
Long after it was heard no more.

George Gordon Byron

The Destruction of Sennacherib

The Assyrian came down like the wolf on the fold,
And his cohorts were gleaming in purple and gold;
And the sheen of their spears was like stars on the sea,
When the blue wave rolls nightly on deep Galilee.

Like the leaves of the forest when Summer is green,
That host with their banners at sunset were seen:
Like the leaves of the forest when Autumn hath blown,
That host on the morrow lay withered and strown.

For the Angel of Death spread his wings on the blast,
And breathed in the face of the foe as he passed;
And the eyes of the sleepers waxed deadly and chill,
And their hearts but once heaved, and for ever grew still!

And there lay the steed with his nostril all wide,
But through it there rolled not the breath of his pride:
And the foam of his gasping lay white on the turf,
And cold as the spray of the rock-beating surf.

And there lay the rider distorted and pale,
With the dew on his brow, and the rust on his mail;
And the tents were all silent, the banners alone,
The lances unlifted, the trumpet unblown.

And the widows of Ashur are loud in their wail,
And the idols are broke in the temple of Baal;
And the might of the Gentile, unsmote by the sword,
Hath melted like snow in the glance of the Lord!

Samuel Taylor Coleridge

Kubla Khan

In Xanadu did Kubla Khan
A stately pleasure dome decree:
Where Alph, the sacred river, ran
Through caverns measureless to man
   Down to a sunless sea.
So twice five miles of fertile ground
With walls and towers were girdled round;
And there were gardens bright with sinuous rills,
Where blossomed many an incense-bearing tree;
And here were forests ancient as the hills,
Enfolding sunny spots of greenery.

But oh! that deep romantic chasm which slanted
Down the green hill athwart a cedarn cover!
A savage place! as holy and enchanted
As e'er beneath a waning moon was haunted
By woman wailing for her demon lover!
And from this chasm, with ceaseless turmoil seething,
As if this earth in fast thick pants were breathing,
A mighty fountain momently was forced:
Amid whose swift half-intermitted burst
Huge fragments vaulted like rebounding hail,
Or chaffy grain beneath the thresher's flail:
And 'mid these dancing rocks at once and ever
It flung up momently the sacred river.
Five miles meandering with a mazy motion
Through wood and dale the sacred river ran,
Then reached the caverns measureless to man,
And sank in tumult to a lifeless ocean;
And 'mid this tumult Kubla heard from far
Ancestral voices prophesying war!

The shadow of the dome of pleasure
Floated midway on the waves;
Where was heard the mingled measure
From the fountain and the caves.
It was a miracle of rare device,
A sunny pleasure-dome with caves of ice!

A damsel with a dulcimer
In a vision once I saw:
It was an Abyssinian maid
And on her dulcimer she played,
Singing of Mount Abora.
Could I revive within me
Her symphony and song,
To such a deep delight 'twould win me,
That with music loud and long,
I would build that dome in air,
That sunny dome! those caves of ice!
And all who heard should see them there,
And all should cry, Beware! Beware!
His flashing eyes, his floating hair!
Weave a circle round him thrice,
And close your eyes with holy dread
For he on honey-dew hath fed,
And drunk the milk of Paradise.

Charles Wolfe

The Burial of Sir John Moore after Corunna

Not a drum was heard, not a funeral note,
As his corse to the rampart we hurried;
Not a soldier discharged his farewell shot
O'er the grave where our hero we buried.

We buried him darkly at dead of night,
The sods with our bayonets turning,
By the struggling moonbeam's misty light
And the lanthern dimly burning.

No useless coffin enclosed his breast,
Nor in sheet nor in shroud we wound him;
But he lay like a warrior taking his rest
With his martial cloak around him.

Few and short were the prayers we said,
And we spoke not a word of sorrow;
But we steadfastly gazed on the face that was dead,
And we bitterly thought of the morrow.

We thought, as we hollowed his narrow bed
And smoothed down his lonely pillow,
That the foe and the stranger would tread o'er his head,
And we far away on the billow!

Lightly they'll talk of the spirit that's gone
And o'er his cold ashes upbraid him,
But little he'll reck, if they let him sleep on
In the grave where a Briton has laid him.

But half of our heavy task was done
  When the clock struck the hour for retiring;
And we heard the distant and random gun
  That the foe was sullenly firing.

Slowly and sadly we laid him down,
  From the field of his fame fresh and gory;
We carved not a line, and we raised not a stone,
  But we left him alone with his glory.

Walter Scott

Proud Maisie

Proud Maisie is in the wood,
 Walking so early;
Sweet Robin sits on the bush,
 Singing so rarely.

'Tell me, thou bonny bird,
 When shall I marry me?' –
'When six braw gentlemen
 Kirkward shall carry ye.'

'Who makes the bridal bed,
 Birdie, say truly?' –
'The grey-headed sexton
 That delves the grave duly.

'The glowworm o'er grave and stone
 Shall light thee steady;
The owl from the steeple sing,
 "Welcome, proud lady."'

Percy Bysshe Shelley

Ozymandias

I met a traveller from an antique land
Who said: Two vast and trunkless legs of stone
Stand in the desert. Near them, on the sand,
Half sunk, a shattered visage lies, whose frown,
And wrinkled lip, and sneer of cold command,
Tell that its sculptor well those passions read
Which yet survive, stamped on these lifeless things,
The hand that mocked them and the heart that fed;
And on the pedestal these words appear:
'My name is Ozymandias, king of kings:
Look on my works, ye Mighty, and despair!'
Nothing beside remains. Round the decay
Of that colossal wreck, boundless and bare
The lone and level sands stretch far away.

John Keats

Ode to a Nightingale

My heart aches, and a drowsy numbness pains
  My sense, as though of hemlock I had drunk,
Or emptied some dull opiate to the drains
  One minute past, and Lethe-wards had sunk:
'Tis not through envy of thy happy lot,
  But being too happy in thine happiness –
    That thou, light-wingèd Dryad of the trees,
        In some melodious plot
  Of beechen green, and shadows numberless,
    Singest of summer in full-throated ease.

O for a draught of vintage! that hath been
  Cooled a long age in the deep-delved earth,
Tasting of Flora and the country green,
  Dance, and Provençal song, and sunburnt mirth!
O for a beaker full of the warm South,
  Full of the true, the blushful Hippocrene,
    With beaded bubbles winking at the brim,
        And purple-stained mouth;
  That I might drink, and leave the world unseen,
    And with thee fade away into the forest dim:

Fade far away, dissolve, and quite forget
  What thou among the leaves hast never known,
The weariness, the fever, and the fret
  Here, where men sit and hear each other groan;
Where palsy shakes a few, sad, last grey hairs,
  Where youth grows pale, and spectre-thin, and dies;
    Where but to think is to be full of sorrow
        And leaden-eyed despairs,

Where Beauty cannot keep her lustrous eyes,
        Or new Love pine at them beyond tomorrow.

Away! away! for I will fly to thee,
    Not charioted by Bacchus and his pards,
But on the viewless wings of Poesy,
    Though the dull brain perplexes and retards:
Already with thee! tender is the night,
    And haply the Queen-Moon is on her throne,
        Clustered around by all her starry Fays;
                            But here there is no light,
    Save what from heaven is with the breezes blown
        Through verdurous glooms and winding mossy ways.

I cannot see what flowers are at my feet,
    Nor what soft incense hangs upon the boughs,
But, in embalmed darkness, guess each sweet
    Wherewith the seasonable month endows
The grass, the thicket, and the fruit tree wild;
    White hawthorn, and the pastoral eglantine;
        Fast fading violets covered up in leaves;
                            And mid-May's eldest child,
    The coming musk-rose, full of dewy wine,
        The murmurous haunt of flies on summer eves.

Darkling I listen; and, for many a time
    I have been half in love with easeful Death,
Called him soft names in many a mused rhyme,
    To take into the air my quiet breath;
Now more than ever seems it rich to die,
    To cease upon the midnight with no pain,
        While thou art pouring forth thy soul abroad
                            In such an ecstasy!
    Still wouldst thou sing, and I have ears in vain –
        To thy high requiem become a sod.

Thou wast not born for death, immortal Bird!
   No hungry generations tread thee down;
The voice I hear this passing night was heard
   In ancient days by emperor and clown:
Perhaps the self-same song that found a path
   Through the sad heart of Ruth, when, sick for home,
      She stood in tears amid the alien corn;
                     The same that oft-times hath
   Charmed magic casements, opening on the foam
      Of perilous seas, in faery lands forlorn.

Forlorn! the very word is like a bell
   To toll me back from thee to my sole self!
Adieu! the fancy cannot cheat so well
   As she is famed to do, deceiving elf.
Adieu! adieu! thy plaintive anthem fades
   Past the near meadows, over the still stream,
      Up the hillside; and now 'tis buried deep
                     In the next valley-glades:
   Was it a vision, or a waking dream?
      Fled is that music: – Do I wake or sleep?

Felicia Hemans

Casabianca

The boy stood on the burning deck,
  Whence all but he had fled;
The flame that lit the battle's wreck,
  Shone round him o'er the dead.

Yet beautiful and bright he stood,
  As born to rule the storm;
A creature of heroic blood,
  A proud, though childlike form.

The flames rolled on – he would not go,
  Without his father's word;
That father, faint in death below,
  His voice no longer heard.

He called aloud – 'Say, father, say
  If yet my task is done?'
He knew not that the chieftain lay
  Unconscious of his son.

'Speak, father!' once again he cried,
  'If I may yet be gone!'
And but the booming shots replied,
  And fast the flames rolled on.

Upon his brow he felt their breath
  And in his waving hair;
And looked from that lone post of death,
  In still, yet brave despair.

And shouted but once more aloud,
  'My father! must I stay?'
While o'er him fast, through sail and shroud,
  The wreathing fires made way.

They wrapped the ship in splendour wild,
  They caught the flag on high,
And streamed above the gallant child,
  Like banners in the sky.

There came a burst of thunder sound –
  The boy – oh! where was he?
Ask of the winds that far around
  With fragments strewed the sea!

With mast, and helm, and pennon fair,
  That well had borne their part,
But the noblest thing which perished there
  Was that young faithful heart.

Thomas Love Peacock

The War Song of Dinas Vawr

The mountain sheep are sweeter,
But the valley sheep are fatter;
We therefore deemed it meeter
To carry off the latter.
We made an expedition;
We met a host and quelled it;
We forced a strong position,
And killed the men who held it.

On Dyfed's richest valley,
Where herds of kine were browsing,
We made a mighty sally,
To furnish our carousing.
Fierce warriors rushed to meet us;
We met them, and o'erthrew them:
They struggled hard to beat us;
But we conquered them, and slew them.

As we drove our prize at leisure,
The king marched forth to catch us:
His rage surpassed all measure,
But his people could not match us.
He fled to his hall-pillars;
And, ere our force we led off,
Some sacked his house and cellars,
While others cut his head off.

We there, in strife bewildering,
Spilt blood enough to swim in:
We orphaned many children,
And widowed many women.

The eagles and the ravens
We glutted with our foemen:
The heroes and the cravens,
The spearmen and the bowmen.

We brought away from battle,
And much their land bemoaned them,
Two thousand head of cattle,
And the head of him who owned them:
Ednyfed, king of Dyfed,
His head was borne before us;
His wine and beasts supplied our feasts,
And his overthrow, our chorus.

John Clare

'I found a ball of grass among the hay'

I found a ball of grass among the hay
And progged it as I passed and went away;
And when I looked I fancied something stirred,
And turned again and hoped to catch the bird –
When out an old mouse bolted in the wheats
With all her young ones hanging at her teats;
She looked so odd and so grotesque to me,
I ran and wondered what the thing could be,
And pushed the knapweed bunches where I stood;
When the mouse hurried from the craking brood.
The young ones squeaked, and when I went away
She found her nest again among the hay.
The water o'er the pebbles scarce could run
And broad old cesspools glittered in the sun.

Robert Browning

Porphyria's Lover

The rain set early in tonight,
    The sullen wind was soon awake,
It tore the elm-tops down for spite,
    And did its worst to vex the lake:
    I listened with heart fit to break.
When glided in Porphyria; straight
    She shut the cold out and the storm,
And kneeled and made the cheerless grate
    Blaze up, and all the cottage warm;
    Which done, she rose, and from her form
Withdrew the dripping cloak and shawl,
    And laid her soiled gloves by, untied
Her hat and let the damp hair fall,
    And, last, she sat down by my side
    And called me. When no voice replied,
She put my arm about her waist,
    And made her smooth white shoulder bare,
And all her yellow hair displaced,
    And, stooping, made my cheek lie there,
    And spread, o'er all, her yellow hair,
Murmuring how she loved me – she
    Too weak, for all her heart's endeavour,
To set its struggling passion free
    From pride, and vainer ties dissever,
    And give herself to me for ever.
But passion sometimes would prevail,
    Nor could tonight's gay feast restrain
A sudden thought of one so pale
    For love of her, and all in vain:
    So, she was come through wind and rain.
Be sure I looked up at her eyes

Happy and proud; at last I knew
Porphyria worshipped me; surprise
Made my heart swell, and still it grew
While I debated what to do.
That moment she was mine, mine, fair,
Perfectly pure and good: I found
A thing to do, and all her hair
In one long yellow string I wound
Three times her little throat around,
And strangled her. No pain felt she;
I am quite sure she felt no pain.
As a shut bud that holds a bee,
I warily oped her lids: again
Laughed the blue eyes without a stain.
And I untightened next the tress
About her neck; her cheek once more
Blushed bright beneath my burning kiss:
I propped her head up as before,
Only, this time my shoulder bore
Her head, which droops upon it still:
The smiling rosy little head,
So glad it has its utmost will,
That all it scorned at once is fled,
And I, its love, am gained instead!
Porphyria's love: she guessed not how
Her darling one wish would be heard.
And thus we sit together now,
And all night long we have not stirred,
And yet God has not said a word!

Alfred Tennyson

Ulysses

It little profits that an idle king,
By this still hearth, among these barren crags,
Matched with an agèd wife, I mete and dole
Unequal laws unto a savage race,
That hoard, and sleep, and feed, and know not me.

I cannot rest from travel; I will drink
Life to the lees: all times I have enjoyed
Greatly, have suffered greatly, both with those
That loved me, and alone; on shore, and when
Through scudding drifts the rainy Hyades
Vext the dim sea: I am become a name;
For always roaming with a hungry heart
Much have I seen and known; cities of men
And manners, climates, councils, governments,
Myself not least, but honoured of them all;
And drunk delight of battle with my peers,
Far on the ringing plains of windy Troy.
I am a part of all that I have met;
Yet all experience is an arch wherethrough
Gleams that untravelled world, whose margin fades
For ever and for ever when I move.
How dull it is to pause, to make an end,
To rust unburnished, not to shine in use!
As though to breathe were life! Life piled on life
Were all too little, and of one to me
Little remains; but every hour is saved
From that eternal silence, something more,
A bringer of new things; and vile it were
For some three suns to store and hoard myself,

And this gray spirit yearning in desire
To follow knowledge, like a sinking star,
Beyond the utmost bound of human thought.

This is my son, mine own Telemachus,
To whom I leave the sceptre and the isle –
Well-loved of me, discerning to fulfil
This labour, by slow prudence to make mild
A rugged people, and through soft degrees
Subdue them to the useful and the good.
Most blameless is he, centred in the sphere
Of common duties, decent not to fail
In offices of tenderness, and pay
Meet adoration to my household gods,
When I am gone. He works his work, I mine.

There lies the port; the vessel puffs her sail:
There gloom the dark broad seas. My mariners,
Souls that have toiled, and wrought, and thought with me –
That ever with a frolic welcome took
The thunder and the sunshine, and opposed
Free hearts, free foreheads – you and I are old;
Old age hath yet his honour and his toil;
Death closes all; but something ere the end,
Some work of noble note, may yet be done,
Not unbecoming men that strove with Gods.
The lights begin to twinkle from the rocks:
The long day wanes: the slow moon climbs: the deep
Moans round with many voices. Come, my friends,
'Tis not too late to seek a newer world.
Push off, and sitting well in order smite
The sounding furrows; for my purpose holds
To sail beyond the sunset, and the baths
Of all the western stars, until I die.
It may be that the gulfs will wash us down:
It may be that we shall touch the Happy Isles,
And see the great Achilles, whom we knew.

Though much is taken, much abides; and though
We are not now that strength which in old days
Moved earth and heaven, that which we are, we are;
One equal temper of heroic hearts,
Made weak by time and fate, but strong in will
To strive, to seek, to find, and not to yield.

Emily Brontë

Remembrance

Cold in the earth – and the deep snow piled above thee,
Far, far removed, cold in the dreary grave!
Have I forgot, my only Love, to love thee,
Severed at last by Time's all-severing wave?

Now, when alone, do my thoughts no longer hover
Over the mountains, on that northern shore,
Resting their wings where heath and fern-leaves cover
Thy noble heart for ever, ever more?

Cold in the earth – and fifteen wild Decembers
From those brown hills have melted into spring:
Faithful, indeed, is the spirit that remembers
After such years of change and suffering!

Sweet Love of youth, forgive, if I forget thee,
While the world's tide is bearing me along;
Other desires and other hopes beset me,
Hopes which obscure, but cannot do thee wrong!

No later light has lightened up my heaven,
No second morn has ever shone for me;
All my life's bliss from thy dear life was given,
All my life's bliss is in the grave with thee.

But, when the days of golden dreams had perished,
And even Despair was powerless to destroy,
Then did I learn how existence could be cherished,
Strengthened, and fed without the aid of joy.

Then did I check the tears of useless passion –
Weaned my young soul from yearning after thine;
Sternly denied its burning wish to hasten
Down to that tomb already more than mine.

And, even yet, I dare not let it languish,
Dare not indulge in memory's rapturous pain;
Once drinking deep of that divinest anguish,
How could I seek the empty world again?

Elizabeth Barrett Browning

Sonnets from the Portuguese XXIV

Let the world's sharpness, like a clasping knife,
Shut in upon itself and do no harm
In this close hand of Love, now soft and warm,
And let us hear no sound of human strife
After the click of the shutting. Life to life –
I lean upon thee, Dear, without alarm,
And feel as safe as guarded by a charm
Against the stab of worldlings, who if rife
Are weak to injure. Very whitely still
The lilies of our lives may reassure
Their blossoms from their roots, accessible
Alone to heavenly dews that drop not fewer,
Growing straight, out of man's reach, on the hill.
God only, who made us rich, can make us poor.

Arthur Hugh Clough

'There is no God'

'There is no God,' the wicked saith,
  'And truly it's a blessing,
For what he might have done with us
  It's better only guessing.'

'There is no God,' a youngster thinks,
  'Or really, if there may be,
He surely did not mean a man
  Always to be a baby.'

'There is no God, or if there is,'
  The tradesman thinks, ''twere funny
If he should take it ill in me
  To make a little money.'

'Whether there be,' the rich man says,
  'It matters very little,
For I and mine, thank somebody,
  Are not in want of victual.'

Some others, also, to themselves,
  Who scarce so much as doubt it,
Think there is none, when they are well,
  And do not think about it.

But country folks who live beneath
  The shadow of the steeple;
The parson and the parson's wife,
  And mostly married people;

Youths green and happy in first love,
   So thankful for illusion;
And men caught out in what the world
   Calls guilt, in first confusion;

And almost every one when age,
   Disease, or sorrows strike him,
Inclines to think there is a God,
   Or something very like Him.

William Barnes

My Orcha'd in Linden Lea

'Ithin the woodlands, flow'ry gleaded,
   By the woak tree's mossy moot,
The sheenen grass-bleades, timber-sheaded,
   Now do quiver under voot;
An' birds do whissle over head,
An' water's bubblen in its bed,
An' there vor me the apple tree
Do lean down low in Linden Lea.

When leaves that leately wer a-springen
   Now do feade 'ithin the copse,
An' painted birds do hush their zingen
   Up upon the timber's tops;
An' brown-leav'd fruit's a-turnen red,
In cloudless zunsheen, over head,
Wi' fruit vor me, the apple tree
Do lean down low in Linden Lea.

Let other vo'k meake money vaster
   In the air o' dark-room'd towns,
I don't dread a peevish measter;
   Though noo man do heed my frowns,
I be free to goo abrode,
Or teake agean my homeward road
To where, vor me, the apple tree
Do lean down low in Linden Lea.

Frederick Tuckerman

'An upper chamber in a darkened house'

An upper chamber in a darkened house,
Where, ere his footsteps reached ripe manhood's brink,
Terror and anguish were his lot to drink;
I cannot rid the thought, nor hold it close
But dimly dream upon that man alone:
Now though the autumn clouds most softly pass,
The cricket chides beneath the doorstep stone
And greener than the season grows the grass.
Nor can I drop my lids, nor shade my brows,
But there he stands beside the lifted sash;
And with a swooning of the heart, I think
Where the black shingles slope to meet the boughs
And, shattered on the roof like smallest snows,
The tiny petals of the mountain-ash.

Adelaide Anne Procter

Envy

He was the first always: Fortune
  Shone bright in his face.
I fought for years; with no effort
  He conquered the place:
We ran; my feet were all bleeding,
  But he won the race.

Spite of his many successes
  Men loved him the same;
My one pale ray of good fortune
  Met scoffing and blame.
When we erred, they gave him pity,
  But me – only shame.

My home was still in the shadow,
  His lay in the sun:
I longed in vain: what he asked for
  It straightway was done.
Once I staked all my heart's treasure,
  We played – and he won.

Yes; and just now I have seen him,
  Cold, smiling, and blest,
Laid in his coffin. God help me!
  While he is at rest,
I am cursed still to live: – even
  Death loved him the best.

Lewis Carroll

'You are old, Father William'

'You are old, Father William,' the young man said,
'And your hair has become very white;
And yet you incessantly stand on your head –
Do you think, at your age, it is right?'

'In my youth,' Father William replied to his son,
'I feared it might injure the brain;
But, now that I'm perfectly sure I have none,
Why, I do it again and again.'

'You are old,' said the youth, 'as I mentioned before,
And have grown most uncommonly fat;
Yet you turned a back-somersault in at the door –
Pray, what is the reason of that?'

'In my youth,' said the sage, as he shook his grey locks,
'I kept all my limbs very supple
By the use of this ointment – one shilling the box –
Allow me to sell you a couple?'

'You are old,' said the youth, 'and your jaws are too weak
For anything tougher than suet;
Yet you finished the goose, with the bones and the beak –
Pray how did you manage to do it?'

'In my youth,' said his father, 'I took to the law,
And argued each case with my wife;
And the muscular strength, which it gave to my jaw
Has lasted the rest of my life.'

‘You are old,’ said the youth, ‘one would hardly suppose
  That your eye was as steady as ever;
Yet you balanced an eel on the end of your nose –
  What made you so awfully clever?’

‘I have answered three questions, and that is enough,’
  Said his father. ‘Don’t give yourself airs!
Do you think I can listen all day to such stuff?
  Be off, or I’ll kick you downstairs!’

Emily Dickinson

Snake

A narrow Fellow in the Grass
Occasionally rides –
You may have met Him – did you not
His notice sudden is –

The Grass divides as with a comb –
A spotted shaft is seen –
And then it closes at your feet
And opens further on –

He likes a Boggy Acre
A Floor too cool for Corn –
Yet when a boy, and Barefoot –
I more than once at Noon,
Have passed, I thought, a whiplash
Unbraiding in the sun
When, stooping to secure it
It wrinkled, and was gone –

Several of Nature's People
I know, and they know me –
I feel for them a transport
Of cordiality –

But never met this Fellow
Attended, or alone,
Without a tighter breathing
And Zero at the Bone.

Matthew Arnold

Dover Beach

The sea is calm tonight.
The tide is full, the moon lies fair
Upon the straits; – on the French coast the light
Gleams and is gone; the cliffs of England stand,
Glimmering and vast, out in the tranquil bay.
Come to the window, sweet is the night-air!
Only, from the long line of spray
Where the sea meets the moon-blanched land,
Listen! you hear the grating roar
Of pebbles which the waves draw back, and fling,
At their return, up the high strand,
Begin, and cease, and then again begin,
With tremulous cadence slow, and bring
The eternal note of sadness in.

Sophocles long ago
Heard it on the Aegean, and it brought
Into his mind the turbid ebb and flow
Of human misery; we
Find also in the sound a thought,
Hearing it by this distant northern sea.

The Sea of Faith
Was once, too, at the full, and round earth's shore
Lay like the folds of a bright girdle furled.
But now I only hear
Its melancholy, long, withdrawing roar,
Retreating, to the breath
Of the night-wind, down the vast edges drear
And naked shingles of the world.

Ah, love, let us be true
To one another! for the world, which seems
To lie before us like a land of dreams,
So various, so beautiful, so new,
Hath really neither joy, nor love, nor light,
Nor certitude, nor peace, nor help for pain;
And we are here as on a darkling plain
Swept with confused alarms of struggle and flight,
Where ignorant armies clash by night.

Walt Whitman

Dirge for Two Veterans

The last sunbeam
Lightly falls from the finished Sabbath,
On the pavement here, and there beyond it is looking,
Down a new-made double grave.

Lo, the moon ascending,
Up from the east the silvery round moon,
Beautiful over the house-tops, ghastly, phantom moon,
Immense and silent moon.

I see a sad procession,
And I hear the sound of coming full-keyed bugles,
All the channels of the city streets they're flooding,
As with voices and with tears.

I hear the great drums pounding,
And the small drums steady whirring,
And every blow of the great convulsive drums,
Strikes me through and through.

For the son is brought with the father,
(In the foremost ranks of the fierce assault they fell,
Two veterans, son and father, dropped together,
And the double grave awaits them.)

Now nearer blow the bugles,
And the drums strike more convulsive,
And the daylight o'er the pavement quite has faded,
And the strong dead-march enwraps me.

In the eastern sky up-buoying,
The sorrowful vast phantom moves illumined,
('Tis some mother's large transparent face,
In heaven brighter growing.)

O strong dead-march you please me!
O moon immense with your silvery face you soothe me!
O my soldiers twain! O my veterans passing to burial!
What I have I also give you.

The moon gives you light,
And the bugles and the drums give you music,
And my heart, O my soldiers, my veterans,
My heart gives you love.

W. E. Henley

Invictus

Out of the night that covers me,
  Black as the pit from pole to pole,
I thank whatever gods may be
  For my unconquerable soul.

In the fell clutch of circumstance
  I have not winced nor cried aloud.
Under the bludgeonings of chance
  My head is bloody, but unbowed.

Beyond this place of wrath and tears
  Looms but the Horror of the shade,
And yet the menace of the years
  Finds and shall find me unafraid.

It matters not how strait the gate,
  How charged with punishments the scroll,
I am the master of my fate:
  I am the captain of my soul.

Algernon Swinburne

A Forsaken Garden (ll. 1–40)

In a coign of the cliff between lowland and highland,
  At the sea-down's edge between windward and lee,
Walled round with rocks as an inland island,
  The ghost of a garden fronts the sea.
A girdle of brushwood and thorn encloses
  The steep square slope of the blossomless bed
Where the weeds that grew green from the graves of its roses
          Now lie dead.

The fields fall southward, abrupt and broken,
  To the low last edge of the long lone land.
If a step should sound or a word be spoken,
  Would a ghost not rise at the strange guest's hand?
So long have the grey bare walks lain guestless,
  Through branches and briars if a man make way,
He shall find no life but the sea-wind's, restless
          Night and day.

The dense hard passage is blind and stifled
  That crawls by a track none turn to climb
To the strait waste place that the years have rifled
  Of all but the thorns that are touched not of time.
The thorns he spares when the rose is taken;
  The rocks are left when he wastes the plain.
The wind that wanders, the weeds wind-shaken,
          These remain.

Not a flower to be pressed of the foot that falls not;
  As the heart of a dead man the seed-plots are dry;
From the thicket of thorns whence the nightingale calls not,
  Could she call, there were never a rose to reply.

Over the meadows that blossom and wither
  Rings but the note of a sea-bird's song;
Only the sun and the rain come hither
          All year long.

The sun burns sere and the rain dishevels
  One gaunt bleak blossom of scentless breath.
Only the wind here hovers and revels
  In a round where life seems barren as death.
Here there was laughing of old, there was weeping,
  Haply, of lovers none ever will know,
Whose eyes went seaward a hundred sleeping
          Years ago.

Gerard Manley Hopkins

Inversnaid

This darksome burn, horseback brown,
His rollrock highroad roaring down,
In coop and in comb the fleece of his foam
Flutes and low to the lake falls home.

A windpuff-bonnet of fáwn-fróth
Turns and twindles over the broth
Of a pool so pitchblack, féll-frówning,
It rounds and rounds Despair to drowning.

Degged with dew, dappled with dew
Are the groins of the braes that the brook treads through,
Wiry heathpacks, flitches of fern,
And the beadbonny ash that sits over the burn.

What would the world be, once bereft
Of wet and of wilderness? Let them be left,
O let them be left, wildness and wet;
Long live the weeds and the wilderness yet.

George Meredith

Lucifer in Starlight

On a starred night Prince Lucifer uprose.
Tired of his dark dominion swung the fiend
Above the rolling ball in cloud part screened,
Where sinners hugged their spectre of repose.
Poor prey to his hot fit of pride were those.
And now upon his western wing he leaned,
Now his huge bulk o'er Afric's sands careened,
Now the black planet shadowed Arctic snows.
Soaring through wider zones that pricked his scars
With memory of the old revolt from Awe,
He reached a middle height, and at the stars,
Which are the brain of heaven, he looked, and sank.
Around the ancient track marched, rank on rank,
The army of unalterable law.

Christina Rossetti

A Frog's Fate

Contemptuous of his home beyond
The village and the village pond,
A large-souled Frog who spurned each byeway
Hopped along the imperial highway.

Nor grunting pig nor barking dog
Could disconcert so great a Frog.
The morning dew was lingering yet,
His sides to cool, his tongue to wet:
The night-dew, when the night should come
A travelled Frog would send him home.

Not so, alas! The wayside grass
Sees him no more: not so, alas!
A broad-wheeled waggon unawares
Ran him down, his joys, his cares.
From dying choke one feeble croak
The Frog's perpetual silence broke: –
'Ye buoyant Frogs, ye great and small,
Even I am mortal after all!
My road to fame turns out a wry way:
I perish on the hideous highway;
Oh for my old familiar byeway!'

The choking Frog sobbed and was gone;
The Waggoner strode whistling on.
Unconscious of the carnage done,
Whistling that Waggoner strode on –
Whistling (it may have happened so)
'A froggy would a-wooing go.'

A hypothetic frog trolled he
Obtuse to a reality.

O rich and poor, O great and small,
Such oversights beset us all.
The mangled Frog abides incog,
The uninteresting actual frog:
The hypothetic frog alone
Is the one frog we dwell upon.

Amy Levy

Philosophy

Ere all the world had grown so drear,
When I was young and you were here,
'Mid summer roses in summer weather,
What pleasant times we've had together!

We were not Phyllis, simple-sweet,
And Corydon; we did not meet
By brook or meadow, but among
A Philistine and flippant throng

Which much we scorned; (less rigorous
It had no scorn at all for us!)
How many an eve of sweet July,
Heedless of Mrs Grundy's eye,

We've scaled the stairway's topmost height,
And sat there talking half the night;
And, gazing on the crowd below,
Thanked Fate and Heaven that made us so; –

To hold the pure delights of brain
Above light loves and sweet champagne.
For, you and I, we did eschew
The egoistic 'I' and 'you;'

And all our observations ran
On Art and Letters, Life and Man.
Proudly we sat, we two, on high,
Throned in our Objectivity;

Scarce friends, not lovers (each avers),
But sexless, safe Philosophers.

Dear Friend, you must not deem me light
If, as I lie and muse tonight,
I give a smile and not a sigh
To thoughts of our Philosophy.

Robert Bridges

London Snow

When men were all asleep the snow came flying,
In large white flakes falling on the city brown,
Stealthily and perpetually settling and loosely lying,
  Hushing the latest traffic of the drowsy town;
Deadening, muffling, stifling its murmurs failing;
Lazily and incessantly floating down and down:
  Silently sifting and veiling road, roof and railing;
Hiding difference, making unevenness even,
Into angles and crevices softly drifting and sailing.
  All night it fell, and when full inches seven
It lay in the depth of its uncompacted lightness,
The clouds blew off from a high and frosty heaven;
  And all woke earlier for the unaccustomed brightness
Of the winter dawning, the strange unheavenly glare:
The eye marvelled – marvelled at the dazzling whiteness;
  The ear hearkened to the stillness of the solemn air;
No sound of wheel rumbling nor of foot falling,
And the busy morning cries came thin and spare.
  Then boys I heard, as they went to school, calling,
They gathered up the crystal manna to freeze
Their tongues with tasting, their hands with snowballing;
  Or rioted in a drift, plunging up to the knees;
Or peering up from under the white-mossed wonder,
'O look at the trees!' they cried, 'O look at the trees!'
  With lessened load a few carts creak and blunder,
Following along the white deserted way,
A country company long dispersed asunder:
  When now already the sun, in pale display
Standing by Paul's high dome, spread forth below
His sparkling beams, and awoke the stir of the day.

For now doors open, and war is waged with the snow;
And trains of sombre men, past tale of number,
Tread long brown paths, as toward their toil they go:
But even for them awhile no cares encumber
Their minds diverted; the daily word is unspoken,
The daily thoughts of labour and sorrow slumber
At the sight of the beauty that greets them, for the charm
they have broken.

Thomas Hardy

Thoughts of Phena

At news of her death

Not a line of her writing have I,
Not a thread of her hair,
No mark of her late time as dame in her dwelling, whereby
I may picture her there;
And in vain do I urge my unsight
To conceive my lost prize
At her close, whom I knew when her dreams were upbrimming with light,
And with laughter her eyes.

What scenes spread around her last days,
Sad, shining, or dim?
Did her gifts and compassions enray and enarch her sweet ways
With an aureate nimb?
Or did life-light decline from her years,
And mischances control
Her full day-star; unease, or regret, or forebodings, or fears
Disennoble her soul?

Thus I do but the phantom retain
Of the maiden of yore
As my relic; yet haply the best of her – fined in my brain
It may be the more
That no line of her writing have I,
Nor a thread of her hair,
No mark of her late time as dame in her dwelling, whereby
I may picture her there.

Robert Louis Stevenson

'Sing me a song of a lad that is gone'

Sing me a song of a lad that is gone,
  Say, could that lad be I?
Merry of soul he sailed on a day
  Over the sea to Skye.

Mull was astern, Rum on the port,
  Eigg on the starboard bow;
Glory of youth glowed in his soul;
  Where is that glory now?

Sing me a song of a lad that is gone,
  Say, could that lad be I?
Merry of soul he sailed on a day
  Over the sea to Skye.

Give me again all that was there,
  Give me the sun that shone!
Give me the eyes, give me the soul,
  Give me the lad that's gone!

Sing me a song of a lad that is gone,
  Say, could that lad be I?
Merry of soul he sailed on a day
  Over the sea to Skye.

Billow and breeze, islands and seas,
  Mountains of rain and sun,
All that was good, all that was fair,
  All that was me is gone.

Mary Elizabeth Coleridge

The Witch

I have walked a great while over the snow,
And I am not tall nor strong.
My clothes are wet, and my teeth are set,
And the way was hard and long.
I have wandered over the fruitful earth,
But I never came here before.
Oh, lift me over the threshold, and let me in at the door!

The cutting wind is a cruel foe.
I dare not stand in the blast.
My hands are stone, and my voice a groan,
And the worst of death is past.
I am but a little maiden still,
My little white feet are sore.
Oh, lift me over the threshold, and let me in at the door!

Her voice was the voice that women have,
Who plead for their heart's desire.
She came – she came – and the quivering flame
Sank and died in the fire.
It never was lit again on my hearth
Since I hurried across the floor,
To lift her over the threshold, and let her in at the door.

Paul Dunbar

Invitation to Love

Come when the nights are bright with stars
Or come when the moon is mellow;
Come when the sun his golden bars
Drops on the hay-field yellow.
Come in the twilight soft and gray,
Come in the night or come in the day,
Come, O Love, whene'er you may,
  And you are welcome, welcome.

You are sweet, O Love, dear Love,
You are soft as the nesting dove.
Come to my heart and bring it rest
As the bird flies home to its welcome nest.

Come when my heart is full of grief
  Or when my heart is merry;
Come with the falling of the leaf
  Or with the reddening cherry.
Come when the year's first blossom blows,
Come when the summer gleams and glows,
Come with the winter's drifting snows,
  And you are welcome, welcome.

Oscar Wilde

The Ballad of Reading Gaol (ll. 1–36)

He did not wear his scarlet coat,
  For blood and wine are red,
And blood and wine were on his hands
  When they found him with the dead,
The poor dead woman whom he loved,
  And murdered in her bed.

He walked amongst the Trial Men
  In a suit of shabby gray;
A cricket cap was on his head,
  And his step seemed light and gay;
But I never saw a man who looked
  So wistfully at the day.

I never saw a man who looked
  With such a wistful eye
Upon that little tent of blue
  Which prisoners call the sky,
And at every drifting cloud that went
  With sails of silver by.

I walked, with other souls in pain,
  Within another ring,
And was wondering if the man had done
  A great or little thing,
When a voice behind me whispered low,
  '*That fellow's got to swing.*'

Dear Christ! the very prison walls
  Suddenly seemed to reel,
And the sky above my head became

Like a casque of scorching steel;
And, though I was a soul in pain,
My pain I could not feel.

I only knew what hunted thought
Quickened his step, and why
He looked upon the garish day
With such a wistful eye;
The man had killed the thing he loved,
And so he had to die.

E. Nesbit

The Things that Matter

Now that I've nearly done my days,
  And grown too stiff to sweep or sew,
I sit and think, till I'm amaze,
  About what lots of things I know:
Things as I've found out one by one –
  And when I'm fast down in the clay,
My knowing things and how they're done
  Will all be lost and thrown away.

There's things, I know, as won't be lost,
  Things as folks write and talk about:
The way to keep your roots from frost,
  And how to get your ink spots out.
What medicine's good for sores and sprains,
  What way to salt your butter down,
What charms will cure your different pains,
  And what will bright your faded gown.

But more important things than these,
  They can't be written in a book:
How fast to boil your greens and peas,
  And how good bacon ought to look;
The feel of real good wearing stuff,
  The kind of apple as will keep,
The look of bread that's rose enough,
  And how to get a child asleep.

Whether the jam is fit to pot,
  Whether the milk is going to turn,
Whether a hen will lay or not,
  Is things as some folks never learn.

I know the weather by the sky,
  I know what herbs grow in what lane;
And if sick men are going to die,
  Or if they'll get about again.

Young wives come in, a-smiling, grave,
  With secrets that they itch to tell:
I know what sort of times they'll have,
  And if they'll have a boy or gell.
And if a lad is ill to bind,
  Or some young maid is hard to lead,
I know when you should speak 'em kind,
  And when it's scolding as they need.

I used to know where birds ud set,
  And likely spots for trout or hare,
And God may want me to forget
  The way to set a line or snare;
But not the way to truss a chick,
  To fry a fish, or baste a roast,
Nor how to tell, when folks are sick,
  What kind of herb will ease them most!

Forgetting seems such silly waste!
  I know so many little things,
And now the Angels will make haste
  To dust it all away with wings!
O God, you made me like to know,
  You kept the things straight in my head,
Please God, if you can make it so,
  Let me know something when I'm dead.

W. E. B. Du Bois

The Song of the Smoke

I am the Smoke King
I am black!
I am swinging in the sky,
I am wringing worlds awry;
I am the thought of the throbbing mills,
I am the soul of the soul-toil kills,
Wraith of the ripple of trading rills;
Up I'm curling from the sod,
I am whirling home to God;
I am the Smoke King
I am black.

I am the Smoke King
I am black!
I am wreathing broken hearts,
I am sheathing love's light darts;
Inspiration of iron times
Wedding the toil of toiling climes,
Shedding the blood of bloodless crimes –
Lurid lowering 'mid the blue,
Torrid towering toward the true,
I am the Smoke King
I am black.

I am the Smoke King
I am black!
I am darkening with song
I am hearkening to wrong!
I will be black as blackness can –
The blacker the mantle, the mightier the man!
For blackness was ancient ere whiteness began.

I am daubing God in night,
I am swabbing Hell in white:
  I am the Smoke King
  I am black.

  I am the Smoke King
  I am black!
I am cursing ruddy morn,
I am hearsing hearts unborn:
  Souls unto me are as stars in a night,
  I whiten my black men – I blacken my white!
  What's the hue of a hide to a man in his might?
Hail! great, gritty, grimy hands –
Sweet Christ, pity toiling lands!
  I am the Smoke King
  I am black.

Rudyard Kipling

The Way through the Woods

They shut the road through the woods
Seventy years ago.
Weather and rain have undone it again,
And now you would never know
There was once a road through the woods
Before they planted the trees.
It is underneath the coppice and heath,
And the thin anemones.
Only the keeper sees
That, where the ring-dove broods,
And the badgers roll at ease,
There was once a road through the woods.

Yet, if you enter the woods
Of a summer evening late,
When the night-air cools on the trout-ringed pools
Where the otter whistles his mate,
(They fear not men in the woods,
Because they see so few)
You will hear the beat of a horse's feet,
And the swish of a skirt in the dew,
Steadily cantering through
The misty solitudes,
As though they perfectly knew
The old lost road through the woods.
But there is no road through the woods.

C. P. Cavafy

The God Abandons Antony

When suddenly, at midnight, you hear
an invisible procession going by
with exquisite music, voices,
don't mourn your luck that's failing now,
work gone wrong, your plans
all proving deceptive – don't mourn them uselessly.
As one long prepared, and graced with courage,
say goodbye to her, the Alexandria that is leaving.
Above all, don't fool yourself, don't say
it was a dream, your ears deceived you:
don't degrade yourself with empty hopes like these.
As one long prepared, and graced with courage,
as is right for you who proved worthy of this kind of city,
go firmly to the window
and listen with deep emotion, but not
with the whining, the pleas of a coward;
listen – your final delectation – to the voices,
to the exquisite music of that strange procession,
and say goodbye to her, to the Alexandria you are losing.

(*Translated by Edmund Keeley and Philip Sherrard*)

Walter de la Mare

Miss Loo

When thin-strewn memory I look through,
I see most clearly poor Miss Loo,
Her tabby cat, her cage of birds,
Her nose, her hair, her muffled words,
And how she'd open her green eyes,
As if in some immense surprise,
Whenever as we sat at tea
She made some small remark to me.

It's always drowsy summer when
From out the past she comes again;
The westering sunshine in a pool
Floats in her parlour still and cool;
While the slim bird its lean wires shakes,
As into piercing song it breaks;
Till Peter's pale-green eyes ajar
Dream, wake; wake, dream, in one brief bar.

And I am sitting, dull and shy,
And she with gaze of vacancy,
And large hands folded on the tray,
Musing the afternoon away;
Her satin bosom heaving slow
With sighs that softly ebb and flow,
And her plain face in such dismay,
It seems unkind to look her way:
Until all cheerful back will come
Her gentle gleaming spirit home:
And one would think that poor Miss Loo
Asked nothing else, if she had you.

G. K. Chesterton

The Rolling English Road

Before the Roman came to Rye or out to Severn strode,
The rolling English drunkard made the rolling English road.
A reeling road, a rolling road, that rambles round the shire,
And after him the parson ran, the sexton and the squire;
A merry road, a mazy road, and such as we did tread
The night we went to Birmingham by way of Beachy Head.

I knew no harm of Bonaparte and plenty of the Squire,
And for to fight the Frenchman I did not much desire;
But I did bash their baggonets because they came arrayed
To straighten out the crooked road an English drunkard made,
Where you and I went down the lane with ale-mugs in our hands,
The night we went to Glastonbury by way of Goodwin Sands.

His sins they were forgiven him; or why do flowers run
Behind him; and the hedges all strengthening in the sun?
The wild thing went from left to right and knew not which was
  which,
But the wild rose was above him when they found him in the ditch.
God pardon us, nor harden us; we did not see so clear
The night we went to Bannockburn by way of Brighton Pier.

My friends, we will not go again or ape an ancient rage,
Or stretch the folly of our youth to be the shame of age,
But walk with clearer eyes and ears this path that wandereth,
And see undrugged in evening light the decent inn of death;
For there is good news yet to hear and fine things to be seen,
Before we go to Paradise by way of Kensal Green.

Amy Lowell

A Blockhead

Before me lies a mass of shapeless days,
  Unseparated atoms, and I must
  Sort them apart and live them. Sifted dust
Covers the formless heap. Reprieves, delays,
There are none, ever. As a monk who prays
  The sliding beads asunder, so I thrust
  Each tasteless particle aside, and just
Begin again the task which never stays.
  And I have known a glory of great suns,
When days flashed by, pulsing with joy and fire!
Drunk bubbled wine in goblets of desire,
  And felt the whipped blood laughing as it runs!
Spilt is that liquor, my too hasty hand
Threw down the cup, and did not understand.

Ezra Pound

The River Merchant's Wife: A Letter

While my hair was still cut straight across my forehead
I played about the front gate, pulling flowers.
You came by on bamboo stilts, playing horse,
You walked about my seat, playing with blue plums.
And we went on living in the village of Chōkan:
Two small people, without dislike or suspicion.

At fourteen I married My Lord you.
I never laughed, being bashful.
Lowering my head, I looked at the wall.
Called to, a thousand times, I never looked back.

At fifteen I stopped scowling,
I desired my dust to be mingled with yours
Forever and forever and forever.
Why should I climb the look out?

At sixteen you departed,
You went into far Ku-tō-yen, by the river of swirling eddies,
And you have been gone five months.
The monkeys make sorrowful noise overhead.

You dragged your feet when you went out.
By the gate now, the moss is grown, the different mosses,
Too deep to clear them away!
The leaves fall early this autumn, in wind.
The paired butterflies are already yellow with August
Over the grass in the West garden;
They hurt me. I grow older.

If you are coming down through the narrows of the river Kiang,
Please let me know beforehand,
And I will come out to meet you
As far as Chō-fū-Sa.

W. H. Davies

The Inquest

I took my oath I would inquire,
   Without affection, hate, or wrath,
Into the death of Ada Wright –
   So help me God! I took that oath.

When I went out to see the corpse,
   The four months' babe that died so young,
I judged it was seven pounds in weight,
   And little more than one foot long.

One eye, that had a yellow lid,
   Was shut – so was the mouth, that smiled;
The left eye open, shining bright –
   It seemed a knowing little child.

For as I looked at that one eye,
   It seemed to laugh, and say with glee:
'What caused my death you'll never know –
   Perhaps my mother murdered me.'

When I went into court again,
   To hear the mother's evidence –
It was a love-child, she explained.
   And smiled, for our intelligence.

'Now, Gentlemen of the Jury,' said
   The coroner – 'this woman's child
By misadventure met its death.'
   'Aye, aye,' said we. The mother smiled.

And I could see that child's one eye
  Which seemed to laugh, and say with glee:
'What caused my death you'll never know –
  Perhaps my mother murdered me.'

HD (Hilda Doolittle)

Sea Rose

Rose, harsh rose,
marred and with stint of petals,
meagre flower, thin,
sparse of leaf,

more precious
than a wet rose
single on a stem –
you are caught in the drift.

Stunted, with small leaf,
you are flung on the sand,
you are lifted
in the crisp sand
that drives in the wind.

Can the spice-rose
drip such acrid fragrance
hardened in a leaf?

Robert Frost

'Out, Out – '

The buzz-saw snarled and rattled in the yard
And made dust and dropped stove-length sticks of wood,
Sweet-scented stuff when the breeze drew across it.
And from there those that lifted eyes could count
Five mountain ranges one behind the other
Under the sunset far into Vermont.
And the saw snarled and rattled, snarled and rattled,
As it ran light, or had to bear a load.
And nothing happened; day was all but done.
Call it a day, I wish they might have said
To please the boy by giving him the half hour
That a boy counts so much when saved from work.
His sister stood beside them in her apron
To tell them 'Supper.' At the word, the saw,
As if to prove saws knew what supper meant,
Leaped out at the boy's hand, or seemed to leap –
He must have given the hand. However it was,
Neither refused the meeting. But the hand!
The boy's first outcry was a rueful laugh,
As he swung toward them holding up the hand,
Half in appeal, but half as if to keep
The life from spilling. Then the boy saw all –
Since he was old enough to know, big boy
Doing a man's work, though a child at heart –
He saw all spoiled. 'Don't let him cut my hand off –
The doctor, when he comes. Don't let him, sister!'
So. But the hand was gone already.
The doctor put him in the dark of ether.
He lay and puffed his lips out with his breath.
And then – the watcher at his pulse took fright.
No one believed. They listened at his heart.

Little – less – nothing! – and that ended it.
No more to build on there. And they, since they
Were not the one dead, turned to their affairs.

Charlotte Mew

Fame

Sometimes in the over-heated house, but not for long,
Smirking and speaking rather loud,
I see myself among the crowd,
Where no one fits the singer to his song,
Or sifts the unpainted from the painted faces
Of the people who are always on my stair;
They were not with me when I walked in heavenly places;
But could I spare
In the blind Earth's great silences and spaces,
The din, the scuffle, the long stare
If I went back and it was not there?
Back to the old known things that are the new,
The folded glory of the gorse, the sweet-briar air,
To the larks that cannot praise us, knowing nothing of what we do,
And the divine, wise trees that do not care.
Yet, to leave Fame, still with such eyes and that bright hair!
God! If I might! And before I go hence
Take in her stead
To our tossed bed,
One little dream, no matter how small, how wild.
Just now, I think I found it in a field, under a fence –
A frail, dead, new-born lamb, ghostly and pitiful and white,
A blot upon the night,
The moon's dropped child!

Anna Wickham

Divorce

A voice from the dark is calling me.
In the close house I nurse a fire.
Out in the dark, cold winds rush free,
To the rock heights of my desire.
I smother in the house in the valley below,
Let me out to the night, let me go, let me go.
Spirits that ride the sweeping blast,
Frozen in rigid tenderness,
Wait! for I leave the fire at last,
My little-love's warm loneliness.
I smother in the house in the valley below.
Let me out to the night, let me go, let me go.

High on the hills are beating drums.
Clear from a line of marching men
To the rock's edge the hero comes.
He calls me, and he calls again.
On the hill there is fighting, victory, or quick death.
In the house is the fire, which I fan with sick breath.
I smother in the house in the valley below,
Let me out to the dark, let me go, let me go.

May Wedderburn Cannan

Rouen

26 April–25 May 1915

Early morning over Rouen, hopeful, high, courageous morning,
And the laughter of adventure and the steepness of the stair,
And the dawn across the river, and the wind across the bridges,
And the empty littered station, and the tired people there.

Can you recall those mornings and the hurry of awakening,
And the long-forgotten wonder if we should miss the way,
And the unfamiliar faces, and the coming of provisions,
And the freshness and the glory of the labour of the day?

Hot noontide over Rouen, and the sun upon the city,
Sun and dust unceasing, and the glare of cloudless skies,
And the voices of the Indians and the endless stream of soldiers,
And the clicking of the tatties, and the buzzing of the flies.

Can you recall those noontides and the reek of steam and coffee,
Heavy-laden noontides with the evening's peace to win,
And the little piles of Woodbines, and the sticky soda bottles,
And the crushes in the 'Parlour', and the letters coming in?

Quiet night-time over Rouen, and the station full of soldiers,
All the youth and pride of England from the ends of all the earth;
And the rifles piled together, and the creaking of the sword-belts,
And the faces bent above them, and the gay, heart-breaking mirth.

Can I forget the passage from the cool white-bedded Aid Post
Past the long sun-blistered coaches of the khaki Red Cross train
To the truck train full of wounded, and the weariness and laughter,
And 'Good-bye, and thank you, Sister', and the empty yards again?

Can you recall the parcels that we made them for the railroad,
Crammed and bulging parcels held together by their string,
And the voices of the sergeants who called the Drafts together,
And the agony and splendour when they stood to save the King?

Can you forget their passing, the cheering and the waving,
The little group of people at the doorway of the shed,
The sudden awful silence when the last train swung to darkness,
And the lonely desolation, and the mocking stars o'erhead?

Can you recall the midnights, and the footsteps of night watchers,
Men who came from darkness and went back to dark again,
And the shadows on the rail-lines and the all inglorious labour,
And the promise of the daylight firing blue the windowpane?

Can you recall the passing through the kitchen door to morning,
Morning very still and solemn breaking slowly on the town,
And the early coastways engines that had met the ships at daybreak,
And the Drafts just out from England, and the day shift coming
  down?

Can you forget returning slowly, stumbling on the cobbles,
And the white-decked Red Cross barges dropping seawards for
  the tide,
And the search for English papers, and the blessed cool of water,
And the peace of half-closed shutters that shut out the world
  outside?

Can I forget the evenings and the sunsets on the island,
And the tall black ships at anchor far below our balcony,
And the distant call of bugles, and the white wine in the glasses,
And the long line of the street lamps, stretching Eastwards to the
  sea?

When the world slips slow to darkness, when the office fire
burns lower,
My heart goes out to Rouen, Rouen all the world away;
When other men remember I remember our Adventure
And the trains that go from Rouen at the ending of the day.

Ivor Gurney

Strange Hells

There are strange hells within the minds war made
Not so often, not so humiliatingly afraid
As one would have expected – the racket and fear guns made.
One hell the Gloucester soldiers they quite put out:
Their first bombardment, when in combined black shout
Of fury, guns aligned, they ducked lower their heads –
And sang with diaphragms fixed beyond all dreads,
That tin and stretched-wire tinkle, that blither of tune:
'Après la guerre fini' till hell all had come down,
Twelve-inch, six-inch, and eighteen pounders hammering hell's
  thunders.
Where are they now, on state-doles, or showing shop-patterns
Or walking town to town sore in borrowed tatterns
Or begged. Some civic routine one never learns.
The heart burns – but has to keep out of the face how heart burns.

Edward Thomas

Lights Out

I have come to the borders of sleep,
The unfathomable deep
Forest where all must lose
Their way, however straight,
Or winding, soon or late;
They cannot choose.

Many a road and track
That, since the dawn's first crack,
Up to the forest brink,
Deceived the travellers
Suddenly now blurs,
And in they sink.

Here love ends,
Despair, ambition ends;
All pleasure and all trouble,
Although most sweet or bitter,
Here ends in sleep that is sweeter
Than tasks most noble.

There is not any book
Or face of dearest look
That I would not turn from now
To go into the unknown
I must enter and leave alone,
I know not how.

The tall forest towers;
Its cloudy foliage lowers

Ahead, shelf above shelf;
Its silence I hear and obey
That I may lose my way
And myself.

Wilfred Owen

The Show

My soul looked down from a vague height, with Death,
As unremembering how I rose or why,
And saw a sad land, weak with sweats of dearth,
Grey, cratered like the moon with hollow woe,
And fitted with great pocks and scabs of plagues.

Across its beard, that horror of harsh wire,
There moved thin caterpillars, slowly uncoiled.
It seemed they pushed themselves to be as plugs
Of ditches, where they writhed and shrivelled, killed.

By them had slimy paths been trailed and scraped
Round myriad warts that might be little hills.

From gloom's last dregs these long-strewn creatures crept,
And vanished out of dawn down hidden holes.

(And smell came up from those foul openings
As out of mouths, or deep wounds deepening.)

On dithering feet upgathered, more and more,
Brown strings, towards strings of grey, with bristling spines,
All migrants from green fields, intent on mire.

Those that were grey, of more abundant spawns,
Ramped on the rest and ate them and were eaten.

I saw their bitten backs curve, loop, and straighten,
I watched those agonies curl, lift, and flatten.

Whereat, in terror what that sight might mean,
I reeled and shivered earthward like a feather.

And Death fell with me, like a deepening moan.

And He, picking a manner of worm, which half had hid
Its bruises in the earth, but crawled no further,
Showed me its feet, the feet of many men,
And the fresh-severed head of it, my head.

W. B. Yeats

The Second Coming

Turning and turning in the widening gyre
The falcon cannot hear the falconer;
Things fall apart; the centre cannot hold;
Mere anarchy is loosed upon the world,
The blood-dimmed tide is loosed, and everywhere
The ceremony of innocence is drowned;
The best lack all conviction, while the worst
Are full of passionate intensity.

Surely some revelation is at hand;
Surely the Second Coming is at hand.
The Second Coming! Hardly are those words out
When a vast image out of *Spiritus Mundi*
Troubles my sight: somewhere in the sands of the desert
A shape with lion body and the head of a man,
A gaze blank and pitiless as the sun,
Is moving its slow thighs, while all about it
Reel shadows of the indignant desert birds.
The darkness drops again; but now I know
That twenty centuries of stony sleep
Were vexed to nightmare by a rocking cradle,
And what rough beast, its hour come round at last,
Slouches towards Bethlehem to be born?

A. E. Housman

'Tell me not here, it needs not saying'

Tell me not here, it needs not saying,
  What tune the enchantress plays
In aftermaths of soft September
  Or under blanching mays,
For she and I were long acquainted
  And I knew all her ways.

On russet floors, by waters idle,
  The pine lets fall its cone;
The cuckoo shouts all day at nothing
  In leafy dells alone;
And traveller's joy beguiles in autumn
  Hearts that have lost their own.

On acres of the seeded grasses
  The changing burnish heaves;
Or marshalled under moons of harvest
  Stand still all night the sheaves;
Or beeches strip in storms for winter
  And stain the wind with leaves.

Possess, as I possessed a season,
  The countries I resign,
Where over elmy plains the highway
  Would mount the hills and shine,
And full of shade the pillared forest
  Would murmur and be mine.

For nature, heartless, witless nature,
   Will neither care nor know
What stranger's feet may find the meadow
   And trespass there and go,
Nor ask amid the dews of morning
   If they are mine or no.

Claude McKay

Harlem Shadows

I hear the halting footsteps of a lass
    In Negro Harlem when the night lets fall
Its veil. I see the shapes of girls who pass
    To bend and barter at desire's call.
Ah, little dark girls who in slippered feet
Go prowling through the night from street to street!

Through the long night until the silver break
    Of day the little gray feet know no rest;
Through the lone night until the last snow-flake
    Has dropped from heaven upon the earth's white breast,
The dusky, half-clad girls of tired feet
Are trudging, thinly shod, from street to street.

Ah, stern harsh world, that in the wretched way
    Of poverty, dishonor and disgrace,
Has pushed the timid little feet of clay,
    The sacred brown feet of my fallen race!
Ah, heart of me, the weary, weary feet
In Harlem wandering from street to street.

Hilaire Belloc

Ha'nacker Mill

Sally is gone that was so kindly,
  Sally is gone from Ha'nacker Hill.
And the Briar grows ever since then so blindly
  And ever since then the clapper is still,
  And the sweeps have fallen from Ha'nacker Mill.

Ha'nacker Hill is in Desolation:
  Ruin a-top and a field unploughed.
And Spirits that call on a fallen nation
  Spirits that loved her calling aloud:
  Spirits abroad in a windy cloud.

Spirits that call and no one answers;
  Ha'nacker's down and England's done.
Wind and Thistle for pipe and dancers
  And never a ploughman under the Sun.
  Never a ploughman. Never a one.

Edna St Vincent Millay

'I, being born a woman and distressed'

I, being born a woman and distressed
By all the needs and notions of my kind,
Am urged by your propinquity to find
Your person fair, and feel a certain zest
To bear your body's weight upon my breast:
So subtly is the fume of life designed,
To clarify the pulse and cloud the mind,
And leave me once again undone, possessed.
Think not for this, however, the poor treason
Of my stout blood against my staggering brain,
I shall remember you with love, or season
My scorn with pity, – let me make it plain:
I find this frenzy insufficient reason
For conversation when we meet again.

T. S. Eliot

Journey of the Magi

'A cold coming we had of it,
Just the worst time of the year
For a journey, and such a long journey:
The ways deep and the weather sharp,
The very dead of winter.'
And the camels galled, sore-footed, refractory,
Lying down in the melting snow.
There were times we regretted
The summer palaces on slopes, the terraces,
And the silken girls bringing sherbet.
Then the camel men cursing and grumbling
And running away, and wanting their liquor and women,
And the night-fires going out, and the lack of shelters,
And the cities hostile and the towns unfriendly
And the villages dirty and charging high prices:
A hard time we had of it.
At the end we preferred to travel all night,
Sleeping in snatches,
With the voices singing in our ears, saying
That this was all folly.

Then at dawn we came down to a temperate valley,
Wet, below the snow line, smelling of vegetation;
With a running stream and a water-mill beating the darkness,
And three trees on the low sky,
And an old white horse galloped away in the meadow.
Then we came to a tavern with vine-leaves over the lintel,
Six hands at an open door dicing for pieces of silver,
And feet kicking the empty wine-skins.
But there was no information, and so we continued

And arrived at evening, not a moment too soon
Finding the place; it was (you may say) satisfactory.

All this was a long time ago, I remember,
And I would do it again, but set down
This set down
This: were we led all that way for
Birth or Death? There was a Birth, certainly,
We had evidence and no doubt. I had seen birth and death,
But had thought they were different; this Birth was
Hard and bitter agony for us, like Death, our death.
We returned to our places, these Kingdoms,
But no longer at ease here, in the old dispensation,
With an alien people clutching their gods.
I should be glad of another death.

Robert Graves

Welsh Incident

'But that was nothing to what things came out
From the sea-caves of Criccieth yonder.'
'What were they? Mermaids? dragons? ghosts?'
'Nothing at all of any things like that.'
'What were they, then?'
'All sorts of queer things,
Things never seen or heard or written about,
Very strange, un-Welsh, utterly peculiar
Things. Oh, solid enough they seemed to touch,
Had anyone dared it. Marvellous creation,
All various shapes and sizes, and no sizes,
All new, each perfectly unlike his neighbour,
Though all came moving slowly out together.'
'Describe just one of them.'
'I am unable.'
'What were their colours?'
'Mostly nameless colours,
Colours you'd like to see; but one was puce
Or perhaps more like crimson, but not purplish.
Some had no colour.'
'Tell me, had they legs?'
'Not a leg or foot among them that I saw.'
'But did these things come out in any order?
What o'clock was it? What was the day of the week?
Who else was present? How was the weather?'
'I was coming to that. It was half-past three
On Easter Tuesday last. The sun was shining.
The Harlech Silver Band played *Marchog Jesu*
On thirty-seven shimmering instruments,
Collecting for Caernarvon's (Fever) Hospital Fund.
The populations of Pwllheli, Criccieth,

Portmadoc, Borth, Tremadoc, Penrhyndeudraeth,
Were all assembled. Criccieth's mayor addressed them
First in good Welsh and then in fluent English,
Twisting his fingers in his chain of office,
Welcoming the things. They came out on the sand,
Not keeping time to the band, moving seaward
Silently at a snail's pace. But at last
The most odd, indescribable thing of all,
Which hardly one man there could see for wonder,
Did something recognizably a something.'
'Well, what?'
'It made a noise.'
'A frightening noise?'
'No, no.'
'A musical noise? A noise of scuffling?
'No, but a very loud, respectable noise –
Like groaning to oneself on Sunday morning
In Chapel, close before the second psalm.'
'What did the mayor do?'
'I was coming to that.'

D. H. Lawrence

Bavarian Gentians

Not every man has gentians in his house
in Soft September, at slow, sad Michaelmas.

Bavarian gentians, big and dark, only dark
darkening the daytime torch-like with the smoking blueness of
 Pluto's gloom,
ribbed and torch-like, with their blaze of darkness spread blue
down flattening into points, flattened under the sweep of white
 day
torch-flower of the blue-smoking darkness, Pluto's dark-blue daze,
black lamps from the halls of Dis, burning dark blue,
giving off darkness, blue darkness, as Demeter's pale lamps give
 off light,
lead me then, lead me the way.

Reach me a gentian, give me a torch!
let me guide myself with the blue, forked torch of this flower
down the darker and darker stairs, where blue is darkened
 on blueness
even where Persephone goes, just now, from the frosted
 September
to the sightless realm where darkness is awake upon the dark
and Persephone herself is but a voice
or a darkness invisible enfolded in the deeper dark
of the arms Plutonic, and pierced with the passion of dense gloom
among the splendour of torches of darkness, shedding darkness
 on the lost bride and her groom.

Dylan Thomas

'The force that through the green fuse drives the flower'

The force that through the green fuse drives the flower
Drives my green age; that blasts the roots of trees
Is my destroyer.
And I am dumb to tell the crooked rose
My youth is bent by the same wintry fever.

The force that drives the water through the rocks
Drives my red blood; that dries the mouthing streams
Turns mine to wax.
And I am dumb to mouth unto my veins
How at the mountain spring the same mouth sucks.

The hand that whirls the water in the pool
Stirs the quicksand; that ropes the blowing wind
Hauls my shroud sail.
And I am dumb to tell the hanging man
How of my clay is made the hangman's lime.

The lips of time leech to the fountain head;
Love drips and gathers, but the fallen blood
Shall calm her sores.
And I am dumb to tell a weather's wind
How time has ticked a heaven round the stars.

And I am dumb to tell the lover's tomb
How at my sheet goes the same crooked worm.

Marianne Moore

Poetry

I, too, dislike it: there are things that are important beyond all
this fiddle.
Reading it, however, with a perfect contempt for it, one
discovers in
it after all, a place for the genuine.
Hands that can grasp, eyes
that can dilate, hair that can rise
if it must, these things are important not because a

high-sounding interpretation can be put upon them but because
they are
useful. When they become so derivative as to become
unintelligible,
the same thing may be said for all of us, that we
do not admire what
we cannot understand: the bat
holding on upside down or in quest of something to

eat, elephants pushing, a wild horse taking a roll, a tireless wolf
under
a tree, the immovable critic twinkling his skin like a horse that
feels a flea, the base-
ball fan, the statistician –
nor is it valid
to discriminate against 'business documents and

school-books'; all these phenomena are important. One must make
a distinction
however: when dragged into prominence by half poets, the result
is not poetry,

nor till the poets among us can be
'literalists of
the imagination –' above
insolence and triviality and can present

for inspection, 'imaginary gardens with real toads in them,' shall
we have
it. In the meantime, if you demand on the one hand,
the raw material of poetry in
all its rawness and
that which is on the other hand
genuine, then you are interested in poetry.

Elizabeth Daryush

Still-Life

Through the open French window the warm sun
lights up the polished breakfast-table, laid
round a bowl of crimson roses, for one –
a service of Worcester porcelain, arrayed
near it a melon, peaches, figs, small hot
rolls in a napkin, fairy rack of toast,
butter in ice, high silver coffee pot,
and, heaped on a salver, the morning's post.

She comes over the lawn, the young heiress,
from her early walk in her garden-wood,
feeling that life's a table set to bless
her delicate desires with all that's good,

that even the unopened future lies
like a love-letter, full of sweet surprise.

John Masefield

Partridges

Here they lie mottled to the ground unseen,
This covey linked together from the nest.
The nosing pointers put them from their rest,
The wings whirr, the guns flash and all has been.

The lucky crumple to the clod, shot clean,
The wounded drop and hurry and lie close;
The sportsmen praise the pointer and his nose,
Until he scents the hiders and is keen.

Tumbled in bag with rabbits, pigeons, hares,
The crumpled corpses have forgotten all
The covey's joys of strong or gliding flight.

But when the planet lamps the coming night,
The few survivors seek those friends of theirs;
The twilight hears and darkness hears them call.

John Betjeman

The Arrest of Oscar Wilde at the Cadogan Hotel

He sipped at a weak hock and seltzer
  As he gazed at the London skies
Through the Nottingham lace of the curtains
  Or was it his bees-winged eyes?

To the right and before him Pont Street
  Did tower in her new built red,
As hard as the morning gaslight
  That shone on his unmade bed,

'I want some more hock in my seltzer,
  And Robbie, please give me your hand –
Is this the end or beginning?
  How can I understand?

'So you've brought me the latest *Yellow Book*:
  And Buchan has got in it now:
Approval of what is approved of
  Is as false as a well-kept vow.

'More hock, Robbie – where is the seltzer?
  Dear boy, pull again at the bell!
They are all little better than *cretins*,
  Though this *is* the Cadogan Hotel.

'One astrakhan coat is at Willis's –
  Another one's at the Savoy:
Do fetch my morocco portmanteau,
  And bring them on later, dear boy.'

A thump, and a murmur of voices –
  ('Oh why must they make such a din?')
As the door of the bedroom swung open
  And TWO PLAIN CLOTHES POLICEMEN came in:

'Mr Woilde, we 'ave come for tew take yew
  Where felons and criminals dwell:
We must ask yew tew leave with us quoietly
  For this *is* the Cadogan Hotel.'

He rose, and he put down *The Yellow Book*.
  He staggered – and, terrible-eyed,
He brushed past the plants on the staircase
  And was helped to a hansom outside.

Louis MacNeice

Bagpipe Music

It's no go the merrygoround, it's no go the rickshaw,
All we want is a limousine and a ticket for the peepshow.
Their knickers are made of crêpe-de-chine, their shoes are made
 of python,
Their halls are lined with tiger rugs and their walls with heads
 of bison.

John MacDonald found a corpse, put it under the sofa,
Waited till it came to life and hit it with a poker,
Sold its eyes for souvenirs, sold its blood for whiskey,
Kept its bones for dumb-bells to use when he was fifty.

It's no go the Yogi-Man, it's no go Blavatsky,
All we want is a bank balance and a bit of skirt in a taxi.

Annie MacDougall went to milk, caught her foot in the heather,
Woke to hear a dance record playing of Old Vienna.
It's no go your maidenheads, it's no go your culture,
All we want is a Dunlop tyre and the devil mend the puncture.

The Laird o'Phelps spent Hogmanay declaring he was sober,
Counted his feet to prove the fact and found he had one foot over.
Mrs Carmichael had her fifth, looked at the job with repulsion,
Said to the midwife 'Take it away; I'm through with
 over-production'.

It's no go the gossip column, it's no go the Ceilidh,
All we want is a mother's help and a sugar-stick for the baby.

Willie Murray cut his thumb, couldn't count the damage,
Took the hide of an Ayrshire cow and used it for a bandage.

His brother caught three hundred cran when the seas were lavish,
Threw the bleeders back in the sea and went upon the parish.

It's no go the Herring Board, it's no go the Bible,
All we want is a packet of fags when our hands are idle.

It's no go the picture palace, it's no go the stadium,
It's no go the country cot with a pot of pink geraniums,
It's no go the Government grants, it's no go the elections,
Sit on your arse for fifty years and hang your hat on a pension.

It's no go my honey love, it's no go my poppet;
Work your hands from day to day, the winds will blow the profit.
The glass is falling hour by hour, the glass will fall forever,
But if you break the bloody glass you won't hold up the weather.

W. H. Auden

Musée des Beaux Arts

About suffering they were never wrong,
The Old Masters: how well they understood
Its human position; how it takes place
While someone else is eating or opening a window or just walking
dully along;
How, when the aged are reverently, passionately waiting
For the miraculous birth, there always must be
Children who did not specially want it to happen, skating
On a pond at the edge of the wood:
They never forgot
That even the dreadful martyrdom must run its course
Anyhow in a corner, some untidy spot
Where the dogs go on with their doggy life and the torturer's horse
Scratches its innocent behind on a tree.

In Breughel's *Icarus*, for instance: how everything turns away
Quite leisurely from the disaster; the ploughman may
Have heard the splash, the forsaken cry,
But for him it was not an important failure; the sun shone
As it had to on the white legs disappearing into the green
Water; and the expensive delicate ship that must have seen
Something amazing, a boy falling out of the sky,
Had somewhere to get to and sailed calmly on.

William Empson

Aubade

Hours before dawn we were woken by the quake.
My house was on a cliff. The thing could take
Bookloads off shelves, break bottles in a row.
Then the long pause and then the bigger shake.
It seemed the best thing to be up and go.

And far too large for my feet to step by.
I hoped that various buildings were brought low.
The heart of standing is you cannot fly.

It seemed quite safe till she got up and dressed.
The guarded tourist makes the guide the test.
Then I said The Garden? Laughing she said No.
Taxi for her and for me healthy rest.
It seemed the best thing to be up and go.

The language problem but you have to try.
Some solid ground for lying could she show?
The heart of standing is you cannot fly.

None of these deaths were her point at all.
The thing was that being woken he would bawl
And finding her not in earshot he would know.
I tried saying Half an Hour to pay this call.
It seemed the best thing to be up and go.

I slept, and blank as that I would yet lie.
Till you have seen what a threat holds below,
The heart of standing is you cannot fly.

Tell me again about Europe and her pains,
Who's tortured by the drought, who by the rains.
Glut me with floods where only the swine can row
Who cuts his throat and let him count his gains.
It seemed the best thing to be up and go.

A bedshift flight to a Far Eastern sky.
Only the same war on a stronger toe.
The heart of standing is you cannot fly.

Tell me more quickly what I lost by this,
Or tell me with less drama what they miss
Who call no die a god for a good throw,
Who say after two aliens had one kiss
It seemed the best thing to be up and go.

But as to risings, I can tell you why.
It is on contradiction that they grow.
It seemed the best thing to be up and go.
Up was the heartening and strong reply.
The heart of standing is we cannot fly.

Alun Lewis

Goodbye

So we must say Goodbye, my darling,
And go, as lovers go, for ever;
Tonight remains, to pack and fix on labels
And make an end of lying down together.

I put a final shilling in the gas,
And watch you slip your dress below your knees
And lie so still I hear your rustling comb
Modulate the autumn in the trees.

And all the countless things I shall remember
Lay mummy-cloths of silence round my head;
I fill the carafe with a drink of water;
You say 'We paid a guinea for this bed,'

And then, 'We'll leave some gas, a little warmth
For the next resident, and these dry flowers,'
And turn your face away, afraid to speak
The big word, that Eternity is ours.

Your kisses close my eyes and yet you stare
As though God struck a child with nameless fears;
Perhaps the water glitters and discloses
Time's chalice and its limpid useless tears.

Everything we renounce except our selves;
Selfishness is the last of all to go;
Our sighs are exhalations of the earth,
Our footprints leave a track across the snow.

We made the universe to be our home,
Our nostrils took the wind to be our breath,
Our hearts are massive towers of delight,
We stride across the seven seas of death.

Yet when all's done you'll keep the emerald
I placed upon your finger in the street;
And I will keep the patches that you sewed
On my old battledress tonight, my sweet.

Henry Reed

Naming of Parts

(from *Lessons of the War*)

Today we have naming of parts. Yesterday,
We had daily cleaning. And tomorrow morning,
We shall have what to do after firing. But today,
Today we have naming of parts. Japonica
Glistens like coral in all the neighbouring gardens,
And today we have naming of parts.

This is the lower sling swivel. And this
Is the upper sling swivel, whose use you will see,
When you are given your slings. And this is the piling swivel,
Which in your case you have not got. The branches
Hold in the gardens their silent, eloquent gestures,
Which in our case we have not got.

This is the safety-catch, which is always released
With an easy flick of the thumb. And please do not let me
See anyone using his finger. You can do it quite easy
If you have any strength in your thumb. The blossoms
Are fragile and motionless, never letting anyone see
Any of them using their finger.

And this you can see is the bolt. The purpose of this
Is to open the breech, as you see. We can slide it
Rapidly backwards and forwards: we call this
Easing the spring. And rapidly backwards and forwards
The early bees are assaulting and fumbling the flowers:
They call it easing the Spring.

They call it easing the Spring: it is perfectly easy
If you have any strength in your thumb: like the bolt,
And the breech, and the cocking-piece, and the point of balance,

Which in our case we have not got; and the almond-blossom
Silent in all of the gardens and the bees going backwards and forwards,
For today we have the naming of parts.

Theodore Roethke

My Papa's Waltz

The whiskey on your breath
Could make a small boy dizzy;
But I hung on like death:
Such waltzing was not easy.

We romped until the pans
Slid from the kitchen shelf;
My mother's countenance
Could not unfrown itself.

The hand that held my wrist
Was battered on one knuckle;
At every step you missed
My right ear scraped a buckle.

You beat time on my head
With a palm caked hard by dirt,
Then waltzed me off to bed
Still clinging to your shirt.

Keith Douglas

How to Kill

Under the parabola of a ball,
a child turning into a man,
I looked into the air too long.
The ball fell in my hand, it sang
in the closed fist: *Open Open*
Behold a gift designed to kill.

Now in my dial of glass appears
the soldier who is going to die.
He smiles, and moves about in ways
his mother knows, habits of his.
The wires touch his face: I cry
NOW. Death, like a familiar, hears

and look, has made a man of dust
of a man of flesh. This sorcery
I do. Being damned, I am amused
to see the centre of love diffused
and the wave of love travel into vacancy.
How easy it is to make a ghost.

The weightless mosquito touches
her tiny shadow on the stone,
and with how like, how infinite
a lightness, man and shadow meet.
They fuse. A shadow is a man
when the mosquito death approaches.

Edith Sitwell

Heart and Mind

SAID the Lion to the Lioness – 'When you are amber dust, –
No more a raging fire like the heat of the Sun
(No liking but all lust) –
Remember still the flowering of the amber blood and bone,
The rippling of bright muscles like a sea,
Remember the rose-prickles of bright paws

Though we shall mate no more
Till the fire of that sun the heart and the moon-cold bone are one.'

Said the Skeleton lying upon the sands of Time –
'The great gold planet that is the mourning heat of the Sun
Is greater than all gold, more powerful
Than the tawny body of a Lion that fire consumes
Like all that grows or leaps . . . so is the heart

More powerful than all dust. Once I was Hercules
Or Samson, strong as the pillars of the seas:
But the flames of the heart consumed me, and the mind
Is but a foolish wind.'

Said the Sun to the Moon – 'When you are but a lonely white crone,
And I, a dead King in my golden armour somewhere in a dark
    wood,
Remember only this of our hopeless love
That never till Time is done
Will the fire of the heart and the fire of the mind be one.'

Elizabeth Bishop

The Fish

I caught a tremendous fish
and held him beside the boat
half out of water, with my hook
fast in a corner of his mouth.
He didn't fight.
He hadn't fought at all.
He hung a grunting weight,
battered and venerable
and homely. Here and there
his brown skin hung in strips
like ancient wallpaper,
and its pattern of darker brown
was like wallpaper:
shapes like full-blown roses
stained and lost through age.
He was speckled with barnacles,
fine rosettes of lime,
and infested
with tiny white sea-lice,
and underneath two or three
rags of green weed hung down.
While his gills were breathing in
the terrible oxygen
– the frightening gills,
fresh and crisp with blood,
that can cut so badly –
I thought of the coarse white flesh
packed in like feathers,
the big bones and the little bones,
the dramatic reds and blacks
of his shiny entrails,

and the pink swim-bladder
like a big peony.
I looked into his eyes
which were far larger than mine
but shallower, and yellowed,
the irises backed and packed
with tarnished tinfoil
seen through the lenses
of old scratched isinglass.
They shifted a little, but not
to return my stare.
– It was more like the tipping
of an object toward the light.
I admired his sullen face,
the mechanism of his jaw,
and then I saw
that from his lower lip
– if you could call it a lip –
grim, wet, and weaponlike,
hung five old pieces of fish-line,
or four and a wire leader
with the swivel still attached,
with all their five big hooks
grown firmly in his mouth.
A green line, frayed at the end
where he broke it, two heavier lines,
and a fine black thread
still crimped from the strain and snap
when it broke and he got away.
Like medals with their ribbons
frayed and wavering,
a five-haired beard of wisdom
trailing from his aching jaw.
I stared and stared
and victory filled up
the little rented boat,
from the pool of bilge

where oil had spread a rainbow
around the rusted engine
to the bailer rusted orange,
the sun-cracked thwarts,
the oarlocks on their strings,
the gunnels – until everything
was rainbow, rainbow, rainbow!
And I let the fish go.

Philip Larkin

Mr Bleaney

'This was Mr Bleaney's room. He stayed
The whole time he was at the Bodies, till
They moved him.' Flowered curtains, thin and frayed,
Fall to within five inches of the sill,

Whose window shows a strip of building land,
Tussocky, littered. 'Mr Bleaney took
My bit of garden properly in hand.'
Bed, upright chair, sixty-watt bulb, no hook

Behind the door, no room for books or bags –
'I'll take it.' So it happens that I lie
Where Mr Bleaney lay, and stub my fags
On the same saucer-souvenir, and try

Stuffing my ears with cotton-wool, to drown
The jabbering set he egged her on to buy.
I know his habits – what time he came down,
His preference for sauce to gravy, why

He kept on plugging at the four aways –
Likewise their yearly frame: the Frinton folk
Who put him up for summer holidays,
And Christmas at his sister's house in Stoke.

But if he stood and watched the frigid wind
Tousling the clouds, lay on the fusty bed
Telling himself that this was home, and grinned,
And shivered, without shaking off the dread

That how we live measures our own nature,
And at his age having no more to show
Than one hired box should make him pretty sure
He warranted no better, I don't know.

Allen Ginsberg

A Supermarket in California

What thoughts I have of you tonight, Walt Whitman, for I walked down the sidestreets under the trees with a headache self-conscious looking at the full moon.

In my hungry fatigue, and shopping for images, I went into the neon fruit supermarket, dreaming of your enumerations!

What peaches and what penumbras! Whole families shopping at night! Aisles full of husbands! Wives in the avocados, babies in the tomatoes! – and you, Garcia Lorca, what were you doing down by the watermelons?

I saw you, Walt Whitman, childless, lonely old grubber, poking among the meats in the refrigerator and eyeing the grocery boys.

I heard you asking questions of each: Who killed the pork chops? What price bananas? Are you my Angel?

I wandered in and out of the brilliant stacks of cans following you, and followed in my imagination by the store detective.

We strode down the open corridors together in our solitary fancy tasting artichokes, possessing every frozen delicacy, and never passing the cashier.

Where are we going, Walt Whitman? The doors close in an hour. Which way does your beard point tonight?

(I touch your book and dream of our odyssey in the supermarket and feel absurd.)

Will we walk all night through solitary streets? The trees add shade to shade, lights out in the houses, we'll both be lonely.

Will we stroll dreaming of the lost America of love past blue automobiles in driveways, home to our silent cottage?

Ah, dear father, graybeard, lonely old courage-teacher, what America did you have when Charon quit poling his ferry and you got out on a smoking bank and stood watching the boat disappear on the black waters of Lethe?

E. J. Scovell

After Midsummer

Love, we curve downwards, we are set to night
After our midsummer of longest light,
After hay harvest, though the days are warmer
And fruit is rounding on the lap of summer.

Still as in youth in this time of our fruition
Thought sifts to space through the words of definition,
But strangeness darkens now to a constant mood
Like hands shone dark with use or hafts of wood;

And over our dense days of activity
Brooding like stillness and satiety
The wonder deepens as clouds mass over corn
That here we are wakened and to this world born

That with its few colours so steeps and dyes
Our hearts, and with its runic signs implies
Meaning we doubt we read, yet love and fear
The forms more for the darkened light they bear.

It was so in youth too; now youth's spaces gone
And death of parents and our time's dark tone
Shadow our days – even children too, whose birth
And care through by-ways bring our thoughts to death;

Whose force of life speaks of the distant future,
Their helplessness of helpless animal nature;
Who, like the old in their shroud of age, close bound
In childhood, impress our natural pattern and end.

The springy twigs arch over walls and beds
Of lilac buddleia, and the long flower-heads
Run down the air like valleys. Not by force
But weight, the flowers of summer bend our course;

And whether we live or die, from this time on
We must know death better; though here as we stand upon
The rounded summit we think how softly the slope
And the sky have changed, and the further dales come up.

Ted Hughes

Wind

This house has been far out at sea all night,
The woods crashing through darkness, the booming hills,
Winds stampeding the fields under the window
Floundering black astride and blinding wet

Till day rose; then under an orange sky
The hills had new places, and wind wielded
Blade-light, luminous and emerald,
Flexing like the lens of a mad eye.

At noon I scaled along the house-side as far as
The coal-house door. I dared once to look up –
Through the brunt wind that dented the balls of my eyes
The tent of the hills drummed and strained its guyrope,

The fields quivering, the skyline a grimace,
At any second to bang and vanish with a flap:
The wind flung a magpie away and a black-
Back gull bent like an iron bar slowly. The house

Rang like some fine green goblet in the note
That any second would shatter it. Now deep
In chairs, in front of the great fire, we grip
Our hearts and cannot entertain book, thought,

Or each other. We watch the fire blazing,
And feel the roots of the house move, but sit on,
Seeing the window tremble to come in,
Hearing the stones cry out under the horizons.

Denise Levertov

To the Snake

Green Snake, when I hung you round my neck
and stroked your cold, pulsing throat
    as you hissed to me, glinting
arrowy gold scales, and I felt
    the weight of you on my shoulders,
and the whispering silver of your dryness
    sounded close at my ears –

Green Snake – I swore to my companions that certainly
    you were harmless! But truly
I had no certainty, and no hope, only desiring
    to hold you, for that joy,
                                        which left
a long wake of pleasure, as the leaves moved
and you faded into the pattern
of grass and shadows, and I returned
smiling and haunted, to a dark morning.

Robert Lowell

Skunk Hour

For Elizabeth Bishop

Nautilus Island's hermit
heiress still lives through winter in her Spartan cottage;
her sheep still graze above the sea.
Her son's a bishop. Her farmer
is first selectman in our village;
she's in her dotage.

Thirsting for
the hierarchic privacy
of Queen Victoria's century,
she buys up all
the eyesores facing her shore,
and lets them fall.

The season's ill –
we've lost our summer millionaire,
who seemed to leap from an L. L. Bean
catalogue. His nine-knot yawl
was auctioned off to lobstermen.
A red fox stain covers Blue Hill.

And now our fairy
decorator brightens his shop for fall;
his fishnet's filled with orange cork,
orange, his cobbler's bench and awl;
there is no money in his work,
he'd rather marry.

One dark night,
my Tudor Ford climbed the hill's skull;

I watched for love-cars. Lights turned down,
they lay together, hull to hull,
where the graveyard shelves on the town . . .
My mind's not right.

A car radio bleats,
'Love, O careless Love . . .' I hear
my ill-spirit sob in each blood cell,
as if my hand were at its throat . . .
I myself am hell;
nobody's here –

only skunks, that search
in the moonlight for a bite to eat.
They march on their soles up Main Street:
white stripes, moonstruck eyes' red fire
under the chalk-dry and spar spire
of the Trinitarian Church.

I stand on top
of our back steps and breathe the rich air –
a mother skunk with her column of kittens swills the garbage pail.
She jabs her wedge-head in a cup
of sour cream, drops her ostrich tail,
and will not scare.

Patrick Kavanagh

Epic

I have lived in important places, times
When great events were decided, who owned
That half a rood of rock, a no-man's land
Surrounded by our pitchfork-armed claims.
I heard the Duffys shouting 'Damn your soul!'
And old McCabe stripped to the waist, seen
Step the plot defying blue cast-steel –
'Here is the march along these iron stones'.
That was the year of the Munich bother. Which
Was more important? I inclined
To lose my faith in Ballyrush and Gortin
Till Homer's ghost came whispering to my mind.
He said: I made the *Iliad* from such
A local row. Gods make their own importance.

Thom Gunn

Considering the Snail

The snail pushes through a green
night, for the grass is heavy
with water and meets over
the bright path he makes, where rain
has darkened the earth's dark. He
moves in a wood of desire,

pale antlers barely stirring
as he hunts. I cannot tell
what power is at work, drenched there
with purpose, knowing nothing.
What is a snail's fury? All
I think is that if later

I parted the blades above
the tunnel and saw the thin
trail of broken white across
litter, I would never have
imagined the slow passion
to that deliberate progress.

Sylvia Plath

Morning Song

Love set you going like a fat gold watch.
The midwife slapped your footsoles, and your bald cry
Took its place among the elements.

Our voices echo, magnifying your arrival. New statue.
In a drafty museum, your nakedness
Shadows our safety. We stand round blankly as walls.

I'm no more your mother
Than the cloud that distils a mirror to reflect its own slow
Effacement at the wind's hand.

All night your moth-breath
Flickers among the flat pink roses. I wake to listen:
A far sea moves in my ear.

One cry, and I stumble from bed, cow-heavy and floral
In my Victorian nightgown.
Your mouth opens clean as a cat's. The window square

Whitens and swallows its dull stars. And now you try
Your handful of notes;
The clear vowels rise like balloons.

Christopher Logue

War Music

(from *Patrocleia*)

Cut to the Fleet:
Then to the strip between the rampart and the ditch.

The air near Ajax was so thick with arrows, that,
As they came, their shanks tickered against each other;
And under them the Trojans swarmed so thick
Ajax outspread his arms, turned his spear flat,
And simply *pushed*. Yet they came clamouring back until
So many Trojans had a go at him
The iron chaps of Ajax' helmet slapped his cheeks
To soft red pulp, and his head reached back and forth
Like a clapper inside a bell made out of sword blades.
Maybe, even with no breath left,
Big Ajax might have stood it yet; yet
Big and all as he was, Prince Hector meant to burn that ship:
And God was pleased to let him.

Pulling the Trojans back a yard or two
He baited Ajax with his throat; and Ajax took.
As the spear lifted, Hector skipped in range;
As Ajax readied, Hector bared his throat again;
And, as Ajax lunged, Prince Hector jived on his right heel
And snicked the haft clean through its neck
Pruning the bronze nose off – Aie! – it was good to watch
Big Ajax and his spear blundering about for, O,
Two seconds went before he noticed it had gone.
But when he noticed it he knew
God stood by Hector's elbow, not by his;
That God was pleased with Hector, not with Ajax;
And, sensibly enough, he fled.

The ship was burned.

R. S. Thomas

On the Farm

There was Dai Puw. He was no good.
They put him in the fields to dock swedes,
And took the knife from him, when he came home
At late evening with a grin
Like the slash of a knife on his face.

There was Llew Puw, and he was no good.
Every evening after the ploughing
With the big tractor he would sit in his chair,
And stare into the tangled fire garden,
Opening his slow lips like a snail.

There was Huw Puw, too. What shall I say?
I have heard him whistling in the hedges
On and on, as though winter
Would never again leave those fields,
And all the trees were deformed.

And lastly there was the girl:
Beauty under some spell of the beast.
Her pale face was the lantern
By which they read in life's dark book
The shrill sentence: God is love.

Rosemary Tonks

Badly Chosen Lover

Criminal, you took a great piece of my life,
And you took it under false pretences,
That piece of time
– In the clear muscles of my brain
I have the lens and jug of it!
Books, thoughts, meals, days, and houses,
Half Europe, spent like a coarse banknote,
You took it – leaving mud and cabbage stumps.

And, Criminal, I damn you for it (very softly).
My spirit broke her fast on you. And, Turk,
You fed her with the breath of your neck
– In my brain's clear retina
I have the stolen love-behaviour.
Your heart, greedy and tepid, brothel-meat,
Gulped it like a flunkey with erotica.
And very softly, Criminal, I *damn* you for it.

John Berryman

'I don't operate often'

(*Dream Songs* No. 67)

I don't operate often. When I do,
persons take note.
Nurses look amazed. They pale.
The patient is brought back to life, or so.
The reason I don't do this more (I quote)
is: I have a living to fail –

because of my wife & son – to keep from earning.
– Mr Bones, I sees that.
They for these operations thanks you, what?
not pays you. – Right.
You have seldom been so understanding.
Now there is further a difficulty with the light:

I am obliged to perform in complete darkness
operations of great delicacy
on my self.
– Mr Bones, you terrifies me.
No wonder they don't pay you. Will you die?
– My
                    friend, I succeeded. Later.

Frank O'Hara

The Day Lady Died

It is 12:20 in New York a Friday
three days after Bastille day, yes
it is 1959 and I go get a shoeshine
because I will get off the 4:19 in Easthampton
at 7:15 and then go straight to dinner
and I don't know the people who will feed me

I walk up the muggy street beginning to sun
and have a hamburger and a malted and buy
an ugly NEW WORLD WRITING to see what the poets
in Ghana are doing these days
                                        I go on to the bank
and Miss Stillwagon (first name Linda I once heard)
doesn't even look up my balance for once in her life
and in the GOLDEN GRIFFIN I get a little Verlaine
for Patsy with drawings by Bonnard although I do
think of Hesiod, trans. Richmond Lattimore or
Brendan Behan's new play or *Le Balcon* or *Les Nègres*
of Genet, but I don't, I stick with Verlaine
after practically going to sleep with quandariness

and for Mike I just stroll into the PARK LANE
Liquor Store and ask for a bottle of Strega and
then I go back where I came from to 6th Avenue
and the tobacconist in the Ziegfeld Theatre and
casually ask for a carton of Gauloises and a carton
of Picayunes, and a NEW YORK POST with her face on it

and I am sweating a lot by now and thinking of
leaning on the john door in the 5 SPOT
while she whispered a song along the keyboard
to Mal Waldron and everyone and I stopped breathing

Basil Bunting

What the Chairman Told Tom

Poetry? It's a hobby.
I run model trains.
Mr Shaw there breeds pigeons.

It's not work. You don't sweat.
Nobody pays for it.
You *could* advertise soap.

Art, that's opera; or repertory –
The Desert Song.
Nancy was in the chorus.

But to ask for twelve pounds a week –
married, aren't you? –
you've got a nerve.

How could I look a bus conductor
in the face
if I paid you twelve pounds?

Who says it's poetry, anyhow?
My ten year old
can do it *and* rhyme.

I get three thousand and expenses,
a car, vouchers,
but I'm an accountant.

They do what I tell them,
my company.
What do *you* do?

Nasty little words, nasty long words,
it's unhealthy.
I want to wash when I meet a poet.

They're Reds, addicts,
all delinquents.
What you write is rot.

Mr Hines says so, and he's a schoolteacher,
he ought to know.
Go and find *work*.

Elma Mitchell

Thoughts after Ruskin

Women reminded him of lilies and roses.
Me they remind rather of blood and soap,
Armed with a warm rag, assaulting noses,
Ears, neck, mouth and all the secret places:

Armed with a sharp knife, cutting up liver,
Holding hearts to bleed under a running tap,
Gutting and stuffing, pickling and preserving,
Scalding, blanching, broiling, pulverizing,
– All the terrible chemistry of their kitchens.

Their distant husbands lean across mahogany
And delicately manipulate the market,
While safe at home, the tender and the gentle
Are killing tiny mice, dead snap by the neck,
Asphyxiating flies, evicting spiders,
Scrubbing, scouring aloud, disturbing cupboards,
Committing things to dustbins, twisting, wringing,
Wrists red and knuckles white and fingers puckered,
Pulpy, tepid. Steering screaming cleaners
Around the snags of furniture, they straighten
And haul out sheets from under the incontinent
And heavy old, stoop to importunate young,
Tugging, folding, tucking, zipping, buttoning,
Spooning in food, encouraging excretion,
Mopping up vomit, stabbing cloth with needles,
Contorting wool around knitting needles,
Creating snug and comfy on their needles.

Their huge hands! their everywhere eyes! their voices
Raised to convey across the hullabaloo,

Their massive thighs and breasts dispensing comfort,
Their bloody passages and hairy crannies,
Their wombs that pocket a man upside down!

And when all's over, off with overalls,
Quickly consulting clocks, they go upstairs,
Sit and sigh a little, brushing hair,
And somehow find, in mirrors, colours, odours,
Their essences of lilies and of roses.

Charles Causley

Ballad of the Bread Man

Mary stood in the kitchen
  Baking a loaf of bread.
An angel flew in through the window.
  'We've a job for you,' he said.

'God in his big gold heaven
  Sitting in his big blue chair,
Wanted a mother for his little son.
  Suddenly saw you there.'

Mary shook and trembled,
  'It isn't true what you say.'
'Don't say that,' said the angel.
  'The baby's on its way.'

Joseph was in the workshop
  Planing a piece of wood.
'The old man's past it,' the neighbours said.
  'That girl's been up to no good.'

'And who was that elegant fellow,'
  They said, 'in the shiny gear?'
The things they said about Gabriel
  Were hardly fit to hear.

Mary never answered,
  Mary never replied.
She kept the information,
  Like the baby, safe inside.

It was the election winter.
  They went to vote in town.
When Mary found her time had come
  The hotels let her down.

The baby was born in an annexe
  Next to the local pub.
At midnight, a delegation
  Turned up from the Farmers' Club.

They talked about an explosion
  That made a hole in the sky,
Said they'd been sent to the Lamb & Flag
  To see God come down from on high.

A few days later a bishop
  And a five-star general were seen
With the head of an African country
  In a bullet-proof limousine.

'We've come,' they said, 'with tokens
  For the little boy to choose.'
Told the tale about war and peace
  In the television news.

After them came the soldiers
  With rifle and bomb and gun,
Looking for enemies of the state.
  The family had packed and gone.

When they got back to the village
  The neighbours said, to a man,
'That boy will never be one of us,
  Though he does what he blessed well can.'

He went round to all the people
  A paper crown on his head.
Here is some bread from my father.
  Take, eat, he said.

Nobody seemed very hungry.
  Nobody seemed to care.
Nobody saw the god in himself
  Quietly standing there.

He finished up in the papers.
  He came to a very bad end.
He was charged with bringing the living to life.
  No man was that prisoner's friend.

There's only one kind of punishment
  To fit that kind of a crime.
They rigged a trial and shot him dead.
  They were only just in time.

They lifted the young man by the leg,
  They lifted him by the arm,
They locked him in a cathedral
  In case he came to harm.

They stored him safe as water
  Under seven rocks.
One Sunday morning he burst out
  Like a jack-in-the-box.

Through the town he went walking.
  He showed them the holes in his head.
Now do you want any loaves? he cried.
  'Not today,' they said.

Edwin Morgan

Strawberries

There were never strawberries
like the ones we had
that sultry afternoon
sitting on the step
of the open french window
facing each other
your knees held in mine
the blue plates in our laps
the strawberries glistening
in the hot sunlight
we dipped them in sugar
looking at each other
not hurrying the feast
for one to come
the empty plates
laid on the stone together
with the two forks crossed
and I bent towards you
sweet in that air
in my arms
abandoned like a child
from your eager mouth
the taste of strawberries
in my memory
lean back again
let me love you

let the sun beat
on our forgetfulness
one hour of all

the heat intense
and summer lightning
on the Kilpatrick hills

let the storm wash the plates

W. S. Graham

The Beast in the Space

Shut up. Shut up. There's nobody here.
If you think you hear somebody knocking
On the other side of the words, pay
No attention. It will be only
The great creature that thumps its tail
On silence on the other side.
If you do not even hear that
I'll give the beast a quick skelp
And through Art you'll hear it yelp.

The beast that lives on silence takes
Its bite out of either side.
It pads and sniffs between us. Now
It comes and laps my meaning up.
Call it over. Call it across
This curious necessary space.
Get off, you terrible inhabiter
Of silence. I'll not have it. Get
Away to whoever it is will have you.

He's gone and if he's gone to you
That's fair enough. For on this side
Of the words it's late. The heavy moth
Bangs on the pane. The whole house
Is sleeping and I remember
I am not here, only the space
I sent the terrible beast across.
Watch. He bites. Listen gently
To any song he snorts or growls
And give him food. He means neither
Well or ill towards you. Above
All, shut up. Give him your love.

Geoffrey Hill

The Kingdom of Offa

(*Mercian Hymns VII*)

Gas-holders, russet among fields. Milldams, marlpools
that lay unstirring. Eel-swarms. Coagulations of
frogs: once with branches and half-bricks, he
battered a ditchful; then sidled away from the
stillness and silence.

Ceolred was his friend and remained so, even after
the day of the lost fighter: a biplane, already
obsolete and irreplaceable, two inches of heavy
snub silver. Ceolred let it spin through a hole
in the classroom-floorboards, softly, into the
rat-droppings and coins.

After school he lured Ceolred, who was sniggering
with fright, down to the old quarries, and flayed
him. Then, leaving Ceolred, he journeyed for hours,
calm and alone, in his private derelict sandlorry
named *Albion*.

Derek Walcott

Sea Canes

Half my friends are dead.
I will make new ones, said earth.
No, give me them back, as they were, instead
with faults and all, I cried.

Tonight I can snatch their talk
from the faint surf's drone
through the canes, but I cannot walk

on the moonlit leaves of ocean
down that white road alone,
or float with the dreaming motion

of owls leaving earth's load.
O earth, the number of friends you keep
exceeds those left to be loved.

The sea canes by the cliff flash green and silver;
they were the seraph lances of my faith,
but out of what is lost grows something stronger

that has the rational radiance of stone,
enduring moonlight, further than despair,
strong as the wind, that through dividing canes

brings those we love before us, as they were,
with faults and all, not nobler, just there.

Stevie Smith

The Galloping Cat

Oh I am a cat that likes to
Gallop about doing good
So
One day when I was
Galloping about doing good, I saw
A Figure in the path; I said:
Get off! (Be-
cause
I am a cat that likes to
Gallop about doing good)
But he did not move, instead
He raised his hand as if
To land me a cuff
So I made to dodge so as to
Prevent him bringing it orf,
Un-for-tune-ately I slid
On a banana skin
Some Ass had left instead
Of putting in the bin. So
His hand caught me on the cheek
I tried
To lay his arm open from wrist to elbow
With my sharp teeth
Because I am
A cat that likes to gallop about doing good.
Would you believe it?
He wasn't there
My teeth met nothing but air,
But a Voice said: Poor cat

(Meaning me) and a soft stroke
Came on me head
Since when
I have been bald.
I regard myself as
A martyr to doing good.
Also I heard a swoosh
As of wings, and saw
A halo shining at the height of
Mrs Gubbins's backyard fence,
So I thought: What's the good
Of galloping about doing good
When angels stand in the path
And do not do as they should
Such as having an arm to be bitten off
All the same I
Intend to go on being
A cat that likes to
Gallop about doing good
So
Now with my bald head I go,
Chopping the untidy flowers down, to and fro,
An' scooping up the grass to show
Underneath
The cinder path of wrath
Ha ha ha ha, ho,
Angels aren't the only ones who do not know
What's what and that
Galloping about doing good
Is a full-time job
That needs
An experienced eye of earthly
Sharpness, worth I dare say
(If you'll forgive a personal note)
A good deal more

Than all that skyey stuff
Of angels that make so bold as
To pity a cat like me that
Gallops about doing good.

Michael Longley

Wounds

Here are two pictures from my father's head –
I have kept them like secrets until now:
First, the Ulster Division at the Somme
Going over the top with 'Fuck the Pope!'
'No Surrender!': a boy about to die,
Screaming 'Give 'em one for the Shankill!'
'Wilder than Gurkhas' were my father's words
Of admiration and bewilderment.
Next comes the London-Scottish padre
Resettling kilts with his swagger-stick,
With a stylish backhand and a prayer.
Over a landscape of dead buttocks
My father followed him for fifty years.
At last, a belated casualty,
He said – lead traces flaring till they hurt –
'I am dying for King and Country, slowly.'
I touched his hand, his thin head I touched.

Now, with military honours of a kind,
With his badges, his medals like rainbows,
His spinning compass, I bury beside him
Three teenage soldiers, bellies full of
Bullets and Irish beer, their flies undone.
A packet of Woodbines I throw in,
A lucifer, the Sacred Heart of Jesus
Paralysed as heavy guns put out
The night-light in a nursery for ever;
Also a bus-conductor's uniform –
He collapsed beside his carpet-slippers
Without a murmur, shot through the head
By a shivering boy who wandered in

Before they could turn the television down
Or tidy away the supper dishes.
To the children, to a bewildered wife,
I think 'Sorry Missus' was what he said.

David Jones

A, a, a, Domine Deus

I said, Ah! What shall I write?
I enquired up and down.
    (He's tricked me before
with his manifold lurking-places.)
I looked for His symbol at the door.
I have looked for a long while
    at the textures and contours.
I have run a hand over the trivial intersections.
I have journeyed among the dead forms
    causation projects from pillar to pylon.
I have tired the eyes of the mind
    regarding the colours and lights.
I have felt for His Wounds
    in nozzles and containers.
I have wondered for the automatic devices.
I have tested the inane patterns
    without prejudice.
I have been on my guard
    not to condemn the unfamiliar.
For it is easy to miss Him
    at the turn of a civilization.

I have watched the wheels go round in case I might see the living creatures like the appearance of lamps, in case I might see the Living God projected from the Machine. I have said to the perfected steel, be my sister and for the glassy towers I thought I felt some beginnings of His creature, but *A, a, a, Domine Deus*, my hands found the glazed work unrefined and the terrible crystal a stage-paste . . . *Eia, Domine Deus.*

Derek Mahon

A Disused Shed in Co. Wexford

Even now there are places where a thought might grow –
Peruvian mines, worked out and abandoned
To a slow clock of condensation,
An echo trapped for ever, and a flutter
Of wild flowers in the lift-shaft,
Indian compounds where the wind dances
And a door bangs with diminished confidence,
Lime crevices behind rippling rain-barrels,
Dog corners for bone burials;
And in a disused shed in Co. Wexford,

Deep in the grounds of a burnt-out hotel,
Among the bathtubs and the washbasins
A thousand mushrooms crowd to a keyhole.
This is the one star in their firmament
Or frames a star within a star.
What should they do there but desire?
So many days beyond the rhododendrons
With the world waltzing in its bowl of cloud,
They have learnt patience and silence
Listening to the rooks querulous in the high wood.

They have been waiting for us in a foetor
Of vegetable sweat since civil war days,
Since the gravel-crunching, interminable departure
Of the expropriated mycologist.
He never came back, and light since then
Is a keyhole rusting gently after rain.
Spiders have spun, flies dusted to mildew
And once a day, perhaps, they have heard something –

A trickle of masonry, a shout from the blue
Or a lorry changing gear at the end of the lane.

There have been deaths, the pale flesh flaking
Into the earth that nourished it;
And nightmares, born of these and the grim
Dominion of stale air and rank moisture.
Those nearest the door grow strong –
'Elbow room! Elbow room!'
The rest, dim in a twilight of crumbling
Utensils and broken pitchers, groaning
For their deliverance, have been so long
Expectant that there is left only the posture.

A half century, without visitors, in the dark –
Poor preparation for the cracking lock
And creak of hinges; magi, moonmen,
Powdery prisoners of the old regime,
Web-throated, stalked like triffids, racked by drought
And insomnia, only the ghost of a scream
At the flash-bulb firing-squad we wake them with
Shows there is life yet in their feverish forms.
Grown beyond nature now, soft food for worms,
They lift frail heads in gravity and good faith.

They are begging us, you see, in their wordless way,
To do something, to speak on their behalf
Or at least not to close the door again.
Lost people of Treblinka and Pompeii!
'Save us, save us,' they seem to say,
'Let the god not abandon us
Who have come so far in darkness and in pain.
We too had our lives to live.
You with your light meter and relaxed itinerary,
Let not our naive labours have been in vain!'

Yehuda Amichai

'My father, in a white space suit'

My father, in a white space suit,
walks around with the light, heavy steps of the dead
over the surface of my life that doesn't
hold onto a thing.

He calls out names: This is the Crater of Childhood.
This is an abyss. This happened at your Bar Mitzvah. These
are white peaks. This is a deep voice
from then. He takes specimens and puts them away in his gear:
sand, words, the sighing stones of my dreams.
He surveys and determines. He calls me
the planet of his longings, land of my childhood, his
childhood, our childhood.

'Learn to play the violin, my son. When you are
grown-up, music will help you
in difficult moments of loneliness and pain.'
That's what he told me once, but I didn't believe him.

And then he floats, how he floats, into the grief
of his endless white death.

(*Translated by Chana Bloch and Stephen Mitchell*)

Anne Stevenson

A Summer Place

(*Vermont, 1974*)

You know that house she called home,
so sleek, so clapboard-white,
that used to be some country jobber's blight
or scab on our hill's arm.
You can see the two cellars of the barn –
stones still squatting where the fellow stacked them.

He worked the place as a farm,
though how, with stones for soil, she never knew.
Partly she hoped he'd been a poet, too.
Why else hang Haystack mountain and its view
from northwest windows?
It was the view she bought it for. He'd gone.
The house sagged on its frame. The barns were down.

The use she saw for it was not to be
of use. A summer place. A lovely
setting where fine minds could graze
at leisure on long summer days
and gather books from bushes, phrase by phrase.
Work would be thought. A tractor bought for play
would scare unnecessary ugly scrub away.

A white gem set on a green silk glove
she bought and owned there.
And summers wore it, just as she would wear
each summer like a dress of sacred air,
until the house was half compounded of
foundations, beams and paint – half of her love.

She lived profoundly, felt, wrote from her heart,
knew each confessional songbird by its voice,
cloistered her garden with bee balm and fanning iris,
sat, stained by sunsets, in a vault of noise,
listening through cricket prayer for whitethroat,
hermit thrush. And couldn't keep it out:
the shade of something wrong, a fear, a doubt.

As though she heard the house stir in its plaster,
stones depart unsteadily from walls,
the woods, unwatched, stretch out their roots like claws
and tear through careful fences, fiercer than saws.
Something alive lived under her mind-cropped pasture,
hated the house. Or worse, loved. Hungering after
its perfectly closed compactness.

She dreamed or daydreamed what it might have come to,
the house itself wanting the view
to take it, and the view's love gathering into
brambles, tendrils, trunks of maples, needing
her every window, entering, seeding.
Fear of attack kept her from sleeping,
kept her awake in her white room, pacing, weeping.

But you see the place still stands there, pretty as new.
Whatever she thought the mountain and trees would do,
they did, and took her with them, and withdrew.

Fleur Adcock

The Ex-Queen among the Astronomers

They serve revolving saucer eyes,
dishes of stars; they wait upon
huge lenses hung aloft to frame
the slow procession of the skies.

They calculate, adjust, record,
watch transits, measure distances.
They carry pocket telescopes
to spy through when they walk abroad.

Spectra possess their eyes; they face
upwards, alert for meteorites,
cherishing little glassy worlds:
receptacles for outer space.

But she, exile, expelled, ex-queen,
swishes among the men of science
waiting for cloudy skies, for nights
when constellations can't be seen.

She wears the rings he let her keep;
she walks as she was taught to walk
for his approval, years ago.
His bitter features taunt her sleep.

And so when these have laid aside
their telescopes, when lids are closed
between machine and sky, she seeks
terrestrial bodies to bestride.

She plucks this one or that among
the astronomers, and is become
his canopy, his occultation;
she sucks at earlobe, penis, tongue

mouthing the tubes of flesh; her hair
crackles, her eyes are comet-sparks.
She brings the distant briefly close
above his dreamy abstract stare.

Elizabeth Bartlett

WEA Course

This evening we are doing Pasternak.
Last week we did Alexander Solzhenitsyn.
Outside this room which has wall to wall carpets
And stands illuminated in its own grounds,
The English autumn dies, modest and well-mannered,
The leaves swept away from the drive, the sun still warm
During the daylight hours, warmth reflected upon the face
Of our tutor, who could be my son, and looks like
D. H. Lawrence.
They should have warned me of Simochka
Who sits on my right in fashionable clothes,
And long blond hair, or Nerzhin,
Who was transferred at the end of chapter nine.
We sit in a circle, but Dante would not have recognized us
As persons with grave and tranquil eyes and great
Authority in our carriage and attitude.
This proves we have actually read *The First Circle*,
But this week I am glad to have travelled
The long train journey without Omar Sharif,
And seen the candles burn, and the iced rowanberries.
Across the room sits Lara, rather silent and also
A librarian, and next to her the Public Prosecutor.
Outside the wind is blowing, and the snow blocks out
This commuter town, silting against the door.
We are trapped, we cannot escape, we grovel
For a few potatoes, a few logs of wood.
Red specks and threads of blood gleam on the snow,
And the sound of gun-fire ends the class as we flee
In cars and on bicycles with our books under our arms.
Next week to Sicily with Lampedusa,
Nunc et in hora mortis nostrae. Amen,

And I shall be cast for the Leopard's wife,
Gesummaria, how far away the snow will seem.
It will be hot wherever we are, and Bendico
Will follow me home through the neon-lighted streets,
His dust will crumble and his smell pursue me,
As Komarovsky pursues me now, in his green car,
Dark as the forests at Varykino, cold as a Russian
Winter, in this Michaelmas weather, cruel and ruthless
As the unseasonable revolution we are all waiting for,
With only a grammar of feeling to defend us.
Ah, Yury, the snow is falling, the stars have gone,
And I am alone; we are lost to each other forever.

Craig Raine

A Martian Sends a Postcard Home

Caxtons are mechanical birds with many wings
and some are treasured for their markings –

they cause the eyes to melt
or the body to shriek without pain.

I have never seen one fly, but
sometimes they perch on the hand.

Mist is when the sky is tired of flight
and rests its soft machine on ground:

then the world is dim and bookish
like engravings under tissue paper.

Rain is when the earth is television.
It has the property of making colours darker.

Model T is a room with the lock inside –
a key is turned to free the world

for movement, so quick there is a film
to watch for anything missed.

But time is tied to the wrist
or kept in a box, ticking with impatience.

In homes, a haunted apparatus sleeps,
that snores when you pick it up.

If the ghost cries, they carry it
to their lips and soothe it to sleep

with sounds. And yet, they wake it up
deliberately, by tickling with a finger.

Only the young are allowed to suffer
openly. Adults go to a punishment room

with water but nothing to eat.
They lock the door and suffer the noises

alone. No one is exempt
and everyone's pain has a different smell.

At night, when all the colours die,
they hide in pairs

and read about themselves –
in colour, with their eyelids shut.

Rita Dove

Ö

Shape the lips to an *o*, say *a*.
That's *island*.

One word of Swedish has changed the whole neighborhood.
When I look up, the yellow house on the corner
is a galleon stranded in flowers. Around it

the wind. Even the high roar of a leaf-mulcher
could be the horn-blast from a ship
as it skirts to the misted shoals.

We don't need much more to keep things going.
Families complete themselves
and refuse to budge from the present,
the present extends its glass forehead to sea
(backyard breezes, scattered cardinals)

and if, one evening, the house on the corner
took off over the marshland,
neither I nor my neighbor
would be amazed. Sometimes

a word is found so right it trembles
at the slightest explanation.
You start out with one thing, end
up with another, and nothing's
like it used to be, not even the future.

Linton Kwesi Johnson

Sonny's Lettah

(*Anti-Sus Poem*)

Brixtan Prison
Jebb Avenue
Landan south-west two
Inglan

Dear Mama,
Good Day.
I hope dat wen
deze few lines reach yu,
they may find yu in di bes af helt.

Mama,
I really don't know how fi tell yu dis,
cause I did mek a salim pramis
fi tek care a likkle Jim
an try mi bes fi look out fi him.

Mama,
I really did try mi bes,
but nondiles
mi sarry fi tell you seh
poor likkle Jim get arres.

It woz di miggle a di rush howah
wen evrybady jus a hosel an a bosel
fi goh home fi dem evenin showah;
mi an Jim stand up
waitin pan a bus,
nat cauzin no fus,
wen all af a sudden
a police van pull-up.

Out jump tree policeman,
di hole a dem carryin batan.
Dem waak straight up to mi an Jim.

One a dem hol awn to Jim
seh him tekin him in;
Jim tell him fi let goh a him
far him noh dhu notn
an him naw teef,
nat even a butn.
Jim start to wriggle
di police start to giggle.

Mama,
mek I tell yu whe dem dhu to Jim
Mama,
mek I tell yu whe dem dhu to him:

dem tump him in him belly
an it turn to jelly
dem lick him pan him back
and him rib get pap
dem lick him pan him hed
but it tuff like led
dem kick him in him seed
an it started to bleed

Mama,
I jus coudn stan-up deh
and noh dhu notn:

soh me jook one in him eye
an him started to cry
mi tump one in him mout
an him started to shout
mi kick one pan him shin
an him started to spin

mi tump him pan him chin
an him drap pan a bin

an crash
an ded.

Mama,
more policeman come dung
an beat mi to di grung;
dem charge Jim fi sus,
dem charge me fi murdah.

Mama,
don fret,
dont get depres
an doun-hearted.
Be af good courage
till I hear fram you.

I remain
your son,
Sonny.

Carolyn Forché

The Colonel

WHAT YOU HAVE HEARD is true. I was in his house. His wife carried a tray of coffee and sugar. His daughter filed her nails, his son went out for the night. There were daily papers, pet dogs, a pistol on the cushion beside him. The moon swung bare on its black cord over the house. On the television was a cop show. It was in English. Broken bottles were embedded in the walls around the house to scoop the kneecaps from a man's legs or cut his hands to lace. On the windows there were gratings like those in liquor stores. We had dinner, rack of lamb, good wine, a gold bell was on the table for calling the maid. The maid brought green mangoes, salt, a type of bread. I was asked how I enjoyed the country. There was a brief commercial in Spanish. His wife took everything away. There was some talk then of how difficult it had become to govern. The parrot said hello on the terrace. The colonel told it to shut up, and pushed himself from the table. My friend said to me with his eyes: say nothing. The colonel returned with a sack used to bring groceries home. He spilled many human ears on the table. They were like dried peach halves. There is no other way to say this. He took one of them in his hands, shook it in our faces, dropped it into a water glass. It came alive there. I am tired of fooling around he said. As for the rights of anyone, tell your people they can go fuck themselves. He swept the ears to the floor with his arm and held the last of his wine in the air. Something for your poetry, no? he said. Some of the ears on the floor caught this scrap of his voice. Some of the ears on the floor were pressed to the ground.

Tony Harrison

Timer

Gold survives the fire that's hot enough
to make you ashes in a standard urn.
An envelope of coarse official buff
contains your wedding ring which wouldn't burn.

Dad told me I'd to tell them at St James's
that the ring should go in the incinerator.
That 'eternity' inscribed with both their names is
his surety that they'd be together, 'later'.

I signed for the parcelled clothing as the son,
the cardy, apron, pants, bra, dress –

The clerk phoned down, *6–8–8–3–1?*
Has she still her ring on? (Slight pause) *Yes!*

It's on my warm palm now, your burnished ring!

I feel your ashes, head, arms, breasts, womb, legs,
sift through its circle slowly, like that thing
you used to let me watch to time the eggs.

Patricia Beer

The Lost Woman

My mother went with no more warning
Than a bright voice and a bad pain.
Home from school on a June morning
And where the brook goes under the lane
I saw the back of a shocking white
Ambulance drawing away from the gate.

She never returned and I never saw
Her buried. So a romance began.
The ivy-mother turned into a tree
That still hops away like a rainbow down
The avenue as I approach.
My tendrils are the ones that clutch.

I made a life for her over the years.
Frustrated no more by a dull marriage
She ran a canteen through several wars.
The wit of a cliché-ridden village
She met her match at an extra-mural
Class and the OU summer school.

Many a hero in his time
And every poet has acquired
A lost woman to haunt the home,
To be compensated and desired,
Who will not alter, who will not grow,
A corpse they need never get to know.

She is nearly always benign. Her habit
Is not to stride at dead of night.
Soft and crepuscular in rabbit-

Light she comes out. Hear how they hate
Themselves for losing her as they did.
Her country is bland and she does not chide.

But my lost woman evermore snaps
From somewhere else: 'You did not love me.
I sacrificed too much perhaps,
I showed you the way to rise above me
And you took it. You are the ghost
With the bat-voice, my dear. *I* am not lost.'

James Fenton

God, A Poem

A nasty surprise in a sandwich,
A drawing-pin caught in your sock,
The limpest of shakes from a hand which
You'd thought would be firm as a rock,

A serious mistake in a nightie,
A grave disappointment all round
Is all that you'll get from th' Almighty,
Is all that you'll get underground.

Oh he *said*: 'If you lay off the crumpet
I'll see you alright in the end.
Just hang on until the last trumpet.
Have faith in me, chum – I'm your friend.'

But if you remind him, he'll tell you:
'I'm sorry, I must have been pissed –
Though your name rings a sort of a bell. You
Should have guessed that I do not exist.

'I didn't exist at Creation,
I didn't exist at the Flood,
And I won't be around for Salvation
To sort out the sheep from the cud –

'Or whatever the phrase is. The fact is
In soteriological terms
I'm a crude existential malpractice
And you are a diet of worms.

‘You’re a nasty surprise in a sandwich.
You’re a drawing-pin caught in my sock.
You’re the limpest of shakes from a hand which
I’d have thought would be firm as a rock,

‘You’re a serious mistake in a nightie,
You’re a grave disappointment all round –
That’s all you are,’ says th’ Almighty,
‘And that’s all that you’ll be underground.’

Peter Porter

Your Attention Please

The Polar DEW has just warned that
A nuclear rocket strike of
At least one thousand megatons
Has been launched by the enemy
Directly at our major cities.
This announcement will take
Two and a quarter minutes to make,
You therefore have a further
Eight and a quarter minutes
To comply with the shelter
Requirements published in the Civil
Defence Code – section Atomic Attack.
A specially shortened Mass
Will be broadcast at the end
Of this announcement –
Protestant and Jewish services
Will begin simultaneously –
Select your wavelength immediately
According to instructions
In the Defence Code. Do not
Take well-loved pets (including birds)
Into your shelter – they will consume
Fresh air. Leave the old and bed-
ridden, you can do nothing for them.
Remember to press the sealing
Switch when everyone is in
The shelter. Set the radiation
Aerial, turn on the geiger barometer.
Turn off your Television now.
Turn off your radio immediately
The Services end. At the same time

Secure explosion plugs in the ears
Of each member of your family. Take
Down your plasma flasks. Give your children
The pills marked one and two
In the C.D. green container, then put
Them to bed. Do not break
The inside airlock seals until
The radiation All Clear shows
(Watch for the cuckoo in your
perspex panel), or your District
Touring Doctor rings your bell.
If before this, your air becomes
Exhausted or if any of your family
Is critically injured, administer
The capsules marked 'Valley Forge'
(Red pocket in No. 1 Survival Kit)
For painless death. (Catholics
Will have been instructed by their priests
What to do in this eventuality.)
This announcement is ending. Our President
Has already given orders for
Massive retaliation – it will be
Decisive. Some of us may die.
Remember, statistically
It is not likely to be you.
All flags are flying fully dressed
On Government buildings – the sun is shining.
Death is the least we have to fear.
We are all in the hands of God,
Whatever happens happens by His Will.
Now go quickly to your shelters.

Kit Wright

The Boys Bump-starting the Hearse

The hearse has stalled in the lane overlooking the river
Where willows are plunging their heads in the bottle-green water
    And bills of green baize drakes kazoo.
    The hearse has stalled and what shall we do?

The old don comes on, a string bag in his strongbox.
He knows what is known about Horace but carries no tool-box.
    Small boys shout in the Cambridge sun.
    The hearse has stalled and what's to be done?

Lime flowers drift in the lane to the baskets of bicycles,
Sticker the wall with yellow and powdery particles.
    Monosyllabic, the driver's curse.
    Everything fires. Except the hearse

Whose gastric and gastric whinnies shoot neutered tom cats
In through the kitchen flaps of back gardens where tomtits
    Wizen away from the dangling crust.
    Who shall restart the returned-to-dust?

Shrill and sudden as birds the boys have planted
Their excellent little shoulders against the lamented
    Who bumps in second. A fart of exhaust.
    On goes the don and the holocaust.

David Dabydeen

Catching Crabs

Ruby and me stalking savannah
Crab season with cutlass and sack like big folk.
Hiding behind stones or clumps of bush
Crabs locked knee-deep in mud mating
And Ruby, seven years old feeling strange at the sex
And me horrified to pick them up
Plunge them into the darkness of bag.
So all day we scout to catch the lonesome ones
Who don't mind cooking because they got no prospect
Of family, and squelching through the mud,
Cutlass clearing bush at our feet,
We come home tired slow, weighed down with plenty
Which Ma throw live into boiling pot piece-piece.
Tonight we'll have one big happy curry feed,
We'll test out who teeth and jaw strongest
Who will grow up to be the biggest
Or who will make most terrible cannibal.

We leave behind a mess of bones and shell
And come to England and America
Where Ruby hustles in a New York tenement
And me writing poetry at Cambridge,
Death long catch Ma, the house boarded up
Breeding wasps, woodlice in its dark-sack belly:
I am afraid to walk through weed yard,
Reach the door, prise open, look,
In case the pot still bubbles magical
On the fireside, and I see Ma
Working a ladle, slow –

Limbed, crustacean-old, alone,
In case the woodsmoke and curry steam
Burn my child-eye and make it cry.

U. A. Fanthorpe

The Cleaner

I've seen it all, you know. Men.
Well, I've been married for thirty-two years,
I can do without them.
I know what they're after.

And these students. They're young, you know.
They don't know what it's all about,
The first years. And these post-grads;
I know what they're after.

They're older, you know. And by Christmas
They've finished here, they've gone. A girl
Can get hurt. I've been here eight years.
I've seen it happen.

Sometimes I say to her friend
You ought to talk to her. Does she know
What she's doing? And the friend'll say
Yes, she does know. Well, I hope I did right.

No need for any of 'em to have a baby,
But do they know? I feel a mother, like.
Once I did ask. I said *Do you know*
And she said *O yes we know how far we're going.*

But these post-grads are older,
They take advantage. These girls, mind,
They're not all as innocent as you'd think.
Twenty stubs in the ashtray.

I can tell a lot from that.

Wendy Cope

Proverbial Ballade

Fine words won't turn the icing pink;
A wild rose has no employees;
Who boils his socks will make them shrink;
Who catches cold is sure to sneeze.
Who has two legs must wash two knees;
Who breaks the egg will find the yolk;
Who locks his door will need his keys –
So say I and so say the folk.

You can't shave with a tiddlywink,
Nor make red wine from garden peas,
Nor show a blindworm how to blink,
Nor teach an old racoon Chinese.
The juiciest orange feels the squeeze;
Who spends his portion will be broke;
Who has no milk can make no cheese –
So say I and so say the folk.

He makes no blot who has no ink,
Nor gathers honey who keeps no bees.
The ship that does not float will sink;
Who'd travel far must cross the seas.
Lone wolves are seldom seen in threes;
A conker ne'er becomes an oak;
Rome wasn't built by chimpanzees –
So say I and so say the folk.

Envoi

Dear friends! If adages like these
Should seem banal, or just a joke,
Remember fish don't grow on trees –
So say I and so say the folk.

Sujata Bhatt

What is Worth Knowing?

That van Gogh's ear, set free
wanted to meet the powerful nose
of Nevsky Avenue.
That Spain has decided to help
NATO. That Spring is supposed to begin
on the 21st March.
That if you put too much salt in the *keema*
just add a few bananas.
That although the Dutch were the first
to help the people of Nicaragua they don't say much
about their history with Indonesia.
That van Gogh collected Japanese prints.
That the Japanese considered
the Dutch to be red-haired barbarians.
That van Gogh's ear remains full of questions
it wants to ask the nose of Nevsky Avenue.
That the vaccinations for cholera, typhoid and yellow fever
are no good – they must be improved.
That red, green and yellow are the most
auspicious colours.
That turmeric and chilli powder are good
disinfectants. Yellow and red.
That often Spring doesn't come
until May. But in some places
it's there in January.
That van Gogh's ear left him because
it wanted to become a snail.
That east and west
meet only in the north and south – but never
in the east or west.
That in March 1986 Darwinism is being

reintroduced in American schools.
That there's a difference
between pigeons and doves, although
a ring-dove is a wood-pigeon.
That the most pleasant thing is to have a fever
of at least 101 – because then the dreams aren't
merely dreams but facts.
That during a fever the soul comes out
for fresh air, that during a fever the soul bothers to
speak to you.
That tigers are courageous and generous-hearted
and never attacked unless provoked –
but leopards,
leopards are malicious and bad-tempered.
That buffaloes too,
water-buffaloes that is, have a short temper.
That a red sky at night is a good sign for sailors,
for sailors . . . what is worth knowing?
What is worth knowing?

Gwendolyn Brooks

Boy Breaking Glass

To Marc Crawford from whom the commission

Whose broken window is a cry of art
(success, that winks aware
as elegance, as a treasonable faith)
is raw: is sonic: is old-eyed première.
Our beautiful flaw and terrible ornament.
Our barbarous and metal little man.

'I shall create! If not a note, a hole.
If not an overture, a desecration.'

Full of pepper and light
and salt and night and cargoes.

'Don't go down the plank
if you see there's no extension.
Each to his grief, each to
his loneliness and fidgety revenge.
Nobody knew where I was and now I am no longer there.'

The only sanity is a cup of tea.
The music is in minors.

Each one other
is having different weather.

'It was you, it was you who threw away my name!
And this is everything I have for me.'

Who has not Congress, lobster, love, luau,
the Regency Room, the Statue of Liberty,
runs. A sloppy amalgamation.
A mistake.
A cliff.
A hymn, a snare, and an exceeding sun.

Kathleen Jamie

The Way We Live

Pass the tambourine, let me bash out praises
to the Lord God of movement, to Absolute
non-friction, flight, and the scarey side:
death by avalanche, birth by failed contraception.
Of chicken tandoori and reggae, loud, from tenements,
commitment, driving fast and unswerving
friendship. Of tee-shirts on pulleys, giros and Bombay,
barmen, dreaming waitresses with many fake-gold
bangles. Of airports, impulse, and waking to uncertainty,
to strip-lights, motorways, or that pantheon –
the mountains. To overdrafts and grafting

and the fit slow pulse of wipers as you're
creeping over Rannoch, while the God of moorland
walks abroad with his entourage of freezing fog,
his bodyguard of snow.
Of endless gloaming in the North, of Asiatic swelter,
to launderettes, anecdotes, passions and exhaustion,
Final Demands and dead men, the skeletal grip
of government. To misery and elation; mixed,
the sod and caprice of landlords.
To the way it fits, the way it is, the way it seems
to be: let me bash out praises – pass the tambourine

Paul Muldoon

Meeting the British

We met the British in the dead of winter.
The sky was lavender

and the snow lavender-blue.
I could hear, far below,

the sound of two streams coming together
(both were frozen over)

and, no less strange,
myself calling out in French

across that forest-
clearing. Neither General Jeffrey Amherst

nor Colonel Henry Bouquet
could stomach our willow-tobacco.

As for the unusual
scent when the Colonel shook out his hand-

kerchief: *C'est la lavande,*
une fleur mauve comme le ciel.

They gave us six fishhooks
and two blankets embroidered with smallpox.

Gillian Clarke

Border

It crumbles
where the land forgets its name
and I'm foreign in my own country.
Fallow, pasture, ploughland
ripped from the hill
beside a broken farm.

The word's exactness
slips from children's tongues.
Saints fade in the parishes.
Fields blur between the scar
of hedgerow and new road.
History forgets itself.

At the garage they're polite.
'Sorry love, no Welsh.'
At the shop I am slapped
by her hard 'What!'
They came for the beauty
but could not hear it speak.

Eavan Boland

The Black Lace Fan My Mother Gave Me

It was the first gift he ever gave her,
buying it for five francs in the Galeries
in prewar Paris. It was stifling.
A starless drought made the nights stormy.

They stayed in the city for the summer.
The met in cafés. She was always early.
He was late. That evening he was later.
They wrapped the fan. He looked at his watch.

She looked down the Boulevard des Capucines.
She ordered more coffee. She stood up.
The streets were emptying. The heat was killing.
She thought the distance smelled of rain and lightning.

These are wild roses, appliquéd on silk by hand,
darkly picked, stitched boldly, quickly.
The rest is tortoiseshell and has the reticent,
clear patience of its element. It is

a worn-out, underwater bullion and it keeps,
even now, an inference of its violation.
The lace is overcast as if the weather
it opened for and offset had entered it.

The past is an empty café terrace.
An airless dusk before thunder. A man running.
And no way to know what happened then –
none at all – unless, of course, you improvise:

the blackbird on this first sultry morning,
in summer, finding buds, worms, fruit,
feels the heat. Suddenly she puts out her wing –
the whole, full, flirtatious span of it.

Carol Ann Duffy

Originally

We came from our own country in a red room
which fell through the fields, our mother singing
our father's name to the turn of the wheels.
My brothers cried, one of them bawling, *Home,*
Home, as the miles rushed back to the city,
the street, the house, the vacant rooms
where we didn't live any more. I stared
at the eyes of a blind toy, holding its paw.

All childhood is an emigration. Some are slow,
leaving you standing, resigned, up an avenue
where no one you know stays. Others are sudden.
Your accent wrong. Corners, which seem familiar,
leading to unimagined pebble-dashed estates, big boys
eating worms and shouting words you don't understand.
My parents' anxiety stirred like a loose tooth
in my head. *I want our own country*, I said.

But then you forget, or don't recall, or change,
and, seeing your brother swallow a slug, feel only
a skelf of shame. I remember my tongue
shedding its skin like a snake, my voice
in the classroom sounding just like the rest. Do I only think
I lost a river, culture, speech, sense of first space
and the right place? Now, *Where do you come from?*
strangers ask. *Originally?* And I hesitate.

Maura Dooley

Explaining Magnetism

Isolated here in the South, fiddling with British Rail
network charts, inhabiting the Underground plan, I learn
again how West means left and East means right.
I used to know that North was always straight ahead,
every map showed that cardinal point, a long feathered
arrow, a capital N. Whichever way I walked the land
restored itself in my own order: true North.

A compass only confused, school got in the way,
pointing at things you couldn't see,
explaining magnetism. In order to find out
I just went straight ahead and up there,
out of sight, was never isolated but isolate.
Down here, we move as one and jump like hamsters,
onto the Circle line. The names don't help much,
recalling that dull board game and me,

broke again, moving a top hat listlessly,
back and forth, left to right, round and round.

Mimi Khalvati

Rubaiyat

Beyond the view of crossroads ringed with breath
her bed appears, the old-rose covers death
has smoothed and stilled; her fingers lie inert,
her nail-file lies beside her in its sheath.

The morning's work over, her final chore
was 'breaking up the sugar' just before
siesta, sitting cross-legged on the carpet,
her slippers lying neatly by the door.

The image of her room behind the pane,
though lost as the winding road shifts its plane,
returns on every straight, like signatures
we trace on glass, forget and find again.

I have inherited her tools: her anvil,
her axe, her old scrolled mat, but not her skill;
and who would choose to chip at sugar-blocks
when sugar-cubes are boxed beside the till?

The scent of lilacs from the road reminds me
of my own garden: a neighbouring tree
grows near the fence. At night its clusters loom
like lantern-moons, pearly-white, unearthly.

I don't mind that the lilac's roots aren't mine.
Its boughs are, and its blooms. It curves its spine
towards my soil and litters it with dying
stars: deadheads I gather up like jasmine.

My grandmother would rise and take my arm,
then sifting through the petals in her palm
would place in mine the whitest of them all:
'Salaam, dokhtaré-mahé-man, salaam!'

'Salaam, my daughter-lovely-as-the-moon!'
Would that the world could see me, Telajune,
through your eyes! Or that I could see a world
that takes such care to tend what fades so soon.

Lavinia Greenlaw

Love from a Foreign City

Dearest, the cockroaches are having babies.
One fell from the ceiling into my gin
with no ill effects. Mother has been.
I showed her the bite marks on the cot
And she gave me the name of her rat-catcher.
He was so impressed by the hole in her u-bend,
he took it home for his personal museum.
I cannot sleep. They are digging up children
on Hackney Marshes. The papers say
when that girl tried to scream for help,
the man cut her tongue out. Not far from here.
There have been more firebombs,
but only at dawn and out in the suburbs.
And a mortar attack. We heard it from the flat,
A thud like someone dropping a table.
They say the pond life coming out of the taps
is completely harmless. A law has been passed
on dangerous dogs: muzzles, tattoos, castration.
When the Labrador over the road jumped up
To say hello to Billie, he wet himself.
The shops in North End Road are all closing.
You can't get your shoes mended anywhere.
The one-way system keeps changing direction,
I get lost a hundred yards from home.
There are parts of the new *A to Z* marked simply
'under development'. Even street names
have been demolished. There is typhoid in Finchley.
Mother has bought me a lavender tree.

Glyn Maxwell

The Eater

Top of the morning, Dogfood Family!
How's the chicken? How's the chicken?
Haven't you grown? Or have you grown,
here in the average kitchen at noontime
    down in the home, at all?

Bang outside, the bank officials
are conga-dancing and in their pinstripe
this is the life! But it isn't your life
out in the swarming city at crushhour
    dodging humans, is it?

Vacant city – where did they find that?
Blossom of litter as the only car
for a man goes by. When the man goes by
his girl will sulkily catch your eye:
    will you catch hers?

Snow-white shop – how do they do that?
Lamb-white medical knowing and gentle
man, advise her, assure and ask her:
do you desire the best for your children
    and theirs? Well *do you*?

Take that journey, delight in chocolate,
you won't find anyone else in the world,
lady, only the man, the sweet man
opening doors and suggesting later
    something – what thing?

Short time no see, Dogfood Family!
How's the chicken? How's the chicken?
How have you done it? Have you done it
with love, regardless of time and income
    and me? Who am I?

I am the eater and I am the eater.
These are my seconds and these are my seconds.
Do you understand that? Do you get that,
you out there where the good things grow
    and rot? Or not?

Jo Shapcott

Phrase Book

I'm standing here inside my skin,
which will do for a Human Remains Pouch
for the moment. Look down there (up here).
Quickly. Slowly. This is my front room

where I'm lost in the action, live from a war,
on screen. I am Englishwoman, I don't understand you,
What's the matter? You are right. You are wrong.
Things are going well (badly). Am I disturbing you?

TV is showing bliss as taught to pilots:
Blend, Low silhouette, Irregular shape, Small,
Secluded. (Please write it down. Please speak slowly.)
Bliss is how it was in this very room

when I raised my body to his mouth,
when he even balanced me in the air,
or at least I thought so and yes the pilots say
yes they have caught it through the Side-Looking

Airborne Radar, and through the J-Stars.
I am expecting a gentleman (a young gentleman,
two gentlemen, some gentlemen). Please send him
(them) up at once. This is really beautiful.

Yes they have seen us, the pilots, in the Kill Box
on their screens, and played the routine for
getting us Stealthed, that is, Cleansed, to you and me,
Taken Out. They know how to move into a single room

like that, to send in with Pinpoint Accuracy, a hundred Harms.
I have two cases and a cardboard box. There is another
bag there. I cannot open my case – look out,
the lock is broken. Have I done enough?

Bliss, the pilots say, is for evasion
and escape. What's love in all this debris?
Just one person pounding another into dust,
into dust. I do not know the word for it yet.

Where is the British Consulate? Please explain.
What does it mean? What must I do? Where
can I find? What have I done? I have done
nothing. Let me pass please. I am an Englishwoman.

Moniza Alvi

The Country at My Shoulder

There's a country at my shoulder,
growing larger – soon it will burst,
rivers will spill out, run down my chest.

My cousin Azam wants visitors to play
ludo with him all the time.
He learns English in a class of seventy.

And I must stand to attention
with the country at my shoulder.
There's an execution in the square –

The woman's dupattas are wet with tears.
The offices have closed
for the white-hot afternoon.

But the women stone-breakers chip away
at boulders, dirt on their bright hems.
They await the men and the trucks.

I try to shake the dust from the country,
smooth it with my hands.
I watch Indian films –

Everyone is very unhappy,
or very happy,
dancing garlanded through parks.

I hear of bribery, family quarrels,
travellers' tales – the stars
are so low you think you can touch them.

Uncle Aqbar drives down the mountain
to arrange his daughter's marriage.
She's studying Christina Rossetti.

When the country bursts, we'll meet.
Uncle Kamil shot a tiger,
it hung over the wardrobe, its jaws

fixed in a roar – I wanted to hide
its head in a towel.
The country has become my body –

I can't break bits off.
The men go home in loose cotton clothes.
In the square there are those who beg –

and those who beg for mercy.
Azam passes the sweetshop,
names the sugar monuments Taj Mahal.

I water the country with English rain,
cover it with English words.
Soon it will burst, or fall like a meteor.

Michael Hofmann

Marvin Gaye

He added the final 'e'
to counteract the imputation of homosexuality.
His father was plain Revd Gay, his son Marvin III.

He slept with his first hooker
in the army, coming off saltpetre.
He thought there was another word for 'virgin' that wasn't
'eunuch'.

Including duets, he had fifty-five chart entries.
His life followed the rhythm of albums and tours.
He had a 'couple of periods of longevity with a woman'.

He preached sex to the cream suits,
the halter tops and the drug-induced personality disorders.
When his hair receded, he grew a woolly hat and beard.

Success was the mother of eccentricity and withdrawal.
In Ostend he felt the eyes of the Belgians on him,
in Topanga someone cut the throats of his two Great Danes.

At forty-four, back in his parents' house,
any one of a number of Marvins might come downstairs.
A dog collar shot a purple dressing-gown, twice.

Jackie Kay

Dusting the Phone

I am spending my time imagining the worst that could happen.
I know this is not a good idea, and that being in love, I could be
spending my time going over the best that has been happening.

The phone rings heralding some disaster. Sirens.
Or it doesn't ring which also means disaster. Sirens.
In which case, who would ring me to tell? Nobody knows.

The future is a long gloved hand. An empty cup.
A marriage. A full house. One night per week
in stranger's white sheets. Forget tomorrow,

You say, don't mention love. I try. It doesn't work.
I assault the postman for a letter. I look for flowers.
I go over and over our times together, re-read them.

This very second I am waiting on the phone.
Silver service. I polish it. I dress for it.
I'll give it extra in return for your call.

Infuriatingly, it sends me hoaxes, wrong numbers;
or worse, calls from boring people. Your voice
disappears into my lonely cotton sheets.

I am trapped in it. I can't move. I want you.
All the time. This is awful – only a photo.
Come on, damn you, ring me. Or else. What?

I don't know what.

Carol Rumens

The Emigrée

There once was a country . . . I left it as a child
but my memory of it is sunlight-clear
for it seems I never saw it in that November
which, I am told, comes to the mildest city.
The worst news I receive of it cannot break
my original view, the bright, filled paperweight.
It may be at war, it may be sick with tyrants,
but I am branded by an impression of sunlight.

The white streets of that city, the graceful slopes
glow even clearer as time rolls its tanks
and the frontiers rise between us, close like waves.
That child's vocabulary I carried here
like a hollow doll, opens and spills a grammar.
Soon I shall have every coloured molecule of it.
It may by now be a lie, banned by the state
but I can't get it off my tongue. It tastes of sunlight.

I have no passport, there's no way back at all
but my city comes to me in its own white plane.
It lies down in front of me, docile as paper;
I comb its hair and love its shining eyes.
My city takes me dancing through the city
of walls. They accuse me of absence, they circle me.
They accuse me of being dark in their free city.
My city hides behind me. They mutter death,
and my shadow falls as evidence of sunlight.

Vicki Feaver

Judith

Wondering how a good woman can murder
I enter the tent of Holofernes,
holding in one hand his long oiled hair
and in the other, raised above
his sleeping, wine-flushed face,
his falchion with its unsheathed
curved blade. And I feel a rush
of tenderness, a longing
to put down my weapon, to lie
sheltered and safe in a warrior's
fumy sweat, under the emerald stars
of his purple and gold canopy,
to melt like a sweet on his tongue
to nothing. And I remember the glare
of the barley field; my husband
pushing away the sponge I pressed
to his burning head; the stubble
puncturing my feet as I ran,
flinging myself on a body
that was already cooling
and stiffening; and the nights
when I lay on the roof – my emptiness
like the emptiness of a temple
with the doors kicked in; and the mornings
when I rolled in the ash of the fire
just to be touched and dirtied
by something. And I bring my blade
down on his neck – and it's easy
like slicing through fish.
And I bring it down again,
cleaving the bone.

Roy Fisher

Birmingham River

Where's Birmingham river? Sunk.
Which river was it? Two. More or less.

History: we're on tribal ground. When they
moved in from the Trent, the first English

entered the holdings and the bodies of the people
who called the waters that kept them alive

Tame, *the Dark River*, these English spread their works
southward then westward, then all ways

for thirty-odd miles, up to the damp tips of the thirty-odd
weak headwaters of the Tame. By all of the Tame

they settled, and sat, named themselves after it:
Tomsaetan. And back down at Tamworth, where the river

almost began to amount to something,
the Mercian kings kept their state. Dark

because there's hardly a still expanse of it
wide enough to catch the sky, the Dark River

mothered the Black Country and all but
vanished underneath it, seeping out from the low hills

by Dudley, by Upper Gornal, by Sedgley, by
Wolverhampton, by Bloxwich, dropping morosely

without a shelf or a race or a dip,
no more than a few feet every mile, fattened

a little from mean streams that join at
Tipton, Bilston, Willenhall, Darlaston,

Oldbury, Wednesbury. From Bescot
she oozes a border round Handsworth

where I was born, snakes through the flat
meadows that turned into Perry Barr,

passes through Witton, heading for the city
but never getting there. A couple of miles out

she catches the timeless, suspended
scent of Nechells and Saltley – coal gas,

sewage, smoke – turns and makes off
for Tamworth, caught on the right shoulder

by the wash that's run under Birmingham,
a slow, petty river with no memory of an ancient

name; a river called *Rea*, meaning *river*,
and misspelt at that. Before they merge

they're both steered straight, in channels
that force them clear of the gasworks. And the Tame

gets marched out of town in the police calm
that hangs under the long legs of the M6.

These living rivers
turgidly watered the fields, gave

drink; drove low-powered mills, shoved
the Soho Works into motion, collected waste

and foul waters. Gave way to steam,
collected sewage, factory poisons. Gave way

to clean Welsh water, kept on collecting
typhoid. Sank out of sight

under streets, highways, the black walls of workshops;
collected metals, chemicals, aquicides. Ceased

to draw lines that weren't cancelled or unwanted; became
drains, with no part in anybody's plan.

James Berry

On an Afternoon Train from Purley to Victoria, 1955

Hello, she said, and startled me.
Nice day. Nice day I agreed.

I am a Quaker she said and Sunday
I was moved in silence
to speak a poem loudly
for racial brotherhood.

I was thoughtful, then said
what poem came on like that?
One the moment inspired she said.
I was again thoughtful.

Inexplicably I saw
empty city streets lit dimly
in a day's first hours.
Alongside in darkness
was my father's big banana field.

Where are you from? she said.
Jamaica I said.
What part of Africa is Jamaica? she said.
Where Ireland is near Lapland I said.
Hard to see why you leave
such sunny country she said.
Snow falls elsewhere I said.
So sincere she was beautiful
as people sat down around us.

Seamus Heaney

St Kevin and the Blackbird

And then there was St Kevin and the blackbird.
The saint is kneeling, arms stretched out, inside
His cell, but the cell is narrow, so

One turned-up palm is out the window, stiff
As a crossbeam, when a blackbird lands
And lays in it and settles down to nest.

Kevin feels the warm eggs, the small breast, the tucked
Neat head and claws and, finding himself linked
Into the network of eternal life,

Is moved to pity: now he must hold his hand
Like a branch out in the sun and rain for weeks
Until the young are hatched and fledged and flown.

*

And since the whole thing's imagined anyhow,
Imagine being Kevin. Which is he?
Self-forgetful or in agony all the time

From the neck on out down through his hurting forearms?
Are his fingers sleeping? Does he still feel his knees?
Or has the shut-eyed blank of underearth

Crept up through him? Is there distance in his head?
Alone and mirrored clear in love's deep river,
'To labour and not to seek reward,' he prays,

A prayer his body makes entirely
For he has forgotten self, forgotten bird
And on the riverbank forgotten the river's name.

Grace Nichols

Blackout

Blackout is endemic to the land.
People have grown sixthsense
and sonic ways, like bats,
emerging out of shadows
into the light of their own flesh.

But the car headlamps coming towards us
make it seem we're in some thirdworld movie,
throwing up potholes and houses exaggeratedly,
the fresh white painted and grey ramshackle
blending into snug relief.

And inside, the children are still hovering,
hopeful moths around the flickerless Box
immune to the cloying stench of toilets
that can't be flushed. The children,
all waiting on electric-spell to come
and trigger a movie, the one featuring America,
played out endlessly in their heads.

While back outside, coconut vendors decapitate
the night, husky heads cutlassed off
in the medieval glow of bottle lamps.

And everywhere there are flittings
and things coming into being,
in a night where football is an act of faith –
a group of young girls
huddled in a questionable doorway;
the sudden dim horizontal of an alleyway;
and the occasional generator-lit big house,

obscenely bright –
hurting the soft iris of darkness
in the worn-out movie, slow reeling

Under the endless cinema of the skies.

Alice Oswald

Wedding

From time to time our love is like a sail
and when the sail begins to alternate
from tack to tack, it's like a swallowtail
and when the swallow flies, it's like a coat;
and if the coat is yours, it has a tear
like a wide mouth and when the mouth begins
to draw the wind, it's like a trumpeter
and when the trumpet blows, it blows like millions . . .
and this, my love, when millions come and go
beyond the need of us, is like a trick;
and when the trick begins, it's like a toe
tip-toeing on a rope, which is like luck;
and when the luck begins, it's like a wedding,
which is like love, which is like everything.

Imtiaz Dharker

Minority

I was born a foreigner.
I carried on from there
to become a foreigner everywhere
I went, even in the place
planted with my relatives,
six-foot tubers sprouting roots,
their fingers and faces pushing up
new shoots of maize and sugar cane.

All kinds of places and groups
of people who have an admirable
history would, almost certainly,
distance themselves from me.

I don't fit,
like a clumsily translated poem;

like food cooked in milk of coconut
where you expected ghee or cream,
the unexpected aftertaste
of cardamom or neem.

There's always that point where
the language flips
into an unfamiliar taste;
where words tumble over
a cunning tripwire on the tongue;
where the frame slips,
the reception of an image

not quite tuned, ghost-outlined,
that signals, in their midst,
an alien.

And so I scratch, scratch
through the night, at this
growing scab on black and white.
Everyone has the right
to infiltrate a piece of paper.
A page doesn't fight back.
And, who knows, these lines
may scratch their way
into your head –
through all the chatter of community,
family, clattering spoons,
children being fed –
immigrate into your bed,
squat in your home,
and in a corner, eat your bread,

until, one day, you meet
the stranger sidling down your street,
realize you know the face
simplified to bone,
look into its outcast eyes
and recognize it as your own.

Paul Farley

A Minute's Silence

The singing stops. Each player finds his spot
around the ten-yard circle that until
tonight seemed redundant, there just for show.
The PA asks us to observe the hush.

We find we're standing in a groundsman's shoes,
the quiet he must be familiar with
while squeaking chalk-paste up the grassy touch,
or overseeing a private ritual

and scattering the last mortal remains
of a diehard fan beneath each home-end stanchion.
No one keeps a count or checks their watch
so space is opened up. It seems to last

a small eternity – the happy hour
that stretches to three, the toast, the final spin.
I observe the silence sneak through turnstiles
and catch on quick – a bar muffles its pumps;

in function rooms, a wedding reception
freezes still as its own photograph;
an awful bagwash winds down mid-cycle –
a Saturday gridlocked, unaccompanied

by hooters or sirens. Like early audiences
we have left the street to its own devices
to watch the flicking shadow of itself
onscreen, the purring spool somehow apart

from all of this. It leaves the one-way system
and finds less work to do outside of town:
a rookery, light aircraft, and the wind
banging gates or moaning through the lines.

(How still without birdsong. It still guts me
to think of all the havoc wreaked each spring
we combed the hedges outside our estate
and stole the still-warm clutches from each nest;

all that music, blown and set in file
on sawdust in a two-pound biscuit tin,
displayed to rivals in attack formation,
a 4–3–3 of fowls and passerines.)

Sooner or later silence reaches the coast
and stops just short of getting its feet wet.
There's something of the Ice Age to all this.
The only sound's the white noise of the sea

that is all song, all talk, all colour, mixed.
Before that whistle bursts a hole and brings
the air rushing back in with arc lighting,
calls for owners of the double parked,

the last verse of 'You'll Never Walk Alone'
(never . . . *the sweet silver song of a lark*)
listen, to where the shore meets the salt water;
a million tiny licking, chopping sounds:

the dead, the never-born, the locked-out souls
are scratching on the thin shell we have grown
around ourselves. Listen. The afternoon
is dark already, and there is a moon.

Jane Draycott

Prince Rupert's Drop

The rapid cooling of this extraordinary glass drop leaves it in a state of enormous tension . . .

It's brilliant. It's a tear you can stand a car

on, the hard eye of a chandelier
ready to break down and cry like a baby, a rare
birth, cooled before its time. It's an ear
of glass accidentally sown in the coldest of water,
that sheer drop, rock solid except for the tail
or neck which will snap like sugar, kick like a mortar
under the surefire touch of your fingernail.

It's the pearl in a will-o'-the-wisp, the lantern asleep
in the ice, the light of St Elmo's fire in your eyes.
It's the roulette burst of a necklace, the snap
of bones in an icicle's finger, the snip of your pliers
at the neck of my heart, the fingertip working the spot
which says 'you are here' until you are suddenly not.

Michael Donaghy

Machines

Dearest, note how these two are alike:
This harpsichord pavane by Purcell
And the racer's twelve-speed bike.

The machinery of grace is always simple.
This chrome trapezoid, one wheel connected
To another of concentric gears,
Which Ptolemy dreamt of and Schwinn perfected,
Is gone. The cyclist, not the cycle, steers.
And in the playing, Purcell's chords are played away.

So this talk, or touch if I were there,
Should work its effortless gadgetry of love,
Like Dante's heaven, and melt into the air.

If it doesn't, of course, I've fallen. So much is chance,
So much agility, desire, and feverish care,
As bicyclists and harpsichordists prove

Who only by moving can balance,
Only by balancing move.

Denise Riley

A Misremembered Lyric

A misremembered lyric: a soft catch of its song
whirrs in my throat. 'Something's gotta hold of my heart
tearing my' soul and my conscience apart, long after
presence is clean gone and leaves unfurnished no
shadow. Rain lyrics. Yes, then the rain lyrics fall.
I don't want absence to be this beautiful.
It shouldn't be; in fact I know it wasn't, while
'everything that consoles is false' is off the point –
you get no consolation anyway until your memory's
dead; or something never had gotten hold of
your heart in the first place, and that's the fear thought.
Do shrimps make good mothers? Yes they do.
There is no beauty out of loss; can't do it –
and once the falling rain starts on the upturned
leaves, and I listen to the rhythm of unhappy pleasure
what I hear is bossy death telling me which way to
go, what I see is a pool with an eye in it. Still let
me know. Looking for a brand-new start. Oh and never
notice yourself ever. As in life you don't.

Benjamin Zephaniah

It's Work

I could hav been a builder
A painter or a swimmer
I dreamt of being a Rasta writer,
I fancied me a farmer
I could never be a barber
Once I was not sure about de future,
Got a sentence an I done it
Still me angry feelings groweth
Now I am jus a different fighter,
I sight de struggle up more clearly
I get younger yearly
An me black heart don't get no lighter.
I will not join de army
I would work wid malt an barley
But here I am checking me roots,
I could work de ital kitchen
But I won't cook dead chicken
An I won't lick nobody's boots,
Yes I could be a beggar
Maybe not a tax collector
But I could be a streetwise snob,
But I'll jus keep reciting de poems dat I am writing
One day I'll hav a proper job.

Sean O'Brien

Cousin Coat

You are my secret coat. You're never dry.
You wear the weight and stink of black canals.
Malodorous companion, we know why
It's taken me so long to see we're pals,
To learn why my acquaintance never sniff
Or send me notes to say I stink of stiff.

But you don't talk, historical bespoke.
You must be worn, be intimate as skin,
And though I never lived what you invoke,
At birth I was already buttoned in.
Your clammy itch became my atmosphere,
An air made half of anger, half of fear.

And what you are is what I tried to shed
In libraries with Donne and Henry James.
You're here to bear a message from the dead
Whose history's dishonoured with their names.
You mean the North, the poor, and the troopers sent
To shoot down those who showed their discontent.

No comfort there for comfy meliorists
Grown weepy over Jarrow photographs.
No comfort when the poor the state enlists
Parade before their fathers' cenotaphs.
No comfort when the strikers all go back
To see which twenty thousand get the sack.

Be with me when they cauterize the facts.
Be with me to the bottom of the page,
Insisting on what history exacts.

Be memory, be conscience, will and rage,
And keep me cold and honest, cousin coat,
So if I lie, I'll know you're at my throat.

Ian Duhig

The Lammas Hireling

After the fair, I'd still a light heart
And a heavy purse, he struck so cheap.
And cattle doted on him: in his time,
Mine only dropped heifers, fat as cream.
Yields doubled. I grew fond of company
That knew when to shut up. Then one night,

Disturbed from dreams of my dear late wife,
I hunted down her torn voice to his pale form.
Stock-still in the light from the dark lantern,
Stark naked but for the fox-trap biting his ankle,
I knew him a warlock, a cow with leather horns.
To go into the hare gets you muckle sorrow,

The wisdom runs, muckle care. I levelled
And blew the small hour through his heart.
The moon came out. By its yellow witness
I saw him fur over like a stone mossing.
His lovely head thinned. His top lip gathered.
His eyes rose like bread. I carried him

In a sack that grew lighter at every step
And dropped him from a bridge. There was no
Splash. Now my herd's elf-shot. I don't dream
But spend my nights casting ball from half-crowns
And my days here. Bless me, Father, I have sinned.
It has been an hour since my last confession.

Don Paterson

Waking with Russell

Whatever the difference is, it all began
the day we woke up face-to-face like lovers
and his four-day-old smile dawned on him again,
possessed him, till it would not fall or waver;
and I pitched back not my old hard-pressed grin
but his own smile, or one I'd rediscovered.
Dear son, I was *mezzo del cammin*
and the true path was as lost to me as ever
when you cut in front and lit it as you ran.
See how the true gift never leaves the giver:
returned and redelivered, it rolled on
until the smile poured through us like a river.
How fine, I thought, this waking amongst men!
I kissed your mouth and pledged myself forever.

Choman Hardi

Two Pages

1. Delivering a message

I was asleep in the middle of a pad
when he started writing on the first page.
The tip of his pen pressed down
forcing pale words into the pages below.
He wrote many versions that night
some very lengthy, others brief.

When my turn came he paused,
palmed his temples, squeezed his eyes,
made himself a calming tea.

She received me early one morning
in a rush, leaving her flat.
She ripped the envelope. Then, gradually,
her steps slowed down,
her fingers tightened around me.

2. Not delivering a message

All my life I waited for words –
a poem, a letter, a mathematical puzzle.

On March 16th 1988
thousands of us were taken on board –
you can't imagine our anticipation.

When they threw us out from high above
we were confused, lost in blankness.

All those clean white pages
parachuting into town . . .

Puzzled faces looked up
expecting a message, but we were blank.

Two hours later they dropped the real thing.
We had been testing the wind direction.
Thousands of people were gassed that day.

Michael Symmons Roberts

Pelt

I found the world's pelt
nailed to the picture-rail
of a box-room in a cheap hotel.

So that's why rivers dry to scabs,
that's why the grass weeps every dawn,
that's why the wind feels raw:

the earth's an open wound,
and here, its skin hangs
like a trophy, atrophied beyond all

taxidermy, shrunk into a hearth rug.
Who fleeced it?
No record in the guest-book.

No one paid, just pocketed the blade
and walked, leaving the bed
untouched, TV pleasing itself.

Maybe there was no knife.
Maybe the world shrugs off a hide
each year to grow a fresh one.

That pelt was thick as reindeer,
so black it flashed with blue.
I tried it on, of course, but no.

Kamau Brathwaite

Bread

Slowly the white dream wrestle(s) to life
hands shaping the salt and the foreign cornfields
the cold flesh kneaded by fingers
is ready for the charcoal for the black wife

of heat the years of green sleeping in the volcano .
the dream becomes tougher. settling into its shape
like a bullfrog. suns rise and electrons
touch it. walls melt into brown. moving to crisp and crackle

breathing edge of the knife of the oven .
noise of the shop. noise of the farmer. market .
on this slab of lord. on this table w/ its oil-skin cloth
on this altar of the bone. this scarifice

of isaac. warm dead. warm merchandise. more than worn merchandise
life
itself. the dream of the soil itself
flesh of the god you break. peace to your lips. strife

of the multitudes who howl all day for its saviour
who need its crumbs as fish. flickering through their green element
need a wide glassy wisdom
to keep their groans alive

and this loaf here. life
now halted. more and more water add-
itive. the dream less clear. the soil more distant
its prayer of table. bless of lips. more hard to reach w/ penn-

ies. the knife
that should have cut it. the hands that should have broken open its victory
of crusts at your throat. balaam watching w/ red leak-
ing eyes. the rats

finding only this young empty husk
sharp-
ening their ratchets. your wife
going out on the streets. searching searching

her feet tapping. the lights of the motor-
cars watching watching round-
ing the shape of her girdle. her back naked

rolled into night into night w/out morning
rolled into dead into dead w/out vision
rolled into life into life w/out dream

Colette Bryce

The Full Indian Rope Trick

There was no secret
murmured down through a long line
of elect; no dark fakir, no flutter
of notes from a pipe,
no proof, no footage of it –
but I did it,

Guildhall Square, noon,
in front of everyone.
There were walls, bells, passers-by;
then a rope, thrown, caught by the sky
and me, young, up and away,
goodbye.

Goodbye, goodbye.
Thin air. First try.
A crowd hushed, squinting eyes
at a full sun. There
on the stones
the slack weight of a rope

coiled in a crate, a braid
eighteen summers long,
and me
I'm long gone,
my one-off trick
unique, unequalled since.

And what would I tell them
given the chance?
It was painful; it took years.

I'm my own witness,
guardian of the fact
that I'm still here.

Owen Sheers

Mametz Wood

For years afterwards the farmers found them –
the wasted young, turning up under their plough blades
as they tended the land back into itself.

A chit of bone, the china plate of a shoulder blade,
the relic of a finger, the blown
and broken bird's egg of a skull,

all mimicked now in flint, breaking blue in white
across this field where they were told to walk, not run,
towards the wood and its nesting machine guns.

And even now the earth stands sentinel,
reaching back into itself for reminders of what happened
like a wound working a foreign body to the surface of the skin.

This morning, twenty men buried in one long grave,
a broken mosaic of bone linked arm in arm,
their skeletons paused mid dance-macabre

in boots that outlasted them,
their socketed heads tilted back at an angle
and their jaws, those that have them, dropped open.

As if the notes they had sung
have only now, with this unearthing,
slipped from their absent tongues.

John Agard

Toussaint L'Ouverture Acknowledges Wordsworth's Sonnet 'To Toussaint L'Ouverture'

I have never walked on Westminster Bridge
or had a close-up view of daffodils.
My childhood's roots are the Haitian hills
where runaway slaves made a freedom pledge
and scarlet poincianas flaunt their scent.
I have never walked on Westminster Bridge
or speak, like you, with Cumbrian accent.

My tongue bridges Europe to Dahomey.
Yet how sweet is the smell of liberty
When human beings share a common garment.
So thanks, brother, for your sonnet's tribute.
May it resound when the Thames' text stays mute.
And what better ground than a city's bridge
for my unchained ghost to trumpet love's decree.

Daljit Nagra

Look We Have Coming to Dover!

So various, so beautiful, so new . . .
– Matthew Arnold, 'Dover Beach'

Stowed in the sea to invade
the lash alfresco of a diesel-breeze
ratcheting speed into the tide, with brunt
gobfuls of surf phlegmed by cushy, come-and-go
tourists prow'd on the cruisers, lording the ministered waves.

Seagull and shoal life
Vexin their blarnies upon our huddled
camouflage past the vast crumble of scummed
cliffs, scramming on mulch as thunder unbladders
yobbish rain and wind on our escape, hutched in a Bedford van.

Seasons or years we reap
inland, unclocked by the national eye
or a stab in the back, teemed for breathing
sweeps of grass through the whistling asthma of parks,
burdened, ennobled, poling sparks across pylon and pylon.

Swarms of us, grafting in
the black within shot of the moon's
spotlight, banking on the miracle of sun –
span its rainbow, passport us to life. Only then
can it be human to hoick ourselves, bare-faced for the clear.

Imagine my love and I,
our sundry others, Blair'd in the cash

of our beeswax'd cars, our crash clothes, free,
we raise our charged glasses over unparasol'd tables
East, babbling our lingoes, flecked by the chalk of Britannia!

Jean Sprackland

The Stopped Train

She stands and knows herself for the first time.
This recognition comes to each of us

sooner or later. When a baby meets a mirror
it enters this same state of rapture.
That's how the train is: stunned
and passionate. She looks, and sees

energy, will, destiny. Sees that she
touches the rails, but is not the rails,
brushes the overhead lines and drinks in power,
is headstrong and pioneering.

Inside, passengers cram the corridors,
sucking ice-cubes, taking turns at the windows.
A woman shouts: Why must you be all so *British*?
The carriage is brash with daylight

like a terrible living-room
filling up with unsaid things:
no one can get a signal here
in this nondescript England of

sly ditches and flat fields, where some
experiment must be taking place and
the only thing moving between the trees is
shadow. This is the Interior,

and if they were to smash the glass with a shoe,
jump down onto the track, set off in a somewhere direction,

they would be struck down
like stranded motorists in Death Valley.

The train has forgotten them.
She is accounting for herself:
steel, glass, plastic, nylon,
an audit of chips and circuits.

She stands and ticks,
letting the heat leak and equalize.

Patience Agbabi

Josephine Baker Finds Herself

She picked me up
like a slow-burning fuse. I was down
that girls' club used to run in Brixton,
on acid for fuel. Lipstick lesbians,
techno so hardcore it's spewing out Audis.
She samples my heartbeat and mixes it with
vodka on the rocks. I'm her light-skinned, negative,
twenty-something, short black wavy-bobbed diva.
She purrs *La Garçonne*, *fancy a drink*? I say
Yes. She's crossing the Star Bar like it's a catwalk. So sleek!
A string of pearls, her flapper dress
studded with low-cut diamonds
through my skin, straight to my heart.
Twenties chic! She works
me up and down. I worship
the way she looks.

The way she looks
me up and down. I worship
twenties chic. She works
through my skin, straight to my heart
studded with low-cut diamonds.
A string of pearls her flapper dress.
Yes! She's crossing the Star Bar like it's a catwalk so sleek
she purrs, la garçonne! *Fancy a drink?* I say.
Twenty-something, short, Black, wavy-bobbed diva:
Vodka on the rocks, I'm her light-skinned negative.
She samples my heartbeat and mixes it with
techno so hardcore it's spewing out Audis
on acid for fuel. *Lipstick Lesbians*,

that girls' club used to run in Brixton
like a slow-burning fuse. I was down.
She picked me up.

Mick Imlah

Maren

You saw so much romance in competition,
like Atlanta before you – a daughter
of thick-witted Schoeness, a Boetian –
they said you'd marry anyone who beat you
in a footrace. Hence our peculiar courtship:

you, crowned once fastest girl over
three thousand metres in Lower Franconia,
myself the great Caledonian bore,
we took to jogging round the astroturf
of Wapping's amenable sports arena.

Plainly, you could have romped ahead
at any point; instead, you made me lead,
woman after my own heart! – dropping
your courteous metres back, as if
feeling the pace, an arrangement

you gilded with 'I can't keep up
when you accelerate!' So we complete
our sixth or seventh lap of the course;
and only when I flag, an end in view,
near to the bags and coats, do you appear

flush at my ear, demanding 'more!'
Together, then, after our fashion:
exchanging oaths like old antagonists,
your Focke-Wulf tailing my Spit
into fresh air and another orbit.

E. A. Markham

A Verandah Ceremony

This is where the kitten died
This is where the kitten died
In the yard below, unfenced
The wild dogs came as if on horses,
Or a Lord's Resistance Army
With machetes, with spears and rifles
The wild dogs came all claws and barking.
This is where the kitten died.

This *new*new kitten three weeks old
Must avoid a kitten's fate
Must clear the house of lizards
Bugs and insects and not stray
Beyond the safety gate where the dogs
All tooth and claw still lie in wait

Where the dogs still lie in wait.

Anthony Joseph

Conductors of His Mystery

(for Albert Joseph)

The day my father came back from the sea
broke and handsome
I saw him walking across the savannah
and knew at once it was him.
His soulful stride, the grace of his hat,
the serifs of his name
~ fluttering ~
in my mouth.

In his bachelor's room in El Socorro that year
he played his 8-tracks through a sawed-off speaker box.
The coil would rattle an the cone would hop
but women from the coconut groves
still came to hear
his traveller's tales.

Shop he say he build by Goose Lane junction.
But it rough from fabricated timber string.
Picka foot jook wood
like what Datsun ship in.

And in this snackette he sold red mango,
mints and tamarind.
Its wire mesh grill hid his suffer well tough.
Till the shop bust,
and he knock out the boards
and roam east
to Enterprise village.

Shack he say he build same cross-cut lumber.
    Wood he say he stitch same carap bush.
Roof he say he throw same galvanize. He got
    ambitious with wood
      in his middle ages.

That night I spent there,
      with the cicadas in that clear village sky,
even though each room was still unfinished
    and each sadness hid. I was with
    my father
    and I would've stayed if he had asked.

Brown suede,
    8 eye high
    desert boots.   Beige
gabardine bells with the 2 inch folds.
He was myth.   The legend of him.
Once I touched the nape of his boot
    to see if my father was real.
Beyond the brown edges of photographs
    and the songs we sang
      to sing him back
          from the sweep and sea agonies
            of his distance.

Landslide scars. He sent no letters.

His small hands were for the fine work of his carpentry.
    His fingers to trace the pitch pine's grain.
        And the raised rivers of his veins,
            the thick rings of his charisma,
                the scars – the maps of his palms –
        were the sweet conductors
                    of his mystery.

            Aiyé Olokun.

He came back smelling of the sea.

Jacob Sam-La Rose

A Life in Dreams

There have been teeth
falling loose from their sockets
like a shower of petals or bones.

There has been treacle;
attempts to run against a gravity wound so tight
tight single steps were futile,
a travelling nowhere,
a running on the spot,
a fanged leer and a gnarled hand
inching ever closer.

There have been glorious revolutions in unnamed countries,
wars against tyrants,
troops like legions of swarming beetles.
There have been blades, flashing at the sun.

Once or twice, a fluency in kung-fu.

Up has mostly been up,
though has been convincingly turned
on its head.

There have been drives down unfamiliar streets,
the front of a car crumpled
like a denim pulled fresh from the wash.
Once, a mobile home.

There have been more than a few kisses. School
classrooms and corridors.
A hiding place in a primary attic.

There have been clothes, forgotten
and remembered too late.
A numbness of gums.

Weightlessness.
Unassisted flight.
Falling but never hitting the ground.
Fear
as solid and real
as table tops or bed-frames.

There has been silence,

the power of sound cleft from the mouth,
the jaw gummed with quiet, the throat
emptied of ammunition.

There has been love.

There have been messages
passed back and forth between hemispheres, metaphors
like acres of fortune cookies.

All this behind shuttered and fluttering eyes
and, I'd wager, some of the best,
where everything moved like snowfall
and time itself was as delicate as a snowflake,
melting on the tongue.

Simon Armitage

The Death of King Arthur (ll. 4209–53)

Being moved into action, Sir Merrak met Mordred,
hit him mightily with a hammered mace;
the border of his helmet he broke clean off
so bright red blood came running down his breastplate.
Mordred wheeled in pain and his face went white,
but like an embattled boar he returned the blow.
Then he flashed a sword of shining silver
that was Arthur's own, and was Uther's, his father,
which was held in high honour in the arsenal at Wallingford;
and the dismal dog dealt out such dreaded dints
that withdrawing was all the other dare do.
For Sir Merrak was a man who was marred by age
and Sir Mordred was mighty and at the peak of manliness.
No one, even a knight, could come within the compass
of the sweep of the sword, or their lifeblood would spill.

Our King watched this happen, and hastened into action,
went forward through the fray by force of his strength,
met with Sir Mordred, and spoke with maddened heart:
'Turn, untrue traitor, your time has come.
By great God, your existence by my hands shall be ended.
All the riches of the realms shall not rescue you from death.'

The King brought Excalibur crashing down,
shearing off cleanly the corner-piece of his shield
and slashing a six-inch wound to his shoulder,
spattering his chain-mail with shimmering scarlet blood.
He shuddered and shook, shrank back just a little,
but then shockingly and sharply in his shining armour
the felon struck forcefully with his fine sword,
slicing through the rib-plates to our Sovereign's side;

through hauberk and heavy armour he opened him up
with a wound to his flesh half a foot wide.
He had dealt him his deathblow, and how dreadful it was
that this dear man should die but for our Deity's will.

Yet with Excalibur he executed an exacting stroke,
thrust his fine shield forward in an act of offence
then slashed off his enemy's sword-hand as he swooped;
an inch from the elbow he hacked it clean off,
chopping through the shining armguard and chain-mail,
so he swooned on the spot then swayed and sank,
and his hand and hilt lay still upon the earth.

Then eagerly Arthur opened his enemy's visor
and buried the bright blade in his body to the handle,
and he squirmed as he died, skewered on the sword.
'It sorrows me, I swear,' said our doomed Sovereign,
'that such a false offender should have so fair a death.'

Jacob Polley

Langley Lane

Stand up straight, my son. Don't slouch.
    Mother, I'm not slouching.
There's nothing you need to hide from me.
    You know I don't like touching.

A mother must – it's in my hands
    to touch what's mine so briefly,
to touch my son for one small proof
    that he's still strong and loves me.

Mother, I wish you weren't at home
    and I could sit in peace.
I'd hoped to meet the dark alone
    and not to cause a fuss.

My son, I'm bound to love no less
    the child who brings me pain.
My son, what spreads across your shirt?
    You need not hide a stain.

What I hide won't be undone
    and I'd not see your face
to spare myself the sight of one
    whose grief is my disgrace.

Take a chair, my son, you're tired.
    Drink a glass of milk.
You're up, you're down. Your brain's still soft.
    Your adulthood half built.

You're pale, my son – you'll fade away:
you need a bite to eat.
Once I was young and like you swayed
unsteady on my feet –

Mother, soon I'll get my rest
so while I can I'll stand.
My son, what's loose at your left wrist?
What's spilling from your hand?

Mother, my hand is full of shame.
It's pouring from my heart.
I've walked it in from Langley Lane
where trouble's known to start.

If trouble starts, you've said to me,
just turn and walk away.
But Langley Lane's blind corner led
to five who blocked my way.

You're on our turf, one said, and spat.
The youngest-looking shoved
me first; I shoved him harder back.
He punched me in the chest.

The leaves were still. The sun came out
to scatter coins of light
and I saw gripped in his right fist
a little silver spike.

A spike at which I stared, surprised –
a bloody silver spike
at which he also stared, surprised,
our two boys' looks alike.

The sun went in. A siren moaned.
Crowds crawled across the blue.
They grabbed my phone. I started home –
what else was there to do?

My son, you walked from Langley Lane?
I walked from Langley Lane.
I took small steps and often stopped
to breathe around the pain.

My son, you walked from Langley Lane.
I walked from Langley Lane.
I held myself to slow the stain
and walked from Langley Lane.

Andrew Motion

The Fish in Australia

Where the mountains crumbled
and yellow desert began,
when the sun began to smoulder
in a vault of indigo,
I left the metalled road
and found a perfect circle
of still and silent water,
fifty yards by fifty,
with hard treeless banks
un-marked by any prints.

Call it a pool of tears
wept by dogs or kangaroos,
or dead transported men.
I considered it a dewpond
but no dew anywhere
ever fell that swarthy colour,
or seemed so like the lid
of a tunnel piercing through
the planet's fiery heart
to the other side and England.

Providence any how
had made me think ahead
and without a moment's pause
I was parked up on the bank,
had my rod and spinner ready,
and was flicking out a cast
to find what rose to me.

Nothing rose, of course.
A kookaburra guffawed
a mile off in the bush
and a million years ago;
a snack of tiny flies
sizzled round my lips;
and as the dying sun
sank deeper in its vault
a gang of eucalypts
in tattered party dresses
seemed to shuffle closer
and show their interest
in hearing how my line
whispered on the water
(now uniformly solid
ancient beaten bronze),
how the reel's neat click
made the spinner plonk down,
how the ratchet whirred
as I reeled in slow enough
to conjure up the monster
that surely slept below.

As I reeled in slow enough
then suddenly too slow,
and the whirling hooks caught hold
of something obstinate.
Not flesh or fish-mouth though.
Too much dead weight for that.
A stone age log perhaps.
A mass at any rate
that would not change its mind
and snapped the flimsy line
which blew back in my face
as light as human hair.

If not myself at least
the pond lay peaceful then,
with sun now turned to dust
and a moon-ghost in its place
as much like company
as anything complete.

Why not, I thought,
why not
despite the loss to me
continue standing here
and still cast out my line,
my frail and useless lash,
with no better reason now
than watch the thing lie down
then lift and lie again,
until such time arrives
as the dark that swallows up
the sky has swallowed me.

Notes

Beowulf *Anonymous/Modern English version by Seamus Heaney*

The Poem *Beowulf*, composed somewhere between AD700 and AD1000 by an unknown poet, is one of the most important works of Anglo-Saxon literature. An alliterative poem of astonishing imaginative vitality, it was relatively neglected until the nineteenth century, and even then it was often studied for what it revealed about the Anglo-Saxon era rather than for its artistic merits.

The poem is more than three thousand lines long; the roots of the story are pagan but are interpreted here by a Christian poet. Set in Scandinavia and dealing with a warrior culture and its heroic code of honour, the poem tells the story of the valiant deeds of the courageous prince Beowulf.

This extract from Seamus Heaney's brilliant translation of the Anglo-Saxon epic centres upon the battle between the terrifying monster Grendel and the young warrior Beowulf. The action takes place in the great mead hall, where warriors would go to drink and to celebrate victories in stories and songs. Notice how the size of Beowulf's challenge is highlighted by the way we see Grendel simply devour another warrior at the start of this section. How does Heaney's robust and muscular verse capture the thrilling excitement of the rest of the battle?

Sir Gawain and the Green Knight *The Gawain Poet*

The Poem Sir Gawain is on a quest that will test his faith and courage. In this extract, he is travelling in arduous conditions to meet with the Green Knight, who had ridden into King Arthur's court and invited any knight brave enough to strike him with an axe, if he is prepared to accept a blow from the Green Knight a year and a day later. Gawain had accepted the challenge by chopping off the Green Knight's head, only to see the mysterious stranger pick it up and remind Gawain of their agreement.

This section of the poem presents Gawain in wild and dangerous country. He has to fight dragons and wolves, wild men and giants, but he is brave and strong and devoted to God. He is nearly slain with the sleet and sleeps on rocks with hard icicles overhead. In peril and pain, he prays to Mary for help and guidance.

Sir Gawain and the Green Knight is medieval alliterative verse, in which the repetition of initial consonant sounds is used to give structure to a line. How does alliteration contribute to the mood and subject matter in this extract?

The Poet The name of the writer of *Sir Gawain and the Green Knight* is not known, but it is thought that he is the author not only of this Arthurian romance dealing with chivalry, honour and religious faith but also of three other major works from the medieval period. He writes with richness, attention to detail and muscularity throughout the manuscript where these poems are found.

The 'Gawain Poet' wrote in a northern Midlands dialect which is significantly different from the more familiar and accessible English of Chaucer. The alliterative verse of *Sir Gawain and the Green Knight* can be traced back to Anglo-Saxon poetic forms and, when the Gawain Poet was writing, it had begun to be less popular. However, in the late 1300s, there was a revival in interest in the form and a number of alliterative poems were written by poets such as the Gawain Poet and William Langland.

The Wife of Bath *Geoffrey Chaucer (c.1343–1400)*

The Poem In The General Prologue to *The Canterbury Tales*, Chaucer introduces the characters as they set off on their pilgrimage to Canterbury. The Wife of Bath is one of the few women in the group and she has had a colourful and adventurous life. We discover that she first married at twelve and has had five husbands; she is an expert in love.

Chaucer describes her skill at cloth-making and sewing and details her elaborate Sunday clothing: her red stockings, her big headscarf, her wimple and her hat as large as a shield. He is less than flattering about her looks: she is ruddy-faced and he tells us she is gap-toothed, an interesting detail that, to a medieval audience, would have suggested that she had a sensuous nature. For a medieval woman, she is remarkably well travelled, having visited some far-flung and famous pilgrimage sites. Pride, piety and sensuousness compete for dominance in the vividly described character Chaucer creates.

The Poet Geoffrey Chaucer was one of the first great writers to produce poetry that established English as a literary language. In the fourteenth century, the official language of the royal court was French, and that of the Church Latin, but Chaucer created works that asserted the legitimacy of the everyday, spoken English of the time.

Chaucer was connected to the royal court and served both Edward III and Richard II as a diplomat and courtier. In 1360, he was captured in one of the battles of the Hundred Years War and was ransomed by the king of France for £16. He travelled in France, Spain and Italy, and was influenced by writers such as the Italian author and humanist Giovanni Boccaccio.

Chaucer was the first poet to be buried in Poets' Corner in Westminster Abbey, and his most famous work is *The Canterbury Tales*, an ambitious, colourful, compassionate but critical portrait of English society at the end of the fourteenth century.

'I syng of a mayden' *Anonymous*

The Poem This Middle English poem is part of a collection of medieval lyrics now held in the British Library. It celebrates the Annunciation, when the angel Gabriel told Mary that she would miraculously conceive and give birth, as a virgin, to the son of God.

Since its rediscovery, many composers have based choral works on this poem, in which the author repeatedly declares that he will 'syng' his tribute to the mother of Jesus. (You can listen to a haunting version sung by the King's College Choir, Cambridge, on YouTube.) What other characteristics of this lyric might encourage musical interpretations?

Notice how the poem celebrates Mary's uniqueness. She is 'makeles' ('matchless' in modern English), while her virginity is stressed through the emphasis on stillness. What images does the poet use to convey the idea that this conception was peaceful and beautiful? This simple and subtle meditation on the Annunciation also reminds us that Mary actively chose to accept her role: 'King of alle kinges/to here sone che chees' ('King of all kings/for her son she chose').

The Poet Anonymous is a well-known and prolific poet. Many of the traditional folk ballads we know today may have begun as songs sung by wandering minstrels; authorship was unimportant. The songs needed to be easily remembered, however, so a simple structure and a degree of repetition were needed. Many of the songs would capture dramatic local tales or legends and would be embellished and refined over the years.

About three quarters of the anonymous lyrics written in English in the fifteenth century, when 'I syng of a mayden' was well known, are devotional and religious. In the seventeenth and eighteenth centuries, many ballads were collected, formally recorded in print and attributed to the versatile 'Anonymous'.

In the nineteenth century, the ballad form was adopted by poets who were definitely not anonymous. Robert Burns, Christina Rossetti and Alfred Tennyson, for example, explored old legends and tragic romances in a number of poems.

'They flee from me that sometime did me seek' *Thomas Wyatt (1503–42)*

The Poem Wyatt's poem begins with an expression of frustration and resentment. Those who once sought him out appear to have abandoned him. The references to 'naked foot' and 'chamber' suggest that he may be referring to intimate relations with women. Where once these women were gentle and submissive, they seem to have tired of him and now seek 'continual change'.

In the middle of the poem, Wyatt reflects upon one particular woman. The language is erotically charged, with references to her physical presence and how she 'sweetly' kisses him. How does Wyatt express a feeling that this is not a secure love based on mutual commitment? Notice how he returns to the idea of the woman searching for new sensations and experiences.

What do you think of the tone of the final two lines, and of Wyatt's depiction of himself and the woman who appears to have forsaken him?

The control of rhythm in the poem is impressive. Look at the first line, which is a perfect example of iambic pentameter, but notice how Wyatt introduces metrical variations in order to avoid monotony. The rhyme scheme is known as 'rhyme royal', and was one used by Chaucer.

The Poet Thomas Wyatt was an accomplished diplomat during Henry VIII's reign and served on missions to France and Italy, where he studied the literature of both countries.

He was suspected at various times of being Anne Boleyn's lover and of treason. Although he did spend some time in the Tower of London, he regained the favour of the king and remained in diplomatic service until his death in 1542.

Through his translations, Wyatt helped bring the Petrarchan sonnet into the English language. He was a charismatic man, who wrote for other educated, sophisticated members of the court. He was not published in his lifetime, but his poems survive in manuscript collections.

Song from *Arcadia* *Philip Sidney (1554–86)*

The Poem This sonnet is a song from Sidney's long pastoral romance *Arcadia*. Arguably written from the point of view of a woman, the poem deals with a perfectly requited love.

Each quatrain leads us deeper into the harmonious love the pair share. The first four lines are bound by rhyme. The following four lines parallel each other: 'His heart in me' is echoed by 'My heart in him'. Then, with the next quatrain, we are spiralled into the state of 'bliss' that is mentioned in the final couplet. We can barely discern the speaker from her lover as 'from me on him his hurt did light'. Who has inflicted the hurt? Whose hurt is it originally? Although the answers are not clear, the poem suggests a state of perfect two-in-oneness has been achieved. The shared hurt simply serves to deepen the connection. In the concluding couplet, we read 'our bliss', implying that there is no longer any separation between the two lovers. The repetition of the first line not only neatly seals the poem but suggests that this love is never-ending.

The Poet A poet, soldier and courtier, Philip Sidney was one of the most celebrated figures of the Elizabethan age. He was a member of a distinguished and talented family; his sister, Mary, the Countess of Pembroke, was a patron of writers and supported her brother as he wrote his great work, *Arcadia*.

Sidney left Oxford before completing his degree and travelled extensively in France, Germany, Austria and Italy with his patron and father-in-law Sir Francis Walsingham. A militant Protestant who fell in and out of favour with Queen Elizabeth I, Sidney was appointed Governor of Flushing in the Netherlands and died after being wounded in the Battle of Zutphen, fighting the Spanish.

He wrote in his hugely influential 'Defence of Poesy' that 'verse far exceedeth prose in the knitting up of memory': an apt claim when his poetry, including *Astrophil and Stella*, with its 108 sonnets and 11 songs, and *Arcadia* are still read today.

'In summer's heat and mid-time of the day'

Christopher Marlowe (1564–93)

The Poem Marlowe's translations of *Amores*, Book 1, by the Roman poet Ovid are among his earliest work.

The poem describes going to bed with Corinna in the middle of the day. Notice the use of the caesuras in the opening lines, which slow down the narrative, suggesting that the bustle of normal life will be left behind for a while. The windows, one closed, one open, create a kind of artificial twilight, and the contemplation of the anonymity this half-light might give to people leads the speaker to think of 'maidens' and 'sport'.

Into this physical and emotional setting walks Corinna. How does the poet describe the woman in lines nine to twelve? Note the references to other women of legendary beauty. In line thirteen the conventional poetic similes are abandoned and replaced by direct action. The poem then goes on to describe the false struggle between the lovers: full of military images and the poet's reaction to the naked Corinna.

How do the iambic pentameters and, in particular, the rhyming couplets contribute to the witty, pithy style of the poem?

The Poet Christopher Marlowe is a highly significant contributor to the Elizabethan dramatic renaissance. The suppleness and energy of his writing almost certainly influenced Shakespeare, and another contemporary poet, Ben Jonson, wrote appreciatively of Marlowe's 'mighty line'.

His writing career was relatively brief, beginning when he was at Cambridge and ending with his violent death in 1593. Some historians suggest that Marlowe may have been a government spy and that his death, which was reported as the outcome of a drunken brawl in a tavern, may have been politically motivated. Details of his short life are surrounded in mystery.

His non-dramatic poetry is best represented by *Hero and Leander* and his witty, sometimes explicit translations of Ovid's *Amores*.

Marlowe's plays have epic scope. *Tamburlaine the Great*, *Edward II* and *The Tragicall History of the Life and Death of Dr Faustus* are all intensely powerful dramas and offer examples of the versatility and richness of blank verse.

Elegy *Chidiock Tichborne (1558–86)*

The Poem The 28-year-old Chidiock Tichborne wrote this poem as he awaited execution for his part in the Babington conspiracy to assassinate Elizabeth I and replace her with the Catholic Mary Queen of Scots.

Notice how measured and balanced the poem is, with its skilful use of antithesis in every line. Even though Tichborne is facing a gruesome death, there is a sense of composure and stoicism. Nevertheless, the poem is imbued with a deep sadness as he contemplates a life cut short. The concluding line in each verse thumps home the inescapable fact that '. . . my life is done'. What is the effect of virtually every word in the poem being monosyllabic?

In the first verse, the poet's frustration is evident in the way he talks about his day being done before he has seen the 'sun', but notice how the tone shifts slightly in the second verse, where his sorrow regarding a life of unfulfilled potential is clear.

In the final verse, where he talks of finding death in his womb, is he perhaps referring to his birth and upbringing as a Catholic?

The Poet When the Protestant Queen Elizabeth I came to the throne, Catholics such as Chidiock Tichborne had a degree of freedom to practise their faith. However, when Elizabeth was excommunicated by the pope in 1570, she retaliated by ending her tolerance of Catholicism in England. Records suggest that Tichborne and his father were questioned on several occasions about their 'popish practices'.

Fatally for Tichborne, he agreed to take part in the Babington Plot to assassinate Elizabeth. The conspiracy was exposed by a double agent and Tichborne and his fellow conspirators were executed in a particularly gruesome fashion, on 20 September 1586. The day before his death Tichborne wrote the elegy for which he is now remembered. The poem was included in a letter he wrote to his wife.

The Good Morrow *John Donne (1572–1631)*

The Poem The words 'Love', 'loved' and 'loves' are mentioned five times, but exactly what kind of love poem is this? 'The Good Morrow', written in the late sixteenth century, appeared in a collection of Donne's poems entitled *Songs and Sonnets*. While the poem clearly has seven more lines than a conventional sonnet and does not follow the form's traditional structure, it does develop an idea or theme in a way that is typical of a sonnet. It is worth trying to trace the way the ingenious argument of the poem evolves. What kind of people are they in stanza one, and what kind of lovers have they become by the end of the third stanza? We are not in a conventional poetic love setting here, with romance and roses. There are biblical allusions to the 'Seven Sleepers' den' and references to maps, sea voyages of discovery and worlds, as Donne explores sensuality and spirituality within love.

The Poet John Donne was educated at both Oxford and Cambridge, and was an experienced traveller, soldier and lawyer by his mid-twenties. However, his promising diplomatic career was halted abruptly when he married the sixteen-year-old niece of his employer's wife. Familial disapproval was so great that Donne was briefly imprisoned. After release, he struggled to support a large family and relied on the help of wealthy friends. His fortunes changed when he converted from Catholicism to the Church of England, and he rose rapidly to the position of Dean of St Paul's Cathedral in London.

A contemporary of Shakespeare, Donne was a prolific writer of sonnets, sermons, pamphlets and elegies. He wrote powerful, persuasive, intellectually robust love poems and questioning religious poetry. Along with other 'metaphysical' poets, he brought new learning and discoveries to his work, using extended metaphors known as 'conceits'. Witty, passionate and self-consciously clever, his work combines profound intellect, originality and feeling.

Walsingham *Walter Ralegh (1552–1618)*

The Poem Ralegh's poem adopts a traditional ballad form with its four-line stanzas and ABAB rhyming pattern and, like many ballads, tells a story and reflects on human nature through dialogue. In this case, questions and answers are exchanged between the initially disconsolate lover and a pilgrim returning from Walsingham, a famous place of pilgrimage in Norfolk.

Notice the conventional description of the 'true love'. She is seen as 'divine', 'angelic', 'a queen' and 'a nymph', but the questioner explains that he has now been abandoned. While some scholars are not convinced that this poem was written by Ralegh, could it perhaps be a coded message to Queen Elizabeth, who not only lavished rewards upon one of her favourite courtiers but also at one point imprisoned him for having a relationship with one of her ladies-in-waiting?

In the ballad, the main speaker explains that he has been rejected because he is old. His loved one does not like the 'falling fruit/From the withered tree'. Consider how the speaker goes on to reflect upon the nature of love and, in particular, the nature of the love felt by 'womenkind'. Note how the final verse begins with a significant 'But'.

The Poet As a successful military adventurer and explorer, author and poet, Walter Ralegh was a notable figure in the court of Queen Elizabeth I. He took expeditions to the New World, searching for El Dorado, and was an early colonizer, while also launching official and unofficial attacks against the Spanish.

By 1585, he had been knighted and was the recipient of many gifts of extensive lands and lucrative trading licences. However, in 1592, Ralegh fell from favour when he secretly married one of Elizabeth's maids of honour and the queen had him imprisoned briefly in the Tower of London.

When Elizabeth died, James I had Ralegh imprisoned once more, in an attempt to appease the Spanish, and on this occasion he remained in captivity for nine years, before being released to lead another expedition, to Guiana in search of gold. The expedition failed, Ralegh attacked a Spanish settlement against the king's wishes and, on his return in 1618, he was executed.

O *Mary Sidney Herbert (1561–1621)*

The Poem Mary Sidney Herbert wrote in the late sixteenth century. Her devout Calvinist form of Protestant belief is captured in this simple poem of faith and obedience.

The poem begins with a conventional image of God lighting the way and establishes the sense that everything the poet does will be in response to God's pure word, which will clear the paths ahead of her and guide her every step.

The second stanza refers to the 'grief' and anguish Mary Sidney Herbert feels. How does this stanza reflect the nature of her relationship with God? In the third stanza, the poet talks of the dangers and temptations that may lie around her. How does she convey her response to those imagined dangers?

In the final stanza, Mary Sidney Herbert proclaims her belief in scripture and the word of God that has been passed down to her. How does she use language to end the poem on a note of passionate, willing subjugation to God's plan?

To what extent do you think the elegant formality and regularity of rhythm and rhyme support the meaning of the poem?

The Poet Mary Sidney Herbert was an influential and talented poet, translator and patron of the arts in Elizabethan England. She was also the sister of the courtier and poet Philip Sidney. She completed the translations of the Psalms into English which he had begun but had been unable to finish before his early death. Mary Sidney Herbert wrote over a hundred Psalm translations, using a remarkable range of verse forms. (A meditation upon the Psalms was seen as an acceptable form of writing for women in the Elizabethan period.)

Mary Sidney Herbert celebrated her brother's life and accomplishments in her verse and acted as a patron to other writers, such as Edmund Spenser, who paid tribute to her brother. She was a highly educated woman, studying not simply scripture and rhetoric but French, Italian and Latin. Even in her own lifetime, she was celebrated as an accomplished poet by male contemporaries.

The Burning Babe *Robert Southwell (1561–95)*

The Poem Written in iambic heptameter couplets, Southwell's poem has an immediately arresting title. Unlike most Christmas poems, which focus on the joy surrounding the birth of Jesus, Southwell presents us with a disturbing image of a burning baby 'scorched with excessive heat' and shedding 'floods of tears'.

Robert Southwell was a young Jesuit priest who was a victim of the persecution of Catholics in Elizabeth's reign. He was brutally tortured and kept in solitary confinement before eventually being hanged, drawn and quartered. It is legitimate to suggest that the tone and content of this poem is influenced by his appalling experiences in captivity.

Notice how the narrator appears as a lost soul in the first line – 'shivering in the snow' – before the dazzling appearance of the burning babe. Consider the images of fire and flames employed by Southwell when he gives the newly born babe a voice in the poem.

In spite of apparent rejection by 'men's defiled souls', the redemptive power of the babe's love and sacrifice is constant and Southwell concludes with a reference to the vision occurring on Christmas Day.

The Poet Robert Southwell wrote most of his poems and prose when working as an underground Jesuit priest in Protestant England at a time when an active Catholic priest's chances of survival were no more than one in three. Educated in Italy, he then attended the Jesuit school in Douai, northern France, before ordination. In 1586, he travelled to England and began his mission, working secretly as a pastor in London. He survived for six years before being captured and enduring sustained torture. His trial and execution took place in 1595.

His prose is admired for its clarity, lucidity and reasonableness of tone. These qualities are seen in his *An Humble Supplication* (1591), which is a powerful and moving response to the royal proclamation that condemned and stigmatized Catholics. Just over fifty of Southwell's poems survive, and all of these explore religious themes.

Robert Southwell was canonized by Pope Paul VI in 1970.

'So oft as I her beauty do behold' *Edmund Spenser (1552–99)*

The Poem

This sonnet is part of a sequence of eighty-nine sonnets that Spenser wrote about his courtship of his second wife, Elizabeth Boyle. These little love poems are written in the tradition of Italian Petrarchan sonnets but, whereas those sonnets tended to deal with an unassailable, idealized object of devotion, Spenser was addressing a very real woman and one he went on to marry.

In Sonnet 55, he begins by wondering what his lady could be made of, because she is both cruel and fair. Look at the way he acknowledges in witty, rhetorical lines how comparisons of his lady with the elements are inadequate. He finally decides that she may be made of 'sky' and the language of the poem employs words such as 'heaven', 'high' and 'pure' in celebration of his 'cruel-fair' love. He hopes that, if she is most like heaven, she will show him heavenly 'mercy' and respond favourably to his protestations of love.

Note the shift in the argument at the start of the second stanza. What is the effect of the elegant, formal use of rhythm and rhyme and, in particular, the final, clinching couplet?

The Poet

Edmund Spenser is often mentioned alongside Shakespeare, Marlowe and Donne as one of the greatest poets of the Elizabethan period.

He is probably best known for his long, allegorical epic poem, *The Faerie Queen*, which was published in the 1590s and dedicated to glorifying the reign of Elizabeth I. In spite of the romantic subject matter of this poem, his sonnet sequences and 'Epithalamion', a traditional optimistic wedding song, Spenser was not a detached and unworldly poet. He was a beneficiary of the Elizabethan conquest of Ireland, receiving confiscated lands, and in 1596 wrote a pamphlet called 'A View of the Present State of Ireland', which advocated a ruthless approach to the 'pacification' of that country.

Spenser was driven from his Irish castle by Irish forces at the end of the century and returned to London, where he died in 1599.

'When that I was and a little tiny boy'

William Shakespeare (1564–1616)

The Poem This song is taken from the final act of Shakespeare's play *Twelfth Night*. It is sung by the 'Clown', or court jester, Feste, in a play that is full of references to music. The opening line offers a sweet image of the little tiny boy, while the surprising 'and' where we might expect a 'but' draws attention to both parts of the line.

The simple lyrical quality of the poem, its rhyme and rhythm patterns and frequent use of repetition all contribute to its song-like qualities.

Consider the tone of the poem and the philosophical aspects of the content. The wind and rain perhaps suggest the difficulties and hardships that are a constant accompaniment to all stages of a person's life. The singer does not rant against the elements but seems to accept them stoically and almost wistfully with a 'hey, ho'.

In the final stanza, the trials and tribulations of life are put to one side for a moment in the hope that the play can provide comfort and pleasure and an escape from the wind and the rain for a short while.

The Poet Born in Stratford-upon-Avon, William Shakespeare was a poet and playwright who lived in the reigns of Elizabeth I and James I. He dominates the story of English literature across the world. His plays remain exceptionally popular, especially his comedies, for example, *A Midsummer Night's Dream*, and his tragedies *Macbeth* and *Hamlet*.

Shakespeare was not only a commercially successful writer of plays for performance in Elizabethan England but also an accomplished actor and shrewd theatrical manager. He was one of the owners of the Globe Theatre for many years. By the time of his death in 1616, he was a man of some wealth and fame.

Although his plays continue to be studied in schools and universities and performed all over the world, Shakespeare is also remembered for his 154 sonnets, which include Sonnet 18, one of his most widely read: 'Shall I compare thee to a summer's day?'

To Celia *Ben Jonson (1573–1637)*

The Poem The poem, addressed to the Celia of the title, is an elaborate appeal for her love and a pledging of the speaker's to her. He first asks for a number of very small tokens of her love for him – he says a look, or a kiss left in a cup, would be enough – then asks her to quench the 'thirst that from the soul doth rise' before declaring that he wouldn't swap anything for a taste of her 'nectar'. What do you think of his argument so far?

In the second stanza, we start to wonder whether the speaker's love for Celia is unrequited. He talks about having sent her a 'rosy wreath', but we soon learn that she 'sent'st it back'. In a perhaps too-clever twist, he asserts that his sending of the wreath was 'not so much honouring' Celia, but more to have it blessed with everlasting life. Even though she 'didst only breathe' on the wreath, the speaker swears it now 'grows, and smells' of Celia rather than itself. What do you think of his argument now? What do you think Celia might have to say in return?

The Poet Ben Jonson was a skilful satirist of contemporary society, producing *Volpone* for the stage in 1605–6 and *The Alchemist* in 1610. It is highly likely that Shakespeare would have appeared in a production of another of Jonson's plays, *Every Man in His Humour*, and, in spite of their professional rivalry, Jonson appeared to hold Shakespeare in high regard. His tribute written on the death of Shakespeare contains the often quoted line 'He was not of an age but for all time.'

Witty, sociable and scornful of ignorance, Jonson attracted an influential circle of friends and admirers known as the 'Tribe of Ben', which included members of the nobility and other writers.

Jonson's poetry is informed by his classical learning; among his well-known poems is his elegant country-house poem 'To Penshurst'. He could also, however, write with touching simplicity in poems such as 'My Picture Left in Scotland' and those written on the death of his children.

Love *George Herbert (1593–1633)*

The Poem This is the third in a series of poems by George Herbert which meditates on the nature of love. 'Love (I)' explores the relationship between mortal and immortal love. 'Love (II)' puzzles out more specifically the relationship between the love of God and human lust. 'Love (III)', this poem, presents a personification of Love, who engages with the speaker in a tender dialogue about his worthiness for love. The language of the poem is religious in tone, but to what extent do you think the poem is religious in theme?

This poem is shaped in a way that is visually arresting, with long lines followed by short lines. Why? How does the meaning ebb and flow between the two very different line lengths?

Notice also that there are three stanzas and that the rhyme scheme of the poem (ABABCC) could be seen as a dance of three steps, with the final two lines of each stanza coming together in a couplet. How does this relate to sound and meaning, and the sense of the poem as a dialogue, even an argument?

The Poet A poet and an Anglican priest, George Herbert was an exceptionally gifted scholar who held important positions at Cambridge University in the 1620s. He was also a Member of Parliament for Montgomery for a short time, and was viewed favourably by King James I. However, after the death of the king, he appears to have given up his secular ambitions and, after taking Holy Orders, he spent the rest of his relatively short life as the rector of a small parish near Salisbury, caring devotedly for his parishioners.

Throughout his life, Herbert wrote religious verse, some of which, like 'The Collar', vividly describes his relationship with God in terms of passionate spiritual conflict. His poetry is technically versatile and full of typically metaphysical, ingenious images. Some of his poems survive as popular hymns, and a stained-glass window in Westminster Abbey in his memory emphasizes his importance within the Anglican Church.

To Althea from Prison *Richard Lovelace (1618–57)*

The Poem A passionate supporter of King Charles I, Lovelace was imprisoned by the Puritans, and it was while in captivity that he imagined in this poem a visit from his beloved Althea.

The poem is full of paradoxes. In the first verse, Lovelace happily submits to a kind of imprisonment created by the wondrous beauty of his Althea. He lies 'tangled in her hair' and 'fettered to her eye' and yet remains as free as the gods. Lovelace's enjoyment of life is recalled in the second stanza through reference to wine and roses and a kind of freedom found in celebration.

Although the poem begins as a passionate love poem, consider how Lovelace's loyalty to the king and his commitment to the Royalist cause are clearly established in the third verse. His endorsement of the king is defiant and uninhibited. He proclaims the 'sweetness, mercy, majesty/And glories of my King.'

Notice how Lovelace forges a triumphant response to the potential disaster of his imprisonment. The frequently quoted first two lines of the final verse sum up his belief in true freedom – the freedom of conscience.

The Poet Richard Lovelace is one of a group of writers known as 'Cavalier Poets'. What they had in common was not only a passionate allegiance to King Charles I but also a belief that the ideal Renaissance man should strive to be a wit, a lover, a courtier, a soldier, a musician and a writer of verses – if these can be produced – while fully engaging with the pleasures of life.

Lovelace was born into a very wealthy family and came to the attention of King Charles and Queen Henrietta Maria while he was still at Oxford. He served in the king's military expeditions to Scotland, and during the Civil War was a general in the Royalist army. Lovelace's involvement in a number of military campaigns led to him receiving serious wounds when fighting at Dunkirk in 1646.

Lovelace used his personal wealth to support the king's cause and died in relative poverty aged thirty-nine.

To the Virgins, to Make Much of Time *Robert Herrick (1591–1674)*

The Poem This poem is frequently anthologized, and its first line is often quoted as a pithy way of saying that we should make the most of the time we have. While this is a valid interpretation of the poem's broad sentiment, the more specific argument of the poem as a whole is that young women should hasten towards marriage before they lose their 'prime'.

There is a song-like quality to the poem, with its jaunty rhythm and rhyme. On the one hand, this seems to reflect the youthful nature of the girls addressed by the speaker; on the other, it seems incongruous with the message that old age and death are both imminent and inevitable. Where do you see the balance between these two elements?

The third stanza suggests that life is 'best' at a younger age. At the time when this poem was written, young women were encouraged to be 'coy' or shy in their public demeanour. The speaker, however, promotes a dynamic and perhaps more exuberant attitude to life, urging the 'youth' to use their time and 'go marry' before it is too late.

The Poet Robert Herrick lived a long life for a seventeenth-century man. He died at the age of eighty-three, having produced well over two thousand poems, many of them written while he was a country parson in Devon. Before that, he had mixed with the literati of London as an enthusiastic disciple of the influential poet Ben Jonson.

Herrick was an ardent Royalist and a traditional Anglican, so it was almost inevitable that he would be expelled from his parish by the Puritans after their victory in the Civil War. In some of his poems he seems to delight in returning to London yet, at the Restoration, he personally petitioned the king to be allowed to go back to his parish, where he resumed his work as parson, remaining there for a further fourteen years, until his death.

Herrick's poems often dealt with religious themes and incorporated his classical learning, but he also wrote lyric poems that dealt with love and desire.

Bermudas *Andrew Marvell (1621–78)*

The Poem The four-line introductory section locates the action of the poem in the Bermudas, which are located off the east coast of America. A group of mariners is giving thanks to God for their safe journey across the Atlantic to islands seen as 'far kinder than our own'. Although this suggests a gentler climate than back in England, the mariners may be hoping to escape from more than just the rain and cold of their home country. Note the mention of the 'rage' of high-ranking clergy in line twelve and the historical fact that some Puritans were fleeing to the New World to escape religious persecution at this time.

The Bermudas the mariners have come to are presented as a kind of paradise. In lines thirteen to twenty-eight Marvell uses colours and descriptions of oranges, pomegranates, melons and figs to give a sense of attractive hue, warmth and abundance. The Bermudas appear like the Kingdom of God made real, and the mariners hope that the word of God will continue to spread beyond the islands.

In the last four lines, the narrative voice returns, helping to frame the mariners' song.

The Poet For some time after his death, Andrew Marvell was remembered as a politician, diplomat, pamphleteer and satirist. He was associated with the anti-Royalist cause in the 1650s and yet served successfully in the Restoration government, representing Hull for many years. Subsequent critical reappraisal of his work has celebrated the wit and elegance of his poetry in pieces such as 'To His Coy Mistress', 'The Garden' and 'Upon Appleton House', which deals with the tension between private and public life.

His even-handedness is seen in his 'Horatian Ode' in praise of Oliver Cromwell, which at the same time contains a tribute to Charles I. While welcoming the Restoration, in verse satires and prose pamphlets he was highly critical of the incompetence and disorder in Charles II's government.

Today Marvell is seen as one of the leading poets of the metaphysical period and a writer of poetry that combines intellectual rigour and the subtle expression of strong emotion.

Epitaph *Katherine Philips (1632–64)*

The Poem Katherine Philips' 'Epitaph' marks the tragic loss of her son, Hector, who died just over a week after his birth. The poem begins conventionally contemplating the transience of youth and beauty, before seemingly moving towards the celebration of birth and the arrival of a son. Note the use of repetition in line 6, and the way the infant is described.

How does Katherine Philips use language in line 10, when we learn of the death of her son? What is the impact of this line? The poet speculates as to why her son may have left this earth so soon. How does she explain in a literary manner why her son broke 'the prison shell'?

The idea of breaking free is reinforced by the reference to 'Hermes Seal'. In Greek myth, the god Hermes was said to have invented a magic seal that would keep vessels airtight. Not even this can restrain the spirit of her son in its journey to Heaven.

The poem ends with a comparison between the glorious sun obscured by a cloud and the infant wrapped in his burial sheet.

The Poet Katherine Philips started writing soon after her marriage in 1648, aged sixteen, to James Philips. He was a prominent supporter of the Parliamentary cause, whereas Katherine enthusiastically welcomed the Restoration of the English monarchy in 1660.

Katherine Philips formed a literary circle of friends known as 'The Society of Friendship', whose members adopted classical pen names when they wrote poetry. She wrote as 'Orinda', and many of her poems were addressed to other women, known, for example, as 'Rosania' and 'Lucasia'. Critics have been intrigued by the nature of the relationships developed by these women, whose feelings are expressed with some intensity, especially in Katherine Philips' poetry.

In addition to writing poetry that was elegant and polished, if somewhat conventional, Katherine Philips was an outstanding linguist and completed many translations of verse and drama from the French. Her talent was widely celebrated by other prominent writers of the period. She died in 1664 of smallpox.

An Exequy to His Matchless Never to be Forgotten Friend

Henry King (1592–1669)

The Poem This is a poem of controlled grief, expressing the poet's longing to be reunited with his dead wife, Anne. This extract begins with the thought that a second marriage will be achieved when age, grief or sickness reunites the poet as dust with his wife's dust that he 'so much loves'.

Notice how King uses the imagery of travel and voyaging when talking about his movement towards death. A night's sleep is an 'eight hours' sail' towards his destination. He speaks of this journey in gentle language that suggests contentment. He will 'swiftly glide' on the tide that takes him ever closer to death and reunion. From the twenty-fifth line in this extract, he suggests that he is ashamed that Anne has taken to the battlefield to engage with death before him, especially as he is so much older than she was. He compares his pulse to the beating of the battle drum, signalling his slow, deliberate march towards their reunion.

He will not contemplate suicide but will live with 'half a heart' until they meet again.

The formal control, tonal restraint and mood of seemingly meditative calm make the poem exceptionally poignant.

The Poet The son of an influential Bishop of London, Henry King followed in his father's footsteps to pursue a career in the Church, which culminated in his appointment as Bishop of Chichester, a position he held during a very turbulent period in British history. His poetry is a chronicle of eventful times. The public, political turmoil of the state was matched by private, personal turmoil for King. Most movingly, he suffered, and wrote about, the death of his young wife, Anne.

His loyalty to the king during the Civil War led to Parliament taking away his estates in 1643, but he lived to be reinstated at Chichester at the time of the Restoration.

King was a friend of the metaphysical poet and Dean of St Paul's Cathedral, John Donne. His poetry employs the sort of extravagant extended metaphors, delight in paradox and self-conscious displays of wit that are characteristic of the metaphysical poets.

Verses upon the Burning of Our House *Anne Bradstreet (1612–72)*

The Poem Anne Bradstreet's poem recounts the dramatic events of one night in 1666 when her house was consumed by fire. After a simple rhyming couplet sets the scene, the poem immediately describes the chaos and confusion prompted by the discovery of the fire. She hears the 'thundering noise' and 'piteous shrieks' but her strong faith is immediately apparent when she writes of how she turns to God to comfort her in her distress. To what extent in lines thirteen to twenty does Anne Bradstreet seem to suggest that the fire is all part of God's plan? Do these lines hint that she is able to find some sense of consolation even in moments of danger and destruction?

Notice how in lines twenty-two to thirty-five she describes a very human and understandable reaction to the loss of things she valued that gave her joy – a 'chest', a 'trunk', all her 'pleasant things' that she will see no more.

However, her seemingly unshakeable faith reasserts itself when she declares, 'all's Vanity', and the poem concludes by reflecting on the permanence of God's 'house', furnished with 'glory'.

The Poet Anne Bradstreet emigrated to America with her family in 1630, on one of the first ships to take Puritans to New England. The journey was arduous, with malnutrition and disease claiming many lives. Anne Bradstreet had eight children with her husband, Simon, who eventually prospered in the new land. She devoted herself to educating her children and expanding her own knowledge by reading books from her father's collection.

In the austere Puritan environment, women were not encouraged to express their views, so Bradstreet wrote cautiously for her family and a close group of friends, with no intention of publishing. However, her brother-in-law, on a trip back to England, independently arranged for some of her poems to be published, making her the first American woman to see her work in print.

Bradstreet continued to write until her death at sixty, while remaining fully aware of the tension in Puritan society between piety and poetry.

Paradise Lost *John Milton (1608–74)*

The Poem John Milton's epic poem, written in blank verse in the 1660s, deals with the great Christian theme of the Fall of Man and the mythical Fall of the Angels led by Satan. In Book I, from which this extract is taken, Milton describes Satan and his comrades languishing in Hell after the disastrous end of their war against God.

Satan is speaking to his second in command, Beelzebub, and reflecting on what has happened to them and their fellow fallen angels after their crushing defeat. How does Satan still find some elements of hope and consolation, in spite of having been cast into the 'mournful gloom'? Consider the significance of Satan's comment 'Better to reign in Hell, than serve in Heaven.'

The Poet Milton was a poet who was actively involved in the world of English politics and government. As the rule of Charles I began to disintegrate, Milton studied, travelled and wrote pamphlets in support of the Puritan and Parliamentary cause. He was outspoken on issues such as divorce, censorship and freedom of expression.

Although seen as a dangerous radical under the monarchy, Milton was rewarded with public office under the Commonwealth and became a secretary in the Foreign Service, making use of his impeccable Latin.

The Restoration of 1660 inevitably saw the Republican Milton fall from favour. By now almost completely blind, he had to dictate his poetry, but he produced much of his major work in this period, including *Paradise Lost* and its sequel, *Paradise Regained*, following the return of the monarchy to his death in 1674.

A Song for St Cecilia's Day *John Dryden (1631–1700)*

The Poem St Cecilia was a Christian martyr who became the patron saint of music. Dryden's poem, written in 1687 to commemorate her saint's day, celebrates and glorifies the power of music, and was set to music for the formal day of celebration on 22 November.

The poem begins by describing the creation of the universe and the role of music in creating harmony. What references to music can you find in this first stanza, and what is the impact of the repetition Dryden uses?

In the second stanza, 'Jubal' refers to the biblical character regarded as the father of music. His invention of the harp and organ encouraged listeners to make connections between music and the Divine.

What aspects of music does Dryden present in the remaining stanzas? Look out for references to war and conflict, love and singing. He mentions trumpets and flutes, violins and the human voice. Notice how he wonders whether the human voice can match 'The sacred organ's praise'.

The Poet John Dryden was one of the dominant literary figures of the English Restoration period. He began his prolific and versatile writing career in the Puritan era before Charles II became king, and wrote verses on the death of Oliver Cromwell. However, he was quick to produce work that celebrated the return of Charles.

The Restoration of the English monarchy allowed the theatres to reopen, and Dryden produced several works for the stage during this time. His most fruitful period of dramatic writing was the 1670s and it culminated in his most successful play, *All for Love*, which was based on the story of Antony and Cleopatra.

In addition to writing for the theatre, Dryden was an essayist, translator, critic, sharp satirist and poet. His long poem *Annus Mirabilis*, commemorating 1666, the year of wonders, with its naval battles and the Great Fire of London, led to him becoming Poet Laureate in 1668.

A Thousand Martyrs *Aphra Behn (1640–89)*

The Poem Many readers will assume that Behn is adopting a male persona here, but we could easily read the poem as written from her own – female – perspective. We are presented with a libertine speaker talking of many lovers. He suggests that, though he has spoken about the pain of love, in fact it is only 'Love's pleasures' that he cares about. As such, he has 'betrayed' 'a thousand beauties'. He claims to have been a callous and deceiving lover, telling 'the fair' about the 'wounds and smart' they long to hear of, then 'laughing' and leaving. Consider how the poem may have been received when it was written in 1688, and how a modern audience might respond.

The poem is written in three elegant sestets. Notice the iambic tetrameter and consider how important form might be to the theme of this particular kind of love and betrayal.

Is this speaker entirely honest? Notice that the final stanza begins with 'Alone'. Is there any sense of regret here? The speaker claims to be 'Without the hell' of love, yet in the same line we find reference to the 'heaven of joy'. Has he also sacrificed his joy with his promiscuous love?

The Poet Aphra Behn was the first female writer to make her living through her art; she was a significant seventeenth-century dramatist, *The Rover* being one of her best-known plays. Little is known of her early life, but we do know that she was an accomplished poet, worked as a scribe for the King's Company players, produced many plays, wrote a novel about an enslaved African prince (*Oroonoko*) and was a spy for the English Crown, operating for a period in the Netherlands.

She caused some scandal, touching as she did on topics of a sexual nature, and during the late nineteenth century her work was largely dismissed for this reason. Behn claimed that no such scandal would have arisen had her plays been penned by a man. Her poetic voice is distinctive and strong. She often comments on contemporary events and situations, and writes from the position of both men and women.

The Mistress *John Wilmot, Earl of Rochester (1647–80)*

The Poem The first line clearly suggests that this is a love poem, but what sort of a love poem is it? We might expect from what we know of Wilmot that the poem would be lustful and witty. If the pain of love is presented, we might imagine this is only so that Wilmot can squeeze exquisite pleasure from his torment. Surprisingly, this is not the case.

Briefly, Wilmot's poem mentions the joys of love: love allows us almost to escape time, it nourishes the soul, it is associated with beauty, and it is a 'treasure'. But the thrust of the poem is the great suffering love brings. Notice how, through absence, love kills the poet's soul, reducing it to a ghost, a 'shade' haunting the 'living tomb of love'. Wilmot associates love with madness, outlining negative emotions, such as 'jealous doubts', 'tormenting fears' and 'anxious cares'. To be in love seems irrational.

Atypically, the poem is not addressed to the beloved, but to the 'wiser men' whose scorn Wilmot anticipates. What answer has he to their 'censure'? That the extent of the pain is the proof that he is really in love, and, crucially, though love creates suffering, it 'make[s] us blest at last'.

The Poet To his many admirers, John Wilmot, 2nd Earl of Rochester, was one of the wittiest men who ever lived and a brilliant poet. A Restoration libertine, unrestrained by moral scruples, Wilmot rose quickly in the court of King Charles II, serving courageously in the navy in the Second Anglo-Dutch War in 1665–7 and attaining the important position of Gentleman of the Bedchamber. Regularly banished from court for writing scandalous satires, Wilmot was as regularly reinstated by a king with a taste for witty entertainment.

To his many detractors, Wilmot was a debauched monster and a scoundrel. Samuel Johnson described him as 'a worthless and dissolute rake', although his contemporary Andrew Marvell praised his satirical writings. He was ignored in the Victorian period, but his reputation as a fine poet was championed by Ezra Pound in the 1920s. Wilmot was just thirty-three when he died, apparently from a combination of sexual diseases and alcoholism.

The Hog, the Sheep and Goat, Carrying to a Fair

Anne Finch (1661–1720)

The Poem This poem is based on the work of the French poet and writer of fables Jean de La Fontaine. The literary genre of fable often uses animals as characters in a short narrative with a clear moral message. The story of the animals being taken to the fair created by Finch offers a slightly darker and more philosophical interpretation of events than the original. Notice how the first verse delays the telling of the story of the journey of the hog, the sheep and the goat by reflecting upon the advantages and disadvantages of foresight.

The hog, or 'swine', fears the worst, knowing that, while the sheep and goat may be prized for their milk and fleece, he will not survive his encounter with the rows of 'dreadful butchers' awaiting his arrival at the fair. Consider the seriousness of the debate between the swine and the driver, couched within the framework of a jaunty and elegantly executed rhyme scheme. The pitiless driver is given the last, thought-provoking words as he asks the swine to consider what benefit will accrue from being certain of his fate. Are those who are blithely unaware of suffering until the last minute more 'fortunate and wise'?

The Poet Anne Finch was an aristocrat acquainted with the most famous poet of the age, Alexander Pope. However, during her lifetime, her poetry was little known and would have remained obscure had not William Wordsworth praised it, particularly her depictions of nature, in an essay included in his *Lyrical Ballads* (written with Samuel Taylor Coleridge). Today, literary academics are again interested in Finch as an example of a neglected female poet who wrote within and against the conventions of contemporary, predominantly male, literary taste.

A spiritual, religious poet, whose work often expresses intense private struggles, Finch seems to have suffered from severe depression. Though she was an aristocrat, her life was certainly not without hardship. In particular, she was a passionate advocate of social justice for women and a staunch, faithful supporter of King James II. After James had been deposed and it was dangerous to be seen to side with him, Finch's support was unwavering.

Epistle to Miss Blount *Alexander Pope (1688–1744)*

The Poem Pope's twenty-five couplets playfully explore the predicament of a young, fashionable woman who is forced to leave the exciting and lively town full of 'opera, park, assembly, play' for the country, where she will be forced to 'Count the slow clock'. How does Pope use language in lines fourteen to twenty-two to present a teasing picture of life in the country as tedious, repetitive and uninspiring?

The poet suggests that romance will not provide a distraction to the under-stimulated Miss Blount, as any potential suitors will be coarse and more interested in hunting and horses than in fashionable young ladies. In line thirty-one the poem returns to thoughts of spectacular city pageants and 'lords and earls and dukes and gartered knights' as it imagines Miss Blount daydreaming of a richer, more animating life.

In the final ten lines, the playful teasing moves towards something more flirtatious and yet sincere sounding. How does Pope seem to identify with Miss Blount? Why is he also pining and wishing he was somewhere else when his friend the poet John Gay taps him on his shoulder?

The Poet Alexander Pope's reputation as an immensely skilful and influential poet, satirist and translator of Homer was established long before his death. Born a Catholic in 1688, at a time when restrictions were still placed upon adherents to the faith, he was largely educated at home. He suffered from a deformity in the spine and, in an age when literary rivalries were vicious, some of his enemies were quick to mock his condition.

However, Pope never lacked friends and allies, and he was part of the Scriblerus Club, which he formed with fellow writers such as Jonathan Swift with the intention of holding folly and false learning up to ridicule.

The Rape of the Lock, a mock-heroic poem about the cutting of a lock of hair, is one of Pope's most famous and frequently read poems, while his poem on the art of writing, *An Essay on Criticism*, contains many of his much-quoted sayings.

A Satirical Elegy on the Death of a Late Famous General

Jonathan Swift (1667–1745)

The Poem An elegy is usually a mournful lamentation for the dead. However, as the title tells us, Swift manipulates the form for satire. Rather than expressing sadness at the passing of the 'late famous general', this speaker's tone is sarcastic and mocking.

Notice the exclamations in the opening lines. What reaction to the news of the duke's death do these imply? The tone from line five becomes conversational to the point of gossip with the casual 'Well, since he's gone . . .' and the conspiratorial 'trust me'.

The form of the poem also seems to mock the deceased. The lines follow an iambic tetrameter with rhyming couplets, perhaps suggesting that the general was unworthy of the iambic pentameter of the classic heroic couplet.

The main section of the poem presents a mean-spirited man whose funeral will be poorly attended. The last eight lines change to a warning, and speak directly to 'all ye empty things', the statesmen, reminding them that all 'honours' ultimately turn to dust.

The Poet Born in Ireland in 1667, Jonathan Swift spent much of his adult life in England. He was actively involved in politics, and in his self-penned epitaph describes himself as a 'champion of liberty'. He was a prolific writer of prose satire and is perhaps most famous for his novel *Gulliver's Travels*. Although often mistaken for a children's book, this was in fact a satirical depiction of human nature.

In his 1729 essay *A Modest Proposal*, much to the outrage of his contemporaries, Swift sardonically proposed cannibalism as a solution to the plight of an impoverished Ireland. His reputation as a writer found him companionship with a group of authors that included Alexander Pope.

Swift's poems, though less well known, also tend towards satire and humour. His tone is generally direct and genial, parodying the styles of numerous poetic forerunners. On a technical level, Swift's poetry appears simple, however his rhetoric is powerful.

The Visit *Mary Leapor (1722–46)*

The Poem Like many writers of her period, Leapor adopts a pastoral-sounding pseudonym. In this case it is Mira, who almost immediately is described as 'poor' and on her way to visit her friend Artemisia. A serving maid who died in relative obscurity, Leapor explores the way in which women are perceived in a male-dominated society.

In a series of comical but rueful couplets she seeks a kind of sanctuary away from the 'penetrating eye' of 'students in physiognomy'. Although this is an eighteenth-century poem, the issues it deals with are strikingly topical and relevant to early-twenty-first-century life. Leapor laments the way women are judged on their looks rather than on their characters. Constantly scrutinized and assessed by men, they are condemned if a hand is freckled or if a nose is anything other than perfectly straight. In a passage of comic hyperbole, Leapor points out the relentlessness of their judges' gaze. They will still search out what they see as physical defects, even in the dark or looking into the 'midday sun'.

How do you respond to the powerful final three-line image concerning sharks and their prey?

The Poet In spite of needing to earn a living as a kitchen maid and her death from measles at the age of twenty-four, Mary Leapor left behind a substantial body of work. Her poetry has increasingly come to be seen as witty, insightful and challenging in its depiction of the world women inhabited in the early eighteenth century.

Leapor had some education, but in terms of her literary writing she was partly self-taught and partly encouraged by benevolent female employers. In some of her poems, Leapor assumes the persona of 'Mira', writing self-deprecatingly about herself and commenting upon the struggles of women living in a paternalistic society.

Her long poem 'Crumble Hall' plays with the genre of 'country-house poetry', where the magnificence of a wealthy patron's estate is normally linked to the impressive virtue of its owner. Leapor subverts this tradition by writing from the perspective of a servant within the great household.

A Receipt to Cure the Vapours *Mary Wortley Montagu (1689–1762)*

The Poem In the early eighteenth century, a 'receipt', as used here, means a remedy, and the term 'the vapours' was used to describe depression and nervousness in women. In the first verse, 'hartshorn tea' is a kind of ammonia-based restorative drink.

Mary Wortley Montagu addresses her friend as Delia, a name taken from Greek myth, a popular literary convention of the time among poets. She is clearly urging her friend not to sink into despair at the loss of a loved one. What does the speaker suggest will happen to her friend if she carries on 'fretting'?

She advises Delia to 'Choose, among the pretty fellows', and urges her to pick someone who is honourable, witty and young. The attention of another man will be the remedy for grief and loss, and she does not seem too concerned about 'All the morals that they tell us'. The relationship between the speaker and the 'they' referred to in this line is worth considering.

What is the tone of the final verse, where it seems that the speaker is suggesting that the remedy should be administered sparingly?

The Poet Mary Wortley Montagu was a prolific writer of letters and is particularly remembered for those she wrote from Turkey, when she was the ambassador's wife in Constantinople. She worked on these letters with the help of notes from her journals, and they were eventually published in 1763, shortly after her death.

In addition to her letter writing and essays, Montagu produced witty adaptations of Virgil and wrote sophisticated poetry in a wide variety of verse forms. She developed a close friendship with the poet Alexander Pope but, after they quarrelled, they engaged in poetic warfare, satirizing each other mercilessly.

Her personal life was unconventional and, although still married, she formed a relationship with an Italian writer. When this was unsuccessful, she lived abroad with an Italian count for a number of years.

She returned to England shortly after the death of her husband, but died seven months later, in 1762.

Elegy Written in a Country Churchyard *Thomas Gray (1716–71)*

The Poem Older readers will be familiar with the start of this poem, as it was regularly recited when poetry recitation was part of the school curriculum. In this extract, Gray reflects on the lives of the humble and unheralded people buried in the country churchyard in which he is standing. An elegy normally mourns the loss of an important, famous person, but this poem is more concerned with 'The short and simple annals of the poor'.

In stanzas nine to eleven, Gray reflects upon the inevitability of death and how, in death, the rich and the poor, the noble and the common man are all the same; while in the second half of this extract, he wonders what talents may have sprung from the hearts and hands of those in the ground if their lives had not been constrained by poverty.

In its measured phrasing and rational approach, the poem reflects the fashions of the Augustan age, but the emotion and individualism in it herald the start of the Romantic period.

The poem uses the 'heroic quatrain', which consists of four lines in iambic pentameter rhyming ABAB. Do the rhythm and rhyme contribute to the mood and meaning of Gray's melancholy, evocative poem?

The Poet Written over several years in the 1740s, Thomas Gray's elegy was eventually published in 1751 and enjoyed phenomenal popularity for the next two hundred years.

Gray was a versatile poet. He wrote elegant lyric and dramatic poems, Latin translations, odes and sonnets which reflected his wide range of interests. As a young man, he travelled widely, going on the Grand Tour of Europe, but he spent much of his life at Pembroke College. In the year he settled in Cambridge, his great friend Richard West died, prompting the writing of the much-admired 'Sonnet on the Death of Mr Richard West'. His reputation was such that he was offered the Poet Laureateship in 1757, but he declined the honour.

Gray never matched the simple profundity of his *Elegy*, but he was an exceptionally learned and significant poet of the late eighteenth century and paved the way for the likes of Wordsworth and Coleridge.

'For I will consider my Cat Jeoffry' *Christopher Smart (1722–71)*

The Poem This passage comes from a longer poem, *Jubilate Agno*, written by Smart during his time in an asylum for the insane. In this section, Smart extols the virtues of his cat, Jeoffry, in a litany that encompasses the fact that the creature 'washes himself', kisses other cats 'in kindness' and has the ability to 'creep'. He implies that the cat is the perfect servant of God in its behaviour and apparent devotion.

Smart was supposedly confined to the asylum as a result of an overt public demonstration of his religious beliefs. This poem can be read as a spiritual celebration, with the cat itself representing nature or a 'divine spirit'. Notice the references to biblical figures and to God throughout the poem.

The poem is distinct in its repeated use of the word 'For' to start each line, echoing language found in the Christian Bible. Are there any claims that Smart makes about his cat that you might disagree with? What effect does this immense piling up of qualities have on you?

The Poet Christopher Smart was born in 1722 and is best remembered for his religious poems *A Song to David* and *Jubilate Agno*, both of which were written during his time at St Luke's Hospital for Lunatics, London. He believed that God created the universe using language, and therefore considered that the work of poets forges a direct connection to the Divine.

As well as writing poetry, during his career Smart wrote copy for magazines, produced translations, songs and satire. He won the Cambridge Seatonian Prize on five occasions, for poetry on 'one or other of the perfections or attributes of the Supreme Being'. Modern admirers and imitators of his work include Allen Ginsberg, Peter Porter and Wendy Cope, while the composer Benjamin Britten used sections of *Jubilate Agno* in musical composition.

Smart incurred large debts during his lifetime, which ultimately saw him imprisoned at King's Bench Prison, where he died in 1771.

On the Death of Dr Robert Levet *Samuel Johnson (1709–84)*

The Poem Robert Levet was described by Johnson as 'an old and faithful friend'. He was part of Johnson's household, acting as a resident doctor and companion for many years until his sudden death in his seventies. He worked tirelessly among the London poor, accepting in payment only what they could afford.

Johnson's elegant, restrained but moving tribute to Levet is written as an ode in the style of the Latin poet Horace. Its four-line stanzas are full of calm, measured, respectful reflections upon Levet's life and work.

What qualities in Levet does Johnson seem particularly to value and record in the first five verses? (Note that 'officious' in the second stanza would not carry the pejorative meaning it has today. Johnson would have meant that Levet was always keen to fulfil a duty or an office.)

While the poem is a dignified tribute to an honest, hardworking man, the reference to the parable of the talents in verse seven perhaps makes us think about how we might best live our lives as we 'toil from day to day'.

The Poet Samuel Johnson is a towering figure in the history of English literature, to the extent that the second half of the eighteenth century has sometimes been described as 'the age of Johnson'. He was a poet, journalist, lexicographer, critic, essayist, biographer and compiler, over eight years, of *The Dictionary of the English Language*, which he completed with the help of six assistants.

After the death of Johnson's wife in 1752, his London household included a variety of domestic servants and companions. His financial position was always precarious, in spite of the success of the *Dictionary*, but this changed when he was awarded a government pension in 1762.

In 1763, he befriended James Boswell, a Scottish lawyer whose *Life of Johnson* contributed to Johnson's fame and reputation when it was published after Johnson's death. They travelled together in the Scottish Highlands and both wrote entertaining accounts of their expedition.

On being Cautioned against Walking on a Headland Overlooking the Sea, because It was Frequented by a Lunatic

Charlotte Smith (1749–1806)

The Poem This sonnet begins with an eight-line question. The speaker has been warned not to go near a cliff overlooking the sea because of the presence of a 'Lunatic', and the octet both questions whether the madman is there and imagines what he might be like.

Note the connection Smith establishes between the stormy conditions and the troubled mental state of the madman, creating a typically Gothic atmosphere. What kind of description of the madman does she offer in the opening eight lines? Are there points of contact between the position of the 'solitary wretch' in society and the solitary poet who is blessed or blighted with a powerful imagination?

Notice how the poem raises issues to do with viewpoint and perspective. In the octet, the poet is 'seeing' the madman in her mind's eye in vivid detail, but in the ninth line the poem shifts to a consideration of self in relation to the madman. '[O]n the giddy brink' seems to suggest her own volatile emotions, and she reveals not fear but 'envy' of the madman. He is not constrained by rationality. In her envy, is there a desire to break free and embrace nature and even danger in the same way?

The Poet Although born into a wealthy family, Charlotte Smith was plagued by debt for much of her life. Married to a reckless man who squandered his money, she spent some time with him in a debtors' prison. With remarkable fortitude, she composed her first book of poems, *Elegiac Sonnets*, in 1784, while in prison, and its success secured her and her husband's freedom and helped revive interest in the sonnet form.

Despite the fact that she had twelve children with her husband, it was a troubled relationship and, after eventually leaving him, she turned to novel writing to raise money. She produced popular fiction at a staggering rate, with a novel appearing, on average, once a year between 1788 and 1798. Her work, which almost certainly influenced Dickens, was sometimes semi-autobiographical and contained elements of the Gothic, with heroines struggling against male oppression and injustice. Her political awareness and radicalism are frequently evident.

Epitaph on a Hare *William Cowper (1731–1800)*

The Poem William Cowper suffered from severe bouts of depression for much of his life and seemed to enjoy keeping a variety of animals as a form of therapeutic distraction. He was given three hares by local villagers, and this poem formally commemorates the death of one, Tiney.

On first reading the 'Epitaph', it might appear to be simply a sincere and charming tribute to a pet. Cowper presents the character of Tiney in an observant and unsentimental manner and seems to appreciate the way in which the hare's antics could soothe his aching heart. However, the ending of the poem is worth considering carefully. Is a more sombre and fatalistic tone introduced? In spite of Cowper's care and protection, he cannot save Tiney from death. The inevitability of death is further emphasized by Cowper reflecting that one of his other hares will soon join Tiney in his grave. Does the ending suggest a pattern of deaths that might also include the death of the poet himself? A poem about a dead pet perhaps offers thoughts on the temporary nature of all life, both animal and human.

The Poet In his descriptions of the English countryside and of scenes from everyday life, William Cowper made a decisive contribution to English poetry, and prepared the ground for successors such as Wordsworth and Coleridge.

A committed evangelical Christian, Cowper also wrote many hymns. 'Light Shining out of Darkness' contains a line that remains well known today: 'God moves in a mysterious way/His wonders to perform.' In spite of his faith, Cowper was plagued by doubts and endured periods of severe depression and insanity in the early 1760s, during which he attempted suicide several times. He found comfort in his friendship with retired clergyman Morley Unwin and his wife, Mary. After Unwin died, he continued to live with Mary, who nursed Cowper through other periods of mental ill-health.

In spite of his battle with depression, Cowper wrote some extremely popular comic poems such as the mock-heroic 'John Gilpin'.

Slavery: A Poem *Hannah More (1745–1833)*

The Poem Hannah More's poem was written in support of William Wilberforce's campaign to abolish slavery. A passionate, poetic explanation of the abolitionists' argument, this extract is part of a 294-line poem. 'Oroonoko', in the fourth line of this extract, is a reference to a novel published in 1688 by Aphra Behn, which describes the suffering of the eponymous 'Royal Slave'. More stresses that this suffering is experienced at the time of writing by 'millions'.

Notice how the poem continually returns to the idea that the colour of a person's skin is irrelevant when considering the worth of a human being. The rhyming couplets reinforce the emphatic message that the people 'dragged' from Africa are not inferior to their captors and oppressors. Look at how More describes, in her words, 'the sable race'. What impression of the people whose 'anguish' she seeks to demonstrate in the poem is created by her use of phrases such as 'rude energy', 'high-souled passion', 'wild vigour'? In the final lines of this extract, examine the references to pride and the meaning of the suggestion that pride is 'In Afric scourged' but in Rome 'deified'.

The Poet A passionate abolitionist and social reformer during the period of slavery, Bristol-born Hannah More was a teacher, playwright and poet. Aged twenty-two, she became engaged to William Turner but, after six years, the wedding had still not taken place. Turner broke off the engagement and paid More £200 a year by way of compensation.

Regular trips to London saw her writing plays and poems and associating with the literary elite of the city. More paid a witty tribute to her circle of friends in her 1784 poem 'Conversation'.

More became increasingly involved with evangelical Christians in the last years of the eighteenth century, including the anti-slavery campaigner William Wilberforce, and produced a vast number of popular, moral and ethical tracts, poems and stories. Philanthropic work in Somerset led to the establishment of a dozen schools in the area by 1800. She lived just long enough to see the abolition of slavery.

The Chimney Sweeper *William Blake (1757–1827)*

The Poem 'The Chimney Sweeper' comes from William Blake's 1789 collection of poems, *Songs of Innocence*. This was later extended to become his most famous work, *Songs of Innocence and Experience*, in which the 'Innocence' poems are often mirrored by the 'Experience' poems to present different views of the human condition. This poem is mirrored by a shorter and bleaker 'Experience' poem.

'The Chimney Sweeper' presents us with a pitiful image of a young 'sweeper' and his friends. As we learn in the opening stanza, a child, often as young as four or five, typically became a chimney sweep when orphaned or sold by impoverished parents. Notice how the sweeper's lisping and mewling ''weep! 'weep!' cries out for our sympathy.

The rhyming couplets and anapaestic metre in this poem might remind us of a nursery rhyme, but how does this contrast with the details? To what extent does Blake present an innocence that has been destroyed?

Despite the harsh reality of working life, this speaker seems to have some acceptance of his lot. Tom Dacre's dream of an 'Angel' and a 'green plain' suggests a spiritual sense of hope for the children. Why is Tom's dream, rather than the speaker's, described?

The Poet An individualist and a highly original thinker, William Blake is a key figure in the English Romantic movement: a mystic, poet, illustrator and radical influenced by the French Revolution.

He first combined his skill as an engraver and his talent for poetic expression in *Songs of Innocence*. On the surface, these short poems have connections with traditional songs and ballads and moralistic poems for children popular in the eighteenth century, but Blake is often communicating something much more original and subversive. The collection was followed a few years later by *Songs of Experience*.

His work makes frequent use of symbols and is often a passionate protest against theological and political tyranny.

A Mother to Her Waking Infant *Joanna Baillie (1762–1851)*

The Poem What expectations does the title of the poem create? Perhaps we might anticipate something rather sweet and sentimental. Romantic poets were especially interested in childhood, often seeing it as a special state of being – innocent, imaginative, close to God. To what extent will Baillie's infant fit this description?

Baillie initially presents a superficially cool, almost detached, assessment of her baby. Among other things, the infant is imperfect (its 'lip' is 'awry') and also weak, helpless and graceless; moreover, it is a limited companion, having 'small understanding', a 'poor tongue' and being 'senseless'; it is also selfish, unbothered by the suffering of others. In summary, an infant is a 'little varlet'.

However, there are hints of the preciousness of the baby to its mother with the references to silk and gold, and the impact the little baby has on others seems overwhelmingly positive. In at least two verses, the mother speaks directly of her love for the baby and looks forward to a time when roles will be reversed and her child will be the one to take care of her.

The Poet Joanna Baillie was a Scottish playwright, critic and poet who lived most of her life in Hampstead, where she was the centre of a rich literary culture. Born into a family of physicians and the daughter of a university professor, Baillie was unusually well educated for a woman of her time. As a teenager, she learned geometry, philosophy and Latin, and she had a lifelong interest in medicine.

Baillie wrote twenty-seven plays and was well known and widely admired during her lifetime. Her poetry was translated into other languages, and both Haydn and Beethoven set her songs to music. Written in an elegant, orderly style, her poetry dealt with heroic historical figures, Scottish songs, nature and childhood.

In addition to her literary work, Baillie was a supporter of other writers and a notable philanthropist who gave away half her earnings to charity. Passionately anti-slavery, she sponsored the first slave narrative published in England.

Song ('Ae fond kiss, and then we sever') *Robert Burns (1759–96)*

The Poem Burns's poem, written in rhyming couplets, explores the pain of parting and lost love and is addressed to Agnes MacLehose. Between 1787 and 1788, they had engaged in a passionate correspondence, but Agnes was a married woman (although estranged from her husband) and propriety dictated that their relationship should be kept secret. In 1791, Agnes, referred to as Nancy in the poem, left Scotland to travel to Jamaica to attempt a reconciliation with her husband.

Note how the poem begins with the action of a kiss but, by the end of the line, we realize that it is not a kiss of greeting, passion or romance, but a farewell kiss. How does Burns convey the finality of this parting and the effect it is having upon him?

In spite of the despair he expresses at the end of the first stanza, he pays tribute to Nancy in the second, declaring that 'Naething could resist my Nancy!' Is there an element of irony in the use of 'my' in this line, given the sense of loss he is experiencing?

In the final stanza, Burns writes with passion but resignation and generosity, even though he talks of 'heart-wrung tears' and 'sighs and groans'.

The Poet Robert Burns started life as a ploughman in Scotland but is now one of the world's most celebrated poets. Every January, his life is remembered with whisky, haggis, singing and dancing on Burns Night.

Perhaps as a distraction from the hard physical work of his early life on the farm, his poetry, and in many ways his life, celebrated the natural world and the pleasures of living life to the full.

His first published collection of poetry was extremely successful and, by the age of twenty-seven, he was a poet of some fame and reputation across Scotland. He began to move in more sophisticated circles, while also engaging in a number of relationships. He remained a radical thinker with a passionate belief in egalitarianism.

Burns lived only for another ten years, but poems such as 'Auld Lang Syne', 'Tam O'Shanter' and 'A Red, Red Rose' ensure that he remains widely read today.

The Rights of Woman *Anna Laetitia Barbauld (1743–1825)*

The Poem Bold and liberating, this rousing poem is written as if declaimed from a soapbox or from the platform of a political meeting; it is a powerful poem that expects to be met with roaring cheers. It is a rallying call to women to rise up to challenge men's power and their 'imperial rule'.

From the start, the mood of the poem is imperative, with its affirmative first word 'Yes' and volley of commanding verbs: 'rise', 'assert', 'Resume', 'Go forth'. In this war of the sexes, the poet tells women that they will fight on their own terms: Barbauld achieves a radical reversal when she instructs women that their feminine virtues – their 'grace', 'Soft melting tones' and 'Blushes' – conventionally construed as weaknesses, are actually strengths. Allied to 'wit and art', these feminine traits are the weapons with which the complacent enemy will be defeated.

But is the whole poem simply a strident call to arms? Notice the shift in tone in the last third, beginning 'But hope not . . .' How does this final section change how we read the rest of the poem?

The Poet Anna Laetitia Barbauld was a celebrated poet, essayist, teacher and children's author who was initially held in high regard by her contemporaries. Admirers included the Romantic poets Wordsworth and Coleridge. In her poems, she challenged gender stereotypes: writing analytically and philosophically, she took on male attitudes by adopting traditionally masculine artistic forms and inhabiting them with female experience. High literary status was an extraordinary achievement for a female poet in a literary landscape dominated by men. A passionate anti-war and anti-slavery campaigner, a religious Dissenter and an influential literary critic, Barbauld ought to have become a major figure in the history of literature.

Although some readers may have been inspired by Barbauld, her revolutionary ideas upset and angered powerful figures in her own time, and Victorian critics either patronized or ignored her. It was not until the late twentieth century that critics re-examined and re-evaluated her distinctive voice.

After Blenheim *Robert Southey (1774–1843)*

The Poem Robert Southey's ballad offers a particular perspective on one of the most famous battles of the eighteenth century. In 1704, in the War of the Spanish Succession, a coalition of forces, including the English, defeated the French and Bavarian armies at Blenheim.

Southey does not describe the battle directly but, through the conversation between an old farmer and his grandchildren, it gradually emerges that the setting is a former battleground. Peterkin has found something 'large . . . and round', which his grandfather explains is a skull, one of many to be found in the earth nearby.

How does Old Kaspar describe the battle and the loss of life? Does he offer any explanation to the children about why the battle was fought? In spite of the graphic description of bodies 'rotting in the sun' and little Wilhelmine's belief that it was a 'wicked thing', the line that Southey frequently repeats has Old Kaspar saying that the battle was 'a famous victory'. Inevitably, we are encouraged to think about the purpose and validity of war. Many years later, Southey altered his pacifist, questioning view of war.

The Poet Robert Southey was an independent-minded young man who was expelled from Westminster School for opposing flogging. He developed radical religious and political ideas and, at one stage, considered emigrating to America with his friend Samuel Taylor Coleridge to set up a utopian commune.

The idea was abandoned, and Southey began writing plays and poems and, in particular, developed the ballad form in poems such as 'After Blenheim' and 'The Inchcape Rock'. He was a prolific writer of verse and histories and an accomplished biographer, who wrote *The Life of Nelson*. If he was not as original and successful in his poetry as contemporaries such as Wordsworth, his prose is highly skilful. Byron called it 'perfect', although he felt that Southey had compromised his beliefs for money and fame.

Southey gradually lost his radical opinions and became much more of an establishment figure. He was appointed Poet Laureate in 1813.

Female Fashions for 1799 *Mary Robinson (1757–1800)*

The Poem Given Mary Robinson's role as a fashion guru, her acerbic attack on the fashions of 1799 might seem surprising. Through the poem, she reveals her disappointment that women are valued more for their appearance than their 'mind' and makes a plea that women ignore the 'CAPRICE' of fashion and present themselves as 'NATURE' intended.

The opening of the poem is deceptive. It appears to applaud the taper-thin silhouette the then current fashion promoted. The second line dismisses any suggestion that the poet is conforming to expectations, however: hats resemble a 'half-pint bason', and Robinson goes on to lambast the clothing and accessories that make a woman appear variously like a '*country clown*' and 'savage SATYR'. The contrast between the various comparisons and the use of capital letters emphasizes how ridiculous Robinson finds the attire.

She puts particular weight on the colour red ('clocks of scarlet', 'POPPIES flaming red', 'deep vermilion red'), perhaps to suggest the moral ambiguity of women who dress themselves for show, and pleads that they avoid spoiling their fair skin with '*rouge*'. The implication is that, if women spent the effort devoted to their clothing on improving their intellect, they would realize how ridiculous they were being made to appear.

The Poet Mary Robinson was a gifted musician, champion of the rights of women, novelist, poet and actress. She was born in Bristol to a wealthy family and received a good education, but her marriage to the thoroughly unreliable Thomas Robinson unravelled when her husband was thrown into debtors' prison while Mary was placed under house arrest.

On her husband's release, Mary went to London and became a Shakespearean actress. Her performance as Perdita in *The Winter's Tale* in 1799 attracted the attention of the Prince of Wales and she became his mistress and a fashion icon in London.

After the Prince had abandoned her, Mary took several other lovers. In 1783, however, she suffered an illness that left her semi-paralysed and, from then on, she devoted her time to writing. She published two plays and eight novels, and her poetry was so well received that she became known as 'the English Sappho'.

Lord Randal *Anonymous*

The Poem Ballads come from the oral tradition, so the rules governing the form of the ballad are not rigid. However, most ballads do conform to a number of conventions. Consider the extent to which 'Lord Randal' obeys certain traditional conventions, such as dramatic, even sensational, subject matter; repetition; a question and answer format; metaphorical phrases such as 'mak my bed soon', which suggests preparation for death; and a simple, emphatic rhythm.

The story features in literature from many countries, and multiple versions exist. Notice how the ballad gradually reveals what has happened to Lord Randal, using only details that drive the plot forward. We learn where he has been, who he met, what he ate and how the remnants of the food were eaten by his bloodhounds, which then died. By the time his mother expresses her fears in the sixth verse, the listeners are already well prepared for the news of Randal's impending death through poisoning.

The Poet Anonymous is a well-known and prolific poet. Many of the traditional folk ballads we know today may have begun as songs sung by wandering minstrels, for which authorship was unimportant. The songs needed to be easily remembered, so a simple structure and repetition were needed. Ballads often captured dramatic local tales or legends and would be embellished and refined over the years. A large number of ballads were collected and formally recorded in print in the seventeenth and eighteenth centuries and attributed to the versatile 'Anonymous'.

In the nineteenth century, the ballad form was adopted by poets who were definitely not anonymous. Robert Burns, Christina Rossetti and Tennyson, for example, all explored old legends and tragic romances in a number of poems.

In the 1960s, the folk singer Bob Dylan modelled his song 'A Hard Rain's a-Gonna Fall' on the ballad 'Lord Randal', in the great tradition of wandering troubadours.

The Wife of Usher's Well *Anonymous*

The Poem The ballad is a popular, poetic form, combining a lilting rhythm with a driving narrative pulse. Usually switching between four-beat lines (tetrameters) and those with three beats (trimeters), ballads often revel in thwarted love, mystery, disaster and murder. This ballad is an engaging example of the form.

Telling the poignant tale of how a woman's sons died at sea, only to be brought back home, temporarily, as ghosts, by the magical power of her grief, the poem suggests an intensity of feeling within the conventions of the genre. Its language is unadorned by poetic flourishings, and the narrative does not halt to establish details of setting, character, mood or theme. Instead, the breezy, earthy feel is generated by the interplay of the familiar ballad rhythm with the use of phonetic spelling and dialect words, so that we truly hear the poem and connect with its story, which is revealed through incremental repetition. The ballad's voice tells this story of one particular woman who is also many women.

The dialect word 'carlin' means 'an old woman', while the hats of 'birk', or birch, her sons wear is a telling reference to the trees which, in legend, surround the gates of Paradise.

The Solitary Reaper *William Wordsworth (1770–1850)*

The Poem Wordsworth offers a definition of poetry as 'the spontaneous overflow of powerful feelings', and this ballad seems to support this view. We are immediately ordered to contemplate the young Scottish girl who is cutting and binding grain on her own. It is worth considering how Wordsworth emphasizes her solitariness in the first verse and how he describes her melancholy but beautiful singing.

The poem is clearly exploring the impact the girl and her song have upon the poet. How would you describe the way in which Wordsworth communicates his response? What kinds of questions does he ask about the nature of her song, which he can hear, but not so well as to be able to make out the words? Is she perhaps singing in a dialect that the poet would not understand?

Wordsworth writes in iambic tetrameters here, and it is not difficult to notice alliteration, hyperbole and rhetorical questions, but what do these features contribute to the ballad?

Wordsworth believed in the power and beauty of nature, and this figure in the landscape reinforces that belief through her haunting and melodious singing.

The Poet William Wordsworth's early poems transformed the way in which poets express themselves. He published the influential *Lyrical Ballads*, with Samuel Taylor Coleridge in 1798, rejecting the contrived, self-consciously poetic language that was fashionable at the time. He believed that poetry could use the real language of ordinary people in a state of 'vivid sensation'. In celebrating nature and human emotions, he was an early leader of the English Romantic movement.

Wordsworth had been caught up in the French Revolution, had fathered an illegitimate daughter with a young Frenchwoman and returned to England with radical and democratic ideas (although his views became increasingly conservative in middle age).

His autobiographical poem *The Prelude* chronicles the spiritual growth and life of the poet, revealing the intense relationship Wordsworth had with nature as he was growing up in the Lake District. He continued to live there for the rest of his life, with his wife, Mary, and his devoted sister, Dorothy.

The Destruction of Sennacherib *George Gordon Byron (1788–1824)*

The Poem Byron's poem is based on a brief biblical story about the defeat of the Assyrians by God's Angel of Death.

At the start of the poem 'Sennacherib', 'The Assyrian' and his followers are preparing to launch an attack upon the Israelites. What kind of imagery does Byron use to describe the attackers and the attacked?

The destruction of the Assyrians is swift and devastating, and is captured in the second verse, with its two balanced couplets, where the green leaves of summer become withered in autumnal desolation. Notice how much of the imagery throughout the poem refers to nature and natural processes. Consider what details of the massacred Assyrian army Byron chooses to dwell upon.

The poem has a distinctive rhythm, which gives a sense of galloping horses. The technical term for this is 'anapaestic tetrameter', which means that Byron has used four feet per line with two unstressed syllables, followed by a stressed syllable in each foot. Interestingly, it is a rhythm that is often used for light or comic verse.

The Poet George Gordon Byron was famously described by Lady Caroline Lamb as 'mad, bad and dangerous to know'. Although he became the 6th Baron Byron of Rochdale in 1798 and attended several sessions in the House of Lords in 1809, he was much more interested in travelling, poetry and love affairs. He travelled extensively through Greece and Turkey, and captured some of his experiences abroad in *Childe Harold's Pilgrimage*. The first two parts, or cantos, were hugely popular and made Byron famous in his own lifetime. He is regarded as one of the five or six leading figures in the English Romantic movement.

Byron continued to travel throughout his life, spending a number of years in Italy, where he wrote much of his poetic masterpiece *Don Juan*. In 1823, he left Italy for Greece, where he planned to fight for Greek independence from the Turks, but he died of a fever in 1824, aged thirty-six.

Kubla Khan *Samuel Taylor Coleridge (1772–1834)*

The Poem According to Coleridge, he composed most of this poem within a dream or vision after having taken 'medicine' for a slight indisposition. We know that Coleridge was addicted to laudanum (a form of opium), and so 'Kubla Khan' tends to be seen as a drug-induced, visionary fragment of a poem. Coleridge said he woke up with two or three hundred lines of poetry fully formed in his head but, after writing down some of them, he was interrupted and could not recapture his intense creative vision.

Kublai Khan, a Mongolian leader in the thirteenth century, conquered China and built a lavish palace known as Xanadu. The first thirty-six lines of the poem focus on Kublai Khan and his creativity, and we could see the whole poem as dealing with the power of artistic creation. Might the river bursting into life and then disappearing be a symbol of the way inspiration might strike a poet?

At line thirty-seven, the poet focuses on a 'damsel with a dulcimer' and, later in the same verse, on his desire to revive her 'symphony and song' so he can emulate Kublai Khan. The Romantic view of the artist as an inspired but tormented genius is vividly described in the last few lines.

The Poet Samuel Taylor Coleridge and his friend William Wordsworth were leading figures in the English Romantic movement. Together, they produced the radical experiments in style and content found in the *Lyrical Ballads* of 1798. Coleridge contributed his most famous poem to the collection – the supernatural 'Rime of the Ancient Mariner'.

Coleridge suffered from ill health for most of his life and became addicted to opium, which perhaps accounts for his relatively small poetic output. However, his contribution to cultural life in the early nineteenth century was still highly significant because of his early radical thinking about democratic living; his literary criticism; his writing on philosophical, political and religious topics; his lectures; and his translations from the German. He was also a charismatic talker, and many younger writers would visit him in his home in Highgate to hear his words of wisdom. In spite of his frequent bouts of sickness, he lived to the age of sixty-two.

The Burial of Sir John Moore after Corunna

Charles Wolfe (1791–1823)

The Poem Wolfe's poem celebrates the valour of the British Lieutenant-General Sir John Moore, who led the retreat to and defence of the port of Corunna while under attack from French troops in 1809. He was killed by cannon shot as he and his men fought a rearguard action that allowed a significant number of his army to embark, in spite of heavy casualties.

There is no time to prepare a burial fit for the soldier the poet describes as a 'hero' in line four, but the insistent rhythm of the lines supplies a drumbeat that was missing from the battlefield.

Wolfe describes the act of burial in the rough ground in terms of sleeping and beds. How do we respond to presenting war and death in this way?

The second line of the last verse draws attention to both the fame and the fatal wounds experienced in the soldier's final battle but the concluding line significantly ends with the idea not only of a lonely final resting place in a foreign field but also a celebration of profound and enduring 'glory'.

The Poet Charles Wolfe was an Irish priest and poet who is best remembered for this extremely popular elegy, which has appeared in many anthologies of poetry throughout the nineteenth and twentieth centuries.

Wolfe was educated at Trinity College, Dublin, and, at one point, it seemed that the brilliantly academic student would study for a fellowship. However, he declined to take his studies further and was ordained as a Church of Ireland priest in 1817. Contemporary records suggest that he was exemplary in this role, full of 'zeal' and 'unaffected benevolence'.

His career was cut short by death through consumption when he was only thirty-one years old. His poetry had been published in periodicals and, in 1825, shortly after his death, a well-received collection of his work appeared, which included this touching, patriotic poem about Sir John Moore. Byron was an admirer of the elegy.

Proud Maisie *Walter Scott (1771–1832)*

The Poem This short poem is set in an almost magical landscape: a lonely woodland, with a 'Sweet Robin' prophesying death. Our heroine, Maisie, is described only as 'Proud', perhaps suggesting youthfulness, or beauty. All this is to come to nothing, though, as the bird warns of a solemn future. There is a contrast between what we might expect from this 'Sweet', 'bonny' creature that is 'Singing so rarely' and the harsh news that he delivers.

Maisie seems to ignore the bird's first hint that she will be carried to the church by 'six braw gentlemen'. Does she assume that these men are suitors rather than coffin bearers? Is this because of her pride? She asks again who she will marry. The robin's response this time is unequivocal: he explains that the only man to make Maisie's bed will be the sexton at her grave. The word 'grave' is repeated in emphasis.

The rhythm of the poem is reminiscent of a bell tolling, perhaps heralding the funeral knell which the robin foretells. Notice the rhyme pattern in the poem and compare it to that of well-known nursery rhymes. What does this poem suggest about the themes of love and death?

The Poet Born in Edinburgh, and trained as a lawyer, Walter Scott became an internationally popular poet, playwright and novelist whose influences include classical myths and legends, the German Romantics and the oral traditions of the Scottish Borders. His first published works were translations, and his most famous writing includes the poems 'The Lady of the Lake' and 'The Lay of the Last Minstrel'.

His poetry is often narrative in style and tends to follow the rhythms and rhymes of the traditional ballad form. Although his poems are intended to be read rather than sung, there is an inherent musicality to the language.

In his forties, Scott concentrated on writing novels, including *Ivanhoe*, *Waverley* and *Rob Roy*, and he is now regarded by many as the father of the modern novel. His influence can be seen in writing by authors such as Elizabeth Gaskell and the Brontë sisters.

Ozymandias *Percy Bysshe Shelley (1792–1822)*

The Poem Ozymandias was the name given to a hugely powerful thirteenth-century BC Egyptian king. It appears that the once magnificent tomb of the pharaoh now lies broken in the desert sands. Only two trunkless legs remain, and a 'shattered visage' half hidden in the sand. How does Shelley reflect in lines four to eight upon the work of the sculptor who created the statue? What aspects of Ozymandias's character has the sculptor captured so perceptively?

The final five lines draw attention to the inscription on the pedestal, which proclaims Ozymandias's power and the futility of trying to emulate his achievements. However, the scene of ruin and decay suggests that even the mighty Ozymandias cannot contend with human mortality and the impermanence of anything other than the natural world. He is reduced to a 'wreck', albeit a 'colossal' one. The final line encourages the reader's eye to turn away from the tomb to contemplate the vast expanse of empty sand stretching away into the distance.

What is the effect of the distancing of the narrative as Shelley imagines a traveller's encounter with the statue and reports his words?

The Poet Percy Bysshe Shelley's revolutionary ideas, independent mind and intellectual curiosity were evident from an early age. His career at Oxford was cut short by his refusal to repudiate the contents of a pamphlet he had written, 'The Necessity of Atheism', and he was estranged from his prosperous family.

He married and had a child with Harriet Westbrook, but abandoned her after falling in love with Mary Wollstonecraft Godwin, the daughter of the philosopher William Godwin, who influenced Shelley's thinking. He eloped with Mary and, during their travels in Europe, formed a close friendship with Byron. Shelley was part of a highly creative literary circle within the English Romantic movement, which included his later wife, Mary, who wrote *Frankenstein*.

It is Shelley's shorter poems that are chiefly read today, including 'Ode to the West Wind', 'To a Skylark' and 'Ozymandias'. He knew John Keats and wrote a passionate elegy on his death, *Adonaïs*.

Ode to a Nightingale *John Keats (1795–1821)*

The Poem One of the most famous poems of the English Romantic movement, 'Ode to a Nightingale' explores the nature of creativity and the transience of life through Keats's response to the song of a nightingale.

In a state of 'drowsy numbness', Keats listens to the bird's song of 'summer' and, in the second and third stanzas, contemplates escaping the pain of life through alcohol. What picture of ageing and the brevity of beauty does he present in the third stanza?

In the following stanzas, Keats rejects alcohol and suggests that he will escape through poetic expression to be with the nightingale; at one point, he contemplates the attraction of slipping into death while listening to the beauty of the bird's song. Keats reflects that the nightingale's song has been heard down the ages by 'emperor and clown', but in the last stanza jolts himself back to present reality with the use of the word 'Forlorn!'

This formal, elaborately patterned ode is written in ten-line stanzas. Consider the effect of the use of iambic pentameter and the consistent rhyme scheme of ABABCDECDE. Note how the eighth line in each stanza is shorter, using three stressed syllables and not five.

The Poet In spite of his early death in 1821 at the age of just twenty-five, John Keats is regarded as one of the major figures of the English Romantic movement. His reputation is based on fifty-four published poems, in a range of poetic forms. In 1819, he produced five great odes, including 'Ode to Autumn'. His development as a poet was remarkably rapid, as he mastered different poetic styles and produced work that was rich in imagery and allusions and communicated a sense of wonder at the human capacity to love and suffer.

Although he trained as an apothecary/surgeon, Keats devoted the last years of his life to poetry, in spite of financial difficulties and the increasing awareness that the tuberculosis he suffered from would kill him.

Keats's passionate, sometimes desperate love for Fanny Brawne inspired many poems and letters. His literary ambitions and ill health, however, meant that they never married.

Casabianca *Felicia Hemans (1793–1835)*

The Poem The opening line of this poem is probably one of the best known lines in English literature, even though many people might not know anything about the rest of the poem, let alone who wrote it. 'Casabianca' was memorized and recited by vast numbers of English-speaking children in the nineteenth and twentieth centuries.

Casabianca was a thirteen-year-old Corsican boy sailor who died at the Battle of the Nile, refusing to leave his ship when it had caught fire. The poem's appeal as a recitation piece in the nineteenth century is fairly obvious. In addition to its easy-to-remember, galloping rhythm, it is a morally uplifting tale of dutiful heroism. But 'Casabianca' contains surprises, and not least in terms of its rhythm. Where are the stresses in that famous first line?

The opening offers an almost nightmarish picture of the young sailor, surrounded by dead bodies illuminated by the encroaching flames. The boy will not leave his post until his father, the admiral of the ship, gives him permission, but the man is already dead.

Consider the dramatic tension in the description of the boy's plight and the graphic account of the boy literally blown to pieces by the exploding ship.

The Poet Felicia Hemans's 'Casabianca' took on such a vibrant life of its own after her death that, somehow, its author became almost irrelevant. In fact, Hemans was an accomplished and prolific poet who wrote over twenty volumes of verse before her death at the age of forty-two.

After she had given birth to five children, Hemans's husband deserted her to live in Italy, and her writing served to help support her large family. She became a literary celebrity, garnering praise from the likes of Wordsworth and George Eliot, but her work was also criticized for its simplicity and sentimentality.

Felicia Hemans may now be a relatively neglected poet, but her popularity and influence in the middle- and upper-class homes of nineteenth-century England should not be underestimated. In more recent times, her sequence of poems recording the experiences of women in the nineteenth century, *Records of Women*, has been much admired.

The War Song of Dinas Vawr *Thomas Love Peacock (1785–1866)*

The Poem This rollicking song can be found within Thomas Love Peacock's entertaining comic novel *The Misfortunes of Elphin* and describes the delight in sheep stealing, blood-spilling, castle-storming and rampaging taken by Welshmen. The poet was not Welsh but had a passionate interest in Welsh myths and legends. The twinkle in the eye of the poem can immediately be seen in the way the Welshmen convey the appropriateness of their actions with a rhyme of 'sweeter' with 'meeter'.

Notice how the ballad form, with its thumping, regular rhythm and rhyme, contributes to the sense of a triumphant song or chant being bellowed out by the carousing rustlers, who brazenly enjoy the 'wine and beasts' they have plundered.

The somewhat comical description of murder and mayhem is sustained throughout the whole poem as children are orphaned, women widowed and a king decapitated. The lexis is relentlessly violent. The opposition is 'killed', 'quelled' and 'conquered'.

The 'War Song' can be enjoyed on a number of levels, including as a satire of some of the 'historical' poems inspired by the success of the novelist Walter Scott.

The Poet Thomas Love Peacock is probably best known today for his novel *Nightmare Abbey*, which cheerfully satirizes the interest of contemporary literature in morbid subjects and Gothic settings. Some of the targets of his broadly affectionate satire were significant literary figures in the early nineteenth century.

Largely self-taught, but intellectually distinguished, he became a successful and important employee of the East India Company, working in London for thirty years. After his retirement, he enjoyed a quiet life with his books and his garden near the Thames, but he died in 1866 from injuries sustained while trying to save his library from a fire.

Most of his seven novels were written between 1815 and 1830; they are sometimes called 'conversation novels'. They are not intricately plotted and the characters are not extensively developed, yet they present the discussions and arguments of a diverse set of people in an appealing and often very funny way.

'I found a ball of grass among the hay' *John Clare (1793–1864)*

The Poem This sonnet, sometimes known as 'The Mouse's Nest', was written in the 1830s by a poet who was distinctly unusual. Unlike many of the highly educated, financially secure poets of the time, John Clare was a farm labourer. He is sometimes described as the 'peasant poet'.

What do you notice about the way Clare describes what he stumbles across and the language he uses? This is a sonnet, but how does the structure differ from that of a conventional sonnet?

John Keats said that Clare's poetry had too much description in it and not enough 'sentiment'. Clare responded by suggesting that city-dwelling poets such as Keats had an unrealistic or fanciful vision of nature. Is there anything about this sonnet that makes you feel that the poet is immersed in the countryside he is describing? Notice how Clare does not attempt to draw a moral at the end of the poem. There is no real sense of the incident having an impact upon the poet. It is as if he is observing and recording, then moving on to the next scene.

The Poet John Clare was a farm labourer who was largely self-educated. He was deeply affected by the Enclosure Act of 1801, when common land was fenced off, halting farming by the general populace, and wrote movingly about the uprooting of trees and hedges and the loss of common land, which changed a centuries-old way of life.

In 1820, Clare's first collection of poems was published. *Poems Descriptive of Rural Life and Scenery* proved extremely popular, and Clare was briefly adopted by fashionable London society. However, subsequent volumes were not successful, as fashions changed and the novelty of reading the work of a 'peasant poet' wore off. Clare became increasingly delusional, distressed by the failure of his literary ambitions and the devastation caused by enclosure.

He spent the last twenty-three years of his life in the Northampton county asylum, where he produced some remarkable, tormented visionary poems, such as 'I Am'.

Porphyria's Lover *Robert Browning (1812–89)*

The Poem Suddenly, in line forty-one, Porphyria is strangled. It is hard not to be shocked by this moment and the simple, matter-of-fact description of the act given by Porphyria's lover in this dramatic monologue. Are we in any way prepared for this abrupt outbreak of violence?

The poem opens with an apparently conventional romantic scene. It is stormy and cold outside, but the beautiful Porphyria appears to bring warmth and comfort to the cottage. The narrator seems to express himself with a steady reasonableness, but the highly patterned rhythm and rhyme scheme hints at an excessive level of control. Are there moments before the murder when you sense that all is not right; that there is an element of menace within the poem?

The character of Porphyria's lover has been interpreted in many ways. Are we in the presence of a deranged psychopath who does not view his act as evil, or is this some bizarre artistic gesture that seeks to preserve Porphyria in a state 'Perfectly pure and good'?

The Poet The romance between Robert Browning and his poet wife, Elizabeth Barrett, inspired a 1930s play and several film and television productions. Behind the drama of their courtship and marriage lies a substantial body of poetry.

Browning was exceptionally well read and reputedly wrote poems as a child. His early work was not successful, but he developed the blank verse dramatic monologue with remarkable skill and subtlety, presenting characters that seem inadvertently to reveal things about themselves.

Browning spent many years with his wife in Italy, living in Florence and absorbing its culture. When Elizabeth died in 1861, he returned to England, and his popularity increased with the publication of the dramatic monologues and an extremely long poem of 21,000 lines, *The Ring and the Book*. It was regarded as a masterpiece in Victorian England but, for most modern readers, it is the dramatic monologues that remain most vibrant, polished and appealing.

Ulysses *Alfred Tennyson (1809–92)*

The Poem This dramatic monologue is spoken by the heroic Ulysses, who has returned to his kingdom after fighting in the Trojan War. How does he describe his domestic life and his relationships with his wife and his people? How does this contrast with what he tells us of his previous adventures and travels in lines seven to twenty-one?

Ulysses seems prepared to leave the management of his kingdom to his son Telemachus while he embarks on a search for new experiences. How does he seem to feel about his son and the way he will rule?

In the final section from line fifty-six, he calls upon the sailors who have fought with him before to join him in one last adventure. It may be dangerous, and he recognizes that they do not have the strength of 'old days', but he urges them to join him with 'heroic hearts'. What is the impact and meaning of the final, forceful line: 'To strive, to seek, to find, and not to yield'?

Consider the use of iambic pentameter and enjambment in the poem and the dramatic-monologue form Tennyson uses. Does the verse seem to move from a kind of soliloquy to a powerful public speech?

The Poet Alfred Tennyson was appointed Poet Laureate after the death of Wordsworth in 1850. By this time he had produced popular early work such as 'Mariana', 'The Lady of Shalott' and 'Locksley Hall' and begun working on 'In Memoriam', an elegy for his friend Arthur Hallam, who died in 1833; this great poem was eventually published in the same year that he became Laureate.

Tennyson is best known for his haunting narratives and emotionally charged lyrics, but also celebrated for his stirring poem of the Crimean War, 'The Charge of the Light Brigade'. He was the pre-eminent poet of the Victorian Age, and was created a baron in 1884.

Remembrance *Emily Brontë (1818–48)*

The Poem Emily Brontë and her sisters created an imaginary world called Gondal and peopled it with princes and princesses. In this world, the Prince Julius is murdered and his wife, the Princess Rosina, laments her loss fifteen years later in the poem 'Remembrance'. Although Gondal and its characters are the creations of the Brontë sisters' imaginations, it may be that Emily Brontë's poem is influenced by personal loss and grief. Does the issue of 'sincerity' affect our response to the poem, or is it irrelevant?

Look at the way certain techniques are used in the first verse to create an atmosphere of solemnity and reflection. Brontë uses repetition very deliberately to emphasize death and love. The rhythm of the poem is exceptionally slow, with frequent end-stopped lines and long vowel sounds. She also uses the caesura several times in these first four lines to slow the pace of the elegy. Consider the extent to which Brontë continues to use these techniques in the rest of the poem.

What conclusions does she seem to draw about death and remembrance by the end of the poem?

The Poet Although Emily Brontë was an accomplished poet, she is best known for her highly original and imaginative novel *Wuthering Heights*.

Emily and her sisters, Charlotte and Anne, initially published their writing under pseudonyms that would disguise their gender, calling themselves Ellis, Currer and Acton Bell.

Emily Brontë was brought up in Haworth on the Yorkshire Moors, where her father was the curate, and her early life was marked by a series of tragic losses. Her mother died when she was three years old, and two sisters died young. Emily and her surviving sisters, along with her only brother, Branwell, created Gondal and wrote extensively about events and relationships within that world.

There is no evidence of romance in Emily's life, and yet she produced, in *Wuthering Heights*, a novel that is full of fierce and striking emotions and in which the wildness and freedom offered by the landscape constantly impress the reader.

Sonnets from the Portuguese XXIV

Elizabeth Barrett Browning (1806–61)

The Poem This is one of forty-four love sonnets written by Elizabeth Barrett Browning. They chronicle the development of her relationship with her husband, the poet Robert Browning. They met at a time when Elizabeth Barrett was physically unwell, spiritually troubled and dominated by a tyrannical father who did not want any of his children to marry.

The sense of a romance evolving in very difficult circumstances is immediately conveyed in the first line. How does Barrett Browning use the extended metaphor of the 'clasping knife' in the poem? Look at the contrast between the warmth and security of the poet's love for Browning and the dangers posed by the world beyond their relationship.

Barrett Browning uses the Petrarchan sonnet form. How do you think the structure of the sonnet supports the meaning? Look for the patterns in the poem. Two groups of four lines are followed by two groups of three lines. Traditionally, in a Petrarchan sonnet the ninth line is significant, as it is a change from one rhyme group to another, while also indicating a change in subject matter. Does this happen here?

The Poet One of twelve children, Elizabeth Barrett Browning suffered with a lung complaint and a spinal injury. She read widely from an early age and completed her first epic poem by the time she was twelve.

After the death of one of her brothers, who was drowned in a sailing accident, Barrett Browning became a virtual recluse in her father's house for a few years, but she continued to write. Her collection of poems published in 1844 was much admired by the poet Robert Browning, and they began to correspond. After 574 letters and 20 months, the couple eloped to Italy, where Elizabeth's health improved and they had a son. Her tyrannical father was vehemently opposed to their marriage.

Barrett Browning's *Sonnets from the Portuguese* was an exploration of her love for her husband. The title is deliberately misleading, suggesting that the poems were translations in order to conceal the intensely personal nature of the poems.

'There is no God' *Arthur Hugh Clough (1819–61)*

The Poem Although in some ways light-hearted and reminiscent in rhythm of a nursery rhyme, Clough's poem raises thought-provoking questions to do with the nature of faith. Notice the way he deftly presents the reactions of different people to the idea of God's existence in the first four stanzas. The 'wicked', a 'youngster', the 'tradesman' and a 'rich man' are all allowed to make their succinct and self-absorbed observations.

In the second half of the poem, the focus is on other people, such as the 'parson', 'married people' and indeed 'almost every one', who, when confronted by age, disease and sorrow, are inclined to think there might just be a God after all, or, as Clough puts it, 'something very like Him'.

The poem offers insights into human nature and the place and importance of faith in people's lives in a style that is light and lively. Is there anything about the poem which makes it seem more like a twentieth- than a nineteenth-century piece of work?

The Poet Arthur Clough suffered from periods of religious doubt throughout his life. His inability to subscribe to the Thirty-nine Articles, which detailed the beliefs of the Church of England, meant that he felt compelled to leave his position as a Fellow at Oriel College, Oxford. He moved to London to become Head of University Hall and then lectured in America before working for the Department of Education back in London. He was interested in radical politics and a tireless supporter of his wife's cousin Florence Nightingale. He is probably best remembered for his uplifting short poem 'Say not the struggle nought availeth'.

Clough's posthumously published collection *Poems* of 1862 was a great success, running to fifteen editions over the following forty years, even though some of his contemporaries may have seen him as an exceptionally learned scholar but a poet of unfulfilled promise. He contracted malaria on a visit to Italy and died at the age of forty-two.

My Orcha'd in Linden Lea *William Barnes (1801–86)*

The Poem This celebration of pastoral beauty and depiction of man in harmony with nature written in a Dorset dialect constantly returns to the image of the apple tree in Linden Lea. It provides not simply food but a kind of spiritual nourishment. The apple tree is always there 'vor me', providing comfort and security and making the speaker appreciate the beauty of his home. Significantly, the apple tree is said to lean towards the speaker, a movement that is captured in mellifluous, alliterative phrases. The poem also conveys the sense of freedom inspired by being at one with nature. The city might offer the chance of making more money, but its attractions and challenges are no competition for the peace and tranquillity found next to the apple tree in Linden Lea, where no peevish employer need be feared.

The use of alliteration and the harmonious balance of individual lines along with a skilfully controlled rhyme scheme give a sense of ease and serenity to the poem, even though there is clearly technical virtuosity on display here.

How does the poet's use of dialect shape your response to the poem?

The Poet William Barnes was a Dorset-dialect poet. An extremely learned man with knowledge of many languages, he worked for some time as a school teacher, running his own schools with his wife, before being ordained into the Church of England.

He is admired for the freshness and vigour of his depictions of the countryside of Dorset, and for his insights into the lives and customs of the people of the county. His use of dialect reflects his fascination with language and his belief in honouring and preserving local traditions.

He published *Poems of Rural Life in the Dorset Dialect* in 1844 and *Hwomely Rhymes* in 1859, by which time he was highly respected by major poets of the period, including Hardy and Tennyson.

'An upper chamber in a darkened house'

Frederick Tuckerman (1821–73)

The Poem The poem employs a conventional fourteen-line structure, but notice its almost anarchic rhyme scheme and the way in which the sonnet form can barely contain the image-rich emotional volatility of the work. This is an unsettling, haunting poem. The world appears disjointed and dislocated. There is an almost filmic quality to the opening, when we immediately find ourselves in a 'darkened house' in an 'upper chamber' and learn about a boy who experienced 'Terror and anguish'. Inevitably, the reference to an upper chamber prompts thoughts of the Passion of Christ and the place where Jesus spent his last evening before his death.

It is autumn, and yet the grass is green. The narrator is transfixed. Is he looking at himself in the third person past? Is this some reaction to a terrible trauma, or some disturbing hallucination? Even the 'swooning of the heart', often a sign of happy romantic love, is seen in this context as evidence of disorientation.

The ending of the sonnet offers no explanation as to what is happening. The soft, delicate petals of the mountain ash, looking like tiny snowflakes, are said to be 'shattered' on the roof.

The Poet Frederick Tuckerman's wife died in childbirth, and a powerful sense of grief and loss permeates many of his poems. He was a poet of the American outdoors, spending much time wandering through the woods and fields of New England, and becoming an expert on flora and fauna. Although he had a law degree from Harvard Law School, he abandoned the profession after a year and devoted himself to his other interests and, in particular, to literature and science.

On a trip to Europe, he developed a close friendship with the poet Alfred Tennyson, but whereas Tennyson was phenomenally successful, Tuckerman struggled to find any kind of readership for his sonnets, his lyrics and his longer poem 'The Cricket'. His one collection, *Poems*, of 1860, was a commercial and critical failure, and it was only after his death that the complexity and originality of his work was appreciated.

Envy *Adelaide Anne Procter (1825–64)*

The Poem This poem could have been a conventional Victorian morality poem about the dangers of being envious. However, Adelaide Anne Procter approaches the theme from a dramatic and unusual perspective. Envy here is personified and, in this concise, taut lyric, the reader witnesses the speaker battling not just against envy but *with* Envy, presented as a male figure that wins every race and is blessed with good fortune. He 'conquered the place' and 'Men loved him'. When he sinned he was pitied, but when she did she was made to feel 'only shame'. She exists in the shadows while he basks in the sun.

What examples of competition does Procter use to reflect both the character of Envy and her own personality and attitudes? Notice how the shorter lines two, four and six in each verse seem to stress unambiguously with their emphatic rhymes the inevitability of Envy's victory.

In the final verse, a startling twist is introduced with Envy apparently defeated by Death, and yet, even at this moment, Envy is still victorious and 'blest'. The speaker is jealous of Envy's escape from life while she remains 'cursed'.

The Poet Adelaide Anne Procter's father was a poet, and her mother actively encouraged her daughter's interest in poetry. She submitted her early work to Charles Dickens's publication *Household Words* under the pseudonym Miss Berwick. When Dickens became aware that Miss Berwick was really Miss Procter, he continued to publish her work in his popular periodicals.

In 1858, Procter published a two-volume collection of poetry, *Legends and Lyrics*. Its appealingly direct language and edifying themes ensured it ran to multiple editions.

A convert to Catholicism, she committed herself to progressive, philanthropic work, arguing for women's equality in property rights, employment and education. She supported Catholic widows and orphans through the Providence Row Night Refuge and was active in the Society to Promote the Employment of Women. In the last ten years of her life, before her early death at thirty-nine, poetry, campaigning for the rights of women and social reform were all inextricably linked.

'You are old, Father William' *Lewis Carroll (1832–98)*

The Poem 'You are old, Father William' is a parody of a pious poem by Robert Southey called 'The Old Man's Comforts', in which Father William explains how his contentment in old age is based on having led a virtuous and restrained life in his youth, when he always 'remembered my God'. Lewis Carroll includes his strongly rhythmical 'Father William' poem in his highly original fantasy novel *Alice's Adventures in Wonderland*, written in the 1860s. He takes Southey's poem and completely subverts it, in a mischievous and amusing manner.

The young man demands answers to his four questions, while relentlessly emphasizing Father William's age. Notice how much of the humour is based on the perception of incongruity. Not many old men would stand on their heads 'incessantly' or enter houses with an athletic 'back-somersault'.

Whereas in the Southey poem, the old man stresses that he led a quiet and dignified life in his youth, Lewis Carroll's Father William seems to be advocating a life full of pleasure, arguing, physical activity and magical ointment. His vigour is undiminished at the end, when he threatens to kick the inquisitive young man downstairs.

The Poet Lewis Carroll was the pseudonym used by Charles Dodgson, who lectured in maths at Oxford University. He is best known for his wonderfully surreal novels *Alice's Adventures in Wonderland* and *Through the Looking-Glass*, but he also wrote popular poems, for example, 'Jabberwocky' and *The Hunting of the Snark*, short stories and books on logic. In addition, he created games and puzzles to help explain the principles of logic and was a highly accomplished photographer.

Lewis Carroll developed parts of *Alice's Adventures in Wonderland* through telling stories to the children of Henry Liddell, a friend and colleague. The Liddell family would become important people in Carroll's life. One of the girls, Alice Liddell, encouraged Carroll to write the story down and, eventually, in 1865, he produced a work that became an enormously popular children's book. Its imaginative playfulness, explorations of logic and illogicality and satirical elements have ensured it is also enjoyed by adults.

Snake *Emily Dickinson (1830–86)*

The Poem Emily Dickinson observes nature in a highly original and distinctive manner. Consider how she reveals the snake to us in the first few verses of description in a way that communicates her fascination with the 'narrow Fellow in the Grass'. Dickinson lived in rural New England and, like the English Romantic poets, she explored her relationship with nature but, often, as in 'Snake', with a mixture of formal and colloquial language and precise, vivid images.

After the first eight lines, where we are introduced to the snake, she recalls childhood experiences in the middle section of the poem. How does she use language here when recalling a previous encounter with a snake?

In the final eight lines, Dickinson reflects upon her encounters with living creatures in nature. Notice how 'Nature's People' has echoes of the use of 'Fellow' in the opening line. Although she talks about 'cordiality' in her relations with nature, she is disturbed by the presence of a snake. Consider the impact and meaning of the final line, where a number is turned into a powerful metaphor.

The Poet Emily Dickinson spent most of her life in Amherst, Massachusetts, where the Dickinsons were respected members of the local community. She spent some time as a young girl at the Amherst Academy and then as an energetic and fully involved member of a female seminary. She was independent-minded and, at a time when a Calvinist declaration of faith in Jesus Christ and readiness to be 'saved' was encouraged, remained true to her own religious principles and would not accept the doctrine of original sin.

However, Dickinson became increasingly reclusive in her late twenties, and there is much speculation as to why she retreated into her family home. Whatever the reason for her seclusion, she continued to produce hundreds of poignant, acutely observed poems. Only a few were published in her lifetime, and it was not until 1955 that the complete works of 1,775 poems became available.

Dover Beach *Matthew Arnold (1822–88)*

The Poem Arnold wrote 'Dover Beach' around 1850, at a time when faith in God and religion seemed threatened by developments in scientific understanding and evolutionary theory. Although it is a poem about Arnold's response to a spiritual crisis, it begins by capturing a moment in the physical world when Arnold is looking out towards France from a Dover beach. How does he convey a sense of tranquillity and intense melancholy in those first fourteen lines? Can a poem be both sad and beautiful? Think about the 'pathetic fallacy', when a poet projects human feelings such as sadness on to inanimate objects, for example, the sea. (Incidentally, notice how the first twenty-eight lines are arranged loosely as two sonnets, and then the final stanza begins a little like a sonnet but, after the first eight lines, it finishes with a powerful, climactic ninth line.)

The poem may deal with 'sadness', 'misery' and 'pain', but there is also hope and consolation as Arnold turns to his companion at the start of the final stanza.

The Poet Matthew Arnold was the son of Thomas Arnold, a famous headmaster at Rugby School, so it is perhaps no surprise that he worked for the nineteenth-century equivalent of Ofsted as an inspector of schools. However, he is much better remembered as a poet, critic and essayist.

Matthew Arnold's poetry is elegant, reflective and meditative, while his commentaries on nineteenth-century culture were extremely influential. His essays on *Culture and Anarchy* (1869) argued that culture did not belong simply to an educated elite. He advocated an openness to change, while being aware, in poems such as 'Dover Beach', of the doubts and uncertainties surrounding faith in turbulent times. The education of the individual was, for Arnold, vital in a journey towards intellectual sweetness and moral light.

His poems continue to be read for the power of their majestic sadness and for the skilful, heartfelt descriptions of nature and significant moments in his life.

Dirge for Two Veterans *Walt Whitman (1819–92)*

The Poem Walt Whitman acted as a volunteer worker in hospitals during the American Civil War and was deeply affected by the suffering he saw.

His 'Dirge for Two Veterans' opens in a tranquil, serene fashion, with a description of the last sunbeam of the sabbath. However, what it illuminates is disturbing, as the poet looks out at 'a new-made double grave' and a funeral procession for a father and son killed in battle. Notice how, at first, he writes very much as an observer but, gradually, as the poem progresses, he becomes more and more involved and emotionally attached to the scene and the sacrifice made by the men.

What is the significance of the frequent references to and descriptions of the moon and drums in the poem?

The emotional intensity of the poem increases as it moves towards resolution. Notice the use of the heartfelt 'O', which appears five times in the last eight lines. Ultimately, Whitman does not reflect upon suffering or waste but chooses to pay tribute to the men in his own way, by giving them what he can – his 'love'.

The Poet At various times, Walt Whitman was a teacher, a journalist, a government official and a clerk. He also spent a significant period in his life working in the hospitals of the American Civil War, and witnessed the acute suffering of casualties.

While employed as a low-level clerk in the Ministry for the Interior, Whitman was fired from his position when a superior disapproved of his first collection of poetry, *Leaves of Grass*, on moral grounds.

The intervention of a friend saw Whitman transferred to the Attorney General's office, and he continued to write and revise new editions of *Leaves of Grass*. His popularity increased with the publication of his tribute on the death of Abraham Lincoln, 'O Captain! My Captain!'

Whitman is regarded as one of America's most significant and popular poets. Stylistically innovative and compassionate in tone, he believed in the vital importance of the relationship between the poet and society.

Invictus *W. E. Henley (1849–1903)*

The Poem 'Invictus' is Latin for 'unconquerable'. Henley wrote this poem about stoicism, courage and refusing to accept defeat while enduring a severely testing time in hospital. He had contracted tuberculosis of the bone in his youth, and the lower part of one of his legs was amputated in his twenties. At one point, it was feared he might lose his other leg.

Written in 1875, but not published until thirteen years later, 'Invictus' was an immediately popular poem. Its uplifting and inspirational qualities saw it frequently appear in poetry anthologies, and it was often memorized and recited in schools up until the 1960s.

Notice how the first verse adopts a humanist position. Reference to a higher power in the midst of suffering is vague – 'whatever gods may be' – while the focus is on his 'unconquerable soul'. The famous line 'My head is bloody, but unbowed' suggests a noble bravery in the face of adversity, while the even more frequently quoted final two lines affirm the power of individuals to shape their own destiny, to accept responsibility and to choose how they will go forward in life.

Is the tone of the poem melodramatic or truly inspirational?

The Poet 'Invictus' has ensured that W. E. Henley is a significant Victorian literary figure, but the phenomenal popularity of this one poem has perhaps led to the neglect of his other work. In fact, Henley was an influential critic, journalist and poet, although a less successful dramatist.

He began work as a journalist, but his career was interrupted by a long stay in hospital. Tuberculosis of the bone had led to the amputation of one leg below the knee, and it was only through innovative treatment by Joseph Lister that his other leg was saved, he produced a series of poems recording his observations and feelings in a variety of poetic forms and using a range of techniques.

Henley was an exceptionally talented critic and journalist, editing a number of magazines throughout his life. He developed a close friendship with Robert Louis Stevenson, who allegedly modelled Long John Silver in *Treasure Island* on the poet.

A Forsaken Garden *Algernon Swinburne (1837–1909)*

The Poem In this poem Swinburne contemplates the transience of love and the inevitability of death through a detailed description of the abandoned garden by the sea. Notice how simply but precisely he locates the forsaken garden for the reader, using the archaic 'coign' to suggest the vantage point once occupied by what is now a 'ghost of a garden'.

How does Swinburne develop a picture of decay and neglect in the first two stanzas? In stanza three, he introduces human figures into a place the 'years have rifled'. How does he present the lovers and their eventual fate?

The rose features prominently in these verses. Consider the symbolic use Swinburne makes of the flower. Are we also encouraged to consider the garden in relation to the Garden of Eden? The biblical garden was also a place of love, but it led to corruption and death. Notice how Swinburne uses the sea as a symbol of permanence to contrast with the temporary beauty of the garden.

Notice, too, how the elaborate, skilfully constructed nature of the poem also contrasts with the disorder and chaos in the garden.

The Poet Algernon Swinburne came from an aristocratic background and drew on a wide range of influences and interests from an early age, including Elizabethan dramatists, Greek and Latin poets and French writers. He was an excitable, extrovert character who made friends with many of the Pre-Raphaelite Brotherhood at Oxford. He professed an addiction to all kinds of vice, although Oscar Wilde thought Swinburne guilty of considerable exaggeration.

Swinburne's early collections of poetry, such as *Poems and Ballads* (1866), were controversial, with their sexually charged sequences, but it was immediately clear that Swinburne was a brilliant technician in terms of rhythm and rhyme, and remarkably versatile. He is credited with inventing the 'roundel' verse form.

Swinburne's alcoholism affected his health, but he was helped to recovery in his forties. He lived another thirty years, becoming more socially respectable and continuing to write poems, verse dramas and a good deal of literary criticism.

Inversnaid *Gerard Manley Hopkins (1844–89)*

The Poem Hopkins's free-flowing but highly rhythmical poem looks in wonder at a stream in the Highlands of Scotland as it plunges over a waterfall into the 'pitchblack' pool. The four verses are packed with alliteration, assonance, repetition, personification, compound words, and dialect and archaic words that give the poem a muscular, passionate energy.

How do you respond to the reference to 'Despair' in verse two? Is Despair drowned in the agitated pool, or are the pool's black depths an image of despair? Consider the playful, experimental use of language and imagery in phrases such as 'féll-frówning' and 'flitches of fern'.

The final stanza conveys the sense of grief and mourning that would be felt if the world were deprived of the wondrous beauty and energy of 'wet and of wilderness'. Hopkins stresses the immense value of a wild and natural landscape, created in his eyes, of course, by God. In 'Inversnaid' we are drawn into an intense creative experience as he gazes in awe at the Divine in the rushing, roaring stream.

The Poet Gerard Manley Hopkins was a remarkably inventive and experimental Victorian poet. In his twenties, he converted to Roman Catholicism and trained as a Jesuit priest, abandoning thoughts of continuing to write. However, several years later, when a ship carrying Franciscan nuns was wrecked at the mouth of the Thames, he wrote 'The Wreck of the *Deutschland*'.

Very little of Hopkins's work was published in his lifetime, as the poet saw a conflict between his religious calling and the self-promotion that publication might suggest. He was a poet of great faith, but also of doubt, as can be seen in his sonnets known as the 'Sonnets of Desolation', or the 'Terrible Sonnets', where he struggles to come to terms with a sense of spiritual anguish.

Hopkins developed innovative techniques in poetry, including 'sprung rhythm', where stresses are counted rather than syllables in a line. His use of language is robust, energetic and, at times, defiantly experimental.

Lucifer in Starlight *George Meredith (1828–1909)*

The Poem In John Milton's *Paradise Lost* the defiant, rebellious angel Lucifer, or Satan, has been cast down into the fiery pits of hell. In Milton's poem the poet proclaims that it is better to reign in hell than serve in heaven, but at the start of Meredith's muscular sonnet, with its robust use of alliteration and assonance, Lucifer is restless and tired of 'his dark dominion'. Notice how 'uprose' in line one describes Lucifer emerging from the depths of hell but also reminds us of his catastrophic uprising against God. The line refers to the stars in the night sky, and stars feature again significantly in line eleven.

Although he has been defeated, Lucifer is still seen as an enormously powerful, menacing force. He is erratic, volatile and hugely formidable; his 'huge bulk' casts a shadow from Africa to the Arctic and complacent sinners are easy prey. But as he soars towards the stars he is reminded of his revolt against God. The stars are the 'brain of heaven'. Are they therefore representative of reason and order; of a moral order that can never be defeated? Notice how, confronted by this 'army of unalterable law', Lucifer can only despair; 'he looked, and sank'.

The Poet George Meredith was a Victorian poet, author and journalist. He published eighteen novels between 1856 and his death in 1909 and, although many had limited commercial and critical success, *The Egoist* (1879) and *Diana of the Crossways* (1885) were well received. At various times Meredith worked as a reader and adviser to publishers, as a war correspondent and as a contributor to and editor of literary journals. He was a skilful essayist and lecturer, and his 'Essay on Comedy' was regarded as a brilliant and insightful piece of work.

Meredith was an accomplished poet. Among his most widely read works is *Modern Love*, an uneven but fascinating account of the break-up of a marriage, clearly based on his own experience. His wife eloped with an artist, abandoning Meredith and their son. The work is written as a sonnet sequence, using the sixteen-line form known as the 'Meredithian sonnet'.

A Frog's Fate *Christina Rossetti (1830–94)*

The Poem Rossetti wrote for both adults and children, but there is often depth and complexity in the poems she wrote for children.

'A Frog's Fate' is, on one level, an amusing piece of light verse describing the adventures of a 'large-souled Frog' who is keen to explore life beyond his village-pond home. Rossetti creates a vivid picture of the frog spurning each 'byeway' in favour of the broad 'imperial highway', undeterred by the sounds of local pigs and dogs. How does Rossetti communicate the frog's sense of ambition and self-importance in the first ten lines?

The frog's excursion into the wider world is cut short by the wheels of a wagon. Consider the tone of the dying words Rossetti gives the frog. Its fate appears all the more unfortunate in that its death is completely unknown to the driver of the wagon, who goes on his way, whistling and singing.

The last six lines are worth exploring. Is Rossetti humorously drawing attention to the problems that arise when danger is overlooked? Should we be content with the familiarity and security of our everyday existence?

The Poet Christina Rossetti was a member of an artistic and extremely creative family. Her brother Dante Gabriel was a poet and painter and a leading figure in the Pre-Raphaelite Brotherhood, which sought to recapture the artistic spirit of the Middle Ages. The deeply religious Christina contributed poems to the Brotherhood's short-lived journal, *The Germ*, and modelled for some of Dante Gabriel's paintings.

She wrote for adults and children, producing poems that are often striking in their sincerity and simplicity and their ability to work on several levels. A good example is her narrative poem 'Goblin Market', written in 1862, which superficially appears to be a fairy-tale about loving sisters and wicked goblins and is full of vivid details, exciting narrative and unusual rhythms. Some readings of the poem, however, see it as being about lesbian eroticism or drug addiction and recovery.

Rossetti's sonnet 'Remember' and her carol 'In the Bleak Midwinter' are both well-loved works.

Philosophy *Amy Levy (1861–89)*

The Poem Written in the late nineteenth century, Amy Levy's poem is a witty, wry and ironic look at the relationship between two 'philosophers'.

The Phyllis and Corydon characters of verse two are lovers from Greek myth, but the poet explains that the context for her relationship is not pretty meadows and streams. In contrast, she has met her love among 'A Philistine and flippant throng'. In saying that she and her lover are not Phyllis and Corydon, is she perhaps also suggesting that this is not a conventional heterosexual love?

There seems to be a self-mocking tone in verses three to six, where Levy writes that she and her lover are interested only in the 'pure delights of the brain'. Is the hyperbole in verse six, where we find them discussing only 'Art and Letters, Life and Man', suggesting that the 'pleasant times' in verse one and the activities that make the poet 'smile' in verse eight are perhaps more physical than philosophical?

Note the innovative and thought-provoking interruption to the seventh stanza and a tripping rhythm that seems entirely appropriate as a vehicle for the poem's droll humour.

The Poet Amy Levy was one of seven children born to a wealthy Anglo-Jewish family. She was in many ways a pioneering woman, becoming in 1879 the first Jewish woman ever to study at Newnham College, Cambridge. She had a wide circle of intellectual friends, but she suffered periodically from bouts of severe depression.

She left university before completing her degree in order to concentrate on her writing and to travel in Germany, Italy and France, often with a female friend.

Her novels deal with the complex issue of Anglo-Jewish identity, while her essays are often concerned with her Jewish heritage and the depiction of Jewish characters in literature. Her poetry includes dramatic monologues and sonnets, and her precocious talent is seen in her first collection, which appeared when she was only twenty.

Amy Levy committed suicide in 1889 by inhaling charcoal fumes at her family home. She was twenty-seven.

London Snow *Robert Bridges (1844–1930)*

The Poem Bridges' quietly observational poem is a description of the transformative effect of nature on the London cityscape. Though the poem seems at first to be rather factual, unfussy and simple, the snow is imbued with life and will, moving 'Stealthily' and 'Lazily'. The magical effect of the snow is heightened through its falling, as if secretly, during the night. By the time people wake the city has already been transformed.

Dutifully, the poet catalogues the effects of snow on the city: its 'hushing' and 'muffling' of sound creating a 'stillness of the solemn air'; the new light of its 'unaccustomed brightness'. Is its major effect, though, as a great leveller of a famously divided city, 'Hiding difference, making unevenness even'?

The major change in this neatly rhymed, well-ordered poem comes when the city wakes to work. Now 'war is waged with the snow'. But even as the busy commerce of the City grinds into action, the sense of the marvellous, and perhaps also the spiritual, lingers. The workers' minds are 'diverted' by 'the beauty that greets them' and, though they must strive to break it, they are working still under the snow's enchantment.

The Poet Robert Bridges worked as a doctor in London hospitals until 1882; he was also a classicist and poet who served as Poet Laureate from 1913 until his death in 1930. Educated at Eton and Corpus Christi College, Oxford, Bridges edited and published the poems of his friend Gerard Manley Hopkins after the latter's premature death.

In the many letters that passed between the two poets after their first meeting as undergraduates in 1863, Bridges emerges as a faithful, gently encouraging friend. However, though he recognized Hopkins's poetic genius, he was alarmed by his bold and unconventional experiments with language and rhythm. In much the same way, he also rejected modernism to develop his own more measured and accessible style. As a poet, he valued precision with language matched by restraint with form, qualities that are displayed in 'London Snow'.

Thoughts of Phena *Thomas Hardy (1840–1928)*

The Poem Tryphena Sparks was Thomas Hardy's cousin, and much speculation has surrounded their relationship. While we cannot be sure exactly what they meant to each other, it is clear from the poem that Hardy was deeply touched by news of her death.

The presentation of the poem on the page is visually striking and the first stanza immediately introduces us to strong rhythms and very irregular lines. Notice the contrast between the realization that Hardy has nothing to remember Tryphena by and his memory of her when she was young. It is as though she had so many hopes and dreams they can be contained only within a line of fifteen syllables.

By the end of the poem Hardy appears to be almost relieved that he has no knowledge of what happened to her ambitions. Why might he take comfort in this ignorance? Look at the final verse, where he talks about his memory of the 'maiden' being 'fined in my brain'. Is he using 'fined' here to mean 'confined', or 'refined', or 'finished', or could it be a combination of all these meanings?

The Poet Thomas Hardy was a Victorian novelist and a twentieth-century poet. He published fourteen novels and over fifty short stories before, remarkably, abandoning his prose writing in favour of his first and enduring love – poetry. His last novels were highly controversial, dealing with love and marriage; divorce; and the hypocrisy of Victorian attitudes towards women. Hardy was uncompromising and sometimes deeply pessimistic, and his final novel, *Jude the Obscure*, caused outrage.

Financially secure, Hardy concentrated from 1898 on poetry, producing over nine hundred poems in the next thirty years. Tirelessly inventive in terms of rhythm and rhyme and the structure and language of his poems, he has influenced later poets such as W. H. Auden and Philip Larkin.

Some of his greatest poems deal with his response to the death of his wife in 1912. The poems that spilled out of him between 1912 and 1913 are technically innovative and suffused with guilt, regret and wonder.

'Sing me a song of a lad that is gone'

Robert Louis Stevenson (1850–94)

The Poem The 'Skye Boat Song' is one of the most famous and frequently sung Scottish folk songs, chronicling the escape of Bonnie Prince Charlie (Charles Edward Stuart) to the Isle of Skye after his defeat at Culloden, aided by the Jacobite heroine Flora MacDonald.

The words of the original 'Skye Boat Song' end with a defiant 'Charlie will come again' and are written from the perspective of an ardent Bonnie Prince loyalist, but in Stevenson's reworked version the tone is somewhat different. Using a similar structure but a less insistent rhyming pattern, Stevenson concentrates on the inner feelings of the defeated prince. Ambition and optimism have been replaced by a sense of weary loss. Notice the use of the repeated 'Give me' in verse four, emphasizing the depth of longing for that earlier time when hope mingled with the expectation of glory.

Whereas the original boat song finishes with a sense of heroic failure and a romantic expression of future victory, Stevenson's ending is poignant and realistic. The speaker realizes that he has lost everything, even his own identity: 'All that was me is gone.' The 'lad' he once was is gone and will never return.

The Poet Born in Scotland, Robert Louis Stevenson was an unconventional and adventurous novelist, poet, essayist, short-story and travel writer with a remarkable gift for captivating story-telling. Some of his prose works, such as *Treasure Island*, *Kidnapped* and *Dr Jekyll and Mr Hyde*, remain enormously popular and have inspired numerous adaptations and film versions.

Stevenson rejected the law for a life as a writer, often travelling to warmer climes for his health. He wrote numerous stories and essays based on his experiences in France and the South Seas. Marrying an American woman took him to San Francisco, where he became stepfather to her two children.

Although the family returned to Europe, Stevenson's health continued to be affected by the climate, and he travelled again to the South Seas and the island of Samoa, immersing himself in the culture. He died there aged forty-four and was buried on a mountaintop overlooking his home.

The Witch *Mary Elizabeth Coleridge (1861–1907)*

The Poem Think of a witch. What comes to mind? Perhaps the hideous, cackling old hags who waylay Macbeth, or maybe the green-skinned, pointy-black-hat-wearing Wicked Witch of the West who frightens Dorothy and her companions in *The Wizard of Oz*? Coleridge's creation is a much subtler one. Should we sympathize with her, or pity her? She is seen against the snow, a small, fragile figure, wet and exhausted. When she pleads to be let in, do we want her to be rescued from the 'cutting wind' so that she can rest her 'little white feet', or is there potentially danger in letting a 'witch' in at the door?

How do you respond to the ambiguity of the third stanza? Why has the speaker allowed the witch in, and what are the repercussions of this action? What might the heart's desire of women be? It is worth noting that the motif of a wanderer or an outsider anxious to be accepted is often found in Mary Coleridge's poems. Could this fascination in the poem with crossing a threshold or stepping over a boundary relate to her own position as a woman and a poet in Victorian society?

The Poet Mary Coleridge was the intellectually gifted great-great-niece of Samuel Taylor Coleridge. Her parents were impressively well connected to writers and musicians in the London of the last half of the nineteenth century.

Mary met weekly with friends in the late 1880s to discuss literature and to read their own creative work. She had already managed to place reviews and essays in various journals before her first novel, *The Seven Sleepers of Ephesus*, was published. Set in Germany, it is a tale full of secret societies, romance and disguise and was generally well received, as were her other historical adventure novels. She wrote poetry throughout her life, and her collection *Fancy's Following* was published in 1896.

A committed Christian, Coleridge taught literature to young women at the Working Women's College for several years. She died after contracting blood poisoning following an operation to remove her appendix.

Invitation to Love *Paul Dunbar (1872–1906)*

The Poem Dunbar's love poem, addressed to his 'dear Love', employs imagery which is often associated with romance. The first three lines mention the sun, moon and stars and elsewhere in the poem there are references to the nesting 'dove', 'blossom', 'heart' and 'summer'. Even when he mentions winter, the atmosphere of the poem is not threatened, as he describes the snows with the soft-sounding word 'drifting'. Notice how the much-repeated 'come', which Dunbar uses seven times in the first octet and five times in the final octet, builds in both cases to the notion that his love will be 'welcome' whenever she does visit him, whatever the time or season.

The quatrain that separates the octets describes the recipient of his love as 'soft' and 'sweet', and he longs for his heart to be brought 'to rest'.

How do the rhythm and rhyme support the simplicity and sincerity of Dunbar's love poem?

The Poet Paul Dunbar was one of the first African-American poets to be widely known and admired in America. His parents were freed slaves and Dunbar used some of their tales of plantation life in his work.

After a successful reading at the World's Fair in Chicago, Dunbar's poems were picked up by national newspapers and magazines. His second collection, *Majors and Minors*, appeared in 1895, with the 'majors' representing poems written in standard English and the 'minors' referring to his very successful dialect poems.

Dunbar's fame spread, and he travelled to England to give readings. On returning to America, he worked at the Library of Congress in Washington DC and married the writer Alice Ruth Moore. However, his health began to deteriorate and, although he continued to be a prolific writer, producing several novels, song lyrics and further collections of poems, he died of tuberculosis in 1906, at the age of thirty-three.

The Ballad of Reading Gaol *Oscar Wilde (1854–1900)*

The Poem This is the opening section of a long poem written by Oscar Wilde after his release from Reading Gaol. He had served a two-year sentence for gross indecency after his homosexuality was exposed in a famous trial. In exile, and shattered by his experiences in gaol, he uses the trial and execution of a soldier for the murder of his wife to reflect upon morality, the death penalty and the penal system.

Notice the rhythm of the ballad. Does the thumping iambic tetrameter perhaps reflect the grinding, laborious hard labour performed by inmates? The yearning for freedom is captured in verses three and four as the prisoners look at the sky while walking in a circle in the prison yard. What is the impact on the narrator in the yard when he learns of the expected fate of the imprisoned soldier?

In a poem that is full of paradoxes, the penultimate line in this extract, 'The man had killed the thing he loved', is repeated elsewhere in the poem. What do you think Wilde means by this line and why might it be such an important line for him?

The Poet Oscar Wilde's imprisonment for homosexuality in 1895 ended a spectacularly successful career. Although he lived for a few more years in exile in France after his release and produced some moving poetry, his life was effectively over.

He had been a remarkably talented and prize-winning student at university in Dublin and Oxford, and embarked on lengthy lecture tours of America, Britain and Ireland. In a society that was suspicious of art, he lived life as an aesthete.

He began to write stories for children and produced his only novel, *The Picture of Dorian Gray*, in 1890. Its homoerotic elements were controversial and were used by the prosecution during Wilde's trial to help prove his guilt.

Between 1892 and 1895 Wilde wrote hugely successful comedies for the stage, including *The Importance of Being Earnest*. His polished, witty and amusing plays offered a satirical perspective on Victorian society and its morals and manners.

The Things that Matter *E. Nesbit (1858–1924)*

The Poem The speaker of the poem is nearing the end of her life and contemplating what she has learned. She thinks about what knowledge will be preserved and also what will be lost with her death. She suggests that some things that people 'write and talk about' will always be known and understood. She talks about first aid, gardening and cooking; practical and domestic issues. But in verse three she considers the things that may be lost when she dies. The list is now full of things that are known through instinct, intuition and experience; things that an individual understands but would find it hard to explain or to write down. It might be the exact moment when the bread should leave the oven or what herbs will make the sick man well. Taking this knowledge from the world seems such a 'silly waste'.

Consider the ending of the poem, when the speaker asks to be allowed to 'know something when I'm dead'. Is the tone comical? Are there profundities and a kind of folk wisdom beneath the cheerful but poignant simplicity of the poem?

The Poet Edith Nesbit was a prolific author of over forty books for children, including the enduringly popular *The Railway Children*.

Her lifestyle, especially for a middle-class Victorian woman, was highly unconventional. A committed socialist and a significant figure within the Fabian Society, Edith Nesbit was seven months pregnant when she married Hubert Bland. Later, she lived in a complex *ménage à trois* with her husband and his mistress which produced five children and was rather different to the idyllic vision of family life she created in her novels.

Nesbit's writing financed the purchase of an impressive house in Kent, where a large circle of friends and admirers was entertained. Established writers such as George Bernard Shaw and H. G. Wells were visitors to the house.

She also wrote novels, short stories and over twenty collections of poetry for adults, which never achieved the commercial and critical success of her much-loved work for children.

The Song of the Smoke *W. E. B. Du Bois (1868–1963)*

The Poem After the emphatic, declamatory, stomping, celebratory opening lines, 'I am the Smoke King/I am black!', short rhymed couplets, boosted by internal rhymes, set the rhythm of the poem pulsating. Notice how 'wringing' echoes 'swinging' and the way this sound pattern is picked up in 'curling' and 'whirling'. These present participles run through each stanza, expressing movement and contributing to the verse's muscular vitality.

A world of industry, strife and suffering is suggested by the smoke, the 'throbbing mills' that lead to the death of the 'soul', the 'iron times', the 'gritty, grimy hands'. And in this crucible of toil is forged Du Bois's characteristic iron conviction, his rallying challenge to conventional, racist colour symbolism: 'The blacker the mantle, the mightier the man!'

Through repetition, the rhythm generates a sense of onward drive, an unstoppable rhetorical momentum pounding towards its clinching climactic final lines. Here blackness and whiteness become indistinguishable, held by the line in perfect balance: 'I whiten my black men – I blacken my white!', and Du Bois's rhetorical question rings out, 'What's the hue of a hide to a man in his might?'

The Poet Sociologist, civil rights campaigner, historian, Harvard graduate, anti-war activist, academic, essayist, novelist, communist and, of course, poet, W. E. B. Du Bois was passionately committed to fighting prejudice and racism in America throughout his long life.

The co-founder of the National Association for the Advancement of Colored People, and of the Pan-African movement, Du Bois spent much of his academic career at the University of Atlanta. He wrote over twenty books, edited fifteen more and published more than a hundred articles and essays in a tireless effort to gain equal treatment for black people in a world dominated by whites and to refute the myths of racial inferiority.

In his nineties, he became a citizen of Ghana, where he died in 1963 and was given a state funeral. In America, fifty years after his death, he is remembered and revered as the outstanding African-American intellectual of the first half of the twentieth century.

The Way through the Woods *Rudyard Kipling (1865–1936)*

The Poem In the first twelve lines Kipling simply and delicately describes the abandoned road in the woods. What details does he present in order to help us picture the scene? What do you notice about the rhythm and the elaborate rhyme scheme, and the way these features support the meaning of the poem? Look at the internal rhyme used in the third and seventh lines in each stanza.

In the second stanza, how does Kipling introduce an element of mystery and intrigue while still employing carefully observed descriptive detail? Note how 'Yet' at the start of the second stanza signals the introduction of new observations and information, while the use of a thirteenth line creates a haunting conclusion to the poem. The drama and tension in the poem are heightened by the sudden auditory and visual impact of the 'beat of a horse's feet' and the 'swish of a skirt'.

Roads and woods can be powerful metaphors in poetry and song. Do you think there is a metaphorical element in this poem, or should we simply enjoy the carefully constructed, mysterious tale of an 'old lost road'?

The Poet Rudyard Kipling's career began to develop when he worked in India for Anglo-Indian newspapers. He was a talented reporter, reviewer, essayist and short-story writer, but his first major success came with poetry after his return to England. The publication of *Barrack-Room Ballads* in 1892, which captured the experiences of soldiers across the British Empire, brought him considerable fame. His appeal was further strengthened by his popular writing for children; *The Jungle Book* was published in 1894.

Kipling suffered devastating personal bereavements, with the loss of one of his daughters when she was six years old, and the death of a son, who was killed in action at the start of the First World War. He was often seen as a 'poet of empire' with conservative views, and his reputation suffered after the First World War and with the advent of modernism, in spite of the impressive range of his work and his skilful craftsmanship.

The God Abandons Antony *C. P. Cavafy (1863–1933)*

The Poem Cavafy's is a mysterious, intense narrative poem in the form of a dramatic monologue. It raises but withholds the answer to a number of pressing questions. Why, for instance, is this 'strange procession' 'invisible'? Where is it going, at 'midnight', making its 'exquisite music'? Who is the 'you' to whom the poem is addressed?

'Antony' is clearly the historical Roman general Marcus Antonius, so 'Alexandria' may be both the city and a metaphor for Cleopatra, Antony's lover. The god leaving, accompanied by music, is Bacchus, Antony's protector. According to the classical writer Plutarch, Bacchus abandoned Antony the night before Alexandria was conquered by his enemies.

Antony is battling with doubt and misfortune. His plans have proved 'deceptive' and his 'work gone wrong'. The poem's calm, firm voice advises him not to mourn, as might be his inclination, but to draw instead on his own qualities, specifically the grace of his courage. He must feel the raw emotions but still keep a dignified public appearance (at the window). Displaying stoical fortitude, Antony must face a series of traumatic losses: of his god, of his lover and of the city they shared.

The Poet C. P. Cavafy is widely considered to be the greatest Greek poet of the twentieth century. A perfectionist as regards his work, which he constantly revised, he published only 154 poems in his lifetime.

From his birth in 1863 to his death aged seventy in 1933, Cavafy lived variously in Alexandria, Constantinople, France and Liverpool, where he spent some time at an English school. The youngest of seven brothers, he worked as a civil servant and as a journalist. His quiet, conventional public persona hid a more complex private life. For instance, Cavafy gambled systematically and seemingly successfully, and he wrote frank, erotic poems about his sexual life. In his lifetime he remained an obscure literary figure whose work was circulated among friends in Alexandria, or published sporadically in newspapers, annuals and magazines. His friendship with the English novelist E. M. Forster led, however, to Cavafy's work being championed.

Miss Loo *Walter de la Mare (1873–1956)*

The Poem Walter de la Mare's poem 'Miss Loo', written in rhyming couplets, was published in his 1912 collection containing his most famous poem, 'The Listeners'.

Consider what attitude towards Miss Loo is suggested by the use of the word 'poor' in the second and penultimate lines. Although the opening, with its reference to 'thin-strewn' memory, might indicate that it will be difficult for the narrator to remember the past with accuracy, the images of Miss Loo he holds in his mind seem vivid.

How does de la Mare use language to place the memories in a particular time and atmosphere? What details of weather and his surroundings does he comment upon as he describes taking tea with Miss Loo?

In the final section of the poem he speculates upon Miss Loo's attitude towards him and her 'gentle gleaming spirit'. Throughout the poem the reader is challenged to determine how de la Mare views Miss Loo.

The Poet Walter de la Mare wrote for both children and adults. He is probably best known for his haunting supernatural poem 'The Listeners', which is regularly anthologized, but he also wrote novels, short stories and essays. He began writing while working in the statistics department of an oil company in London.

His novels, such as *The Return*, often deal with a heightened reality that contains elements of fantasy and the supernatural. *Memoirs of a Midget* was very well received, with one reviewer calling it 'the most notable achievement in prose fiction of our generation'.

De la Mare's poetry is sometimes compared to the work of Thomas Hardy and William Blake. He often created a dream-like atmosphere in his poems and was concerned with themes of mortality and the imagination.

In his thirties, he became financially secure and was able to devote his life to writing until his death in 1956.

The Rolling English Road *G. K. Chesterton (1874–1936)*

The Poem Chesterton's life-affirming, rollicking defence of individuality and ordinary pleasures, enhanced by a mug or two of ale, was first published in 1913. Originally known as 'A Song of Temperance Reform', it was written as an entertaining warning against adopting the kind of anti-alcohol laws that would be passed during Prohibition in the USA.

Celebrating with affection the work of the 'English drunkard' who built roads that meander across the countryside, Chesterton crams his fourteen-syllable lines with alliteration. The defence of the road builder is proudly patriotic, as the poem takes a swipe at the potential invasion of the 'Frenchman', who may have come to 'straighten out' the crooked road. The speaker reflects not only upon the simple pleasures of drink and the appeal of the winding English road but also the activities of his youth. He has wandered and rambled through the country with an 'ale-mug' in his hand, taking routes that would not be recommended by a satellite-navigation system. Now an older man, he does not wish to be 'the shame of age' and so some restraint is appropriate, but he still hopes that much fun is to be had before he and his friends go to Paradise.

The Poet G. K. Chesterton is probably best known for his popular priest-detective Father Brown, who appeared in over fifty short stories. However, he was also a poet, biographer, essayist, dramatist, critic, journalist, advocate of a political movement called 'Distributism' and, after his conversion to Catholicism in 1922, an influential writer on theological issues.

While Chesterton could move confidently and successfully between different literary genres, his journalism was at the heart of his life as a writer. He produced thousands of articles, combining humour and seriousness, on a huge variety of topics, for the *Illustrated London News* and the *Daily News*. For a while, he even had his own idiosyncratic newspaper, *G. K.'s Weekly*. He travelled widely on lecture engagements and was a powerful orator. Not renowned for his organizational skills, Chesterton would occasionally write his articles in Fleet Street bars and in railway-station waiting rooms, having missed his train.

A Blockhead *Amy Lowell (1874–1925)*

The Poem Amy Lowell's sonnet begins with the speaker presenting a picture of a life that is full of monotony and drudgery. Her days are 'shapeless' and covered in 'dust'. One day is almost indistinguishable from another and her actions appear mechanical and repetitive as she sifts and sorts a joyless life. Notice how there is something almost scientific and cold about the diction, with references to 'atoms' and 'particles'. She compares her actions to those of a monk counting prayers on a rosary with movements that are repeated time and time again.

However, in the ninth line, which often represents a change of direction in sonnets, the poet recollects a very different time of passion and excitement. The poem is now full of references to 'joy' and 'fire', 'wine' and 'desire'; to a time of 'glory'.

In the final couplet the speaker reflects that she did not make the most of the days that pulsed with energetic life. What has she failed to 'understand', as she puts it, in the final word of the sonnet?

The Poet Amy Lowell was born into an affluent Massachusetts family and educated at home and in private schools in Boston. Her financial resources helped her develop a liberated and unconventional lifestyle.

Amy Lowell once remarked that God had made her a business-woman and she had made herself a poet. Over a relatively brief period she produced over 650 poems but also worked energetically to publicize and promote modern trends in poetry. In particular, she embraced imagism within the modernist movement, and in 1914 became friends with Ezra Pound, one of its leading proponents. Lowell edited a number of collections of imagist poetry.

She published extensively between 1915 and her death in 1925. She lectured, promoted the work of other poets she admired and wrote literary criticism, including a lengthy biography of John Keats. Lowell was posthumously awarded the Pulitzer Prize for Poetry in 1926 for her collection of poems *What's O'Clock*.

The River Merchant's Wife: A Letter *Ezra Pound (1885–1972)*

The Poem In a series of precise and vivid images, Pound's translation of a Chinese poem by Li Po captures the past and present feelings of the river merchant's wife for her husband.

How does Pound convey the sense of innocent enjoyment in each other's presence when the merchant and his future wife meet as children in their village? Look at the repetition of the verb to 'play' in the first few lines.

Married at fourteen to her 'Lord', the merchant's wife appears unhappy in her first year of marriage but, by fifteen, she has stopped 'scowling'. Pound gives an impression of her deepening love for her husband and unqualified emotional commitment to him when she looks beyond life to their 'dust' mingling 'forever'. What is the effect of 'forever' being repeated three times in line thirteen?

The tone of tender melancholy is evident in the second half of the poem, when the merchant's wife recalls her husband's departure and references to nature emphasize the passing of time. The poignant ending sees her longing for his return and expressing her desire to travel out to meet him on his journey home to her.

The Poet Although born and educated in America, Ezra Pound spent much of his life in Europe. He came to London in 1908, where he was highly influential in shaping the character of poetry in this period.

Pound was part of the modernist movement and developed imagism, a strand of modernism which encouraged poets to write with economy of language and to record observed detail through precise, visual images.

Hugh Selwyn Mauberley, dealing with the life of a disillusioned poet, was published in 1920, when Pound left England for Paris and then Italy. During the war his support for Mussolini and his pro-Fascist broadcasts led to his arrest. He was deemed not sane enough to stand trial and was hospitalized in Washington DC for the next thirteen years, before his release saw him return permanently to Italy.

He continued working on his long, ambitious, epic poem *The Cantos* from 1925 until the start of the 1960s.

The Inquest *W. H. Davies (1871–1940)*

The Poem The seven four-line stanzas rhyming or half rhyming ABCB have echoes of a traditional ballad and, like some ballads, the poem deals with a disturbing incident. The speaker is a juror in a coroner's court and describes the inquest into the death of a baby.

The viewing of the dead baby is described in an emotionally detached way in the second verse, and yet the third verse focuses on the still-open left eye and speculates as to what this might mean. In a somewhat macabre section the speaker imagines the baby communicating with him through the open eye, which seems to be laughing or gleeful. The fourth verse plants the idea in the reader's mind that this might be a case of infanticide, an idea that is reinforced by the mother's smile as she gives evidence about the death of 'a love-child'. Notice how the seventh and final stanza is almost a repetition of the fourth stanza. What is the effect of this repetition in terms of the mystery and moral ambiguity of the poem?

The Poet The Welsh poet W. H. Davies wrote the famous poem 'Leisure', which begins: 'What is this life if, full of care / We have no time to stand and stare.' The poem's theme is reflected in Davies's own outdoor life, which was unconventional. Leaving Wales, he worked and begged his way across America, losing a leg in an accident when jumping from a train. He returned to England and, unfit for physical work, dedicated himself to making a living as a writer. His first collection of poems attracted influential admirers, such as George Bernard Shaw, who helped Davies publish a successful memoir, *The Autobiography of a Super Tramp*, which dealt with his life travelling across America.

By 1929 his popularity and literary reputation led to the award of an honorary degree from the University of Wales and, ten years later, his home town of Newport unveiled a plaque in his honour.

Sea Rose *HD* (*Hilda Doolittle*) *(1886–1961)*

The Poem Think of a rose. Think of how roses are conventionally described in poetry. You might imagine perfume, sensuality, thorns, love, perhaps as in Burns's 'O my love is like a red, red rose'. Characteristically, Doolittle replaces the conventional poetic symbol of the red rose with a less favoured, less praised variety, the sea rose. Thus she implies a critique of conventional poetic taste and practice and indicates her own, different aesthetic.

What qualities does the sea rose possess to distinguish it from its more celebrated kin? Notice the adjectives: 'harsh', 'meagre', 'sparse', 'Stunted', 'small'. It may be 'marred', it may be vulnerable and exposed to the violence of the elements ('caught' and 'flung'), it may be alone ('single'), but the sea rose is tenacious and tough; 'hardened', it endures. Instead of gorgeous perfume, its fragrance is 'acrid', a smell not always thought attractive, but one that is certainly potent.

Clearly the sea rose is an analogue, a metaphor. For the poet herself, perhaps, or for the poetry she writes? For both? The poem is delicate, fragile-looking, spare, stoical, as if sculpted in air.

The Poet Feminist icon, friend and patient of Sigmund Freud, famous bohemian, Hilda Doolittle was an innovative, celebrated American poet and the first woman to win the Award of Merit Medal from the American Academy of Arts and Letters.

Doolittle married once and had a number of heterosexual and lesbian relationships in her life. She was closely associated with Ezra Pound and with imagism, which was characterized by its stringent rules of directness and compression and its rejection of conventional poetic language and metres. Pared down, often focused on a specific object, Doolittle's verse displays a spare, almost gaunt quality, an economy of language wholly in line with the imagist manifesto.

Doolittle had a deep interest in Ancient Greek literature and her work often made reference to Greek mythology. The imagist vogue for sparseness and compression is exemplified by the fact that Pound advised Hilda Doolittle to change her poetic name to just the letters HD.

'Out, Out – ' *Robert Frost (1874–1963)*

The Poem The poem begins by depicting the dominant presence of the buzz-saw before dwelling on the landscape for several lines. The focus then returns to personifying the saw that 'snarled and rattled', introducing a sense of menace and danger to the poem. Even so, there is also an atmosphere of work coming to an end and relaxation as the boy's sister comes out to call him in for 'Supper'.

At this moment the fatal accident happens. How does Frost describe the moment when the boy's hand is caught by the saw, and the boy's reaction? What do you think of the tone of the poem in this section, lines sixteen to twenty-six?

The doctor cannot save the boy and the last seven lines record the boy slipping into death while those around him 'turned to their affairs'. Consider the tone of the ending. Is it deliberately and ironically detached?

It has been suggested that, as the poem was written during the First World War, it might be a commentary on the destruction of innocence and the callous disregard for life seen in this war.

The title is a reference to Macbeth and his response to his wife's death, 'Out, out, brief candle . . .'

The Poet Robert Frost was a dominant figure in American cultural life throughout the first half of the twentieth century. On his death in 1963 President Kennedy talked about Frost leaving behind him 'imperishable verse' that gives 'joy and understanding'.

Frost's first volumes of poetry were published in New England but became a more widely known poet when he moved for a few years to England and met poets such as Ezra Pound and Robert Graves.

Frost believed that a perfect poem was a fusion of emotion and thought. It is the lucid combination of feeling and intellect in his poems that helped him become so successful and ensured the popularity of poems such as 'The Road Not Taken'. While skilfully handling traditional verse forms, he captured the rhythms and texture of ordinary language. He delighted in the rural landscape of New England but could also explore profound issues of life and death with gravity and wit.

Fame *Charlotte Mew (1869–1928)*

The Poem In 'Fame' the speaker struggles with self-identification. In the 'over-heated house', how does she depict herself? She contrasts her experience of showing off in a crowd of people, courting fame perhaps, with when she walked in 'heavenly places', free to be creative and expressive. She feels the tension between 'silences and spaces' and the 'din' and the 'scuffle'. How is nature depicted in the central section, when she talks about the air and larks and trees?

The speaker exclaims excitedly about the prospect of leaving 'Fame' and replacing it with 'One little dream'. The dream turns into a nightmare when, in line twenty-two, the speaker describes finding the dream in a field under a fence. It is 'A frail, dead, new-born lamb'. The image becomes even more disturbing and haunting when the poem concludes with two more descriptions of the dead dream. It is a 'blot upon the night' and 'The moon's dropped child!' What might these challenging metaphors represent? Are they referring to the blocking of the creative aspirations of the female poet or simply to the impossibility of being true to oneself?

The Poet Charlotte Mew was surrounded by mental ill health and death from a young age. Three brothers died while she was still a child and two other siblings were committed to mental institutions. She vowed never to marry, fearful of the mental ill health any children she had might develop.

Mew was not a prolific writer but began intermittently publishing poetry and short fiction in magazines. She achieved some recognition after her narrative poem 'The Farmer's Bride' appeared in a journal in 1912, and she began to be invited to readings and gatherings in influential literary circles in London. Her first collection of poetry sold slowly, but a revised edition published in England and America attracted interest and praise.

In 1923 literary friends used their influence to secure Mew a small government pension, but she became increasingly isolated and delusional. She entered a nursing home in 1928 but committed suicide by drinking disinfectant.

Divorce *Anna Wickham (1884–1947)*

The Poem It is very easy to think of the title of this poem as referring to a marital divorce, but it is also helpful to think of the word 'Divorce' in terms of a separating or breaking away from something.

The speaker in this ingeniously rhymed poem is feeling restricted and constrained in the house in the valley but is aware of potential freedom outside. 'A voice from the dark is calling' yet the speaker is not frightened. They yearn to be let free, into a night they associate with liberty and desire.

Notice how the poem turns on the exclamation 'Wait!' in line nine, when the speaker appears ready to break away from the smothering house and the fire which has been fanned with their 'sick breath'. Look at the images of drums and war in the second half of the poem. The speaker's escape is into an exciting, if dangerous, world, but this is preferable to a life of suffocating loneliness. They are drawn to the call of the 'hero' at the rock's edge.

The poem concludes with the repeated refrain and the urgent, passionate plea 'let me go, let me go.'

The Poet Born in London, raised in Australia, Edith Harper adopted the pseudonym Anna Wickham to write her poetry – partly, it seems, to assuage her husband, who found Edith's work so threatening he had her forcibly admitted to a mental hospital when she refused to stop writing. Unhappily married, struggling intermittently with mental illness and her bisexuality, Harper/Wickham had a troubled, turbulent life, one that ended prematurely, with her suicide in 1947.

At nearly six foot tall and fond of pubs, pies and a pint of bitter, Harper cut a somewhat eccentric, energetic bohemian figure on the London literary scene. Although in her lifetime she found it difficult to get her poems published, she is seen today as a courageous and accomplished early feminist writer. Her many literary friends included D. H. Lawrence, as well as the American poet Hilda Doolittle, with whom she had a brief affair.

Rouen *May Wedderburn Cannan (1893–1973)*

The Poem 'Rouen' recalls a momentous time in May Wedderburn Cannan's life during the First World War, when she worked in a canteen providing meals for soldiers arriving there from England.

Notice how she uses the rhetorical device known as 'anaphora', in which a sequence of words at the beginning of a line – in this case, 'And the' – is repeated. The Greek word means a 'carrying back', and we as readers are carried back to a time in her life which is not about the trenches and the intense suffering we have come to expect from First World War poetry but about 'the laughter of adventure'.

The poet is writing not as a passive observer from the safety of her comfortable Oxford home but as an active participant in what she felt was an important cause. While the poem conveys her sense of exhilaration in the 'glory of the labour of the day', she revealingly describes the 'mirth' as 'heart-breaking'. She is clearly moved by people's heroic ability to laugh in the face of extreme and painful adversity. The singing of the national anthem by the soldiers prompts a sense of both 'agony and splendour'. She is not blind to the sacrifices and terrifying challenges facing these men.

The Poet May Wedderburn Cannan not only wrote about life before, during and after the First World War but also played an active part in the war effort. She travelled to Rouen in 1915 to work in the canteen at the railhead, helping to feed thousands of British troops.

She returned to England to join her father, who was Dean of Trinity College, Oxford, and secretary of the Oxford University Press, before returning to work at the War Office Department in Paris. Tragically, although he survived the war, her fiancé, Bevil Quiller-Couch, died in the Spanish flu pandemic of 1919.

Her semi-autobiographical novel, *The Lonely Generation*, was published in 1934, while her autobiography, *Grey Ghosts and Voices*, did not appear until 1976, three years after her death.

Her poems are honest, touching, poignant reflections on love, bereavement and sacrifice. Looking back on her life, she commented, 'At least I wrote a salute to my generation.'

Strange Hells *Ivor Gurney (1890–1937)*

The Poem 'Strange Hells' is one of the poems Gurney wrote in response to his experiences in the First World War. Look at the first three lines of this unconventionally structured sonnet and consider the shifts in feeling and thinking. Notice how our expectations of the poet being plunged into the nightmarish hell of war are not necessarily met when, in the third line, Gurney writes about not being as afraid 'As one would have expected'.

However, the central section of the poem deals with the 'hell' of enduring a bombardment in the trenches when the regiment tries to drown out the sound of the guns by singing. In line ten, the impact of the bombardment is emphasized by the use of repeated sounds.

In the last four lines of the sonnet, we jump forward to dwell briefly on the survivors who have returned home. How does Gurney depict the soldiers who have survived the war? The poem concludes with the idea of the heart burning but the need to 'keep out of the face how heart burns'. Why might Gurney suggest this need for concealment?

The Poet Ivor Gurney suffered periods of mental ill health before the First World War, but his condition had deteriorated significantly by the end of the conflict. He had joined up after initially being rejected and was subsequently wounded and gassed.

At the end of the war he had a number of temporary jobs, but his mental instability worsened and he was committed to a mental asylum in 1922. Gurney never fully recovered and died in an asylum in Kent in 1937 from tuberculosis. He almost certainly suffered from some form of bi-polar disorder.

Gurney was not only a poet but also an extremely gifted composer. Although tormented by mental illness, he wrote over two hundred musical pieces and hundreds of poems. During his lifetime he was probably best known for his music, but after his death his friends ensured that his poetic work was collected and preserved and its originality and value have been increasingly widely recognized.

Lights Out *Edward Thomas (1878–1917)*

The Poem This meditation on sleep as welcome rest and as the ultimate rest of death was written during the First World War when Thomas was serving in France. He did not survive the war.

Thomas compares the moment just before falling into a deep sleep to reaching the border of a dense forest. Notice the use of the image of a road or track, which suggests a journey or a purposeful sense of direction, and yet in this poem the road does not lead to anywhere but oblivion.

Consider the third verse, where Thomas seems to confront directly the prospect of death. What does the poem suggest will end with death?

In the penultimate verse Thomas appears to be choosing to turn from the known world of books and people to embrace the unknown, and he expresses a powerful realization that he must do this 'alone', repeatedly using the active pronoun 'I'.

The poem ends with the paradox of hearing silence and Thomas's reference once again to the forest, with all its traditional associations of enchantment, mystery and danger.

The Poet Edward Thomas is often thought of as a war writer, but by 1914 he was already the father of three children and had been supporting his family for some years through book reviewing and writing essays (especially about the English countryside) and biographies. His novel *The Happy-Go-Lucky Morgans* was published in 1913.

He began to produce poetry in 1914, partly encouraged by his friendship with the American poet Robert Frost, who was living near Thomas in England at the time. Frost urged Thomas to move with his family to New England, but Thomas enlisted in 1915. He was killed by a shell blast in France in 1917.

He wrote many poems between 1915 and 1917, recording both his experiences of wartime and his response to the countryside with the kind of meditative thoughtfulness seen in one of his most widely read and loved poems, 'Adlestrop'.

The Show *Wilfred Owen (1893–1918)*

The Poem 'The show', in euphemistic army slang, refers to a battle. Owen in this poem paints a graphic picture of the living hell that is war. He begins by suggesting that he is observing the scene of battle with 'Death'. How does he give the sense of looking down from 'a vague height' on a world at war?

Notice how Owen deliberately uses deeply repellent images. The land is full of 'scabs'; hills are described as 'myriad warts'; and the figures in the landscape appear as grotesque, terrifying creatures. They are barely recognizable as men as they creep through the mud and ditches and the foul stench of 'wounds deepening'. The men he is observing give glimpses of bodies that may be human, but even their backs are 'bitten', in a world that seems to be devouring itself.

The appalling sights Owen records of a dislocated and disjointed world are reinforced by the structure of the poem, with its irregular stanzas and half-rhymes such as 'Death'/'dearth'; 'why'/'woe'.

Consider the last five lines of the poem, where Owen descends with Death into the battlefield like a fall in a nightmare. What is the significance of what Death shows Owen in the last two lines?

The Poet Wilfred Owen's was one of the most passionate and eloquent voices of the First World War. His poems were written in a period of intense creativity between 1917 and 1918.

Appalled by the suffering and waste of human life in a conflict that seemed increasingly futile, Owen set out to show what he called the 'pity of war'.

In 1917 he was wounded, suffered shell shock and was sent to a Scottish military hospital, where he met and was influenced by Siegfried Sassoon. On his return to the Front, Owen's courage and leadership were recognized with the award of the Military Cross. He did not survive the war, dying in action just days before the end of hostilities.

His work is full of compassion and outrage and is technically highly skilful. Perhaps more than any other poet of the First World War, he was able to show the reality and horror of war.

The Second Coming *W. B. Yeats (1865–1939)*

The Poem When Yeats wrote 'The Second Coming' the First World War had just ended, memories of the Easter Rising in Ireland were still vivid and revolution had broken out in Russia. The world appeared to be in a state of flux and chaos.

The 'Second Coming' refers to the idea that Jesus will return to Earth towards the end of time to bring justice and order. However, Yeats does not express a Christian interpretation of these final days. He believed in a complicated set of ideas to do with 'gyres', intersecting cone-shaped spirals representing various elemental historical and individual forces offering transitions into new worlds. The opening eight lines of the poem offer a complex vision of an apocalypse.

In the second section Yeats presents a disturbing image of a sphinx 'out of *Spiritus Mundi*', which, literally, means 'spirit of the world' but here refers to Yeats's belief that every mind is linked to a single vast intelligence. This glimpse of the new order after two thousand years of Christianity is not a comforting one; Yeats concludes by wondering about the nature of this 'rough beast' that 'Slouches towards Bethlehem to be born'.

The Poet W. B. Yeats was born in Dublin and was a major contributor to the literary revival in Ireland in the second half of the nineteenth century. He was deeply influenced by Irish mythology and was keen to resist the cultural influences of English dominance in Ireland.

In the 1890s his creative output became prolific, with several collections of poetry, plays dealing with Irish legends and mysticism and books about Irish folklore. In 1889 he met his muse, Maud Gonne, whose character and political activism deeply influenced him.

Yeats's work became more political in response to the events that led to the Easter Rising, which he commemorated in 'Easter 1916'. He entered political life when he was appointed to the Senate of the Irish Free State in 1922.

Yeats's later works continued to explore the relationship between art and life through symbol and powerful images. He was awarded the Nobel Prize for Literature in 1923.

'Tell me not here, it needs not saying' *A. E. Housman (1859–1936)*

The Poem This poem is one of forty-one Housman published in 1922 as *Last Poems*. His only other collection, the exceptionally successful *A Shropshire Lad*, had been published twenty-six years earlier. On learning of the imminent death of his great friend Moses Jackson, whom he had met at Oxford, Housman assembled the *Last Poems* so that Jackson could read them before he died. 'Tell me not here, it needs not saying' is written with a calm elegance and beautiful ease as Housman reflects upon nature. Revealingly, in the second line he refers to nature as the 'enchantress', a woman who may fascinate and charm but may also break a heart.

Consider the picture of nature Housman paints in the first three verses before he makes it clear that he does not see the working of a divine purpose in nature. This is not a pantheistic view. On the contrary, Housman sees nature as detached and indifferent to man. 'Heartless, witless nature' will be oblivious to those who walk among her forests and meadows.

The Poet A. E. Housman published only two collections of poetry during his lifetime. Even though his first book, *A Shropshire Lad*, sold extremely well, the poet committed himself to a life of classical scholarship. Educated at Oxford, he performed erratically in his final exams, before working in the Patent Office in London for several years. During this time he studied the great Greek and Roman poets so successfully that he was appointed Professor of Latin at University College, London. Later he fulfilled a similar role at Cambridge University, where he remained until his death.

He was regarded as a highly meticulous and exceptionally brilliant scholar, but he was a reserved and somewhat reclusive man. *A Shropshire Lad* gave a glimpse into an interior life he would normally have kept hidden. His poems deal with unrequited love, war, the natural world and the transience of youth and beauty, and are written in tones of nostalgia, resignation and regret.

Harlem Shadows *Claude McKay (1889–1948)*

The Poem McKay's neatly rhymed eighteen-line poem expresses his characteristic sympathy for people exploited, marginalized and condemned by society. In this instance he writes with great gentleness and pity about the plight of female prostitutes.

How does the poet inspire sympathy for these women? Look at how they are described as being like children. The adjective 'little' is repeated in each stanza. Repetition of the phrase 'street to street' at the end of each stanza conveys the idea that the women are trapped in this life. Notice how they also seem reluctant to do this degrading work; their footsteps are 'halting', their feet 'timid'. They are vulnerable, alone and 'weary, weary', an adjective that suggests physical tiredness but also tiredness with their lives. Most importantly, McKay states that the women have been forced into their degradation by social traumas, such as 'poverty'.

McKay employs synecdoche: the women's tired feet stand in for their exploitation. In turn, the women represent the whole 'fallen [black] race'. Finally, in its turn, the black race here represents all minorities exploited and degraded by a 'harsh world'.

The Poet Born in Jamaica, Claude McKay left home in 1912 and, at the age of twenty-one, arrived in America. In the USA he was shocked by the virulent racism and the bitter reality of segregation. In response, he wrote defiant protest poems and actively supported black working-class movements.

McKay travelled to Russia and England in the early 1920s, before publishing an award-winning novel, *Home to Harlem*, the first commercially successful novel by a black writer, and over time he became a strong influence on the Harlem Renaissance, a cultural and artistic movement in the 1920s and '30s that promoted black consciousness.

A journalist, novelist, short-story writer, political idealist, convert to Roman Catholicism as well as a poet, McKay dedicated his life to art, using his writing as a way of fighting against bigotry and the racist stereotyping of black people. In 2002 he was included on a list of a Hundred Great African-Americans.

Ha'nacker Mill *Hilaire Belloc (1870–1953)*

The Poem 'Ha'nacker Mill' was inspired by the fate of an actual mill that Belloc knew in Sussex. The working mill had been struck by lightning in 1905 and was badly damaged. By the time Belloc, a great lover of the Sussex Downs, came across it in the 1920s, it was derelict.

How does Belloc convey the state of the mill in the first verse? Notice how the first word of the poem, repeated at the start of the second line, is a woman's name, which serves to lend warmth and humanity to the picture of the ruined mill: 'Sally is gone that was so kindly'.

In lines eight to eleven Belloc repeats the word 'Spirits' several times, the word, which suggests emotion and character, also introducing the idea of the mill almost being haunted by a richer past. The neatly crafted three verses with their simple, robust rhymes offer a contrast in form with the now-dilapidated mill.

In the final stanza the poem states emphatically, 'England's done', and the use of 'never' drives home the picture of abandonment and desolation. Is Belloc mourning not just the destruction of a mill but the passing of a way of life?

The Poet Hilaire Belloc was an extremely versatile writer, who is best known for his original light verse for children. He was a passionate debater, becoming President of the Oxford Union in the 1890s, an accomplished historian and essayist and an MP representing Salford for four years. Much of his work is underpinned by his staunch and orthodox Catholic faith.

French-born, Belloc became a British citizen in 1902. He developed a great passion for the English countryside, especially Sussex, where he spent part of his childhood and settled in 1906.

His *Cautionary Tales for Children* remains popular, and contains titles such as 'Matilda: Who told Lies and was Burned to Death', 'Jim: Who ran away from his Nurse and was Eaten by a Lion' and 'Rebecca: Who slammed Doors for Fun and Perished Miserably'. The titles might give an indication that the tales appeal to adults as well as children.

'I, being born a woman and distressed'

Edna St Vincent Millay (1892–1950)

The Poem The sonnet form is traditionally employed to declare love for someone or something. Here, however, Edna St Vincent Millay uses the fourteen-line form to claim that her 'staggering brain' can at times be overcome by lust. The poem implicitly mocks the idea in Millay's contemporary society that women should be demure and fragile.

Consider the importance of the word 'born' in the title. Is Millay suggesting she can't help her actions because she is a woman (and is therefore deemed incapable of using reason to tame her senses), or is there irony here? What tone do you think is being employed in the first eight lines of the poem? Is it humorous or serious? Is the speaker close to or at a distance from the lover she dismisses?

Notice how the voice changes at the start of the last six lines of the poem. 'Think not for this, however' is assertive and uses the language of reasoned argument, establishing that, although her brain is 'staggering', her 'stout blood' will enable her to resist future temptation. Such stoutness is evident in her colloquial directness: 'let me make it plain'. How convinced are you by her claims?

The Poet Edna St Vincent Millay was an American poet who combined accomplishment in traditional forms with progressive attitudes. She also became known for her open bisexuality and her pacifism during the First World War. She was much admired as a reader of her poetry.

Millay's childhood was unconventional. After her parents' divorce, she travelled with her mother and sisters from town to town, living in poverty but always with a trunk of great literature. By the age of eight, Edna had had her first poem published.

Millay's poetry was bold and non-conformist in its time: her collection *A Few Figs from Thistles* met with some disapproval for its exploration of female sexuality. Millay also wrote verse dramas, including the pacifist play *Aria da Capo*. She nonetheless participated in the war effort during the Second World War by creating propaganda. Despite her receiving universal acclaim and many prestigious prizes, her reputation declined and has only more recently been reclaimed.

Journey of the Magi *T. S. Eliot (1888–1965)*

The Poem T. S. Eliot's dramatic monologue focuses upon the famous biblical story of the three kings from the East travelling to Bethlehem to pay homage to the baby Jesus. He imagines one of the kings giving an account of the journey.

Within the Christian tradition, the journey of the Magi is associated with celebration and wonder and gifts of gold, frankincense and myrrh. However, this seems like an arduous journey. What details in the first twenty lines suggest that the kings had 'a hard time' of it?

In lines twenty-one to thirty-one, they arrive at their destination. Given what we know of the life and death of Christ, what is the significance of some of the images in this section, such as 'the three trees on the low sky' and the hands 'dicing for pieces of silver'?

In the last twelve lines we learn that the kings were deeply affected and changed by their experience. The birth of Christ heralds the start of a new order and new truth, and yet the kings have to return to their kingdoms and to 'an alien people clutching their gods'.

The Poet T. S. Eliot was a poet, verse dramatist and literary critic who grew up in America and studied at Harvard, the Sorbonne and Oxford. He settled in England in 1914 and worked initially in teaching and banking. Later, he became a significant figure in the publishing firm Faber and Faber.

His first collection of poems, *Prufrock and Other Observations*, in 1917, was an immediate success and established him as a leading figure in the modernist movement, which sought to break with literary traditions in an era of technological advancements and global conflict.

In 1922 Eliot published *The Waste Land*, one of the most influential and important poems of the twentieth century. Stylistically complex and innovative, it uses myth and symbolism to express the crisis in postwar modern life and culture. Between the publication of *The Waste Land* and his death in 1965, Eliot was a consistently dominant figure in Western culture.

Welsh Incident *Robert Graves (1895–1985)*

The Poem Robert Graves once said that he wrote 'Welsh Incident' in a Welsh accent. Notice the use of Welsh place names and the lyrical rhythm of a poem which begins mid-conversation.

One of the speakers is describing the 'things' that came out of the sea-caves of Criccieth, while the other speaker we hear is clearly fascinated and anxious to hear more about these creatures. The urgent questions and demands for further information expressed by the listener contrast with the detailed but leisurely account given by the eyewitness to this remarkable incident. This is a person who knows he has an astonishing story to tell, and he is not going to be rushed.

In an interview, Graves said that 'Welsh Incident' was 'pleasant joking' and a 'satire'. What human characteristics do you think Graves is gently satirizing in this poem?

The poem does not build up to a dramatic revelation. The conclusion is in keeping with the comic tone of the poem. The listener is still firing off questions and the eyewitness is still in eloquent command of his story and will tell it in his own way: '"What did the mayor do"?'/'"I was coming to that."'

The Poet Robert Graves was born in 1895, one of ten children. His father was an academic and Irish poet who loved Celtic poetry and myth, and this influence can be seen in Graves's work.

Graves won a scholarship to study at Oxford in 1913 but, with the outbreak of the First World War, he enlisted, writing verse consistently throughout the conflict. By 1918 he had already published three volumes of poetry.

He married that year and then took up a fellowship at Oxford, while continuing to write and publish. His meeting in 1926 with the American poet Laura Riding was significant in terms of his personal life and the nature of his poetry. In 1929 he left England to live and write in Majorca.

Graves published a successful autobiography, *Goodbye to All That*, in 1929 and the historical novel *I, Claudius* in 1934, which became an internationally popular television series in the 1970s.

Bavarian Gentians *D. H. Lawrence (1885–1930)*

The Poem Gentians are deep-blue plants with trumpet-shaped flowers. Lawrence's poem seems to be prompted by careful scrutiny of them, but it quickly moves beyond imaginative description of a pretty flower into an exploration of themes of life and death, sex and identity.

The melancholy opening has a seductive, languorous atmosphere, and it becomes apparent that the gentians are needed by Lawrence as a 'torch' as he moves down the 'darker stairs'. Lawrence wrote 'Bavarian Gentians' towards the end of his life and there is a sense of journeying in the poem.

Look at the way Lawrence has set out the poem on the page and the effect of constant repetition of 'blue'/'blueness' and 'dark'/ 'darkness'. Life and death, light and darkness, are constantly explored.

Clearly, the poem is full of allusions to Greek mythology, and the story of Persephone is worth researching further. The sexual imagery in the second half of the poem is significant.

The Poet A miner's son from Nottingham, D. H. Lawrence was a prolific writer of short stories, essays, poems and novels before his death at the age of forty-four in 1930. He was a rebellious, restless and polemical figure who was viewed with suspicion by the establishment, especially after his marriage in 1914 to the German Frieda von Richthofen.

The earlier novels – *Sons and Lovers*, *The Rainbow* and *Women in Love* – see Lawrence exploring relationships with realism and intensity. Philosophically, his novels warn against the danger of overemphasizing the importance of the mind at the expense of the body. His belief in the importance of touch and intimacy is seen in some of the depictions of sex in the novels that made Lawrence a controversial figure in his lifetime. *Lady Chatterley's Lover* was attacked for its sexual content and was banned until 1960, when Penguin won the right to publish the book after a sensational trial.

'The force that through the green fuse drives the flower'

Dylan Thomas (1914–53)

The Poem Dylan Thomas's poem deals with the endless cycle of life and death in a series of immensely rich and vivid images that examine nature, mortality, love and what it means to be alive. There is a restless muscularity about much of the poem as soon as the sense of an unstoppable, powerful force is introduced in line one. It 'blasts' the roots of trees and is the speaker's 'destroyer'.

What connections does Thomas see between nature and man in the first two verses, and what is the impact of the repeated use of 'drives'? Note how the sense of regular, repeated processes in nature is reinforced by the use of repetition in the poem. The four main verses begin with 'The' and the final lines of verses two, three and four begin with 'How', while the fourth lines begin with 'And'. The third line in each verse is shortened.

What images of an explosive force and energy that can be destructive as well as creative do you see in the poem? What do you think is the significance of the 'crooked worm' in the final line?

The Poet Dylan Thomas was a Welsh poet born in Swansea who wrote only in English. His highly acclaimed first collection, *18 Poems*, appeared when he was just twenty, in 1934. In an age of stripped-down modernism, his passionate, vivid, lyrical work made a significant impression in literary circles in Wales and England. Subsequent collections contained poems that remain extremely well known today, such as 'Fern Hill', 'And Death Shall Have No Dominion' and 'Do Not Go Gentle into That Good Night'.

In 1937 Thomas married Caitlin Macnamara and began a relationship that was consistently tempestuous and marked by passion, drunkenness and infidelities until Thomas's death in 1953, when he was on a performance tour of America. As an unpredictable but mesmerizing performer of his own work, Thomas made many broadcasts for the radio, and one of his most famous works is the radio play *Under Milk Wood*.

Poetry *Marianne Moore (1887–1972)*

The Poem This teasing, playful poem, with its epigrams and refusal to conform to any conventional view of what poetry should be, starts with a disarming, 'I, too, dislike it'. Is it poetry, or some aspect of poetry, that she dislikes? Is it the reader or someone else who is included by the word 'too'?

The question demanded of and by this poem is 'What is poetry?' Is Moore offering us a solution, or leading us into further confusion? The poem offers no glib, satisfying answers but instead encourages further questioning and debate. It explores obscurity in poetry and considers through examples taken from various walks of life how we tend to 'not admire what/we cannot understand'. The poem does not offer an elitist view of poetry – '"business documents and school-books"' must not be discriminated against – but at the beginning and end of the poem Moore stresses the value of that which is 'genuine'. She encourages poets to be '"literalists of the imagination"', a phrase she borrowed from Yeats, and to create '"imaginary gardens with real toads in them"'.

Moore reworked this poem several times and, by 1935, it had been reduced to three lines.

The Poet Born in Missouri and educated at Bryn Mawr College in Pennsylvania, Marianne Moore began to publish her poetry when she was twenty-eight years old. She joined company with William Carlos Williams, T. S. Eliot, Ezra Pound and others in her attempts to break with tradition and discover new ways to write poetry. She contributed to and eventually became editor of the prestigious literary magazine *Dial*.

She won many awards for her work, including the Pulitzer Prize, the Helen Haire Levinson Prize and the National Book Award. In New York she became something of a celebrity figure, well known for her quirky tricorn hat and cape. An avid fan of baseball and athletics, Moore was invited to throw the ceremonial first pitch for the 1968 season at the Yankee Stadium.

Her poetry is characterized by acute observations and her preoccupation with relationships between the common and uncommon. Her style is often humorous and clever.

Still-Life *Elizabeth Daryush (1887–1977)*

The Poem Elizabeth Daryush's sonnet presents in its opening eight lines a seductive picture of wealth and luxury through a description of a breakfast table immaculately laid out for one person. Roses and polished wood, fine porcelain and an abundance of fresh fruit, butter cooled by ice and a silver coffee pot are all bathed by a warm sun. How does Daryush's choice of words appeal to the senses when you read these opening lines?

In the next four lines the poem reveals that this exquisitely presented breakfast is to be enjoyed by the 'young heiress' who is returning from her early-morning walk. What insight into her beliefs and aspirations is given in lines eleven and twelve?

The final couplet is intriguing. Line eight refers to the morning's post heaped on a salver and the final image of the poem compares the 'unopened future' to a love letter full of 'sweet surprise'. Is the use of 'lies' deliberately hinting that what the future holds for this wealthy and privileged young woman may not be as serene as she might hope?

The Poet Elizabeth Daryush was the daughter of the Poet Laureate Robert Bridges and initially published her first two collections in the 1920s under the name Elizabeth Bridges. She married Ali Akbar Daryush in her mid-thirties and lived for several years in what was then Persia.

Her early work was fairly conventional and appeared to be more influenced by nineteenth-century models than by the modernism of the 1920s. Her diction is sometimes described as strangely archaic, and this has perhaps contributed to her being one of the more unfairly neglected poets of the twentieth century. Her poetry is often full of feeling and melancholy and is concerned with nature, love and mortality and the response of the individual to the world and its pleasures and challenges.

Her work was often overlooked in her lifetime, but her *Selected Poems* and *Collected Poems* were published in the 1970s, shortly before her death.

Partridges *John Masefield (1878–1967)*

The Poem Masefield's skilfully rhymed sonnet is a closely observed picture of a partridge shoot. A 'covey' is a small flock of partridges and the 'nosing pointers' are the gundogs that help the hunters locate and flush out the well-camouflaged, ground-nesting birds.

The hunting action is condensed by Masefield into one succinct line at the end of the first verse, which describes the flapping of the wings of the partridges and the flash of the shotguns. The second verse, with its confident use of alliteration and assonance, neatly captures the immediate aftermath of the volley of shots. Dogs are praised, while some of the birds are dead – 'shot clean' – and some wounded. Masefield contrasts the plight of the shot birds carried home in a sack full of rabbits and pigeons with a time before the hunt when the covey would have enjoyed 'strong or gliding flight'. As darkness falls, described in the evocative line 'when the planet lamps the coming night', the poem leaves us with a glimpse of the 'survivors' and a haunting image of the 'darkness' hearing them call.

The Poet John Masefield was Poet Laureate from 1930 to 1967. He was a versatile poet, novelist and journalist, and wrote and lectured for the government during the First World War after supporting the war effort as a hospital orderly in France.

Masefield went to sea at a young age but saw no future as a sailor and on one voyage to America deserted ship in New York. He read insatiably, and his poems began to be published in periodicals, followed by a first collection of poetry when he was twenty-four. Novels followed, and narrative poems, so that by 1912, when he was awarded a major literary prize, Masefield was a successful and well-known writer.

Nearly a hundred years before Poetry By Heart, Masefield organized the Oxford Recitations in the 1920s, an annual contest designed to 'discover good speakers of verse' and to 'encourage the beautiful speaking of verse'.

The Arrest of Oscar Wilde at the Cadogan Hotel

John Betjeman (1906–84)

The Poem Betjeman imagines the moment when the dramatist, writer and flamboyant wit Oscar Wilde is arrested by police on 6 April 1895. Wilde was charged with gross indecency and, at a time when homosexuality was illegal, he was sentenced to two years' hard labour. The prison regime was brutal and, although he was released in 1897, he died three years later in exile in France.

Notice the way the poem presents three voices and how significant rhythm and rhyme are within it. The relatively emotionless voice of the narrator describes the scene inside the Cadogan Hotel, where Wilde is waiting with his friend Robbie Ross for the inevitable arrival of the police. The second voice we hear is Wilde's. How does Betjeman depict the writer at a moment of crisis? Finally, Betjeman introduces the policemen, giving them language that emphasizes the gulf between the sophisticated and effete writer and the working-class police. Why do you think there is an almost pantomime quality to the way the police speak?

The Poet By the time of his death in 1984, John Betjeman was a 'national treasure'. His poetry was popular and accessible, and he was known not only as the Poet Laureate (between 1972 and 1984) but also as a distinctive and entertaining television and radio presenter. His poems are often gently funny and nostalgic and, in a period when many poets were experimenting with form and style, his work explored more traditional poetic forms.

A consummate performer of his own work, he recorded four albums, including *Banana Blush*, in which he reads his poems over a backing of jazz music. His *Collected Poems* reveal his accomplished technical ability and his compassionate, whimsical approach to satire. In *Summoned by Bells*, his blank-verse autobiography, he looks back on his life from his middle-class childhood in Edwardian London through to his time at Oxford University.

Bagpipe Music *Louis MacNeice (1907–63)*

The Poem Louis MacNeice wrote this poem at the end of the 1930s on a visit to the Western Isles of Scotland. The exuberantly rhymed poem careers across the page at breakneck speed, never dwelling too long on any one image or character.

Think of the associations that attach themselves to the image of Scottish bagpipes. How does the sound of the lines attempt to suggest the bagpipe music of the title?

Beneath the exuberant wordplay, lilting rhythm and accounts of bizarre and comical human behaviour, MacNeice touches upon what he sees as the cultural decline of the Highlands and Islands in the 1930s. John MacDonald, Annie MacDougall and Willie Murray, with their traditional Scottish names, appear to be characters caught up in an almost surreal world but, beneath a comical, nonsensical surface, is MacNeice hinting at a clash between a dying folk culture and a new, commercially focused urban culture? As the poem gallops along at great pace, he seems to take a genial but slightly world-weary swipe at a huge range of issues. Bureaucracy, tourism, fake spirituality and politics are all caught up in the repeated refrain of 'It's no go'.

The Poet Louis MacNeice is often associated with a group of highly influential poets such as W. H. Auden and Stephen Spender, who emerged as innovative and significant writers in the 1930s.

MacNeice was born in Belfast, studied at Oxford and lectured in classics in Birmingham and London. He spent a good part of his career working as a producer and writer for the BBC. Some of his best plays were originally written for radio.

His *Poems* of 1935 established him as an important new writer. MacNeice went on to produce translations, prose works and even an eccentric kind of travel book chronicling a trip to Iceland with W. H. Auden, *Letters from Iceland*; but he is best remembered for his meticulously crafted poems such as 'Snow', 'Sunlight on the Garden' and 'Bagpipe Music'.

Musée des Beaux Arts *W. H. Auden (1907–73)*

The Poem Auden's poem was inspired by the poet looking at paintings in a museum gallery by the Old Masters (the great artists of the Renaissance who depicted scenes, for example, from Christ's life and early Christendom). In the first thirteen lines, consider what is happening in the paintings he is viewing. What is going on around the 'miraculous birth' and the 'dreadful martyrdom'?

Auden is particularly struck by Breughel's *The Fall of Icarus*. The painting captures the moment when, having flown too close to the sun on wings held together by wax, Icarus plunges into the sea. We might think that this disaster would be the focal point of the painting, but it clearly isn't. What view of life and death is conveyed as we see the painting through Auden's eyes?

The tone of the poem appears almost nonchalant in places. How does this fit with the themes in the poem? (You can see the painting online if you search for *The Fall of Icarus*.)

The Poet Many people will know W. H. Auden's poem 'Funeral Blues', because it featured in the successful film *Four Weddings and a Funeral*. This popularity makes it seem exceptional, but in fact it is characteristic of much of Auden's work, which combines a high level of technical skill with wit, compassion and grace.

Auden was the leading figure in the second generation of modernist poets writing after Eliot, who produced poetry that was often ironic but not unfeeling; full of allusions and concerned with the purpose of literature in a world that seemed to be disintegrating.

In 1939 Auden moved to America and he continued to exert a major influence on poets on both sides of the Atlantic.

Aubade *William Empson (1906–84)*

The Poem 'Aubade' is traditionally a dawn song where the lover laments the fact that dawn will separate him and his lover and bring an end to their night of passion. Empson's poem was written in Tokyo in 1933 and captures the moment when he and his Japanese lover were woken by an earthquake. The opening line describes their initial experience of the quake in plain, almost matter-of-fact terms: 'Hours before dawn we were woken by the quake.'

Biographies of Empson suggest that his lover was employed as a nanny and, in the poem, she feels the need to return to the house where she works in order to comfort the child she is looking after. Is the earthquake perhaps a symbol of the coming war between Britain and Japan, a war that would make a relationship with a Japanese woman difficult?

The poem repays multiple readings so that the richness of the symbolism and ambiguity can be felt, if not always securely understood. References to sexual desire run through the poem, while the connections and tensions between two languages and two cultures at a time of crisis are explored.

The Poet William Empson was a remarkably influential critic and a writer of poems that are often strikingly unsentimental and demonstrate an air of rational objectivity. He taught in China and Japan and worked for the BBC before becoming Professor of English Literature at Sheffield University. Empson was idiosyncratic, and a fierce opponent of Christianity, and his poetry and criticism display a consistent intellectual precision.

The school of literary criticism known as 'New Criticism' was strengthened by Empson's persuasive work *Seven Types of Ambiguity*, one of the most important texts in the field of literary criticism, which explains how meaning is carried in poetic language. Empson began formulating the ideas in *Seven Types of Ambiguity* while still at Cambridge, where he switched from studying Maths to English. His college expelled him in the 1920s for allegedly having condoms in his room but, fifty years later, awarded him an honorary fellowship in the year that also saw him knighted.

Goodbye *Alun Lewis (1915–44)*

The Poem This poem describes a familiar scene from novels and films: a lover going off to war and saying goodbye to his beloved, with both characters aware that these could be their last moments together. The first half of the poem presents an intimate domestic interior, drawing us into this private space, particularly through the use of small, normally insignificant details, such as the fixing of 'labels', putting a 'final shilling in the gas', the quiet sounds of 'rustling' and the woman undressing.

In this first half everything is understated. We are not told what the two characters are feeling. Emotion is made more powerful for being held in check. Look, for instance, at the line, 'make an end of lying down together'.

The closeness of the lovers and their tenderness combine with the quiet modulation of the verse. Subtle hints at separation and fear about the future gather in the poem. The overall effect is of a great elegiac groundswell that builds as the poem progresses. Notice how in the second half of the poem, starting with the religious word 'Eternity', the verse moves outwards towards the universal, before we are returned back once more into the poignantly specific.

The Poet Regarded as a major poet of the Second World War, Alun Lewis grew up in the coalmining villages of South Wales but wrote only in English. After winning a scholarship to grammar school, Lewis went on to gain a first-class degree in history at the University of Aberystwyth and worked at various times as a journalist and teacher. He was also a writer of short stories.

Although he was a socialist and sympathetic to pacifism, Lewis joined the British Army after the outbreak of the Second World War. He served with the Royal Engineers and died of a gunshot wound to the head in Burma in 1944, which may have been suicide or the result of a tragic accident. Many of his best-known poems concern his experience of the war.

Naming of Parts *Henry Reed (1914–86)*

The Poem 'Naming of Parts' forms Part I of a six-poem collection called *Lessons of the War*, each a parody of British Army training during the Second World War. There are two juxtaposing voices in this poem, the first being that of a training instructor delivering a lecture on the parts of a rifle. The second voice, which comes in halfway through the fourth line of each stanza, is more lyrical and seems to be that of the recruit, daydreaming about a beloved garden.

The lecturer's language is direct, literally the 'naming of parts' of the rifle. Noticeably, parts of the rifle which the soldiers 'have not got' are also named, such as 'the piling swivel'. The British Army at the time was under-equipped and the poem emphasizes how poorly prepared the men were for war. They, like the blossoms, are 'fragile' and, like the bees, 'fumbling'.

The contrast between the instructor and the images of nature is profound. The 'naming of parts' at this stage refers to the gun. Is there an implication it will later refer to bodies?

The Poet Henry Reed studied language and literature at Birmingham University, where he associated with W. H. Auden, Louis MacNeice and Walter Allen. He worked as a teacher and journalist until 1941 and served as a translator during the Second World War.

Lessons of the War is Reed's most well-known poem and also one of the most distinctive poems of the war. He mimics the speech of army instructors, precisely echoing the vocal rhythms and including military jargon. The contrast between this seemingly prosaic language and the lyrical, meditative voice that also appears in the poem leads to a poignant exploration of the individual's experience. Reed's *Collected Poems* was published posthumously in 1991.

As well as poetry, Reed produced a number of verse dramas and witty radio plays, including a dramatization of *Moby-Dick*. He also worked on a biography of Hardy for many years, though, eventually, he abandoned this project.

My Papa's Waltz *Theodore Roethke (1908–63)*

The Poem Written in a rhythm that imitates the movement of a waltz, Roethke's poem recalls a moment from his childhood when he dances with his father in the kitchen of their home. Note the use of 'My' in the title. The word is not essential to the meaning of the title, but does it suggest a tender possessiveness in how he recollects his father?

Roethke's father died when his son was only fourteen and the impact of that loss perhaps explains the presence of a powerful simile in line three, when the poet talks about hanging on 'like death' as they playfully and clumsily dance.

The sober mother's disapproval can be sensed in line eight. Her face cannot 'unfrown' itself as the horseplay continues. The details Roethke remembers seem to try to capture the physical presence of his father and the physical connection between them – the hand gripping his wrist; the buckle of his father's belt scraping his ear; and the sensation of his father beating time to the waltz on his head.

Does the use of 'clinging' in the final line suggest that, in adulthood, the speaker does not want to let go of this memory?

The Poet Theodore Roethke was born in Michigan and spent a good deal of his childhood in the extensive commercial greenhouses owned by his father and uncle. Roethke's work displays a fascination with the natural world and, clearly, the environment of his early years influenced his writing. The death of his father when he was fourteen also had a profound impact upon Roethke's work.

Roethke had a number of teaching and lecturing positions in the 1930s and '40s, in spite of suffering from a recurrent manic depressive illness. He published his first collection, *Open House*, in 1941 when he was teaching at Pennsylvania State University. W. H. Auden called it 'completely successful'.

The Lost Son and Other Poems followed seven years later and contains his 'Greenhouse' poems, which revisit his childhood experiences. *The Waking: Poems 1933–1953*, published in 1953, won the Pulitzer Prize for Poetry, while *Words for the Wind* won many prizes in 1957.

How to Kill *Keith Douglas (1920–44)*

The Poem Douglas wrote 'How to Kill' during the Second World War. He had left Oxford and enlisted at the outbreak of war.

Although the title seems to suggest an instruction will follow, the poem reflects in a deliberately impersonal way on the act of killing. In the opening verse the movement from childhood to adulthood is mentioned. Where once the object in his hand was a harmless ball for throwing, he now grips perhaps a grenade or gun, something '*designed to kill*'.

In the second verse and the run-on line into the beginning of the third verse, how does Douglas describe the moment of fixing an enemy soldier in his gunsight? What is the impact of the reference to 'mother' in this section of the poem?

In verse three, why might the narrator speak of himself as 'damned'? Consider the contrast in this verse between 'flesh' and 'dust' and the impact this war and moments of death have upon 'love'.

In the final verse, how does Douglas use thoughts of the mosquito to describe death in the context of a war that inevitably dehumanizes combatants?

The Poet Keith Douglas was twenty-four when he died in the D-Day invasion of Normandy in 1944. A student at Oxford when war broke out, he had already established a reputation as an immensely promising poet. One of his Oxford poems, 'Canoe', contrasts the pleasure of punting on the river with the approaching 'thunder' of war.

Douglas enlisted immediately in 1939 and, after training, was stationed in North Africa. He wrote some of his poems and a memoir of the desert campaign while recovering from injuries sustained in the advance on Tripoli in 1943. He had been an intrepid soldier, at one point abandoning relatively safe duties at his regimental headquarters in order to join troops at the Front.

Douglas's war poetry was not overtly emotional but, as he said in a letter to a friend, his focus on external observations and impressions was an attempt to 'write true things, significant things'.

Heart and Mind *Edith Sitwell (1887–1964)*

The Poem This is a poem that explores erotic love and mortality through allegorical figures. Sitwell writes of the Sun and the Moon, the Lion and Lioness, and the Skeleton.

Look at the initial conversation between the Lion and the Lioness in the first stanza. How does Sitwell use language to present a picture of youthful vitality, strength and energy? We are plunged immediately into the Lion's address to the Lioness, who is asked to think of a time when she is 'amber dust'. Note the frequent use of 'amber' and 'gold' in the poem. What is the effect of the contrasting image at the end of line seven?

In the third stanza, the Skeleton speaks of being consumed by the 'flames of the heart'. He compares his former self to Hercules and Samson, heroic figures from Greek myth and the Bible, who were immensely strong and both slayers of lions but unable to defeat time.

In his words to the Moon, the Sun also speaks of death, decay and a 'hopeless love', and the impossibility of the heart and mind being one. Notice the evocative use of colour throughout the poem.

The Poet Born in 1887, Edith Sitwell endured an unhappy childhood in Renishaw Hall, near Sheffield, with affluent but neglectful parents. She managed to escape to London with the help of her governess and, from 1914, the two women lived in a small flat in London, where Sitwell would preside over gatherings of artists and writers.

After publishing her first book of poems and editing an important poetry magazine, *Wheels*, she was seen in the 1920s as an important and influential poet. Her work was often ambitious and experimental, employing allegory and symbolism, and she cultivated a personal image that was often described as 'eccentric'. She preferred to say that she was simply 'more alive' than other people.

Sitwell is probably best remembered for *Façade*, a series of poems recited over music, and for the dramatic and immensely powerful poem written about the Blitz in London, 'Still Falls the Rain'.

The Fish *Elizabeth Bishop (1911–79)*

The Poem 'The Fish' has a deceptive ease of utterance, an exactness of observation and an almost hypnotic emotional steadiness in the way it tells its story.

On one level, the poem simply describes in vivid detail the catching and letting go of an old fish that has defeated and escaped from at least five anglers in the past. However, on another level, as the poem encourages us to look over the side of a boat at a fish and the water around it, we are perhaps simultaneously peering into other structures, relating to the mysterious forces in language and the creative process. What does Bishop catch along with the fish? Is it poetry itself? Is it this poem? Notice how, in a self-deprecating touch, the boat is characterized by its rustiness.

The poem develops a sense of poise, of balance, a feeling of rightness, even though there is a sense of danger and suffering within its lines. We are gradually brought towards the moment when 'everything was rainbow, rainbow, rainbow' and the beautiful simplicity of the ending when the narrator decides to let the fish go.

The Poet Recipient of many awards for her work, including the Pulitzer Prize for Poetry, Elizabeth Bishop was a close friend of the poets Marianne Moore and Robert Lowell. After being brought up by her grandparents, Bishop travelled extensively, financing her journeys with an inheritance. She became particularly interested in the languages and literature of Latin America, and lived for fifteen years in Brazil. Later in life, she combined writing with teaching in higher education institutions, including Harvard.

While poets around her practised 'confessional' poetry, Bishop always remained reticent and controlled in her verse. Her poetry encourages us to 'focus not on but with her'. Her style is characterized by her precise, meticulous descriptions of the physical world. Peculiarly lucid, her poems explore dislocation and the struggle to find a place to belong in the world. Indeed, Bishop described herself to a close friend as the 'loneliest person who ever lived'.

Mr Bleaney *Philip Larkin (1922–85)*

The Poem In the final stanza Philip Larkin talks about the extent to which 'how we live measures our own nature'. In the mid-1950s the speaker of the poem is renting a room previously occupied by a Mr Bleaney and, as he glances around the room and talks with his landlady, a picture of Mr Bleaney and the dingy room emerges. What do we learn about the former tenant and the way he lived his life from the first five stanzas? How does the landlady view Mr Bleaney?

The sudden statement 'I'll take it' in the third stanza might surprise us, given the description of the room, but the narrator is clearly increasingly identifying with Mr Bleaney and his lonely, predictable life. Does the form and structure of the poem reinforce the sense of a monotonous life in the poem?

Notice how the pace of the poem increases in the penultimate stanza with the use of enjambment, as it moves towards a more urgent conclusion as the narrator confronts the reality of his situation. Even so, the final words of the poem are tentative and hesitant, and return to the weariness of tone seen earlier in the poem: 'I don't know'.

The Poet Philip Larkin's four main volumes of poetry cover only about a hundred pages and were produced over forty years, but he is still regarded as one of the finest poets of postwar Britain. He was a technically accomplished poet and valued clarity and precision in his work. He could write with strict metres and polished rhymes and yet still incorporate the sounds and voices of modern life. He was an astute observer of people and places, situations and events.

Larkin was a shy, undemonstrative man who spent most of his working life as the librarian at the University of Hull. He did not travel widely, or tour or perform. His poems are not full of linguistic fireworks, and some may see in them a kind of unsettling, melancholy pessimism. However, they are beautifully crafted and accessible and unfailingly honest in the way they look at modern life.

A Supermarket in California *Allen Ginsberg (1926–97)*

The Poem Ginsberg's poem is partly an homage to Walt Whitman, one of his literary heroes, and partly a critique of the growth of consumerism and industrialization. These two aspects are linked, as Whitman was concerned with the danger posed to nature and a 'natural' way of living by an increasingly industrialized society.

Why does Ginsberg refer to the 'neon fruit' in the supermarket, and why might he be astonished by 'Whole families shopping at night'? In this odd fantasy of Ginsberg's, another hero of free thinking, left-wing Spanish poet and playwright Garcia Lorca, suddenly appears as well.

The start of the second section touches upon Whitman's alleged homosexuality as Ginsberg imagines following the dead poet down the aisles. As they walk, 'tasting' and 'possessing', what picture of the supermarket and its contents is presented?

The final section talks of a 'lost America' and compares the nation to Hades, where Charon would ferry souls on the River Styx to their destiny. What ideas does the poem leave the reader with in the last line, with the reference to the River Lethe in Hades, which, according to Greek myth, would cause complete forgetfulness?

The Poet Allen Ginsberg was a leading figure within the Beat Generation, a group of artists and writers in the 1950s who reacted against the consumer culture of post-war American society and the prudery of an older generation. The writer of *On the Road*, Jack Kerouac, coined the phrase the 'Beats', and he and Ginsberg are often regarded as the unofficial co-founders of the Beat Generation.

The opening line of Ginsberg's controversial poem *Howl* is often quoted as an example of its tone and content: 'I saw the best minds of my generation destroyed by madness, starving hysterical naked'.

Like many of the Beat poets, Ginsberg experimented with hallucinogenic drugs and, in the 1960s, he represented a bridge between the Beat movement of the 1950s and hippie culture. He was still performing just months before his death at the age of seventy.

After Midsummer *E. J. Scovell (1907–99)*

The Poem Consider the significance of the word 'After' in the title. Midsummer is associated with a celebration of love and fertility and the warming, nourishing power of the sun, but this poem begins at a point after midsummer, when the sun will go into a gradual decline and nights will grow longer. There is a sense of maturity and abundance in the first verse, with references to the harvest and fruit, but the poem quickly moves on to consideration of what it feels like to be alive and born into the world. The sense of time passing is captured, however, in verse five, when thoughts turn to 'death'.

The penultimate verse draws attention to the richness of nature and the super-abundance of summer flowers just after the midsummer point, prompting the poet to reflect in the final verse that 'We must know death better'. Does this suggest that a turning point in the year, and perhaps in a life, has been reached and that death must be the inevitable destination? However, notice that, as 'we stand upon/The rounded summit', very little has changed in nature all around that summit. The slope and the sky have mutated, but only softly, and the distant dales have 'come up'.

The Poet E. J. Scovell's work did not easily align itself with any particular movement in twentieth-century poetry, and she was never a 'fashionable' or a political poet. A contemporary of Auden, she did not publish her first collection until 1944, when she was thirty-seven years old. She produced just four more original collections of verse over a period of a further forty-two years, but her later collections show no decline in her powers as an observant, sensitive, lyrical poet with a love of rhythm and rhyme. In addition to writing her own poetry, she produced some much-admired translations of poems by the Italian poet Pascoli.

Scovell was born in Sheffield and educated at Somerville College, Oxford. After marrying an ecologist, she spent some time supporting her husband's research in the West Indies and the South and Central American rainforests. She died in Oxford in 1999 at the age of ninety-two.

Wind *Ted Hughes (1930–98)*

The Poem In 'Wind' Hughes explores the power of nature and the vulnerability and insignificance of humankind through his depiction of a storm that seems to move 'the roots of the house'. The images of a house 'far out at sea', hills straining in the wind and in danger of escaping their tethered place, and 'Winds stampeding' have the quality of nightmare about them. This is a nature poem, but not one that aspires to traditional pastoral conventions.

Hughes makes the storm vividly alive and immediate to us. We hear 'crashing' woods and 'booming' hills. We feel the speaker's eyeballs 'dented' by its force when he goes outside. The wind is violent, ruthless and reckless in its destruction: look at the disturbing image of its 'Blade-light' in the second stanza and of the 'gull bent like an iron bar' in the fourth. The house has so far stood up to the onslaught, but it is a finely balanced and fragile situation, a 'fine green goblet' which could be shattered at any moment by the wind's pitch.

The speaker is paralysed by the wind: he and his companion 'cannot entertain book, /thought, Or each other'. What sense do you make of being 'left' in this scene?

The Poet A former Poet Laureate, Ted Hughes was one of the most influential English poets of the twentieth century. While at Cambridge University he met and later married the American scholar and poet Sylvia Plath. For many years after Plath's suicide Hughes remained virtually silent about her, despite accusations that he had contributed to his wife's tragic death. Shortly before he died Hughes surprised the literary world by publishing *Birthday Letters*, a collection of poems about his relationship with Plath.

Earlier in his career Hughes wrote nature poetry, but his poems about his native Yorkshire landscape and its animals were very different from the pastoral conventions of English poetry; charged with the intensity of the mythic, his work was rawer, darker and more violent. Drawing on Anglo-Saxon, the language Hughes used often has a rough-hewn physicality that gives his verse a monumental quality.

To the Snake *Denise Levertov (1923–97)*

The Poem On one level, 'To the Snake' vividly describes a 'Green Snake'. Note the use of sibilance (repetition of 's' sounds) to create a powerful description of the hiss of the snake in the poem. Levertov uses words like 'pulsing', 'scales', 'swore', 'smiling' and 'grass'.

The poem seems to work on a series of contrasts and a sense of attraction and repulsion. The snake is not draped around the neck but 'hung'. The tender word 'stroked' is used to describe touching the throat of the snake, which is 'cold', suggesting a lack of emotion and life, but the snake is also 'pulsing', which clearly gives the idea of warmth and life. She assures her friends that the snake is harmless, but even she is not convinced that she will not be harmed. She moves into a dark morning 'smiling' but also 'haunted'.

Consider the use of symbolism in the poem. The American dollar is sometimes called a 'greenback'. Might this be a poem about the seductive power and danger of gambling? What else might be associated with 'green'? Shakespeare wrote about jealousy as a 'green-eyed monster'. The snake, of course, is strongly associated with the temptation in the Garden of Eden.

The Poet Denise Levertov was born and educated at home in England. She was determined to be a writer from an early age, and her first book, *The Double Image*, was published when she was only twenty-three.

She worked as a civilian nurse during the Second World War and married an American shortly after the end of the war, before moving permanently to America. Her early work was relatively formal and in the tradition of Neo-Romanticism popular in the 1940s.

From the 1960s onwards Levertov became more politically active, and this is reflected in her work. She responded in her poetry to the Vietnam War and explored issues such as feminism, religion and the role of the individual within society.

She worked for much of the last part of her life in American universities and published over twenty collections of poetry, translations and criticism before her death in 1997.

Skunk Hour *Robert Lowell (1917–77)*

The Poem 'Skunk Hour' is taken from Robert Lowell's extremely influential collection *Life Studies*, published in 1959.

Consider the shifting tone of the poem. It begins with a detached description of the 'hermit/heiress' and her actions in the first two verses, but at the start of the third verse Lowell states that the 'season's ill'. This sombre line is reinforced by the description of the futility of the decorator's actions.

Notice the movement towards more personal and even confessional writing in verse five, which begins with an echo of the line written by another poet/mystic, St John of the Cross, 'One dark night', dealing with troubling, spiritual struggle.

The move towards the expression of a state of lonely, bleak despair is seen in verse six, and yet in verse seven the speaker corrects his statement that 'nobody's here' when he notices the skunks and describes the action of one skunk in visually arresting images.

Is there a connection between the isolated poet's condition and the traditionally shunned skunk? In a poem that deals with the pain of living, is there a sense of hope in the final line that states the skunk 'will not scare'?

The Poet Robert Lowell is often associated with the 'confessional' poets of the 1950s and '60s, whose work was sometimes unflinchingly self-revelatory, but Lowell's poetry underwent many changes and developments between the 1940s and his death in 1977.

Born into a prosperous family in Boston, he dropped out of Harvard but went on to graduate in classics from Kenyon College in Ohio. He served some time in prison as a conscientious objector in the Second World War and remained politically active throughout his life.

He published *Lord Weary's Castle* in 1946, and its rich and sometimes violent imagery and rigorously controlled use of form saw the collection win the Pulitzer Prize for Poetry. Lowell suffered from mental ill health for many years and, after the deaths of his father and mother in the 1950s, his work became more intimate and 'confessional', employing looser forms and rhythms.

Epic *Patrick Kavanagh (1904–67)*

The Poem Although the 'epic' of the title might conventionally imply a long poem of heroic couplets and subject matter, this poem takes the short fourteen-line form of a sonnet. This, too, appears to be inverted: where we might expect a poem on the theme of love, Kavanagh offers a local dispute over land, 'half a rood of rock'; the colloquial voices of the 'Duffys shouting "Damn your soul!"' and the response from 'old McCabe'. Instead of a more conventional rhyme scheme, Kavanagh uses half-rhymes.

We might start to think about these inversions and variations in the light of the poem's ending, in which Homer's ghost appears to the poet and whispers that his epic poem *Iliad* was made from just such local disputes and details. How convinced do you think the poet is in the final line? His subject might, similarly, be local lives and people's domestic conflicts, but does his choice of the sonnet form suggest a very different stance to it? Does the looser application of the sonnet's conventions suggest that, although some things are similar, others are not the same in an Ireland where a world war can be dismissed as 'the Munich bother'?

The Poet Born in County Monaghan in Ireland in 1904, Patrick Kavanagh is known for poems that deal with the hardships of rural Irish life in an uncompromising way. Kavanagh was well placed to write such poetry: he grew up in a poor farming community and left school at the age of thirteen to work on his father's smallholding. His long poem *The Great Hunger* depicted the desperately gruelling existence of one peasant during the Famine.

Kavanagh struggled with the literary establishment in Dublin, where he eventually moved to pursue his literary ambitions. He was disillusioned by the values of this society and felt patronized as a 'peasant poet' rather than treated as a major poet. He is now among the most popular poets in Ireland: in 2000, ten of his poems were in the top fifty favourite Irish poems in the *Irish Times*, second only to the great Irish poet W. B. Yeats.

Considering the Snail *Thom Gunn (1929–2004)*

The Poem Thinking of a snail, what comes into your mind? An enemy of plants and vegetables? Something comical, repulsive or edible?

The closely observed snail in the first verse of this poem is seen deep within nature. Gunn writes of 'grass', 'water', 'rain' and 'a wood', but the snail's journey is anything but easy. He 'pushes' through the night, and the grass is heavy with rain, making progress even slower than usual. Does Gunn's choice of a strictly observed seven-syllable line with its odd line breaks and enjambment give a sense of the snail's difficult but deliberate journey?

It is, of course, very tempting to see the poem in metaphorical terms. Is the snail's journey applicable to the way a person might choose to approach life? Patient, persevering and focused, does the snail offer an example of an inherent passion to succeed? Is the journey every bit as important as the destination?

The Poet Born in Kent, Thom Gunn moved to America in 1958 after National Service and a degree at Cambridge, and settled in San Francisco for the rest of his life.

His first two collections of poetry were seen as impressive and unsettling works of exceptional promise that looked at rebellion and violence in verse that was formal and controlled. His poetry shows a willingness to write in both highly metrical and free verse.

Gunn taught in America for a while but then devoted himself to writing full time. America in the late 1960s and '70s allowed him to publicly acknowledge his homosexuality, and the work of his middle period reflects his experimentation with drugs and involvement with aspects of a hippie counterculture. However, as the AIDS epidemic began to kill many of his friends in the 1980s, he produced poems that were full of heartbreaking loss and sadness.

Morning Song *Sylvia Plath (1932–63)*

The Poem Consider the opening line and the striking image that compares the newborn baby to a 'fat gold watch'. The three words vividly but unsentimentally suggest shape and preciousness, while the implied ticking of a watch is associated with the heartbeat of the baby and reinforced by the monosyllabic nature of eight of the ten syllables of the opening line. The title of the poem implies hope and celebration, but we quickly see and hear words of detachment and exhaustion. Notice how we never learn anything about the baby or its gender. What do you make of the tone of the poem?

After the rather impersonal comparison with a watch, the baby is described as a 'New statue' and its mouth as 'clean as a cat's'. Any thought that the reference to the baby's 'moth-breath' might lead to a consideration of its vulnerability is banished when Plath responds to the baby's cry by stumbling from her bed, 'cow-heavy'.

How do you respond to the final stanza and the description of the crying of the baby when 'The clear vowels rise like balloons'?

The Poet Born in America, Sylvia Plath was an exceptionally talented student who studied at Cambridge on a Fulbright Scholarship. While in England she met and married the poet Ted Hughes, and they had two children in the early 1960s.

Her first collection of poems, *The Colossus,* was followed by her semi-autobiographical novel, *The Bell Jar,* which deals in part with her clinical depression. Plath had made earlier suicide attempts but, in 1963, separated from Hughes and living with two small children in a flat in London during one of the bitterest winters on record, she killed herself.

Her collection of poems *Ariel* was published after her death and shows the influence of 'confessional' poets such as Robert Lowell in its intensely personal examination of all aspects of her life, including her battle with depression. The poems are strikingly original and at times both painfully raw in their presentation of deep emotion and extremely skilfully crafted.

War Music *Christopher Logue (1926–2011)*

The Poem *War Music* is Christopher Logue's 'account' of Homer's *Iliad*. Rather than a direct translation of the original Greek poem, Logue has reworked it into dramatic narrative verse of his own.

This extract comes from Logue's *Patrocleia*, which is based on Book XVI of the *Iliad*. In this extract we meet Ajax, the Greek hero, noted for his strength, and Hector, a Trojan prince, in the midst of a battle. Notice the cinematic style of the line 'Cut to the Fleet'. This suggests that we are in the director's seat, a reference to modern times and a clear shift in perspective from Ancient Greece.

The sound of the arrows battering Ajax echoes in the assonance of 'thick' and 'tickered'. The image of Ajax's head ringing in his helmet is both comic and brutal. Hector taunts Ajax then slices the 'bronze nose' off Ajax's spear. At this Ajax realizes he is defeated and flees. What do you make of the simple finality of 'The ship was burned'?

The Poet Born in Portsmouth, Christopher Logue was educated at Prior Park College in Bath and Portsmouth Grammar School. He joined the Black Watch regiment in the 1940s, although he was court-martialled after claiming he intended to sell stolen army documents. In 1951 he moved to Paris, and subsequently lived in London.

Referring to himself as a 'rewrite man', he was well known for his versions of Homer's *Iliad*, which he worked on from the 1950s. He claimed that there would be no literature without plagiarism and, in his rewriting of the *Iliad*, he both omitted and created various characters and scenes. He wrote screenplays and fiction as well as poetry and won the Whitbread Poetry Award for his collection *Cold Calls: War Music Continued* in 2006.

On the Farm *R. S. Thomas (1913–2000)*

The Poem The first three stanzas of this apparently simple yet deeply moving poem introduce male members of the Puw family of farmers. Thomas captures the speech patterns of a Welsh speaker, but who is he? What is his relation to the people he observes and comments on? Consider how much this poem tells us about life 'on the farm' and how much it reveals about the judgements of the speaker.

The names of the Puw family members are all monosyllabic Welsh names, and there is something limited in the rhymes of 'Llew Puw' and 'Huw Puw', perhaps reflecting a simplicity of thought or lack of imagination. According to the speaker, each of them is, in his own way, 'no good'. Notice the similes associated with the first two characters and what is suggested by them: the 'slash of a knife' and 'a snail'.

Finally, we are told 'there was the girl', who is not given a name, but is 'the' girl not 'a' girl, someone known but whose relationship is unspecified. Why might that be? Which beast do you imagine her to be 'under some spell' of? What is the effect of the adjective 'shrill' in the final line?

The Poet R. S. Thomas was awarded the Lannan Lifetime Achievement Award for Literature in 1996, when he was eighty-three years old. His poetry, written in English, uses straightforward language to present the people and sometimes harsh country settings of his native Wales. His subject matter might be considered bleak, but his poetry has quiet, life-affirming undertones.

Thomas was born the son of a sailor and spent much of his young life moving between port towns. In 1936 he was ordained in the Anglican Church and began work as a priest in the Welsh mining village of Chirk. Throughout his time in the priesthood he moved among rural communities, finding inspiration for his poetry among the peasants and farm settings he encountered.

Badly Chosen Lover *Rosemary Tonks (1932–2014)*

The Poem Amidst some striking and surreal images, poignancy is generated by the sense of the poetic persona's suffering. Complex, uncertain feelings also seem to lie under the angry, emotional surface. For example, in a poem whose two stanzas neatly balance each other, the potent anger of 'Criminal, I damn you for it' is counterbalanced, perhaps even contradicted, by the final words of the line, '(very softly)'.

Is this phrase evidence that the anger is mixed with residual tenderness? The tone of this poem is hard to pin down and perhaps softness can, like quietness, be menacing, for the poem ends with an emphatic denunciation of the lover's behaviour when the speaker damns him. The title, though, suggests she does not shirk responsibility for the part she played in this disastrous relationship. Her choice was 'badly' made.

The sequence of surreal images, in which parts of the body are mixed, such as 'I have the lens and jug of it!' and 'my brain's clear retina', suggest displacement and confusion. There is something undeniably disturbing in the series of images that culminates in the lover imagined as a sort of greedy vampire, or a cannibal consuming the speaker's 'spirit' and 'brain'.

The Poet Rosemary Tonks produced two slim volumes of verse and several novels between 1963 and 1974 while living an affluent, sociable life, then disappeared entirely from view. At the age of twenty she married a wealthy banker, and his work took them to Karachi, before they returned to live in Hampstead. It seems that in the early 1970s Tonks became disillusioned with modern life, retreated from the world completely and stopped publishing. She lived an exceptionally private and reclusive existence for the next forty years, while rumours periodically emerged regarding her whereabouts. It was only after her death in 2014 that it became clear she had been living alone in a house in Bournemouth since 1981.

Influenced by French symbolist and surrealist poets, Tonks has a distinct style and voice and is a poet of urban life and, specifically, London life. She writes lyrically, colloquially and dramatically about relationships in the city.

'I don't operate often' *John Berryman (1914–72)*

The Poem Berryman once wrote that his *Dream Songs* sequence was not meant to be easily understood but 'to terrify and to comfort'. At first reading, it may certainly seem difficult to decipher what Berryman is writing about, but the more the poem is read and heard, the more most readers begin to engage with the dark, disordered, odd world that Berryman is creating. The poems in this song sequence deal with a character called 'Henry' who resembles Berryman but, according to the poet, is only a fictional, unreliable version of himself.

A poet is perhaps a kind of doctor – maybe a witchdoctor – and a lyric poet writes about himself, creating spells about himself which have the power to heal in some way; to heal his society perhaps. He is 'obliged' by his calling; it is what he does and what he is. The operations (poems) are performed 'on my self' (using the materials of his life experience). And poetry, famously, hardly ever pays very well.

The voice in Berryman's *Dream Songs* is that of a trickster; it is and is not Berryman himself. The world tricksters create is carnivalesque, grotesque, by turns manic and sad, but always interesting.

The Poet Winner of the Pulitzer Prize in 1965, John Berryman was an American poet closely associated with the 'confessional' school of poetry. When he was only twelve years old, his father committed suicide – a tragedy that he returned to again and again in his poetry.

Berryman combined writing with an academic career, teaching for many years at the University of Minnesota.

His most celebrated collection, *77 Dream Songs*, was published in 1964. Although regarded as a confessional poet, his best works always have an extra dimension, where the 'I' is not straightforwardly just the personality of the poet. Berryman's style, with its sudden shifts of tone and neurotic, edgy syntax, can be unsettling. In a single poem he can ricochet alarmingly between high lyricism and low comedy, leaving the reader disorientated, but also engaged. His struggle against depression and alcoholism ended when he committed suicide in 1972.

The Day Lady Died *Frank O'Hara (1926–66)*

The Poem This poem is an elegy to the great jazz singer Billie Holiday. Mal Waldron, mentioned in the last line, was her accompanist. However, Holiday's death is only mentioned obliquely at the end of the poem, when the poet picks up the newspaper. O'Hara excludes any of the language and details we might normally expect in an elegy.

Instead, his poem seems to be a list of insignificant, loosely connected events that happened on that particular day. The dominant conjunction is the simplest one in English, 'and', a conjunction that tells us only that one thing happened after another. The connections between details of the poem seem arbitrary. The poet tells us how he ate a burger, visited the bank and bought some French cigarettes and a book.

Notice the use of dates, times, places and names, such as 'Patsy' and 'Mike'. Perhaps they give the impression that we are gaining unmediated access to the poet's life; that O'Hara is being artless and honest and therefore can be trusted. Is the impact of the last lines also made more powerful through contrast with the apparent insignificance of what has gone before?

The Poet An American writer and influential art critic, Frank O'Hara was associated with the New York School of Poetry. He was particularly influenced by abstract expressionism and was a friend of many famous painters. Fundamentally, though, O'Hara was a city poet, and his city was New York.

Towards the end of the Second World War, O'Hara joined the US Navy. In 1946 he took advantage of the GI Bill, which provided benefits to returning war veterans, and completed a BA at Harvard. In 1951 he earned an MA from the University of Michigan, winning a prestigious prize for his creative writing. He moved to New York and worked at the front desk of the Museum of Modern Art while continuing to write poetry and articles for art journals. He died, aged just forty, in a bizarre accident, when he was hit by a dune buggy on the beach at Fire Island, off Long Island.

What the Chairman Told Tom *Basil Bunting (1900–1985)*

The Poem What is the value of poetry? To the speaker of Bunting's humorous dramatic monologue, poetry is a complete waste of time and effort, an excuse to avoid doing work in the real world.

Bunting creates and dramatizes a scenario in which the poet is put in the humbling position of asking for work. Notice how the poet is insulted, demeaned and humiliated at will by the speaker. He is told that what he writes is 'rot', and that a 'ten year old' could do better. Bluntly expressing common prejudices against poetry, the accountant is presented as conceited and boorish.

It is quite clear that the speaker is responding dismissively to what the poet says. Why doesn't Bunting give the poet a voice? What is the effect of excluding the poet's part of this conversation?

Written in short, unrhymed tercets which fit neatly the curt, matter-of-fact phrasing of the accountant, the poem seems to show the entirely unequal relationship between the two characters and, by implication, more widely, between the world of finance and the world of art. However, the poet has the last ironic laugh, turning the accountant's words into poetry and rebutting his argument. Bunting takes his poetic revenge.

The Poet It was only after the publication of his modernist masterpiece *Briggflatts* in 1966 that the Northumbrian poet Basil Bunting secured his place as an important contributor to twentieth-century poetry. A Quaker whose pacifism led to his imprisonment as a conscientious objector for six months during the First World War and a nomadic wanderer whose travels took him to Italy, France, the USA and Persia, Bunting earned a living at times as a journalist. Fluent in classical Persian, he also worked for a period in Persia as a translator for the RAF in the Second World War and continued to work for the British Embassy until 1952.

Bunting met Ezra Pound in 1923 and the two poets became close friends, in spite of political differences, bringing Bunting into contact with an avant-garde literary scene. He was an accomplished reader of his own verse and believed strongly in the sonic qualities of poetry.

Thoughts after Ruskin *Elma Mitchell (1919–2000)*

The Poem John Ruskin was the most celebrated writer and art critic of Victorian times. He viewed women in a romanticized and idealized manner and his own relationships with them were extremely problematic. The 'after' in the title is something of a joke, as this poem is no imitation of Ruskin's view of the place of women in the world. The opening takes a traditional, shallow and condescending view of women as smelling of 'lilies and roses' and then confronts the reality of a woman's existence in muscular descriptions full of energy, urgency and violence.

Notice the astonishing number of dynamic action verbs describing what 'tender' and 'gentle' women really do. 'Gutting', 'stuffing', 'zipping' and 'Spooning' are just four of about thirty you could find in the poem. The phrase 'bloody passages and hairy crannies' may be a reference to the story of Ruskin's unconsummated marriage to Effie Gray and the idea, disputed by some critics, that he was shocked by the sight of his wife's pubic hair and the bodily function of menstruation.

The poem ends with women conscious of the imminent arrival of husbands home from work rushing upstairs to transform themselves into the 'essences of lilies and roses'.

The Poet Elma Mitchell was born in Scotland, but after studying English at Oxford she spent most of her life in England. She qualified as a librarian at University College, London, and worked for the BBC during the Second World War. She went on to become a writer and translator, working from her home in Somerset.

Mitchell featured in the second Penguin Modern Poets series, alongside U. A. Fanthorpe and Charles Causley, and produced three well-received collections of rhythmically skilful and compassionate poetry. She won the Camden Festival Poetry Prize in 1969, the Cheltenham Poetry Festival competition in 1977 and the Cholmondeley Award in 1999.

She did not give many public readings but, when she did, she was a powerful and charismatic performer of her own work.

'Thoughts after Ruskin' is probably her most widely known poem and one which attracted much attention and critical praise when it was published in the late 1960s.

Ballad of the Bread Man *Charles Causley (1917–2003)*

The Poem Charles Causley's reimagining of the birth, life and death of Christ in a modern setting uses a traditional ballad form. This ancient form of poetry, often dealing with themes of universal significance, is perhaps particularly appropriate for the retelling of this story.

Consider the significance of the description of Jesus as the 'bread man'. What references to bread appear in the Bible and what are the symbolic associations with bread in the Christian faith?

The appearance of the angel Gabriel to Mary is dealt with in a light-hearted colloquial fashion, but notice how verse six suggests seriousness and tenderness in the way Mary keeps the information 'Like the baby, safe inside'.

The three wise men in Causley's version become a bishop, a general and the head of an African country, and Christ's story is reported in newspapers and on television. The rejection of Christ's message and his execution and resurrection are described in the same simple, rhythmical, emphatic style Causley uses throughout the poem.

What is the impact of the ending of the poem when the risen Christ's offer of bread is met with the reply, 'Not today'?

The Poet Charles Causley spent most of his life in Cornwall and was fascinated by the folklore of the region. He served in the navy during the Second World War and wrote about his experiences in a book of short stories at the start of his writing career.

He worked as a teacher in Cornwall after the war and remained exceptionally loyal to the county of his birth, although he did make visits to Australia and Canada to lecture after his early retirement from teaching. He was greatly in demand for poetry readings and broadcasts.

Causley wrote for both adults and children in a number of poetic genres. Some of his poems were enormously popular, for example the story of poor 'Timothy Winters', which is regularly anthologized.

Strawberries *Edwin Morgan (1920–2010)*

The Poem 'Strawberries' captures a moment of immensely vivid memory, with Morgan recalling an afternoon of freedom and passion eating strawberries and making love.

The intensity and importance of the experience is established immediately when he states emphatically that no strawberries had ever been as sweet and luscious as the ones the lovers ate that 'sultry afternoon'. The heat of the day and the gathering storm suggest their rising desire and passion. The poem moves from the past tense to the present, as if trying to recapture the moment in the act of writing: 'lean back again/let me love you'.

The shape of the poem on the page and the detail of the two forks laid on the plate, suggesting sameness, might indicate that this is a homosexual relationship. Is this significant, or are the themes in this poem universal and applicable to any sexuality or gender?

Note the lack of punctuation, which gives the poem a fluidity of movement that reflects the freedom enjoyed by the lovers, while the language and imagery constantly appeal to the senses. What does the final dramatic line suggest about the lovers' passion and the act of memory?

The Poet Edwin Morgan was born in Glasgow and lived there throughout his long life, apart from his war years in Egypt and the Lebanon. His work is rooted in his knowledge and love of Glasgow and Scotland, but he was also deeply interested in international developments in poetry. His mastery of classic forms is seen in *Sonnets from Scotland*, which was published in the 1980s.

Although Morgan built a relatively conventional career as an academic in Glasgow, he was an inventive and inquiring poet, writing about science and technology, history and popular culture, as well as the traditional subjects of poetry such as love. The repressive, legislation and attitudes towards homosexuality in the first half of Morgan's life led to his love poems being deliberately ambiguous in terms of gender.

Morgan was honoured by his home city when he became its first Poet Laureate in 1999, and in 2004 he held the post of Scots Makar (national poet of Scotland).

The Beast in the Space *W. S. Graham (1918–86)*

The Poem 'The Beast in the Space' opens with one half of a conversation that may have been going on for some time, and it appears the reader is being addressed. The boldness of Graham's impolite command to 'Shut up. Shut up' is immediately arresting.

Graham creates a sense of mystery through spatial vagueness: 'There's nobody here', he tells us. Later on he says, 'I remember/I am not here'. Notice how he also refers to the 'other side of the words'. Where is the 'here' and the 'other side' of the words? It seems that Graham imagines the writer on one side and the reader on the other. The 'beast' inhabits the space between and, at times, Graham actively sends the beast across the space towards the reader. Although the beast is 'terrible', what he 'snorts' or 'growls' is a 'song' and, revealingly, what Graham asks the reader to give the beast in silence is 'love'. Only if we are silent will we be able to hear the 'beast'.

The poem is deftly written and enticingly inscrutable, encouraging a response that explores the relationship between the writer and the reader; the reciter and the listener.

The Poet Scottish poet W. S. Graham left school at fourteen to train as a structural engineer in preparation for a career in shipbuilding. A year at college studying philosophy and literature inspired him, however, to change course and become a writer. Graham brought out his first collection in 1942.

Graham was a friend of Dylan Thomas, and his early poems share the Welsh poet's richness of language, but, as Graham's poetry developed, his language grew sparer and less sonorous.

In 1943 Graham moved into a caravan in Cornwall, where he lived for the rest of his life, working occasionally as a fisherman or coastguard and continuing to write.

Although he did not achieve great literary success in his own lifetime, he was championed by influential figures such as the playwright Harold Pinter. Graham is now considered an important twentieth-century romantic modernist. Many of his poems explore the medium of language.

The Kingdom of Offa *Geoffrey Hill (b.1932)*

The Poem *Mercian Hymns* is a collection of thirty connected poems that lie somewhere between prose and poetry. Hill refers to them as 'versets'. They focus upon Offa, King of Mercia between 758 and his death in 796. He is remembered for the massive dyke that marks, to some extent, the border between England and Wales. Hill interweaves his own experiences and memories from the 1930s and '40s with elements taken from what is known about Offa's career.

Think of the 'he' in the prose poems as both the young Hill and the legendary king. In Hymn VII, look for the Saxon/twentieth century fusion in the poem. What is conjured up by 'biplane', 'Gas-holders', 'sandlorry' and words rooted in an ancient past such as 'flayed', 'milldams' and 'Ceolred' (one of the earlier Mercian kings)? The synthesis of an ancient past with a recent past may even be captured in the one word 'flay', which can mean to remove the skin but was also used hyperbolically in Hill's childhood with the meaning to 'beat up' someone.

In exploring a cultural and political past in a poem full of intriguing sound patterns, Hill gives us complex insights into his childhood and the making of a poet.

The Poet Geoffrey Hill was elected Professor of Poetry at Oxford University in 2010 and knighted in 2012, marking his position as one of the most significant poets writing in English over the last fifty years. His critical fame is greater than his popular readership, but his uncompromisingly robust and often unpredictable poetry commands widespread respect.

Publishing poetry while still at Oxford in the 1950s, Hill followed an academic career, teaching at various times in higher education in Leeds, Cambridge, Bristol and Boston.

Hill's powerful and tightly controlled poetic voice can be heard in over twenty volumes of poetry. His work is erudite, full of allusions, musicality and rhetorical devices. He believes that complexity, or what some people might call 'difficulty', in poetry acknowledges intelligence and curiosity in the potential reader.

Hill is also a distinguished essayist, winning the Truman Capote Award for Literary Criticism in 2008 for his *Collected Critical Writings*.

Sea Canes *Derek Walcott (b.1930)*

The Poem The profoundly serious and contemplative nature of 'Sea Canes' is captured in its slow rhythms, full and half-rhymes and its elegiac tone.

The poem opens with the poet in conversation with the 'earth', pleading for the return of friends who have died. The passage of time has meant that the number of friends left alive above ground is exceeded by the number buried in the earth. Notice how in a poem that is very much about coming to terms with death the references are often appropriately elemental. The earth, moonlight, the wind and the ocean are almost gently placed within the poem.

The sea canes, powerful symbols of strength and regrowth, first occur in the poem as filters of the surf's sound, creating in the poet's mind the voices of his dead friends. On line fourteen they are suddenly visual, 'flash green and silver', and this shift mirrors a change in the poet. He has moved to a visionary state 'further than despair'.

In finally comparing that state to the wind moving through the canes, Walcott brings us back full circle to those voices in the wind that conjure up loved ones 'as they were', unchanged.

The Poet Born in St Lucia, Derek Walcott won the Nobel Prize for Literature in 1992 and, in his career to date, he has published over fifty books, mainly of poetry and plays. He is Professor of Poetry at the University of Essex.

His masterpiece is *Omeros*, in which he assimilates the European literary tradition, adapting it to a Caribbean context. Combining Dante's terza rima verse form from *The Divine Comedy* with Homer's stories and characters, Walcott forges a link between the experiences of Caribbean fishermen and those of the great Homeric heroes.

As a post-colonial writer, Walcott has a complex, nuanced relationship with the English language and with European art forms. Rather than seeing this colonial cultural heritage only as the remnants of cultural oppression, Walcott draws on it as a resource. Lush and lyrical, his precisely observed, sensual, painterly poems infuse English with the rich cadences of the Caribbean.

The Galloping Cat *Stevie Smith (1902–71)*

The Poem In this loosely structured, energetic, narrative free-verse poem, a talking cat that moves like a horse confronts on a path a 'Figure' who turns out not to be there. Dodging an imagined blow, the cat slips on a banana skin. Then our narrator attempts to strike the mysterious figure, but finds herself striking empty air, at which point a voice says 'Poor cat' and the cat is stroked, resulting in baldness (of course!). As if that is not enough, the cat then hears the rush of wings and sees 'A halo shining at the height of/Mrs Gubbins's backyard fence'. From the evidence of lack of intervention by the Divine to deliver justice on earth, the narrator cat draws the conclusion that he must carry on 'galloping' around, doing 'good'.

Throughout this absurd, metaphysical, morality animal fable, the cat speaks in an erratic register, ranging from upper middle class ('bringing it orf') to teenspeak ('all that skyey stuff'). Fairy tale, social commentary, speculation about God and nursery rhyme are all commingled to peculiar and entertaining effect as the self-righteous and the self-satisfied are mercilessly lampooned in the shape of the insufferable galloping cat.

The Poet An accomplished, entertaining reader of her own verse and winner of the Queen's Gold Medal for Poetry, Stevie Smith is probably best known for her poem 'Not Waving, but Drowning', which regularly features in anthologies of the nation's favourite poetry. Born in Hull, Smith spent most of her life in London, where she worked as a secretary for the magazine publisher George Newnes and lived a seemingly quiet, secluded life. She wrote three novels but is more celebrated for the poetry she began to write in her twenties and for the quirky line drawings she produced to accompany her words. As she grew older, Stevie Smith seemed to settle into the literary persona of an eccentric but formidably sharp spinster.

Characteristically, Smith's playful, witty work mixes the serious with the whimsical, lightness with darkness, the formal with the colloquial. The effect is often peculiar and unsettling; at times comical and at others eerie.

Wounds *Michael Longley (b.1939)*

The Poem This elegiac poem is filled with characters and their voices. As well as the poet, we have his father, the Ulster Division, 'a boy about to die', a 'London-Scottish padre', three English soldiers, a bus conductor and the 'shivering boy' who is his killer. What do all these characters have in common? Are they all victims? The poem raises but does not answer the question of whether it is ethically right to say they are all victims of conflict.

The first half of the poem focuses on the father's experiences of the First World War. The second connects these experiences to 'the Troubles' in Northern Ireland. The settings and nature of the characters' deaths appear to be very different; the first half of the poem takes place on the battlefield, whereas the killing of the bus conductor occurs in a vividly realized domestic context.

Formally, the first half of the poem is mirrored by the second. Notice, too, how Longley makes further links between the two events, such as the use of the word 'boy' to describe the soldier and, controversially, the bus conductor's murderer.

The Poet Born in Belfast, Michael Longley is an award-winning Irish poet who is a contemporary of Seamus Heaney and Derek Mahon. An influential figure, he has worked as Director of Literature and the Traditional Arts for the Arts Council of Northern Ireland. In 2001 he was awarded the Queen's Gold Medal for Poetry.

Longley studied classics at Trinity College, Dublin, and the influence of classical literature is apparent in most of his poetry. He often makes links between the world of Homer and other classical authors and the contemporary reality of life in Northern Ireland and the Irish Republic, particularly in terms of conflict, revenge and reconciliation. The focus on conflict in his poetry is, however, counterbalanced by close observation and the celebration of nature.

It is perhaps as an elegist that he is most celebrated, as a poet whose compassion for the victims of conflict sweeps aside sectarian divisions.

A, a, a, Domine Deus *David Jones (1895–1974)*

The Poem The narrator of this lament is on a quest for inspiration, a spiritual search to find in the everyday modern reality of 'pylon[s]', 'nozzles' and 'automatic devices' something of worth and meaning. The forlorn nature of the quest is conveyed by repetition of the phrase 'I have' followed by verbs in the past tense such as 'run', 'journeyed', 'tired', 'felt'. However, the poet perseveres, and it is clear from the title, with its cry to the Lord God ('Domine Deus'), the reference to 'His symbol' in the fifth line and the way the speaker has 'felt for His Wounds/in nozzles and containers' that the search for Christ is what preoccupies a despairing poet. The title makes reference to the prophet Jeremiah, who felt inadequate when called to speak for God.

Notice how the poet narrator tries to remain responsive, alert to potential signs of Christ's presence. He has been on his 'guard' and is prepared to explore 'manifold lurking-places'. But, try as he might, the poem ends with the poet apparently defeated in his quest. Dropping into prose, he cannot find God behind a shallow world. The 'terrible crystal' (a reference to Ezekiel, Chapter 1) is merely 'stage-paste'.

The Poet David Jones was a visionary visual artist and poet who served in the trenches as an ordinary soldier from 1915 until 1918, was wounded at the Battle of the Somme and spent more time on active service than any of the other First World War poets.

Jones grew up in London and studied at Camberwell School of Art. His father was Welsh and, from his early childhood, Jones saw himself as Welsh, developing an interest in the country's history and literature. His poetry often draws on this, and on the vernaculars of cockneys and Welsh hill farmers encountered in his regiment.

He published his first major work in 1937 and continued painting, drawing and writing poetry in between episodes of depression caused by what would now be termed post-traumatic stress.

In 1921 Jones converted to Roman Catholicism, believing that 'the Mass makes sense of everything'.

A Disused Shed in Co. Wexford *Derek Mahon (b.1941)*

The Poem The first line of Mahon's poem, written not long after Bloody Sunday (30 January 1972, on which twenty-six civil rights protesters and bystanders were shot by soldiers of the British Army, thirteen fatally), announces the idea that obscure, out-of-the-way places might allow the poet a freedom for new thinking: 'Even now there are places where a thought might grow'. In these ignored spaces, new perspectives might emerge that were unavailable from more conventional vantage points. Forgotten places are characterized as being undemonstrative, diffident, quiet and humble as an old 'shed'. They are places where 'a door bangs with diminished confidence'.

Here, in a shed, the poet discovers his central metaphor of the long-abandoned mushrooms. Personified, they 'crowd' towards a keyhole, which is their only source of light, the 'one star' in their darkened world. Notice how the mushrooms are described as prisoners. Their suffering and stoicism is emphasized; they may have 'learnt patience and silence' but they suffer 'deaths', 'drought' and 'insomnia' in the long wait for deliverance.

The full significance of what these mushrooms symbolize is not revealed until the last stanza. Surreally, we hear the voices of the mushrooms. In the historical context of loss, exploitation and destruction, the poem reaches out to the neglected and abandoned.

The Poet Born in Belfast, a contemporary of Seamus Heaney and Michael Longley, Derek Mahon studied at Trinity College, Dublin, and at the Sorbonne. After graduating, he travelled and worked in Canada, the United States and London, and he now lives in the Republic of Ireland. In 2007 he was awarded the David Cohen Prize for Literature.

In his scrupulously crafted poems, Mahon often explores large, universal ideas through the prism of close examination of small, seemingly insignificant details. Something of an exile from his native Protestant culture, Mahon is able to view this world from an outsider's perspective.

'My father, in a white space suit' *Yehuda Amichai (1924–2000)*

The Poem Gently surreal, this moving elegy explores the complex relationship between a father and his son. In some ways the father is presented as an attractive, authoritative figure. He is associated with the glamour of space exploration, for example, and he acts as a sort of scientific tour guide to life, naming its features in a factual way, as if they were features of the moon: 'This is the Crater of Childhood.'

But there are more troubling resonances: the spaceman image suggests emotional distance between father and son; childhood is described as a 'Crater' and, even more ominously, as an 'abyss'. Whereas the father is a powerfully active force in the poem, his son is so passive he has become the moon's surface, trodden on, mapped, examined by the spaceman. In writing the poem, the poet repeats this passivity by withholding any commentary on the relationship he describes.

And isn't this father, in his white space suit, a surrogate for the ultimate father, God? At the end of the poem, is God dead?

The Poet Born in Germany to Orthodox Jewish parents, Yehuda Amichai moved with his family to Jerusalem, where he attended a religious school. He fought with the British Army in the Second World War and later in the Israeli War of Independence, the Sinai War and the Yom Kippur War. In between, he studied the Bible and Hebrew literature and started to write and publish his poems. He taught literature at the University of California, Berkeley, at New York University and at the Hebrew University of Jerusalem.

With clear but tender intelligence, Amichai's poems characteristically probe philosophical issues in a down-to-earth style, taking the reader on a voyage through religious doubt accompanied by an observant, perceptive and evidently wise guide.

Amichai was greatly admired by the poet Ted Hughes. His work has been translated into more than forty languages and awarded many prestigious national and international poetry prizes.

A Summer Place *Anne Stevenson (b.1933)*

The Poem The narrator in this poem is recalling the occupant of what appears to be a tumbledown but attractive and charming Vermont house. The owner, 'a poet', recalled in the poem bought the house from a farmer but had no intention of working the land from the new home, in its 'lovely setting'. The twelfth line simply states, 'It was the view she bought it for.' Notice the lyrical, delicate description of the way the new occupant lives in the house, seeing it as a place 'where fine minds could graze'.

Summer with flowers and birdsong is tenderly evoked until, unexpectedly, in line thirty-two a sense of unease enters the poem: 'the shade of something wrong, a fear, a doubt.' The environment suddenly appears menacing and disturbing. Consider the ways in which Stevenson conveys the sense of a creeping, advancing danger as the new owner endures sleepless nights in her room, 'pacing' and 'weeping'.

Look at the final triplet, where the neat rhymes reinforce the simple, almost matter-of-fact conclusion revealing that the house and landscape remain the same but the owner has gone.

The Poet Born in England of American parents, Anne Stevenson was educated at the University of Michigan, where she initially studied music and literature before completing an MA in English in the early 1960s. Since 1971 she has spent most of her life in England, making frequent trips back to America.

Living for various periods in Scotland, Oxford, Cambridge, Hay-on-Wye, Wales and now Durham, Anne Stevenson has produced sixteen collections of poetry. *Poems 1955–2005* contains nearly all the poems from her earlier books.

She has written about other poets, including Elizabeth Bishop, and in particular Sylvia Plath. Her biography of Plath, *Bitter Fame*, was controversial when it was published in 1989 but has increasingly been seen as a perceptive and intelligent account of Plath's life.

Stevenson's sharply observed, questioning, musical poetry has been awarded a number of prizes, among them the Neglected Masters Award from the Poetry Foundation of America in 2007.

The Ex-Queen among the Astronomers *Fleur Adcock (b.1934)*

The Poem In her richly described and playful poem Fleur Adcock imagines an ex-queen among a group of male astronomers. These scientists are seen as servants rather than masters of celestial objects and the physical universe: 'They serve revolving saucer eyes.' Is Adcock placing them in the traditionally subservient position of women rather than presenting them as masterful males? They 'calculate, adjust, record' and, in an image with perhaps sexual overtones, Adcock writes that they are merely 'receptacles'. Meanwhile, the ex-queen passes among them. She has been abandoned and exiled by her husband after a life of dutiful obedience to his wishes and now 'His bitter features taunt her sleep.'

But notice how suddenly and perhaps unexpectedly in the last three stanzas the queen is transformed into a dynamic and powerful force. She 'seeks', 'plucks' and 'sucks'. Her hair 'crackles' and her eyes are described as 'comet-sparks'. She becomes almost predatory as she takes 'this one or that' among the astronomers, emphasizing her authority.

The poem subtly and vividly explores stereotyping and sexual politics within a work that deliberately contains echoes of Metaphysical poetry.

The Poet Fleur Adcock was born in New Zealand but emigrated to England in 1963. Initially she worked as a librarian, becoming a writer in the 1970s. She has written ten volumes of poetry, and her collected works, *Poems 1966–2000*, was published in 2000. She was awarded an OBE in 1996 and the Queen's Gold Medal for Poetry that same year.

Her restrained, almost conversational poems are skilfully crafted and deal with a wide range of issues. Perhaps not surprisingly for a poet who emigrated, identity, roots and rootlessness are important themes in her poetry. Adcock also writes about childhood, women in society and the complexity of relationships between men and women. Her tone is never strident or hectoring. Instead she seeks to engage the reader or listener in a quiet and intimate conversation.

WEA Course *Elizabeth Bartlett (1924–2008)*

The Poem The WEA of the title stands for the Workers' Educational Association, which was founded in 1903 and is the UK's largest voluntary-sector provider of adult education. It specializes in providing educational opportunities for adults facing social and economic disadvantage.

The poem is set in a WEA literature evening class. Last week the group worked on the Russian novelist Alexander Solzhenitsyn and on the evening captured in this poem they are looking at Boris Pasternak's novel *Dr Zhivago*.

Notice how Bartlett is both a participant in the course and an observer wittily commenting on her fellow students and her teacher and blurring the lines between the reality of the educational class and the imagined worlds of literature. Many of the references to names such as Komarovsky and Yury (Dr Zhivago), and descriptive details, for example, 'iced rowanberries', can be traced back to Pasternak's novel. Next week they will be studying the Italian author Lampedusa, who wrote *The Leopard*. The Latin in line thirty-one, 'Nunc et in hora mortis nostrae. Amen' ('Now and at the hour of our death. Amen'), is the opening line of that novel.

Does a darkness descend upon the poem in the final third? The weather is 'cruel' and 'ruthless' and the 'stars have gone'. Where has this immersion in literature taken the poet?

The Poet Elizabeth Bartlett published her first collection of poetry in her mid-fifties. Her final volume of verse appeared on her eightieth birthday, in 2004.

She came from a working-class background in the south of England and worked for many years in the health service. Her clear-sighted, powerful poems often deal with the lives of the lonely and disadvantaged. She herself suffered hardship growing up and left school at fifteen. At nineteen, she was married and a mother, and soon working hard to support her family.

She lived in the same house in West Sussex for fifty years, and most of her poems in her four collections were written in the same room within this house.

A Martian Sends a Postcard Home *Craig Raine (b.1944)*

The Poem This poem seeks to describe human behaviour and objects as if they are being seen for the first time by a visiting Martian. Consequently, the tone is detached and objective, but also quizzical. The ordinary and commonplace are illuminated by a fresh perspective in seventeen unrhymed couplets. While the poem is almost like a series of riddles that invite the reader to decipher them, the use of language is original and evocative. Books are described as 'Caxtons' in a reference to William Caxton, who developed the printing press, and here they are mechanical birds with many wings. The act of holding a book when reading is seen as one of the mechanical birds perching on a hand. The description of a land under mist is written with economical and lyrical delicacy.

Consider some of the other aspects of human behaviour the Martian records. What is the 'haunted apparatus' and why do adults go to a 'punishment room' with water? This playful, humorous and ironic poem ends with a beautiful, tender description of sleeping and dreaming at night, when 'all the colours die'.

The Poet Craig Raine was educated at Oxford and, in addition to his career as a poet and, more recently, a novelist, he has been the poetry editor of Faber and Faber and an academic at New College, Oxford, where he is now Emeritus Professor. He is founder and editor of the literary magazine *Areté*. His first collection of poetry was published in 1978, and he has gone on to produce eleven collections, in addition to two novels and some literary criticism. He has written extensively on T. S. Eliot.

Raine is well known as one of the exponents of 'Martian' poetry. Through unusual, ingenious and sometimes humorous visual images, Raine attempts to make readers look at the familiar in fresh, illuminating ways. The poem in this anthology inspired the 'Martian' description of the work of a number of writers in the late 1970s and early '80s, whose poems were full of striking, surreal images.

Ö *Rita Dove (b.1952)*

The Poem Named after the Swedish word for 'island', Dove's stately, unhurried free-verse poem dramatizes the potential of language to transform the world. Here just a single foreign word is enough to change a 'whole neighborhood'. How exactly can that happen?

The philosopher Ludwig Wittgenstein said 'the limits of my language are the limits of my world'. It follows from this that, if you expand your language, you expand your world. Notice how Dove's acquisition of new language enriches her perceptions – so much so that a house becomes a 'galleon stranded in flowers' and the sound of a leaf mulcher is transformed into the 'horn-blast' of a ship in the mist.

A word from a different culture refreshes the poet's imagination, and the ordinary is defamiliarized into the marvellous: 'nothing's/like it used to be'. Is Dove perhaps suggesting that this is also the function of art? By defamiliarizing what has become invisible to us, art recovers our sense of wonder at the world. Such a change, Dove seems to be saying, can permanently alter perceptions and shape 'even the future'.

The Poet Critic and poet Rita Dove studied English at Miami University and won a prestigious Fulbright Scholarship to study literature in Germany. Winner of the Pulitzer Prize for her verse-novel *Thomas and Beulah*, she became in 1993 the youngest ever American Poet Laureate and the first black American to be elected to this post. Currently, Dove, who has been awarded twenty-four honorary doctorates, is Commonwealth Professor of English at the University of Virginia.

Dove is a sensual, lyrical poet, and her poems often explore female black experience and social history. Her intimate style is said to be capable of dissolving the barriers between the present and the past. Featuring famous black American women, such as Rosa Parks and Billie Holiday, as well as more anonymous, everyday characters, her poems explore what Dove calls the 'underside of history'.

Rita Dove is the editor of *The Penguin Anthology of Twentieth-Century American Poetry.*

Sonny's Lettah *Linton Kwesi Johnson (b.1952)*

The Poem Many of Linton Kwesi Johnson's early poems deal with the conflict between members of the black British community and a police force which, in the 1970s in particular, was guilty of institutionalized racism. 'Sonny's Lettah' draws attention to the Sus, or 'Suspected Person', Law, which in effect led to police stopping, searching and arresting a disproportionate number of black youths. Johnson translates a typical written form – the letter – into an oral tale, differentiating the stanzas of the poem through rhythm, timbre and intonation in performance.

Sonny's report to his mother on the attack suffered by his little brother and his own impulsive reaction to the policemen's violence begins with conventional, affectionate but respectful formality. As the violence is described, however, the beat of the poem becomes more emphatic and the conflict is captured in the rhythm Johnson creates.

As the poem progresses we learn that one of the policemen has died and Sonny has been charged with murder. The alternate 'an' and 'mi' lines describing the fight create a picture of a macabre rhythmical dance with a deeply tragic end when the policeman, 'an crash/an ded'. The poem concludes with a return to the affectionate formality of the opening.

The Poet Born in Jamaica in 1952, Linton Kwesi Johnson is a poet and performer whose work focuses on issues of race and social injustice. Johnson moved to Britain in 1963 and many of his poems explore the experience of being Jamaican in this country. His performances are hugely popular for the way they combine recitation of his poems with dub reggae.

Overtly political, Johnson's poetry seeks to make a difference in the world. The protest dimension of his work is counterbalanced by the poet's delight in language, especially its rhythms. However, language in his poems is also, in itself, political. Johnson's use of Jamaican patois expresses resistance to cultural standardization.

In 2012 Linton Kwesi Johnson was given the Golden PEN Award by English PEN for a 'lifetime's distinguished service to literature'. He is the second living poet, and the only black poet, to have had his poems published in the Penguin Modern Classics series.

The Colonel *Carolyn Forché (b.1950)*

The Poem Like reportage from the front line, there is nothing fanciful about this poem; its prose style suggests that it is focused entirely on telling the truth. This is a poem about brutality and about hearing as a form of witness.

Its first line implies a conversation. Seemingly under pressure, the narrator of the poem and a companion are justifying to a listener their visit to the colonel's home. Through short, blunt statements, Forché swiftly builds tension. Notice how the narrative voice focuses resolutely on reporting what is happening as factually and unemotionally as possible.

Withholding their reaction to the events they witness makes the reader edge imaginatively into this gap. Tension increases on seeing the 'pistol' and mounts still further when we hear about the 'Broken bottles'. We feel the strain as they eat the fine meal and drink the good wine in a seemingly polite and civilized manner before the horrific introduction of the sack of ears.

In an arresting magic-realist image, some of the severed ears are said still, miraculously, to hear. This image takes us back to the poem's opening line. People will hear this story, the poem promises, and news of the colonel and his atrocities will emerge.

The Poet Carolyn Forché is an award-winning American poet, translator, editor and human rights campaigner whose work bears witness to, and confronts, the suffering caused by exile, torture and war. In 1994 she brought together 140 poems from five continents that bore 'witness' to this suffering in her groundbreaking anthology *Against Forgetting*.

Her exceptionally promising first collection of poetry was published in 1975 when she was only twenty-four years old, but it was after she received a Guggenheim Fellowship to travel to El Salvador with Amnesty International that her poetry began to fuse the personal and the political. Her experiences were captured in the collection *The Country Between Us* (1981), which chronicles the awakening of a political consciousness.

Timer *Tony Harrison (b.1937)*

The Poem 'Timer', from Harrison's 1981 collection, *The School of Eloquence*, is one of a long sequence of poems that explores the poet's relationship with his parents. It deals with the death of his mother, focusing on her wedding ring, which would not burn, and the emotions this prompts. Notice the unusual sonnet form Harrison uses. It is a sixteen-line version of the form made popular by the nineteenth-century poet George Meredith. Harrison's brilliant handling of polysyllabic and colloquial rhymes ('St James's's' with 'their names is' and 'incinerator' with 'together "later"') give the sense of an ordinary man expressing his thoughts in his own authentic voice.

His father is present in the poem when Harrison talks of how his father wanted his wife's 'eternity' ring to go in the incinerator as a symbolic gesture of a future togetherness. Holding the burnished ring, Harrison can almost 'feel' the physical presence of his mother, and the poem ends with a remembered moment of gentle intimacy involving watching the sand of his mother's egg timer. Inevitably, given the topic of the poem, the egg timer takes on a deeper, metaphorical significance within this poignant and unsentimental poem.

The Poet Regarded by many as one of the major poets of the last fifty years, Tony Harrison was born in Leeds in 1937 and attended the local grammar school before studying classics at Leeds University. His early poetry explored the tension between his working-class upbringing and the culture he was introduced to through education in verse that is both moving and technically accomplished in its precise control of rhythm and rhyme.

His long, ambitious poem *v.*, written during the miners' strike of 1984–5, was highly controversial. Inspired by the vandalizing of his parents' grave by football hooligans, Harrison reflects on his feelings of outrage within the context of a profound meditation upon social conflict and the waste of human potential.

Harrison has translated Greek drama, written for the theatre, adapting the medieval mystery plays, and directed a film of his own poem *Prometheus*. He is one of the most distinctive voices writing in English today.

The Lost Woman *Patricia Beer (1924–99)*

The Poem Notice the form of this poem. Six stanzas of six lines follow the same neat and regular rhyme scheme. The rhyme scheme is like a dance of separation and reunion; in each stanza four cross-rhymed lines culminate in a couplet.

The overall impression of this formal design is of control and balance. However, the sound qualities of the rhymes run counter to all this good order. Beer frequently uses half-rhymes, as if the words are slightly off key, slightly out of control. Is the effect quietly unsettling, even a little sinister?

Tension is also evident in the tone and language. At first Beer's language is ordinary and understated: 'My mother went' is a seemingly rather cold, euphemistic way of saying 'My mother died'. The poem's title also suggests emotional detachment and distance, depersonalizing the tragic experience. Why didn't Beer call the poem 'My Mother'? In contrast, the fairy-tale imagery of metamorphosis, 'the ivy-mother turned into a tree', hints at darker, richer undercurrents and a more complex emotional impact: 'My tendrils . . . clutch.'

These tensions culminate in the startling reversal at the end of the poem, when suddenly it is the poet who is presented as a 'ghost' with the eerie 'bat-voice'.

The Poet Born into a Plymouth Brethren family in Devon, Patricia Beer was an English poet, novelist, memoirist, essayist and literary academic. She recalls her childhood in her vivid autobiography, *Mrs Beer's House*.

For many years after her graduation from the universities of Exeter and Oxford, Beer worked as a teacher of literature, firstly in the universities of Padua and Rome and later as senior lecturer in English at Goldsmiths College in London. Her celebrated collection of essays *Reader, I Married Him* explores the presentation of female characters in the works of the great female novelists.

Death and the haunting of the living by the dead were subjects Beer returned to repeatedly in her seven collections of poetry, and these themes can be seen clearly in 'The Lost Woman'. She wrote an historical novel set in Devon and lived the last thirty years of her life in the county of her birth.

God, A Poem *James Fenton (b.1949)*

The Poem The poem rests on a powerful paradox. An apparently non-existent entity is proclaiming that he does not exist, thereby implying that he actually does exist, at least enough to have a voice and to speak in rhyme. The circularity is intriguing.

'God, A Poem' is a deceptively simple example of a genre that employs a playfully ironic treatment of serious themes. The poem begins in a cheerful, jaunty manner, the apparent light-heartedness enhanced by the regular three-beat lines, but it develops into a strange, nightmarish vision with references to the dead and decaying body, 'a diet of worms'.

Notice how the poem subtly modifies and repeats the first two verses at the end and, in doing so, gives God, literally, the last word.

'Soteriology' is the study of religious doctrines of salvation and, although the word is introduced to comic effect in a verse that audaciously rhymes 'The fact is' with 'malpractice', it is in keeping with the more serious undertones in the poem.

The relationship between expectations and reality is humorously but pointedly explored throughout: 'You're a nasty surprise in a sandwich.'

The Poet A poetic prodigy who published his first collection when he was just twenty-three years old and winner of the Queen's Gold Medal for Poetry, James Fenton is a poet, journalist, critic, academic and dramatist. He has served as Professor of Poetry at the University of Oxford and worked in high-profile journalistic roles. As well as having been employed as the political correspondent for the *New Statesman*, he has also worked as a war reporter and foreign correspondent.

A witty, playful poet, Fenton is always serious about the purpose of art. Influenced by W. H. Auden, he sees poetry as a public and political art form. Fenton tends to use ordinary, 'unpoetic' language in extraordinary, often athletic ways. He has a precise, musical ear for rhythm and his poems are driven by the powerful forward momentum of his metre. As well as private subjects, Fenton's interests in geopolitics are often reflected in his poetry.

Your Attention Please *Peter Porter (1929–2010)*

The Poem Porter's searingly ironic indictment of the arms race begins with the chilling announcement that a nuclear strike has been launched against 'our major cities'. The 'Polar DEW' refers to the string of radar stations located in the Arctic region of Canada that was supposed to give Distant Early Warning (DEW) against an impending Soviet nuclear strike.

The poem mimics the language and seriousness of a public information broadcast while incorporating moments of ludicrousness. The 'All Clear' will be signalled by 'the cuckoo in your/perspex panel' while the sheltering population may receive a visit from their 'District/Touring Doctor'. Orders and instructions are given in a calm, robotic, impersonal manner. Beneath the measured, clinical announcement that suggests everything has been prepared for lies the prospect of mass death and destruction.

The poem raises many questions about the relationship between communities and their leaders. Even at this moment of near-disaster the announcer is reassuring the people that retaliation will be 'Massive'. If the poem seems far-fetched in 2014, it is worth remembering that as recently as 1980 the government issued every household in Britain with a pamphlet advising how to keep 'your home and your family as safe as possible under nuclear attack'.

The Poet Between 1960 and his death in 2010 Peter Porter published seventeen collections of verse, establishing a reputation as a writer of philosophical and ironic poetry.

He was born and brought up in Australia, but in his mid-twenties he moved permanently to England and began to associate with a number of ex-Cambridge poets known as 'The Group' who would meet regularly to share and criticize each other's work.

His personal life was marked by tragedy in 1974 when his first wife committed suicide. A number of his poems explore his grief and sense of loss, but he devoted himself to bringing up his two young daughters and continued to work at writing and editing poetry, contributing to newspapers and magazines and broadcasting on radio and television.

In the 1990s he received various awards from Australia and in 2002 he was presented with the Queen's Gold Medal for Poetry.

The Boys Bump-starting the Hearse *Kit Wright (b.1944)*

The Poem 'Bump-starting' is a surprising phrase to find in a title that contains the word 'hearse' with all its solemn and sombre associations. Does the conjunction of the two immediately suggest a comical rather than a tragic scene?

The characters certainly seem types drawn from comedy, such as the otherworldly and bookish Cambridge don incapable of dealing with a practical challenge. We also have the poor 'neutered tom cat'. Wright skilfully paints a picture of a sun-dappled Cambridge, noting the 'bottle-green water' of the river and the 'Lime flowers' drifting in the lane. Are the descriptions of nature around the central scene merely decorative, or do they have any other function?

The language is exuberantly rhythmical and audaciously rhymed: 'drakes kazoo'/'what shall we do?'; 'bicycles'/'particles'. Moreover, Wright uses a word savoured by generations of schoolboys for its comic ripeness in the phrase: 'A fart of exhaust'.

However, not everything in this poem is gently funny. Throughout, we have the presence of the hearse, which seems to represent the dead person himself. Notice how the hearse is called 'the lamented', while the last word of the poem, 'holocaust', introduces a set of profoundly serious associations.

The Poet A master of puns, rhymes and word play, Kit Wright has won many awards during his career, including an Arts Council Writer's award and the Hawthornden Prize. Wright has produced books for both children and adults and is a highly entertaining performer of his own work.

After a scholarship to Oxford, Wright was employed as a lecturer in Canada. On his return to England he worked for the Poetry Society before becoming a full-time writer.

Wright's poetry displays an elegant ease with form. He has a jaunty way with rhythm and rhyme, one that can mislead the reader into assuming they are reading light or comical verse. At times he uses the deliberate contrast between content and style to powerful effect. An entertaining debunker of artistic pretentiousness, Wright often produces poetry that is both extravagantly funny and deeply serious.

Catching Crabs *David Dabydeen (b.1955)*

The Poem Written in the artless present-tense voice of a child recounting a happy memory, the first stanza lulls us. Here we have a boy and his sister roaming at liberty in nature, carrying cutlasses like pirates, hunting for crabs, seemingly without a worry in the world. Their childishness has an innocent charm; they catch only the crabs they imagine 'don't mind' being cooked 'because they got no prospect/Of family'. And the stanza culminates with a feast as the family devours their bounty in 'one big happy curry feed'.

Then time races forward. In the blink of an eye we have jumped ahead years – decades, in fact. In one long, brutal sentence we discover the children have grown up, parted, that Ruby's life has soured and that their mother is now long dead. And in the creepy old house, the poet fears, or perhaps hopes, the ancient ghost of his mother may still be taking care of him, cooking the crab curry. Notice how the description of the mother as 'crustacean-old' takes us back to the more carefree opening, when the writer and his sister were out on the savannah hunting for the crabs.

The Poet Born in Guyana in 1955, David Dabydeen is a prize-winning novelist, critic, poet and academic. Since 2010 he has been Guyana's ambassador to China. He co-edited *The Oxford Companion to Black British History* and in 2008 published his sixth novel, *Molly and the Muslim Stick*. He was a consultant on Channel 4's three-part series on interracial sex, *Forbidden Fruit,* was awarded the 2004 Raja Rao Award for Literature and is a professor at the University of Warwick.

Dabydeen spent some of his school years at the Ernest Bevin comprehensive school in Balham after moving to England when he was thirteen. He went to Cambridge University, despite being put into care at fifteen, and from there went on to University College, London, and to Oxford University. As well as writing many acclaimed novels, his long poem *Turner*, a response to J. M. W. Turner's famous painting *The Slave Ship*, is both powerful and moving.

The Cleaner *U. A. Fanthorpe (1929–2009)*

The Poem Fanthorpe's poem is a dramatic monologue written in the voice of a cleaner working at a university hall of residence. The cleaner performs a sort of choric role; outside of the main action (the world of the students), she provides a commentary on it, a seemingly neutral and impartial observer. As a cleaner, the narrator has, however, privileged access to the private world, the inside story of what really goes on in those student rooms.

How would you describe her tone? Sad, concerned, caring, judgemental, cynical?

In her own mind the cleaner is a realist, someone who has learned her lessons from the University of Life: 'I've seen it all, you know. Men.' The cleaner's knowledge and experience are contrasted ironically with the innocence of the female students: 'They don't know what it's all about.'

Is the cleaner a comic creation, a dully conventional woman with stereotypical ideas about men and women, unable to appreciate the value of an academic education? Can we just dismiss what she says? Or is there something more troubling in her comment that 'a girl/Can get hurt'?

The Poet Fellow of the Royal Society of Literature and the first woman to compete for the post of Professor of Poetry at Oxford University, U. A. Fanthorpe was a much-loved, popular poet. Her wry, witty verse was always accessible to the non-specialist reader, amassing for her a wide and loyal readership.

For sixteen years she worked as a teacher at Cheltenham Ladies' College before becoming, in her own words, a 'middle-aged dropout'. She started writing only after resigning from her teaching post, taking up instead employment as a secretary, receptionist and, most significantly for her writing, as a hospital clerk.

A debunker of pretension, Fanthorpe had a satirical, Larkinesque eye for the absurd, the pompous and the foolish. However, her manner was gentler, more humorous, warmer and more humane. And even when sticking her elegant knife in, Fanthorpe maintained the poise of her civilized, understated, very English style.

Proverbial Ballade *Wendy Cope (b.1945)*

The Poem A ballade is a verse form usually consisting of three eight- or ten-line stanzas with a brief envoi (postscript) that sums up the poem. Each stanza and the envoi end with the same one-line refrain, in this case, 'So say I and so say the folk.' The refrain points to the gently comic intentions of the poem. Folk wisdom neatly encapsulated in proverbial sayings is lightly satirized in a poem that perfectly observes the rhythm and rhyme of the ballade form.

Do the rhythm and content of the lines conjure up memories of other sayings with which we are familiar? For example, 'No use crying over spilt milk' and 'There are plenty more fish in the sea' are probably sayings that have been repeated countless times and are pithy comments designed to console or reassure. In Cope's poem her collections of sayings appear to be proverbial statements, but closer scrutiny reveals them to be hilariously meaningless or mind-numbingly banal, for instance, 'Who has no milk can make no cheese'; 'Who catches cold is sure to sneeze.' In the envoi Cope addresses the reader and can't resist one more joke about fish not growing on trees.

The Poet Born in Kent and educated at Oxford, Wendy Cope trained and worked as a teacher before becoming a writer. She has subsequently worked as a television critic and editor of a number of poetry anthologies, but it is as a writer of witty, humorous and thought-provoking poetry that she is best known.

Wendy Cope's published output is relatively small, but her three full collections over the last twenty-five years have been well received. *Making Cocoa for Kingsley Amis* (1986), where this poem appeared, was full of witty parodies of poetic greats such as Seamus Heaney and sold exceptionally well. She has proved to be a poet whose work is admired by critics and enjoyed by significant numbers of the poetry-reading public, who have responded enthusiastically to her wry observations on human relationships.

What is Worth Knowing? *Sujata Bhatt (b.1956)*

The Poem This poem is a list of responses to the question of the title, 'What is Worth Knowing?' The answers range from practical to surreal, from global to individual in scale. The first line sets the tone as somewhat absurd, and the plaintive plea of the final lines, in which 'What is worth knowing?' is repeated, suggests that any response to this question might ultimately be absurd.

Like a van Gogh painting, the poem seems to swirl around, shifting subjects from superstition to tradition, to cooking, politics and wildlife. The topic comes back repeatedly to van Gogh's ear. What is the effect of this?

The poem is sensual in its imagery, and vibrant colours dominate. There is an almost frantic feel to the list, as if the speaker is recalling memories and truths or moving in and out from reality to dream state. Is this a memory of a fever or a reflection on the absurdity of existence?

Bhatt seems to invite the whole world – 'the Dutch', 'Nicaragua', 'Indonesia', 'the Japanese', America,'east and west', 'north and south' – to answer the question, leading the reader to consider a personal response.

The Poet Sujata Bhatt was born in India to a traditional Gujarati Brahmin family. She lived there until she was twelve, when her family emigrated to the United States. Her first collection of poetry, *Brunizem* (1988), won both the Commonwealth Poetry Prize and the Hunt Bartlett Award. Subsequent collections have won the Cholmondeley Award and the Italian Tratti Poetry Prize.

Though she is widely travelled, her writing is, nonetheless, shaped by her childhood experiences in India, which she remembers with great fondness. She says her 'imagination seems to be continually sparked by those early years in India'. She draws on Indian traditions and Gujarati folk tales and poems but is also influenced by Christina Rossetti and Walter de la Mare. The semi-autobiographical voice of many of her poems is, she says, 'not exactly the "I" who lives in the world'. Her colour-rich, sensual work often explores issues of identity, language and culture.

Boy Breaking Glass *Gwendolyn Brooks (1917–2000)*

The Poem Marc Crawford, to whom this poem is dedicated, was a black writer and editor who suggested Brooks write about inequality. The poem features a boy whose attempts at self-expression are manifested in the breaking of windows, his twisted 'cry of art' not a 'note' or an 'overture' but 'a hole' and 'a desecration'. In this first separated couplet we hear the boy's cry, and in the oppositions of his claims we see the frustration of a creative urge that is seeking an outlet.

The fourth stanza expresses an existential crisis with 'grief' and 'loneliness' pervading the experience of the speaker. Notice the sense of outrage in the final outburst from the boy, the accusation in the repeated 'It was you' and the belief that he is a victim of social injustice. The partially alliterative list in the final stanza highlights comforts to which the boy's life gives him no access, but the list slides from obvious luxury to words with more unsettling connotations: 'mistake' and 'cliff'. How do you understand this shift?

The Poet Gwendolyn Brooks was born in Topeka, Kansas, in 1917. She became the first black author to win the Pulitzer Prize for her writing and also the first black woman to hold the position of poetry consultant to the Library of Congress. As Poet Laureate of the State of Illinois, Brooks encouraged many aspiring poets, often funding prizes herself.

Her first poem was published when she was thirteen years old and by the time she was seventeen her poems were being published regularly. Many of her later poems deal with the civil rights activism of the 1960s and reflect her experience as an African-American woman in a society largely dominated by white men.

Her poetry often paints realistic and raw portraits of individuals, using a variety of forms. Her only novel, *Maud Martha*, was published in the 1950s and features a black female protagonist.

The Way We Live *Kathleen Jamie (b.1962)*

The Poem Superficially, Jamie's list poem seems to be just a series of random words and ideas thrown together and held in shape only by the driving rhythm and frequent enjambment. Look, for instance, at phrases like 'chicken tandoori and reggae' and 'launderettes, anecdotes'. However, an energetic celebration of the incongruous mix of things, what Louis MacNeice called 'the drunkenness of things being various', is integral to the theme of the poem.

Under the apparent randomness, patterns of language connections begin to appear. Notice, for example, the chain linking 'giros' to 'overdrafts', 'Final Demands' and the 'caprice of landlords'. Or how the language of transport, of journeys, is conveyed through 'driving fast', 'airports' and 'motorways'. This language of travel is held in tension with images of home. The poem encompasses 'Bombay' as well as 'Rannoch', 'Asiatic swelter' as well as the 'endless gloaming' of Scottish weather.

The poem draws attention to the disjointed strangeness of life in language that is sometimes grand and sometimes uncompromisingly banal. A celebratory tone is conveyed with the references to 'tambourine' and 'praises' to the Lord, suggesting a religious element, but, equally, could it be a more general tribute to the chaotic beauty of human existence?

The Poet Kathleen Jamie is a Scottish poet, essayist and travel writer. She won the Forward Prize for Best Collection in 2004 and currently holds the position of Chair of Creative Writing at Stirling University.

Jamie's early work focused on issues of identity, especially on female identity and her Scottishness. Many of these poems celebrate female power, but also explore the more troubling experience of entrapment. Recently, her work has focused less on identity and more on nature and what the poet describes as 'some idea of what is true and sanctified or sanctifiable'. Written in a spare, lyrical style, her nature poems are constructed from close observation of natural phenomena.

Running throughout Jamie's work is a tension between the tug of home and the pull of adventure and engaging with other cultures. A similar tension can be found in her language, which can switch in a single poem between English and Scots.

Meeting the British *Paul Muldoon (b.1951)*

The Poem This imagined account of the meeting between Native Americans and British colonizers in the 1760s is full of a sense of unease and dislocation until the final word of the poem directly confronts the chilling horror of what the colonizers are doing. The Native Americans had trade links with French forces who were at war with the British, and initially the speaker of the poem calls out in French, only to discover British officers.

The encounter is compared to two streams coming together but, significantly, they are both frozen over and the time is the 'dead' of winter. Notice the use of half-rhyme to emphasize a lack of harmony and the way two famous army officers who were implicated in the plan to use an early form of biological warfare are mentioned.

What is the significance of the frequently mentioned lavender in the poem and what is the effect of splitting the word 'handkerchief' across two couplets?

Does the use of French spoken to a Native American by a British officer in the eighth couplet draw attention to a theme of colonial invasion in the poem?

The Poet Paul Muldoon was born and educated in Northern Ireland and worked for the BBC for a number of years as a producer. He moved to America in 1987 and is a professor at Princeton University and poetry editor of the *New Yorker*. He was Professor of Poetry at the University of Oxford between 1999 and 2004.

Muldoon has won many major literary prizes, including the Pulitzer Prize for Poetry in 2003. His work is technically highly accomplished, witty, full of intriguing allusions and often ambitious in the range of ideas with which it engages. His long postmodern poem *Madoc: A Mystery*, which explores colonization, is a good example of the stimulating scope and complexity of his writing.

Muldoon has also written children's books, translations, literary criticism and librettos for several operas, as well as collaborating on lyrics for rock musicians such as the late Warren Zevon.

Border *Gillian Clarke (b.1937)*

The Poem When responding to Gillian Clarke's 'Border' it is worth knowing that she is a Welsh poet. Born in Cardiff to Welsh-speaking parents and now living in the coastal county of Ceredigion in mid-west Wales, she is a bilingual poet.

Consider the associations that spring from that single-word title. The separation of two political or geographical areas probably comes to mind and, as we read this poem, the border between two languages, Welsh and English, is clearly also being explored, along with the border between the rural and the urban. The countryside appears threatened. The farm is 'broken' and the hedgerow is a 'scar'. The third line conveys an unsettling sense of isolation: 'I'm foreign in my own country.'

The final verse uses the everyday experiences of going to a garage and a shop to highlight a sense of alienation. The use of Welsh is met with incomprehension and even hostility. How do you respond to the lines that suggest that the likes of the garage and shop workers 'came for the beauty/but could not hear it speak'?

The Poet In 2008 Gillian Clarke was appointed National Poet of Wales, having been the Capital Poet for Cardiff in 2005 and 2006. She is a writer who believes in the richness and power of both Welsh and English. She once said that she felt Welsh was the language in which Wales speaks to itself and English the language it uses to speak to the world. The interplay between the past and the present, the land and the people who inhabit it, is often seen in her work.

In addition to writing many volumes of poetry Gillian Clarke has worked as a playwright, broadcaster, editor, lecturer, translator and creative-writing tutor. In 2010 she was awarded the Queen's Gold Medal for Poetry.

The Black Lace Fan My Mother Gave Me *Eavan Boland (b.1944)*

The Poem As the title tells us, the object in question is a lace fan. Meditating on this heirloom leads the poet back into a story from the past. It is a seemingly romantic story of a man and a woman set in prewar Paris and centres on 'the first gift he ever gave her'. However, this is not a sentimental poem. The mood is inevitably influenced by references to 'violation' and the 'worn-out', 'overcast' nature of the lace.

Notice how the story is conveyed in short, curt sentences; carefully presented snapshots, like frames from a film: 'She stood up', 'The streets were emptying.' Though we are shown the actions and are allowed some access to the woman's thoughts, we are left to guess at their significance. The heat and the gathering storm suggest a powerful passion is lying just beneath the surface of the words.

Snapping out of the past, the poet examines the fan, as if for clues, like a detective. With its 'darkly picked' 'wild roses' and 'silk', the fan is exotic and potentially erotic.

The poet knows that the past is another country, remote and irrecoverable. The narrative remains unresolved. Only imagination can leap into this breach.

The Poet A celebrated Irish poet and essayist who has lectured at many universities, Eavan Boland spent her childhood in London and New York. Returning to Dublin as a student, she published her first collection of poems at the precocious age of eighteen while studying for a degree at Trinity College. She featured in the Penguin Modern Poets series alongside Vicki Feaver and Carol Ann Duffy in 1995 and has published over thirty books of poetry and literary criticism.

Preoccupied with issues of language, place, history and identity, Boland's work explores the poetry of ordinary, everyday experience. She is prepared to write unflinchingly about private and taboo subjects, such as infanticide and domestic violence. For Boland the private and the personal can be political. In particular, her poetry often confronts and subverts traditional, conservative concepts of womanhood.

She is a professor at Stanford University and divides her time between Dublin and California.

Originally *Carol Ann Duffy (b.1955)*

The Poem A poem about a family relocation begins with an evocative reference to the 'red room'. Is this on one level not only the car in which they are travelling to a new home but also a deliberate reference to other red rooms in literature, such as the one in *Jane Eyre* which becomes synonymous with suffering and anxiety? Duffy reconstructs a seemingly traumatic childhood event from a position of adult awareness and experience, allowing her to make the profoundly reflective and telling statement in the second verse: 'All childhood is an emigration.'

The difficulty of adapting to a new home, a new neighbourhood and a new dialect is captured in the second stanza, when the child is still disorientated and longing for her 'own country'. However, in the space between stanzas two and three the process of partial acclimatization has taken place and Duffy comments, 'But then you forget, or don't recall, or change'. The child starts to lose her accent and is now unsure about what exactly she has lost or maybe gained. Even so, when people ask her where she comes from '*Originally*', she will still 'hesitate'.

The Poet Carol Ann Duffy is a playwright, children's writer and poet whose many bestselling books include *Mean Time* and *Rapture*. She was born in Glasgow and studied at Liverpool University, is currently the Director of the Writing School at Manchester Metropolitan University and their Professor of Contemporary Poetry and was appointed Poet Laureate in 2009, the first female poet to hold the position.

Often written in a demotic style with a wide range of cultural references, Duffy's poems explore political, philosophical and social issues relating to gender, identity and inequality. She is particularly known for her exploration of feminine archetypes, her subversion of gender stereotypes and for her dramatic monologues, which were often written in the voices of characters who are marginalized, ignored or demonized by mainstream society.

Explaining Magnetism *Maura Dooley (b.1957)*

The Poem In this poem we find ourselves being led, like the speaker, into a place of aimlessness, as the poet takes us from 'British Rail/network charts' to an unspecified 'dull board game' (a reference to Monopoly). The image of the compass is repeated throughout and suggests that the speaker is seeking direction. However, she seems more interested in the aesthetics of 'a long feathered/arrow' than the specifics of finding her way. Think about the 'true North' mentioned at the end of the first stanza. Does this imply she once had found her own truth?

The movement of the Underground trains is reflected in the rhythm of the poem, adding a jolting and unstable sensation. The speaker's mental map of London seems to be based on Monopoly and she seems as unenthused about being 'in the South' as she did as a child playing the 'dull' board game. Her memory, like the train line, is circular and she moves from the present to the past, 'back and forth, left to right, round and round'. Note the distinction she draws between being 'isolated' and 'isolate' in line twelve and the multiple meanings of 'broke again' in the penultimate line.

The Poet Maura Dooley grew up in Bristol, though she was born in Truro and is of Irish descent. She is a freelance writer and a lecturer in creative writing at Goldsmiths College in London. She has published several collections of poetry, two of which have previously been shortlisted for the T. S. Eliot Prize. She has worked as an arts administrator and has close connections with the Poetry Society and the Arvon Foundation.

Her poetry is often personal, dealing with memory, complex emotions, journeys and our experience of time. 'Explaining Magnetism' is the title poem of her first full-length collection, which was published in 1991. She described it as being 'full of compass points: journeys into different parts of these islands and beyond. Into the past, into other people and into myself.'

Dooley often takes everyday images and uses them to dive under the surface to a subtle and seemingly collective version of reality.

Rubaiyat *Mimi Khalvati (b.1944)*

The Poem A rubaiyat is a Persian verse form, made famous in the Western world by Edward FitzGerald's English translation of the *Rubaiyat of Omar Khayyam*. A demanding form, it has a four-line stanza, or quatrain, with the first, second and fourth lines rhyming.

Khalvati's poem is a gentle, moving elegy to her grandmother. The poem bridges the enormous gap between the two women and the worlds they live in. Whereas Khalvati has become a celebrated poet, her grandmother appears to have worked as a servant, doing the menial, repetitive task of breaking up pieces of sugar. The poet honours and praises the skill involved in this task and compares her own comparative lack of dexterity. Though their worlds seem to be very different, the poem finds links between them. For instance, the 'care' the grandmother takes to 'tend what fades so soon' is mirrored by the care the poet takes to preserve her grandmother's memory.

There is a quietly magical, sensual quality to this poem. Notice, for instance, how the bed 'appears'. The most arresting image is of the lilac tree in a neighbour's garden. How do you think this tree might relate to the poet and her grandmother?

The Poet Actor, director and poet, Mimi Khalvati was born in Tehran in 1944 but went to a boarding school on the Isle of Wight until she was seventeen. Returning to England in her mid-twenties, she has published a number of collections of poetry, and co-founded an organization specializing in teaching poetry writing.

Khalvati is particularly interested in the creative opportunities, as well as the tensions, in her mix of English and Persian influences. This cultural cross-fertilization is evident in her use of Persian poetic forms such as the rubaiyat and ghazal and her extensive use of the sonnet and the villanelle.

She refers to her poems as dreaming spaces. Elegantly and precisely constructed, they often focus on small sensual details to evoke times, places and her experiences as a woman.

Love from a Foreign City *Lavinia Greenlaw (b.1962)*

'he Poem We are used to seeing and hearing reports of cities struggling somewhere far off in the world under a violent siege. Greenlaw's poem is shocking because it brings this situation home. London is defamiliarized as a city slowly degenerating, becoming violent and dangerous, overrun by cockroaches and rats. Trapped within this city is the quietly despairing voice of a woman trying desperately to remain calm and plucky; seeking not to alarm too much the 'Dearest' to whom the poem is addressed.

At first the situation seems almost comical. The cockroach falling into the gin, for example, is said to produce 'no ill effects'. However, the details grow more disturbing as the poem progresses: evidence of the 'bite marks of a rat' on the baby's cot is followed by the gruesome Gothic horror of a girl having her 'tongue cut out', then firebombs and a 'mortar attack'. We are given no sense of a cause or the identity of the enemy.

Notice how the form reflects the courageous attempts of the narrator to stay calm and measured, while all around her things are falling apart.

At the end of this dramatic monologue, the speaker's mother brings her a lavender tree, the flowers of which are said to calm the nerves.

The Poet Lavinia Greenlaw was born in London into a family of doctors and scientists. An essayist, librettist, playwright, poet and novelist whose first novel won the Prix du Premier Roman Étranger in France, Greenlaw is also an accomplished writer of non-fiction. A winner of a number of prizes and scholarships, including the Ted Hughes Award for new work in poetry for her sound work *Audio Obscura*, she was Professor of Poetry at the University of East Anglia before taking up a Wellcome Foundation Scholarship in 2013.

The first writer in residence at the Science Museum in London, Greenlaw is widely associated with writing about science. Her scientific background is reflected in the subjects of her early poetry and the cool, precise, observational style of her writing. Her latest book, *A Double Sorrow* (2014), is inspired by Chaucer's *Troilus and Criseyde*.

The Eater *Glyn Maxwell (b.1962)*

The Poem In 'The Eater' we are presented with a swirling and surreal city life. The frequent exclamations bring an immediate vibrancy, perhaps echoing the noise and bustle of cars and people. The reader is challenged throughout by questions, sometimes within and always at the end of each stanza. The use of the personal pronoun 'you' at times feels like reported speech, at others like direct address. Is it friendly or demanding?

The metre of each stanza shifts like the 'swarming city' with its 'bank officials' and 'crushhour'. The pattern of the first stanza is almost repeated in the penultimate, though the final line of this quintain stops us short with the question 'Who am I?' Again, the question is multi-layered and could be asked of the speaker and the reader alike.

Notice the repetitions in the middle of each stanza. What is the significance of this? Is it suggesting the circular pattern of city life or of time itself?

Consider also the enjambment and caesura in this poem. Maxwell says that, as a poet, 'line-break is all you've got'. How do the line breaks affect our experience of this poem?

The Poet Glyn Maxwell is an award-winning poet, playwright and librettist. He won the Somerset Maugham Award for his 1992 collection of poetry, *Out of the Rain*, and twenty years later his critical work *On Poetry* is seen as an exceptionally illuminating guide to the art form.

Born in England to Welsh parents, Maxwell read English at Oxford and completed his MA in poetry and drama at Boston University.

His poetry draws on traditional poetic forms, using the voices of various fictional and mythical personas to relate narratives. He is influenced by his performance work and says that he does not believe in a poetic voice unless 'I feel the breath in it, I feel the bloodstream in it.'

Phrase Book *Jo Shapcott (b.1953)*

The Poem Military euphemisms such as 'collateral damage' often hide the reality they are supposed to describe. Shapcott's dramatic monologue imagines a confused and increasingly distressed woman trying desperately to decipher military jargon as the world of her TV set appears to enter her domestic existence.

The scenario seems to be that an English woman is trapped somehow within a military conflict. She is trying to understand what is happening, but needs a phrase book in order to translate military jargon into ordinary language: 'Please write it down. Please speak slowly.' The language of propaganda and the sophisticated, graphic media coverage from war zones combine with the speaker's sense of her own physicality and humanity to create an unsettling, disorientating atmosphere.

Notice how the word 'bliss' is used to express the collision of two very different frames of reference: to the military pilots it is an acronym, a reminder of the evasive strategies needed to escape enemy fire when seeking shelter ('Blend, Low silhouette, Irregular shape, Small, Secluded' location); to the woman it is a word that evokes an erotic vision of tenderness and pleasure. If the meaning of 'bliss' can become distorted, the poet/narrator wonders, what about the word 'love'?

The Poet Recipient of the Queen's Gold Medal for Poetry, Jo Shapcott is Professor of Poetry at Royal Holloway College, University of London. She has won many prizes for her work, including the Forward Prize for Best Collection, the Costa Book Award and, on two occasions, the National Poetry Competition. She was educated at Trinity College, Dublin, and undertook postgraduate studies at Oxford, where she focused on the work of Elizabeth Bishop, and at Harvard, where she was taught by Seamus Heaney.

Interested in science, sexual politics, identity, perspective, language and power, Shapcott often explores her subjects from an unusual perspective, writing in one poem about the thoughts of a water particle, and in a series of others adopting the voice of a brain-diseased cow.

The Country at My Shoulder *Moniza Alvi (b.1941)*

The Poem When Moniza Alvi was young, her family moved from Pakistan to England. She published her collection of poems *The Country at My Shoulder* in 1993, before she had revisited the country of her birth. In this poem we see the influence a country can have on a person's identity, even without them physically having been there.

'Country at my shoulder' is repeated twice in the poem. To have something 'on' one's shoulder might suggest a great weight of responsibility. However, Alvi's country, with all its social and political complexity, is 'at' her shoulder. Notice the word 'burst' in the first and final stanzas. What is it that will cause the country to explode in this way?

We are drawn into stories that the speaker seems to have overheard about her faraway cousins and uncles. The names 'Azam', 'Aqbar', and 'Kamil' are scattered, hinting that the speaker longs to be closer to these family members whose 'quarrels,/travellers' tales' she hears about.

In the final stanza we are offered a surreal image of 'the country' being planted as if the speaker were covering it with soil and watering it. Notice the sense of anticipation in the final stanza.

The Poet Moniza Alvi was born in Pakistan. Her family moved to Hertfordshire when she was a few months old. She worked as a secondary school teacher in London before publishing her poetry. Today, she works as a freelance writer and tutor at the Poetry School, which provides poetry development programmes for adults.

Alvi has published several collections of poetry, many of them dealing with divisions and identity. She often writes about otherness and explores the boundaries between inner and outer worlds. Her poetry is written in English, but infused with words and vibrant images from her homeland.

In 1994 Alvi was included in the Poetry Society's New Generation Poets list. In 2002 she received a Cholmondeley Award for her poetry.

Marvin Gaye *Michael Hofmann (b.1957)*

The Poem Marvin Gaye was a Motown singer well known for hit songs such as 'I Heard It through the Grapevine'. Later in his career he suffered from paranoia and in 1984 he was shot dead by his minister father, Marvin Gay Senior.

This poem, a series of unsettling statements about Gaye's life, takes a detached tone and seems more fragmented biography than eulogy. In the first stanza the word 'final' seems to pre-empt the shooting in the last line. Notice the details that are included. It might be interesting also to consider which aspects of a life this poem leaves out.

The half-rhymes throughout offer a languid feel, perhaps echoing the music Gaye was famous for making. The 'personality disorders' of stanza four are presented vividly in the next stanza, with 'the eyes of the Belgians' and the unexpected violence towards the 'two Great Danes' in Topanga.

In the final line the reader is drawn far away from the reality of the violence, as the details of the father shooting his son are reduced to synecdoche. The father becomes 'a dog collar' and the great soul singer a 'purple dressing-gown'.

The Poet Michael Hofmann, who works as a translator and writer, was born in West Germany and grew up in England. His father was a novelist who wrote twelve novels in as many years, and his grandfather edited an encyclopaedia.

He studied at the University of Cambridge and published his first collection of poetry in 1983. He has won several awards for his writing, including the Cholmondeley Award, the Geoffrey Faber Memorial Prize for Poetry and, for his translation of his father's novel *The Film Explainer*, the Independent Foreign Fiction Prize.

The poem 'Marvin Gaye' comes from his third collection, *Corona, Corona* (1993), which features travel poems and character sketches. Hofmann frequently alludes to his difficult relationship with his father, and a common theme in his deft, skilful poetry is that we are doomed to make the same mistakes as our predecessors.

Dusting the Phone *Jackie Kay (b.1961)*

The Poem Kay's poem dramatizes a familiar situation: the narrator of the poem is waiting desperately for her lover to ring and make contact. Left in a state of dreadful suspense, she knows that if the phone rings it will presage disaster, and if it does not that will presage disaster too.

So, this is a love poem. But what sort of experience of love is this? There does not appear to be much enjoyment, or intellectual or erotic pleasure. Instead this is a poem about the pain, the torture, the worry and heartache of being in love. Notice how the narrator is so desperate for some news of the beloved that she 'assault[s] the postman for a letter'.

The feeling is all-consuming, the poem implies; the narrator feels 'trapped' and powerless in a way that is captured in the hanging question at the end of the poem. She demands a phone call, 'Or else. What?'

In this poem written in loose tercets, Kay's language and situation are made up from the ordinary, mundane and everyday. Yet within this ordinariness is the potentially overwhelming emotional and universal experience of love.

The Poet A novelist, short-story writer and poet, Jackie Kay is a black Scottish writer who was adopted as a child by two white Scottish communists. The subjects of her adoption, the experience of growing up as a black child in a white community and of her loving if unconventional family, have been important ones in her work. Indeed, the complex nature of identity and a celebration of cultural plurality are major themes that run through her writing. Kay, who is Professor of Creative Writing at Newcastle University, has recently written about her search for her birth parents in *Red Road Dust*.

Kay's work is energetic, often humorous, and generally written in the cadences of familiar speech; many of her poems are mini-dramas involving the voices of a range of characters.

The Emigrée *Carol Rumens (b.1944)*

The Poem 'The Emigrée' is taken from Carol Rumens's *Thinking of Skins*, published in 1993. An emigrée is normally a person forced to leave a country for political or social reasons, but might there be a metaphorical use of the term here?

The poem begins with memories of a country left 'as a child'. Whatever news the speaker receives of this country cannot detract from the impression of sunlight she associates with that place. Is it a memory of a country, or perhaps of a time or a person?

The second verse speaks of time threatening her and uses the language of yearning for something banned by the state. Is this a forbidden or unattainable love?

The third verse begins with a simple, melancholy statement that there is no passport to allow a 'way back'. And yet the narrator writes of being visited by her 'city' and talks of her relationship with this city in terms of love and devotion. The 'city of walls' is introduced at the end of the poem and appears menacing and threatening. Darkness, death and shadows feature in the last four lines but is the final word, 'sunlight', significantly optimistic?

The Poet Online readers of the *Guardian* will know Carol Rumens as the person who writes perceptive and entertaining analyses of whatever 'Poem of the Week' comes before her generous, critical eye. However, she is also a distinguished academic, an award-winning poet who published her first full-length collection of verse in 1974, a novelist and editor of a number of poetry anthologies. She has also written short stories and a number of plays, as well as collaborating on translations of Russian writers.

Her career in higher education has seen her work as the first director of the Philip Larkin Centre for Poetry and Creative Writing at the University of Hull, and her reputation as a poet and critic has led to her appointments at the University of Hull and the University of Bangor as Visiting Professor of Creative Writing.

Judith *Vicki Feaver (b.1943)*

The Poem 'Judith' is a dramatic monologue written in the voice of the biblical character of that name. In the Apocrypha, Judith is a Jewish heroine who kills Holofernes, the general of the army besieging her people. Her husband died in the barley harvest and she has mourned his loss for many years.

In the first line of the poem it is almost as if the poet herself is trying to reconcile how a woman can be both good and a murderer, before imaginatively inhabiting the mind of Judith as she enters Holofernes' tent.

Notice the complexity of feelings in Judith which Feaver describes between lines seven and thirteen. The desire to be taken care of and protected; to 'melt' into Holofernes and into a sweet oblivion is powerfully conveyed before the memory of her loss, her husband's suffering and her devastating sense of loneliness and isolation returns. Without him she would roll in the ashes of a fire just 'to be touched and dirtied by something'.

Consider the act of murder as described by Feaver in the last five lines and the impact of the use of the word 'cleaving' in the final line.

The Poet Vicki Feaver's first collection of poems, *Close Relatives*, was published in 1981 and was followed by two more volumes in 1994 and 2006. Individual poems from her collections have won prestigious prizes, including the Forward Poetry Prize (for 'Judith') and the Arvon Foundation Poetry Competition (for 'Lily Pond').

Vicki Feaver is Emeritus Professor at the University of Chichester, where she taught creative writing for a number of years. Her poised, sometimes confessional poetry powerfully explores relationships and female creativity. She combines the magical and the practical, the exotically sensual and the domestic.

Vicki Feaver now lives in Scotland. Her latest collection of poetry, *Like a Fiend Hid in a Cloud*, was published in 2013 to coincide with her seventieth birthday.

Birmingham River *Roy Fisher (b.1930)*

The Poem The River Thames has been eulogized in verse many times. Less celebrated are the rivers of Birmingham, the Tame and the prosaically named Rea (meaning 'river'). It is characteristic of Fisher's writing to focus on his own cultural and geographical context and on something disregarded and unvalued.

The tone of the poem at times is almost conversational in its use of contractions as the path of the little-known rivers is mapped. If it is a celebration of these unnoticed rivers, what are the qualities Fisher focuses on? Look at that emphatically isolated verb, 'Sunk'. These rivers have gone underground and 'sunk', which might carry the connotation of 'defeated'. They also repeatedly 'Gave way to' other forces and are 'marched' out by police. They become the repository for waste and industrial pollution and the 'drains, with no part in anybody's plan'.

These are not grand, showy, extravagant qualities. Nor are these adjectives normally associated with the proper names of places Fisher incorporates into his poem. Rarely can Wolverhampton or Dudley have featured in English poetry.

So in this controlled but limber poem, written in unshowy, unrhymed couplets, Fisher is celebrating an unconventional heroism, a heroism that is modest and stoic and which endures.

The Poet Roy Fisher's working-class Birmingham background forms an important subject in his poetic work. Teacher and jazz pianist as well as writer, Fisher is associated with the British Poetry Revival of the 1960s and '70s. Influenced by modernism, the Revival poets sought to challenge the dominance of 'the Movement', a stylistically and politically conservative genre of poetry that had held sway in Britain for a couple of decades after the Second World War.

Fisher's poetic aesthetic is also influenced by American poetry, in particular the work of William Carlos Williams and the Black Mountain Poets. He shares with these poets a preference for free verse, where the form of the poem is improvised to fit the content. His work, published in a dozen books over the last fifty years, offers an oblique angle on the familiar, focusing on the often uncelebrated, unseen or ignored.

On an Afternoon Train from Purley to Victoria, 1955

James Berry (b.1924)

The Poem Berry confronts ignorant, unintended racism in this poem with amused compassion. The woman who sits down beside him on the train and starts up a conversation is a Quaker. Quakers are normally seen as great advocates of human rights and social justice, so the nature of the conversation that follows is ironic. Quakers worship communally by waiting in silence until someone is moved by the spirit to speak. Clearly, this has happened to the woman, who tells Berry that she spoke on Sunday in support of 'racial brotherhood'.

Notice the third verse, where Berry reflects upon his earlier life in Jamaica and his father's banana field. What might have prompted that recollection?

The woman's precarious grasp of geography is revealed when she confuses Africa and Jamaica, but Berry is not offended. He responds to her in a gentle, humorous way and one which no doubt passes lightly over the woman's head. The charms of snow are contrasted symbolically with the attractiveness of a sunny climate before Berry concludes the poem by choosing to focus on the woman's sincerity rather than her ignorance. Does the idea of people sitting down 'around us' in the last line suggest an element of harmony and understanding?

The Poet James Berry was brought up in Jamaica and was fascinated by words and stories from an early age. However, he saw few opportunities to flourish in the town of his birth, where access to books was limited, and he set sail for England in 1948.

Working by day and studying in the evening, he began to write, and by the late 1970s he was ready to embark on a career that has seen him publish several collections of poetry for adults, stories and poems for children and two highly influential anthologies of British/West Indian writing. His work explores a wide range of subjects, including his West Indian roots, the experiences of the West Indian community in England and relationships between communities. There is anger at injustice and oppression but also a celebration of generosity and unity among communities.

St Kevin and the Blackbird *Seamus Heaney (1939–2013)*

The Poem One of the fascinating things about Heaney's playful, compassionate response to the legend of the Irish Kevin and the blackbird is the way that it confronts and accepts the plain fabrication of the story. The fact that it is made up makes it all the more interesting, since that focuses the reader on the real question of the purpose of the story. A true story never quite has that stylized edge, that cool detachment we sense in an allegorical tale like this.

Having neatly described the remarkable nesting of the bird in Kevin's outstretched hand when the saint is linked to 'the network of eternal life', Heaney presents a series of questions almost like a catechism: 'Does he still feel his knees?'; 'Is there distance in his head?'

The picture of St Kevin universalizes the ideas of suffering, nurturing and enduring, and it universalizes their connections. Another saint's prayer, '"To labour and not to seek reward"', attributed to St Ignatius of Loyola, the founder of the Jesuits, encapsulates St Kevin's philosophy.

The poem ends fittingly in an atmosphere of mysticism and self-forgetfulness.

The Poet Winner of the Nobel Prize for Literature in 1995 and Professor of Poetry at Oxford and Harvard universities, Seamus Heaney was the best-known and most celebrated poet of the last fifty years. His death in 2013 prompted tributes from across the world.

Beginning with *Death of a Naturalist* in 1966, Heaney's early work excavated his past, exploring themes of childhood and growing up. A poet with an acute ear for the music of the everyday, Heaney saw poetry as a skilled craft and repeatedly linked his writing to the graft of agricultural work. Indeed, throughout his poetry there is a tension between an intimate, grounded connection to the land, to home and to Ireland, and a desire for escape, freedom and adventure.

Born near the Irish borders, Heaney also wrote about 'the Troubles', sometimes obliquely in his bog poems, sometimes more directly, in elegies to victims of the conflict.

Blackout *Grace Nichols (b.1950)*

The Poem There is something eerie about this poem, with people 'emerging out of shadows' and 'grey ramshackle' houses, like scenes in a horror film. 'Blackout' can refer to a lack of electricity but also to a period of blank memory, usually due to excessive use of drugs or alcohol. Is Nichols implying that the capitalized 'Box', or television, is a drug for the people, causing them to forget the 'cloying stench' of their reality?

The picture painted here is grim and 'medieval'. The violent image of the coconut vendors who 'decapitate/the night' makes us fear for the heads of the children 'all waiting'. Nichols creates a sense of anticipation and breathlessness with repeated lines starting with 'And'.

The 'generator-lit big house' stands out, emphasizing the darkness that surrounds it. Rather than an image of hope, this light appears 'obscenely bright', ostentatious in its contrast to the world around. There seems to be an injustice in the distribution of the coveted electricity and, by implication, of wealth. The 'worn-out movie' seems to refer to the narrative of wealth and poverty which humanity repeatedly plays out, with the single line at the end of the poem reminiscent of rolling film credits.

The Poet Grace Nichols won the Commonwealth Poetry Prize in 1983 with her first collection of poetry, *I is a Long-memoried Woman*. This collection was also dramatized by the BBC and adapted for film. Since then she has published numerous collections, many of them inspired by her Caribbean roots. She writes about the experiences of women and immigrants, weaving in Guyanese and Native American myths and folklore. Her writing is lively and musical, often echoing the oral traditions and rhythms of the Caribbean. She combines standard English and Creole to explore themes of alienation, separation, connection and spirituality. She also writes for children and has produced poetry and entertaining short stories for a younger audience.

Nichols was born in Georgetown, Guyana, and worked there as a teacher and journalist. In 1977 she moved to the UK, where she still lives, with her partner and fellow Guyanese poet, John Agard.

Wedding *Alice Oswald (b.1966)*

The Poem This sonnet begins with a line of iambic pentameter which has echoes of many conventional lines of poetry which seek to describe and define love. In this case, 'our love is like a sail', but there is no attempt to extend the simile. Instead the poem offers comparison after comparison and transformation after transformation. The sail becomes a swallowtail, a coat, a tear, a mouth and a trumpeter.

How does the poem encourage the reader to consider the changes and transformations that love brings and the way art attempts to make sense of those transformations? Love, time and timelessness in the context of shared, universal human experience are explored in a tone of breathless, wind-buffeted exhilaration. The final couplet brings together wedding and love and the all-encompassing word 'everything', suggesting both a sense of wonder and the cyclical nature of human experience.

Look at the way Oswald uses variations within the sonnet form to support the meaning of the poem.

The Poet Alice Oswald read classics at Oxford before training and working as a gardener with, originally, no intention of becoming a full-time poet.

However, her first collection of poetry was shortlisted for the Forward Poetry Prize for Best First Collection in 1996, and her second book, *Dart*, which explored the River Dart in Devon through poetry and prose, won the T. S. Eliot Prize for Poetry. Her 2011 work *Memorial* is based on Homer's *Iliad* and deals powerfully with death and how the dead might be memorialized.

Oswald's belief in the importance of rhythm is evident throughout her work and in her admiration for writers such as Milton and Beckett, where rhythmical control of language is significant. Her almost visionary appreciation of nature and her understanding of the historical significance of the landscape along with her deft control of tone are widely admired.

Minority *Imtiaz Dharker (b.1954)*

The Poem The opening line of the poem introduces its theme of separation and otherness. The speaker repeats the word 'foreigner', emphasizing their isolation from their own family. They are certain that 'All kinds of places and groups' 'distance themselves' from them.

Notice how different the similes in the third and fourth stanzas seem. The first – 'like a clumsily translated poem' – appeals to the intellect, whereas the second – 'like food cooked in milk of coconut' – adds a sensual experience of foreignness. Notice also the isolation of the third stanza and the separation created between these two similes.

We are presented with images connected with the mouth, as if the processes of eating and speaking have become interchangeable for the speaker. As well as 'the unexpected aftertaste/of cardamom or neem', the speaker writes how 'language flips/into an unfamiliar taste'. What does this suggest about identity and culture?

Later the speaker seems to find an internal reconciliation in writing. The assonance of 'scratch', 'chatter' and 'clattering' builds up a momentum that reflects the speaker's move away from otherness to a final acceptance. Through the use of direct address, the final stanza invites the reader to share in the experience of being the 'outcast'.

The Poet Imtiaz Dharker's poetry often deals with themes of identity, separation and home, reflecting the experiences of her own life. Born in Pakistan, she moved to Scotland when she was very young and was brought up in Glasgow. She currently lives between India, London and Wales. She describes herself as a 'Scottish Muslim Calvinist'.

As well as poetry, Dharker also produces drawings and documentary films. She had her first solo exhibition in 1982 and has created over three hundred films. Her five collections of poetry to date all include her own artwork and she often combines art exhibitions with poetry readings. In her art and writing Dharker challenges us to question how we live on an individual and global scale and how we respond to others and ourselves.

Imtiaz Dharker is a Fellow of the Royal Society of Literature and in 2013 was Poet in Residence at the Cambridge University Library.

A Minute's Silence *Paul Farley (b.1965)*

The Poem The setting of this beautifully observed poem at a Liverpool football match tells us something significant about the poet and his concerns. The central conceit of Farley's poem is silence becoming alive, escaping the ground, sweeping outwards through space and backwards through time, until it reaches the coast and comes back again. The silence creates a 'space' that has been 'opened up' in which time seems suspended (wonderfully caught in the paradoxical phrase 'small eternity') and into which the poet's imagination moves.

Notice how Farley uses synaesthesia, the mixing of senses, so that sound becomes physical and a 'space' (the whistle, for example, 'bursts a hole'). Silence is also characterized as being 'observed', as if it is a visual phenomenon, and it gets 'its feet wet'.

The classic Liverpool supporters' anthem 'You'll Never Walk Alone' is woven into the last section of the poem, inevitably arousing thoughts of communal grief and celebration.

This is a poem of rich sounds – 'a million tiny licking, chopping sounds' of the surf – and of rich memories. Farley finishes it in imperative mood. What do you take to be the message of those last, enigmatic lines?

The Poet Born in Liverpool in 1965, Paul Farley is a poet and broadcaster who studied painting at the Chelsea School of Art. He is currently Professor of Poetry at the University of Lancaster.

Farley's award-winning poetry is particularly characterized by his use of the mundane and the ordinary as a gateway for poetic exploration. Culturally wide-ranging, his poems often feature a familiar contemporary world as a starting point for reflections on issues such as history and identity.

Critics celebrate Farley's adeptness at filling traditional closed forms with a modern idiom and his running of the cadences of speech across the strictures of metre. In general, there is a poignant, touching strain to Farley's formally elegant, engaging and rather cinematic style of writing.

Prince Rupert's Drop *Jane Draycott (b.1954)*

The Poem Formed when molten glass is dropped into cold water, a 'Prince Rupert's drop' is a jewel-like, tadpole-shaped droplet of glass that is both incredibly strong and very fragile. The italicized line at the beginning of the poem suggests the poet's interest in this, but the poem swiftly reveals that the interest lies not in glass-making so much as the states of tension the phenomenon encourages the poet to consider.

The poem is a string of bright visual metaphors in which the drop is imagined variously as an 'eye', an 'ear' and a 'lantern'. But it is the running play of sounds that links the language together and gives it rhythmic impact.

A sonic chain stretches between the monosyllables 'drop', 'rock', 'neck', 'like', 'kick', 'nick' and 'snap'; another between 'sugar', 'mortar' and 'surefire'. Notice how the violent verb 'snap' is repeated and the way in which 'your' takes the fascination with the drop into a more personal realm and one that makes us think of love and loss. The final couplet of the poem might suggest a harmonious ending, but the emphatic 'spot'/'not' rhyme emphasizes the sense of someone being present one moment and gone a moment later.

The Poet Jane Draycott teaches creative writing at Oxford and the University of Lancaster and is an academic and poet with a particular interest in sound art and collaborative work. Her award-winning sound recordings with Elizabeth James have been performed on BBC Radio, and Draycott has also worked with film makers and digital artists. Her most recent writer-in-residence assignment was in Amsterdam in 2013.

Nominated three times for the Forward Prize for Poetry, her first two full collections, *Prince Rupert's Drop* and *The Night Tree*, were both Poetry Book Society Recommendations. Her latest collection, *Over*, was shortlisted for the T. S. Eliot Prize. Her work has a mesmeric intensity and blends feelings with ideas in ways that are inventive and arresting.

She was nominated as one of the Poetry Book Society's Next Generation Poets in 2004. Draycott's most recent book is an acclaimed translation of the anonymous medieval poem *Pearl*.

Machines *Michael Donaghy (1954–2004)*

The Poem 'Machines' presents an elaborate and ingenious comparison between a piece of slow, stately Purcell music played on the harpsichord and a twelve-speed racing bike. This kind of extended, skilfully sustained comparison, sometimes known as a 'conceit', was made popular by the likes of John Donne, writing in the seventeenth century. Donaghy, writing in the late twentieth century, was an admirer of Donne and his fellow Metaphysical poets.

Note the fusion of intellect and emotion in the poem. It begins with an address to a loved one, 'Dearest', but immediately moves in to the conceit. Ptolemy's geocentric model of the universe and the bicycle engineer Schwinn are mentioned in the same line as the poem explores 'The machinery of grace'.

Line ten, with its reference to 'this talk', suggests a more direct appeal to his 'Dearest'. What might the poet be hoping for if the 'effortless gadgetry of love' works as smoothly and successfully as a beautiful piece of music or a precisely engineered bicycle wheel?

The themes of movement and progression are captured in the final line, which is, like the whole poem, carefully balanced. The lovers, cyclists and harpsichordists all know that they 'only by moving can balance,/Only by balancing move.'

The Poet Michael Donaghy was born and educated in America but moved to London in his early thirties. He grew up in the Bronx in New York in an area of racial tension and violence, but became an enthusiastic reader of poetry in public libraries. He even continued to read while working as a doorman, keeping copies of poems under his hat.

In England he taught at City University and Birkbeck College in London and was a critic and poetry editor. Donaghy was also an accomplished musician, specializing in traditional Irish music.

His first full-length collection of poetry, *Shibboleth*, won literary prizes, as did subsequent collections, and he was greatly admired as a performer of his own work, which he always recited from memory.

Donaghy's work can be both playful and melancholic, streetwise and exceptionally learned. His collected poems were published posthumously in 2009 after his sudden death in 2004.

A Misremembered Lyric *Denise Riley (b.1948)*

The Poem Woven through this poem are snippets of song lyrics 'misremembered', as the title tells us. Lines from a song by Greenaway and Cook and performed by Gene Pitney are changed in the speaker's recollection. Instead of 'Something's gotten hold of my heart' she offers 'gotta', and rather than 'keeping my soul' Riley uses the more emotive 'tearing'. In the original song, 'soul and senses' are kept apart. What difference does the speaker's version of 'soul and conscience' suggest? Are the lyrics 'misremembered' or stored in a more appropriate version in the memory?

Another song that is invoked by the speaker is the Cascades' 'Rhythm of the Rain'. Where the song lyrics 'listen to the rhythm of the falling rain', here, 'I listen to the rhythm of unhappy pleasure.' She also asks, 'Do shrimps make good mothers?', which is the title of a popular comic song of the 1920s. Notice the way the speaker's thoughts seem to 'whirr' between song lyrics, stitching very different songs together into an emotional patchwork that neither consoles, nor keeps off 'falling rain' nor offers 'a brand-new start'.

The Poet Denise Riley is a poet who has also written extensively on philosophy, history and feminist theory. Born in Carlisle, she studied at both Cambridge and Oxford. She was Professor of English Literature and Director of the Creative Writing MA (Poetry) at the University of East Anglia, and taught for several years at Cornell University. She has been a Writer in Residence at the Tate Gallery, London, but returned to the University of East Anglia as Professor of Poetry and History of Ideas in 2013.

In 2012, after more than a decade when she had not published a new poem, she produced a set of twenty linked short poems called *A Part Song*, dealing with the death of her adult son. Resisting any description of the sequence as elegy or lament, she seeks to explore her altered experience of time. *A Part Song* won the 2012 Forward Prize for Best Single Poem.

It's Work *Benjamin Zephaniah (b.1958)*

The Poem Zephaniah's light-hearted, humorous poem is about the choices he did or did not make in his life and, in this way, it is an autobiographical poem revealing the character of its creator.

The range of possibilities was, and is, wide. If he had told careers advisers that he would like to be either a 'farmer' or a 'Rasta writer', they may well have been nonplussed. What we do not do defines us as much as what we do. We learn about Zephaniah's character and values through the fact that he was not interested in joining the army or in becoming a tax collector. This all fits with the fact that the poet is a pacificist and a vegan with socialist political leanings.

The poem ends with a simple statement of belief in the importance and validity of the role of the poet and an ironic echoing of the voices that would not see poetry as a 'proper job'.

Of course, who we are is also revealed by what we say and how we say it. Zephaniah rejects the conventions of standard English, of standard spelling, choosing instead to write phonetically in his own distinct British-Afro-Caribbean voice.

The Poet Benjamin Zephaniah is one of the best-known and most distinctive poets writing today. In addition to his success as a poet, with more than a dozen published collections, Zephaniah has written a number of novels. He left school when he was just thirteen and, after a sometimes troubled childhood growing up in Birmingham, discovered poetry through writing lyrics for reggae music.

A charismatic performer of his verse, Zephaniah has an extraordinary ear for rhythm. His poems are often inspired by the sonic patterns of words he hears spoken. Extemporizing or riffing on this pattern allows him to develop poems that are accessible and thought-provoking. Political issues inspire him to write; his dub style of poetry is politically engaged, particularly in terms of race and human rights. Though Zephaniah tackles difficult political subjects, his poems are also often engagingly funny.

Cousin Coat *Sean O'Brien (b.1952)*

The Poem O'Brien says this poem is 'about an invisible coat which I eventually discovered I'd been wearing all my life and was not allowed to remove'. It seems to be a statement of his intent and purpose as a poet.

The formality of the poem, with its steady iambic pentameter and consistent rhyme scheme, reflects the serious tone and the constant presence of the 'secret coat'. The language is sometimes colloquial. The coat gives a 'clammy itch', compelling the speaker to work to give voice to the poor and persecuted in history even though there was a time when he sought to escape into libraries and the literature of Donne and Henry James.

In the third and fourth stanzas he lists those he feels obliged to represent. We see a compassion for the 'North, the poor', while a reference to 'Jarrow' places the speaker's perceived task firmly within the politics and history of his northern home. Progress, he seems to suggest, has been limited since the Jarrow March.

Notice how the final stanza is like a prayer with its repeated plea 'Be with me' and a passionate request for the coat to keep his poetic voice 'honest'.

The Poet Sean O'Brien has won the Forward Prize for Poetry three times, in addition to numerous other awards for his six collections of poetry. He is also a critic, academic, novelist and short-story writer.

He grew up in Hull before moving to Newcastle upon Tyne, where he has lived since 1990. He studied at Cambridge and taught for several years in East Sussex. He is Professor of Creative Writing at Newcastle University and had previously been Professor of Poetry at Sheffield Hallam University.

O'Brien is an unashamedly political writer, and his technically accomplished poetry is typically based in the post-industrial North-east and examines the interplay of past and present. He examines, often with wit and humour, a quintessential England of allotments, football and old industrial towns. He also explores the experiences of individuals during different points in history, looking at the effects of collective narrative on individual lives.

The Lammas Hireling *Ian Duhig (b.1954)*

The Poem Lammas is a traditional festival that marks the beginning of the harvest season. The 'he' of this poem is a hireling presumably taken on to help with this busy farming time. Things start well, and the hireling is popular with the cattle, which 'doted on him'. However, this mysterious narrative poem immersed in folklore takes a turn for the macabre at the end of the first stanza following the anecdotal 'Then one night'.

In a classic example of the archetypal intruder, the hireling is caught 'Stark naked but for the fox-trap biting his ankle.' What follows leaves the speaker in a state of such ineradicable guilt that he feels compelled to spend his life in confession.

Notice how the colloquial tone draws us into the narrative, with the phrase 'muckle' (a large amount) adding to a sense of alienating otherworldliness. The cows 'only dropped heifers' in the company of the hireling, as if he were a good-luck charm. However, the speaker's 'dear late wife' leads him from a dream to the 'warlock' and, suddenly, the hireling's body is dropped over the bridge and the 'herd's elf-shot' (riddled with disease). What happened?

The Poet Ian Duhig is a freelance teacher and writer of poetry and short stories. He often draws on his Irish roots in his poetry, writing about myths and legends with a lilting musicality reminiscent of the speech patterns of Ireland. He skilfully incorporates elements of traditional ballad forms, songs and hymns into modern contexts. His style is often humorous and his subject matter is diverse.

He was born in England to a large Irish family and currently lives in Leeds. He spent fifteen years working in a homeless hostel, an experience which has informed his writing.

Duhig has won the National Poetry Competition twice, and his collection *The Lammas Hireling* was shortlisted for both the T. S. Eliot and Forward prizes.

Waking with Russell *Don Paterson (b.1963)*

The Poem Sonnets are a popular form for love poetry. This sonnet, with its subtle ABAB rhyme scheme, plays on that idea: the first two lines suggest guardedly that the poet is in bed with a lover, whom we know from the title is called Russell. It is not until the third line that we realize he is alone with his new baby. The baby's smile transfixes his father so much that his own smile is transformed from his usual 'hard-pressed grin' to something more fresh and joyous, an innocent smile 'rediscovered'.

Paterson was '*mezzo del cammin*', or halfway down the road of life, suggesting he was approaching middle age when he became a father. Before the birth of his son he felt he had lost the 'true path', but the poem expresses the sudden delight he finds when, continuing the road imagery, the baby's arrival 'cut in front' (overtook him) and lit up the road ahead.

There is great tenderness throughout the poem, and this is underlined in the final line as the stresses of the regular iambic pentameter rhythm gently fall on the key words: 'I *kissed* your *mouth* and *pledged* my*self* for*ev*er'.

The Poet Don Paterson was born in Scotland but moved to London in 1984 to work as a jazz guitarist. He published his first collection in 1993, and his many awards include the Queen's Gold Medal for Poetry in 2010 and the T. S. Eliot Prize on two occasions (1997 and 2003).

He is Professor of Poetry at the University of St Andrews, having returned to live in Scotland, and, besides writing poetry, he edits anthologies and writes drama for the theatre and for radio. He has been poetry editor for the publisher Picador Macmillan for many years. He is fascinated by the aphorism and has produced a compendium and two books of aphorisms. The language of his poetry can switch effortlessly between the erudite and the colloquial, between playful postmodernism and heartfelt lyricism. He continues to combine writing poetry, composing and performing music and teaching in higher education.

Two Pages *Choman Hardi (b.1974)*

The Poem This is a poem of two halves, each telling a seemingly separate story. In the first we are presented with the outline of a narrative. Though we cannot work out exactly what has happened, we know that the male character has written something that distresses the female recipient. So this is a story, it appears, of some sort of betrayal.

The second half refers to a specific historical event, a poison-gas attack on the Iraqi Kurds of Halabja by forces controlled by Saddam Hussein. Over two decades later this aerial attack remains the largest chemical-weapon assault on a civilian population in history, resulting in over five thousand dead.

Hardi tells both stories from similar, slightly unusual perspectives. In the first narrative the pad of paper appears to be the narrator; in the second the paper itself speaks. What do you think is achieved by her unusual choices of narrator? How do these two stories, one personal and fictional, the other geopolitical and historical, relate to each other?

Sometimes telling a story from the perspective of a naïve, innocent participant can make it more poignant. To what extent is this true in the case of 'Two Pages'?

The Poet Raised in Iraq and Iran, Choman Hardi is a Kurdish poet, painter and translator who moved to the United Kingdom in 1993, where she studied philosophy and psychology at the universities of Oxford, University College, London, and Kent.

Hardi is a poet who draws on her personal experiences, using poetry as a method for seeing things in fresh ways with fresh language. She had published two books in Kurdish by the time she was twenty-five, but began to write more in English after the year 2000. Her second language has allowed her some critical distance from her often painful, personal subjects, and her characteristic tone is quiet and civilized, even when considering brutality.

Hardi is a former chair of Exiled Writers Ink, a collaboration between established refugee authors writing in another language as well as English.

Pelt *Michael Symmons Roberts (b.1963)*

The Poem 'Pelt' is the first poem from Michael Symmons Roberts's 2004 collection *Corpus*. The speaker in this poem claims to have discovered the 'pelt' of the world. Pelts are the skins of animals shot by hunters and sometimes displayed as trophies. The speaker seems surprised to find this particular skin in a 'cheap hotel' and wonders 'Who fleeced it?' The conclusion he draws is that the earth's 'open wound' – its weeping grass, raw wind and scabbed riverbeds – is the product of this lack of an outer skin.

Roberts explores but cannot find who has done this to the world; there is no obvious evidence. Towards the end of the poem the speaker wonders whether instead of some malevolent human agency, the world 'shrugs off a hide/each year'. There is a contrast between the certainty of the second stanza and the hesitant, repeated 'maybe's of the penultimate one. In a surreal moment at the end the speaker tries wearing the pelt, but concludes it is not for him. What else contributes to a sense of the surreal in this poem? What does this contribute to your understanding of the poem?

The Poet Michael Symmons Roberts was born in Preston and spent his early childhood in Lancashire before moving south to Berkshire. After graduating from Oxford University, where he read philosophy and theology, he trained as a newspaper journalist and then worked for several years for the BBC, before concentrating on his own writing. He has written novels, radio plays and libretti as well as several collections of poems. His choral work has been produced by the BBC Proms, and he has also written operas in a continuing collaboration with the composer James Macmillan. Roberts is Professor of Poetry at Manchester Metropolitan University and has been described as a religious poet for a secular age.

In his lyric poetry he examines the everyday. His language, as can be seen in 'Pelt', tends to be matter-of-fact and straightforward, and his common themes include science, medicine, religion and a sense of grace.

Bread *Kamau Brathwaite (b.1930)*

The Poem Brathwaite coined the term 'Sycorax style' to describe an aspect of his rebellion against the rules of standard English. 'Sycorax style' refers to Brathwaite's non-standard use of fonts, typography, breaks, icons and images in his poems.

Notice all the different ways in which Brathwaite deviates from standard English in 'Bread'. He cuts lines in unusual places, uses non-standard spelling, such as 'scarifice' for 'sacrifice', and incomplete sentences. Rather than being used to mark units of sense, punctuation is employed as a rhythmic device, shaping units of breath.

The poem is compelling, with its stark, almost hypnotic, rhythm. The key early phrases would appear to be 'the white dream', 'the foreign cornfields', 'the black wife'. Do the references to the bread carry deeper, metaphorical meanings? That 'you' in 'flesh of the god you break' in line sixteen is the first personal pronoun in the poem. Suddenly, we the reader, almost halfway through the poem, feel accused. Life-giving gestures and rituals appear now to become dangerous and even murderous. References to knives and cutting and rats litter the ending of the poem, while the menacing lights of the cars are constantly 'watching'.

The Poet Born in Barbados in 1930, Edward Kamau Brathwaite is one of the most influential Caribbean writers of the twentieth century. Educated at Harrison College in Barbados, at Cambridge and at Sussex, where he completed a PhD in philosophy, he was the co-founder of the Caribbean Artists' Movement. Currently, he is Professor of Comparative Literature at New York University.

A post-colonial poet, Brathwaite writes extensively about Caribbean history and identity. For post-colonial writers, the use of English and European art forms is problematic. English is the language of the colonizers, but it is also a language that allows communication with the world. Addressing this issue, Brathwaite re-colonizes the English language, writing in what he calls a revolutionary 'nation language'. Though he uses English vocabulary, his spelling and grammar, for example, are non-standard. More importantly, the syntax and rhythms of his verse are deeply influenced by African culture, by blues music and by jazz.

The Full Indian Rope Trick *Colette Bryce (b.1970)*

The Poem The Full Indian Rope Trick is a magic trick that was reportedly performed by a fakir – a wandering Sufi monk. He would cause a rope to rise up from the ground as he played a musical pipe, and his young accomplice would miraculously climb to the top. In the 1930s a disbelieving collection of magicians offered a reward to anyone who could perform the trick. Bryce starts her poem with reference to this challenge, saying there was 'no secret', 'no dark fakir' and 'no footage'. The speaker's rope is 'caught by the sky' and they climb up, repeating 'goodbye'. What is it that the speaker is leaving behind?

The poem itself seems to lift into the air with the energy of its language and rhyme. 'Passers-by', 'caught by the sky', 'First try' and 'squinting eyes' loop through the second and third stanzas like a coiled rope.

Notice the contradictions in the poem. The speaker is both 'long gone' and 'still here'. They complete the trick 'First try' and yet it also took years. What do these paradoxes suggest about the speaker's magical rite of passage?

The Poet Colette Bryce was born in 1970 in Derry, Northern Ireland, though later moved to London, Scotland and the North-east. She was the Fellow in Creative Writing at the University of Dundee from 2003 to 2005 and North-east Literary Fellow at the University of Newcastle from 2005 to 2007. She currently works as a freelance writer, teaches for various organizations such as the Arvon Foundation and is poetry editor of *Poetry London*.

Her first collection of poetry, *The Heel of Bernadette*, was published in 2000. 'The Full Indian Rope Trick' is the title poem of her second, which is filled with images of miracles and magic. This collection examines the experience of being trapped and looks with energy and passion at the need to find escape. This poem won her the National Poetry Competition in 2003 and in 2008 it was voted the favourite winning poem of the last thirty years.

Mametz Wood *Owen Sheers (b.1974)*

The Poem During the Battle of the Somme, the 38th Welsh Division was ordered to take Mametz Wood. The objective was finally achieved a week later – largely due to the help of another battalion of Welsh soldiers – but over four thousand men were lost.

The poem describes how farmers ploughing today regularly find the remains of those gunned-down soldiers. There is an extended metaphor of the land being injured, with the farmers tending it back to itself, helping to rid it of wounds.

There is little left of 'the wasted young'. Sheers emphasizes the fragility of their remains in the second stanza. In the third he points out the ugly irony that the lumps of flint lying in the soil, blue and white, resemble what is left of the men's bones.

Towards the end, Sheers focuses on a new and particularly gruesome discovery of 'twenty men buried in one long grave'. He pauses on vivid details such as the fact that their boots outlasted their bodies. There is ugly comedy: they appear 'paused mid dance-macabre', a poignant contrast to the activity they were actually involved in when they died.

The Poet Owen Sheers was born in Fiji in 1974 but brought up in South Wales. He studied at New College, Oxford, and at the University of East Anglia.

A prolific writer in many genres, he is not only an award-winning poet but also a successful film writer, dramatist, novelist and biographer. His first novel, *Resistance*, has been translated into ten languages and made into a film with a screenplay written by Sheers himself. He regularly appears on BBC Radio 3 and 4, and was recently Poet in Residence for the Welsh Rugby Union. His most recent collection of poems, *Skirrid Hill*, won a Somerset Maugham Award.

His verse drama *Pink Mist*, dealing with soldiers returning from active service in Afghanistan, was commissioned by Radio 4 and his play *The Two Worlds of Charlie F*, which also deals with wounded servicemen, has toured nationally.

Toussaint L'Ouverture Acknowledges Wordsworth's Sonnet 'To Toussaint l'Ouverture' *John Agard (b.1949)*

The Poem Agard's poems often enact cultural hybridity through his 'mashing up' of languages, particularly standard English with Caribbean Creole. In this poem, however, the hybridity is formal, rather than linguistic. We have a dramatic monologue in the form of a sonnet in which Agard ventriloquizes the voice of Touissant L'Ouverture. L'Ouverture was the leader of the first successful slave-led rebellion. In 1791 slaves in Haiti revolted against their French colonial masters and, with some help from the British, defeated Napoleon's forces, eventually securing independence from France in 1804.

In 1802 the English Romantic poet William Wordsworth wrote a poem celebrating L'Ouverture, suggesting that his example of a noble struggle for justice would inspire future generations. Agard's poem makes reference to a number of famous images from Wordsworth's poems, such as daffodils and Westminster Bridge (from 'Upon Westminster Bridge'). The poem is built on a series of contrasts between the lives of the two poets. Unlike Wordsworth, for instance, L'Ouverture 'never walked on Westminster Bridge'.

Underneath these superficial differences, Agard suggests, is a deeper brotherhood between L'Ouverture and Wordsworth. Any reader of 'Upon Westminster Bridge' will recognize how fitting Agard's choice of metaphor is: 'When human beings share a common garment.'

The Poet Born in Guyana, John Agard emigrated to England in 1977. A poet, playwright and short-story writer who has written many books for both adults and children, he is an exuberant, flamboyant performer of his poetry, known for his interest in social justice and his humorous, compassionate poems.

Agard writes about issues of identity, language, colonialism and history, often employing a language that fuses English with Caribbean Creole; in this way he makes himself a champion of multiculturalism. In 2012 he was awarded the Queen's Gold Medal for Poetry.

Look We Have Coming to Dover! *Daljit Nagra (b.1966)*

The Poem The poem is in a dialogue with one written over 150 years earlier by Matthew Arnold. In 'Dover Beach' the melancholic poet stands at the edge of civilized England imagining the withdrawal of religion from our shores and the descent into conflict and disorder he thinks must follow. Nagra's cleverly shaped poem also dramatizes a withdrawal, as one idea of England is replaced by another.

In 'Dover Beach' the surrounding sea is presented as being beautiful, calm and tranquil. In Nagra's poem the sea has 'gobfuls' in its 'phlegmed water'; Dover's cliffs are crumbling and 'scummed'. The landscape has become polluted by an ugly hostility to immigrants and even the thunder 'unbladders/yobbish rain'.

Consider how the immigrants are described. 'Stowed in the sea' and 'hutched', they try to go under the radar. They are doing something dangerous, fearing a 'stab in the back' or being caught in the 'spotlight' of the moon. Nagra also uses the sort of metaphors employed insidiously by racists to whip up fear of immigration. He imagines that immigrants 'invade' in dehumanized 'Swarms'.

Just as in 'Dover Beach', the poet turns to his 'love' at the end. Is there a sense of hope in the final verse?

The Poet Winner of Forward prizes for Best Poem and Best First Collection in 2007, Daljit Nagra is a poet whose parents moved from India to England in the 1960s. Brought up in Sheffield and in London, he now lives and teaches in the capital.

In his carefully crafted poetry, Nagra explores the challenging experiences of British-born Asians and through this presents a fresh portrait of modern Britain. His mixing of cultures and language is most obvious in his use of 'Punglish', a form of Indian English, influenced by the language of the Punjab. Often in dramatic-monologue form, his poems also combine references to things quintessentially English (Dover beach, Ford Grenadas, alcopops) with things quintessentially Indian (saris, rickshaws) or, at least, Anglo-Indian (corner shops).

Nagra's work is generally celebratory. Variably voiced, often humorous, the poems themselves are testament to the enriching creative possibilities of cultural hybridity.

The Stopped Train *Jean Sprackland (b.1962)*

The Poem Jean Sprackland's poem 'The Stopped Train' appears in her 2007 collection *Tilt*. The train of the title is personified as a woman and has stopped still in a moment of 'recognition'. At this point of sudden self-awareness the train 'has forgotten' the passengers who 'cram the corridors', 'stunned' as she comes to know herself 'for the first time'. How does Sprackland present the passengers? How do their reactions to their situation compare to what has happened to the train?

The train's realization of her power and strength contrasts with the scene inside the carriage – 'a terrible living-room/filling up with unsaid things' – and with the 'nondescript England' that surrounds them, as alien and hostile to the passengers as California's Death Valley. How do these contrasts affect your view of the train?

Notice how the first and final stanzas are each two lines in length, each starting with 'She stands'; they are parallel like train tracks, holding the experience of the train and the passengers between them in this moment. The list in the penultimate stanza shifts the poem from the depiction of a spiritual experience to an acknowledgement of the physical, as if the train is now aware of herself as a whole. But why a train? Why 'she'?

The Poet Jean Sprackland grew up in Burton upon Trent, before studying English and philosophy at the University of Kent at Canterbury. She began to write poetry at the age of thirty, publishing her first collection, *Tattoos for Mother's Day*, in 1993. Her third volume of poems, *Tilt*, won the Costa Poetry Prize in 2007. Sprackland's non-fiction work *Strands* was inspired by the years she spent living near Ainsdale Sands on the Sefton coast and won the Portico Prize for Literature in 2012.

Sprackland's poetry often pays attention to moments of almost holy mystery in our everyday lives, reaching past what can be said to something ineffable just beyond.

She is currently Reader in Poetry at Manchester Metropolitan University, a trustee of the Poetry Archive and a tutor for Arvon writing courses. She selected with Andrew Motion the poems contained in this *Poetry By Heart* anthology.

Josephine Baker Finds Herself *Patience Agbabi (b.1965)*

The Poem The form of this poem is striking. Notice how the second stanza is a mirror image of the first one, with the line 'the way she looks' acting as a sort of hinge. The technical skill of constructing a palindrome like this, in which sentences have got to make sense in both orders, backwards as well as forwards, is considerable.

The title refers to the legendary American-born singer, actress and dancer Josephine Baker, who found fame and success initially in France in the 1920s. The term '*La Garçonne*' refers to a sexually liberated woman of the period.

Clearly, this monologue dramatizes the traditional poetic subject of falling in love, but the conventional scenario is given a few unconventional tweaks. Firstly, the relationship is set in the modern, urban setting of a nightclub in Brixton where the 'techno [is] so hardcore' it turns sound into complex mechanical objects. Secondly, and more importantly, the two characters are both female. Thirdly, by meeting the lover, the protagonist finds herself.

Notice how the line 'I'm her light-skinned negative' adapts a familiar romantic motif of lovers being two halves of the same person, and so connects the love theme to the poem's title.

The Poet Poet and performer Patience Agbabi was born in London to Nigerian parents. Fostered by white parents, she grew up in Colwyn Bay, where, as a teenager, she fell in love with Northern Soul music and Geoffrey Chaucer. (Her modern retelling of Chaucer's tales was published in 2014.)

After studying English at Oxford and completing an MA in creative writing at Sussex University, Agbabi has lectured in creative writing at various universities.

Agbabi describes herself as 'bi-cultural and bisexual', and her poems often explore issues of gender, sexuality, race and identity. A formalist poet fascinated by transformations and transgressions, Agbabi adopts and adapts traditional poetic forms such as the dramatic monologue and crosses back and forth over the divide between performance and 'written for the page' poetry.

Maren *Mick Imlah (1956–2009)*

The Poem Maren is the name of Mick Imlah's partner, whom he met while working at *The Times Literary Supplement*. This poem is one of a few personal poems included in his collection *The Lost Leader*, which was published a year before Imlah died.

The poem, a direct address to Maren, starts with admiration of her competitive spirit 'like Atlanta'. Imlah alludes to his partner's German heritage through the words 'Schoeness', 'Boetian', 'Lower Franconia' and later the German plane the 'Focke-Wulf'. His own Scottish background is captured in 'Caledonian bore', while the playful references to battling planes continue with the allusion to his 'Spit' [fire]. There is a gentle humour and humility in the race that is described. Imlah writes self-deprecatingly and knows that Maren 'could have romped ahead'.

The direct address, the personal references and almost secret language create a sense of looking in on an intimate relationship that, when this poem was published, had a very real sense of 'an end in view'.

Notice how half-rhymes throughout the poem seem to build up towards the closer rhyme of the final two lines. Consider how this might reflect the relationship. Is 'another orbit' love, bliss, death or something else?

The Poet Mick Imlah published only two collections of poetry during his lifetime: *Birthmarks* in 1998 and *The Lost Leader* in 2008, which won the Forward Prize for Best Collection.

Imlah was born in Aberdeen, Scotland, but when he was ten the family moved south to Kent and he was educated at Dulwich College and then Oxford, where he was part of an influential circle of writers. He later edited the *Poetry Review* and worked as poetry editor for *The Times Literary Supplement* for many years. He continued to work in the final stages of the motor neurone disease from which he died in 2009.

After *Birthmarks*, Imlah published only occasional poems in the *TLS* for many years, before his ambitious, coherent, subtle and tender collection *The Lost Leader* confirmed his reputation as one of the finest poets of his generation. His poetry is characterized by a bleak fatalism, inventiveness and ironic intelligence.

A Verandah Ceremony *E. A. Markham (1939–2008)*

The Poem The poem is informed by the war in Uganda and the vicious brutality inflicted on its people by the Lord's Resistance Army. Markham uses a powerful metaphor in describing how the little vulnerable kitten is torn apart by wild dogs. At one point he compares the savagery of the dogs explicitly to 'a Lord's Resistance Army'. The claws and barking of the wild dogs mirror the weapons of death carried by the soldiers – machetes, spears and rifles.

The use of the kitten inevitably invites comparison with children. A feature of the way the Lord's Resistance Army operates is to target children, with thousands abducted, tortured and used as child soldiers.

Notice how Markham talks of the yard where the kitten died as being 'unfenced'. Are there echoes here of the defencelessness of a people who are being terrorized by the rebel army? What is the impact of Markham's use of repetition with the line 'This is where the kitten died'?

Consider the effect of the haunting last line, significantly separated from the rest of the poem: '*Where the dogs still lie in wait.*'

The Poet E. A. Markham was born in the West Indies and came to England in 1956. He was a lecturer at Kilburn Polytechnic and then founded the Caribbean Theatre Workshop, which toured in the West Indies in the early 1970s.

Markham is best remembered for his witty, sagacious, playful poetry, found in over twenty collections, and his ability to inhabit different personae. He prefaced one collection of poetry with an autobiographical note entitled 'Many Voices. Many Lives', which neatly sums up his life and work.

He edited two major anthologies of Caribbean writing and also wrote highly regarded short stories. He held creative-writing fellowships at various universities and was made Professor Emeritus at Sheffield Hallam in 2005.

Markham always travelled extensively and worked for periods in Germany and Papua New Guinea. He lived for most of his life in England although he moved to Paris three years before his death in 2008.

Conductors of His Mystery *Anthony Joseph (b.1966)*

The Poem At its heart the poem tells a simple, universal story about a father and his son. A fragmentary narrative is sketched out in which the father leaves and then later returns to his family and his home, 'broke and handsome'. Crucial elements of the narrative are left out, such as an explanation of why the father left or what prompted his return. Instead of concrete detail we have subtextual hints, such as the 'wire mesh' of his shop which 'hid his suffer' and a reference to the 'sadness hid'. The 'Shack' he built remained unfinished and is recalled by the son as a place where he stayed briefly with his father at one point. He would have remained there had his father 'asked'. The father is captured as 'legend' and 'myth' but also as 'real' and a subject of touching fascination.

The poem is set in two locations and its language follows a similar double pattern, a home language and a more exotic one. Notice how after the standard English of the first few stanzas the poem shifts with 'Shop he say he build'.

The Poet Anthony Joseph is a poet, novelist, academic and musician who moved from Trinidad to the UK in 1989. A lecturer in creative writing at Birkbeck College, he is particularly interested in the point at which poetry becomes music.

His written work and performance occupies a space between surrealism, jazz and the rhythms of Caribbean speech and music. He is the author of four poetry collections and has released four acclaimed albums. His doctoral thesis explores the life of the Trinidadian calypsonian Lord Kitchener. In 2005 he was selected by the Arts Council of England as one of fifty black and Asian writers who have made major contributions to contemporary British literature.

In his poems Joseph attempts to synthesize the speech rhythms of Trinidad with surrealist and postmodernist techniques. Into this hybrid experimental mix Joseph adds the language and rhythms of the Baptist Church and what he calls 'spontaneous language'.

A Life in Dreams *Jacob Sam-La Rose (b.1976)*

he Poem Sigmund Freud famously argued for the significance of dreams in our lives and, clearly, Sam-La Rose is constructing his poem from familiar dream imagery such as teeth falling out and persecution dreams of being pursued while unable to move quickly because of being stuck in a swamp of 'treacle'. The dreams may be frightening and close to nightmares when a 'fanged leer' and a 'gnarled hand' move menacingly closer, but the poem also captures those dreams that can prompt involuntary smiles and amused pleasure: the dreamer as hero waging war against tyrants and a talented swordsman and a kung-fu master also people the narrative of the poem. The poem recognizes how dreams can take people back to long-forgotten experiences in 'classrooms and corridors' and moments of romance: 'more than a few kisses'.

Notice how Sam-La Rose uses figurative language to convey the distorted, strange-familiar world of dreams. Through simile he turns 'Fear', for example, into an object, 'as solid . . . as table tops'. And in the sensual final image, time becomes solid, but as ephemeral as snow: 'time itself was as delicate as a snowflake/melting on the tongue'.

The Poet Born and raised in South-east London, the poet, educator and editor Jacob Sam-La Rose is a much-admired performer of his own work and has appeared at a wide range of venues and festivals in this country and abroad. He has developed spoken-word programmes with organizations such as the British Council, the National Theatre and the Arvon Foundation, and is particularly well known for his work with youth 'slam' poetry initiatives.

He is recognized as a passionate mentor and supporter of young and emerging poets and an advocate for the positive impact of new technology on literary and artistic practice and collaboration. He has run workshops at hundreds of schools.

His first full-length collection of poetry, *Breaking Silence*, was shortlisted for the Forward Poetry Prize, while his earlier pamphlet, 'Communion', was a Poetry Book Society selection in 2007.

The Death of King Arthur *Simon Armitage (b.1963)*

The Poem This is Simon Armitage's translation of a 1,000-year-old poem, the *Alliterative Morte Arthure*, the author of which is anonymous. As the title suggests, the original was written in alliterative lines and presents stories culminating in the death of King Arthur. In this version, Armitage has retained many of these stylistic patterns, to present a poem that is both true to the original and engaging for modern readers.

In this section of the poem we witness a violent battlefield scene in which Arthur is mortally wounded by his enemy, Mordred. Despite being dealt a wound that is 'half a foot wide', King Arthur finds strength to continue the fight and strikes Mordred 'with Excalibur', his famous sword. He cuts Mordred's arm off from the elbow and then buries 'the bright blade in his body to the handle'.

This poem is one that comes to life when read aloud with alliteration, onomatopoeia and poetic rhythms, adding to the gruesome pleasure of an epic tale.

The Poet One of the most popular and widely read of modern poets, Simon Armitage was born in Huddersfield and studied at Portsmouth University before completing an MA at Manchester University. He worked as a probation officer until 1994 and his early poetry was often inspired by his experiences in the probation service. Currently, he is Professor of Poetry at Sheffield University.

A poet with a particularly acute ear for the rhythms of everyday language, Armitage often writes in a modern, spoken idiom. A charismatic performer of his poetry, with a dry, deadpan delivery, Armitage won widespread acclaim for his retelling of the medieval poem *Sir Gawain and the Green Knight*. As well as his prize-winning poetry, Armitage writes regularly for radio, television, the theatre and film. He won an Ivor Novello Award for his song lyrics for the Channel 4 film *Feltham Sings*.

Langley Lane *Jacob Polley (b.1975)*

The Poem This poem uses a traditional ballad form to tell the modern story of a boy who has been stabbed for being found by other boys on what they consider to be their 'turf'. What has happened is not immediately obvious either to his mother or the reader, as at first the boy speaks elliptically to hide his 'shame'.

In the opening line the mother reprimands the boy for 'slouching'. Her voice is initially dominant, having more lines, repeatedly referring to 'my', 'me' and 'mine' and issuing instructions. The mother recognizes her son's tiredness and swaying but attributes this to the wrong causes, such as his 'half built' adulthood. How do her questions reinforce this sense of the distance between their lives despite their closeness at this moment?

When the gravity of the situation becomes apparent, the son describes the fight. Note how the enjambment in stanza eleven echoes the shove. Nature is then 'still' in reaction to the stabbing; the realization of what has happened takes the boys by surprise, and this is reflected in the pace of the next two stanzas. The mother's voice returns: how does her repetition of 'you walked from Langley Lane' create pathos?

The Poet Jacob Polley has published three collections of poetry, beginning with *The Brink* in 2003. All three were enthusiastically reviewed and established him as an important figure within contemporary poetry. In 2004 he appeared on the influential 'Next Generation' list of poets produced by the Poetry Book Society.

His first novel, *Talk of the Town*, was published in 2009 and won the 2010 Somerset Maugham Award.

He taught at Trinity College, Cambridge, as the Visiting Fellow Commoner in Creative Arts between 2005 and 2007, and was Arts Queensland's poet in residence in 2011.

Polley's observations of the natural world are often precise and haunting and expressed in technically skilful lyrics. He offers an unexpected perspective on everyday things and in his latest collection explores the folklore and mythic traditions of his native Cumbria.

The Fish in Australia *Andrew Motion (b.1952)*

The Poem In this poem a man driving through an Australian desert landscape at sunset pulls off the road and finds a lake, a 'perfect circle/of still and silent water'. It is an unpromising prospect, with 'hard treeless banks' and the water a 'swarthy colour', reminding him of the tears of 'dogs or kangaroos/or dead transported men'. Nonetheless, he takes out fishing gear and casts his line for what he might find in the water.

There is an otherworldliness to the poem, with its pond that might be a secret tunnel, its whispering gang of trees and the 'moon-ghost'. Time is both now and 'a million years ago'; we feel the drag of 'mass' and a line 'as light as human hair'; he catches nothing with his 'frail and useless lash' but casts again, not in the hope of a catch but to tease the 'monster' below. What exactly is it he is fishing for as the light fades?

The first three stanzas of the poem have a certain excitement of anticipation. What happens to that in the longer, middle stanza? How does the mood change after that? Should we fear the impending darkness?

The Poet Andrew Motion was born in London and brought up in rural Essex. He published his first collection of poems in 1976, and since then has won a number of prizes, including the Somerset Maugham Award and the Whitbread Prize for biography. He was UK Poet Laureate from 1999 to 2009, co-founded the Poetry Archive and Poetry By Heart, and was knighted for his services to poetry in 2009. He is Professor of Creative Writing at Royal Holloway College, University of London.

In addition to poetry, Motion has also written a childhood memoir, biographies of Philip Larkin and John Keats, and fiction, including his follow-ups to *Treasure Island – Silver* (2012) and *The New World* (2014).

Acknowledgements

Fleur Adcock: 'The Ex-Queen among the Astronomers' from *Poems 1960–2000*, Bloodaxe Books, 2000; John Agard: 'Toussaint L'Ouverture Acknowledges Wordsworth's Sonnet "To Toussaint L'Ouverture"' from *Alternative Anthem: Selected Poems with Live DVD*, Bloodaxe Books, 2009; Patience Agbabi: 'Josephine Baker Finds Herself' from *Bloodshot Monochrome*, Canongate, 2008; Moniza Alvi: 'The Country at My Shoulder' from *Split World: Poems 1990–2005*, Bloodaxe Books, 2008; Yehuda Amichai: 'My father, in a white space suit' from *Selected Poems*, edited by Ted Hughes and Daniel Weissbort, Faber and Faber, London, and *The Selected Poetry of Yehuda Amichai*, translated by Chana Bloch and Stephen Mitchell, University of California Press, Berkeley, Los Angeles. Reprinted by permission of Hana Amichai and the Estate of Yehuda Amichai; Simon Armitage: extract from *The Death of King Arthur*, Faber and Faber, 2012, and extract from *Sir Gawain and the Green Knight*, Faber and Faber, 2009; W. H. Auden: 'Musée des Beaux Arts' from *Collected Poems*, Faber and Faber, 1994; Elizabeth Bartlett: 'WEA Course' from *Two Women Dancing: New and Selected Poems*, Bloodaxe Books, 1995; Patricia Beer: 'The Lost Woman' from *The Lie of the Land*, Carcanet, 1983; Hilaire Belloc: 'Ha'nacker Mill' from *Sonnets and Verse*, reprinted by permission of Peters Fraser & Dunlop (www.petersfraserdunlop.com) on behalf of the Estate of Hilaire Belloc; James Berry: 'On an Afternoon Train from Purley to Victoria, 1955' from *A Story I Am In*, Bloodaxe Books, 2011; John Berryman: 'I don't operate often' (*Dream Songs* No. 67) from *77 Dream Songs*, Faber and Faber, 2001, reprinted by permission of Faber and Faber and Farrar, Straus and Giroux; John Betjeman: 'The Arrest of Oscar Wilde at the Cadogan Hotel' from *Collected Poems*, John Murray, 2006; Sujata Bhatt: 'What is Worth Knowing?' from *Brunizem*,

Carcanet, 1986; Elizabeth Bishop: 'The Fish' from *Complete Poems*, Chatto, 2004, reprinted by permission of Farrar, Straus and Giroux; Eavan Boland: 'The Black Lace Fan My Mother Gave Me' from *Outside History: Selected Poems 1980–90*, Carcanet, 1990, reprinted by permission of Carcanet and W. W. Norton & Company, Inc.; Kamau Brathwaite: 'Bread' from *Born to Slow Horses* © Kamau Brathwaite. Reprinted by permission of Wesleyan University Press; Gwendolyn Brooks: 'Boy Breaking Glass', reprinted by consent of Brooks Permissions; Colette Bryce: 'The Full Indian Rope Trick' from *The Full Indian Rope Trick*, Picador, 2004; Basil Bunting: 'What the Chairman Told Tom' from *Complete Poems*, Bloodaxe Books, 2000; May Wedderburn Cannan: 'Rouen', reprinted by kind permission of Clara Abrahams; Charles Causley: 'Ballad of the Bread Man' from *Collected Poems 1951–2000*, Picador, 2000; C. P. Cavafy: 'The God Abandons Antony' from *Collected Poems*, translated by Edward Keeley and Philip Sherrard, edited by George Savidis, Princeton University Press, 1992 © C.P. Cavafy 1948/54/63/66/68. Reproduced by permission of the Estate of C.P. Cavafy c/o Rogers, Coleridge & White, 20 Powis Mews, London, W11 1JN; Gillian Clarke: 'Border' from *Collected Poems*, Carcanet, 1989; Wendy Cope: 'Proverbial Ballade' from *Making Cocoa for Kingsley Amis*, Faber and Faber, 1986; David Dabydeen: 'Catching Crabs' from *Turner: New and Selected Poems*, Peepal Tree Press, 2003; Elizabeth Daryush: 'Still-Life' from *Collected Poems*, Carcanet, 1976; Walter de la Mare: 'Miss Loo', by kind permission of the Estate of Walter de la Mare c/o The Society of Authors; Imtiaz Dharker: 'Minority' from *Postcards from God*, Bloodaxe Books, 1997; Michael Donaghy: 'Machines' from *Conjure*, Picador, 2000; Maura Dooley: 'Explaining Magnetism' from *Sound Barrier: Poems, 1982–2002*, Bloodaxe Books, 2002; Rita Dove: 'Ö' from *The Yellow House on the Corner*, Carnegie Mellon University Press, 1980. Reprinted by permission of the author; Jane Draycott: 'Prince Rupert's Drop' from *Prince Rupert's Drop*, Carcanet, 1999; Carol Ann Duffy: 'Originally' from *The Other Country*, Picador, 2010 © Carol Ann Duffy, 1990. Reproduced by permission of the author c/o Rogers, Coleridge & White Ltd, 20 Powis Mews, London W11 1JN; Ian Duhig: 'The Lammas Hireling' from *The Lammas Hireling*, Picador, 2013; T.S. Eliot: 'Journey of the Magi' from *Collected Poems 1909–1962*, Faber and Faber, 2002; William Empson: 'Aubade' from *The Complete Poems*, Penguin, 2001. Reprinted with permission of Curtis Brown Group Ltd, London, on behalf of the Estate of William Empson. Copyright © William Empson, 1949; U.A. Fanthorpe: 'The Cleaner' from *New and Collected Poems*, Enitharmon Press, 2012; Paul Farley: 'A Minute's Silence' from *The Boy from the Chemist is Here to See You*, Picador, 1998; Vicki Feaver: 'Judith' from *The Handless Maiden*, Jonathan Cape, 1994. Reprinted by permission of The Random House Group Limited; James Fenton: 'God, A Poem' from *The Memory of War and Children in Exile*, Penguin, 1984, reprinted by permission of United Agents; Roy Fisher: 'Birmingham River' from *The Long & the Short of It: Poems 1955–2010*, Bloodaxe Books, 2012; Carolyn Forché: 'The Colonel' from *The Country Between Us*, HarperCollins, 1981 © Carolyn Forché. Originally appeared in Women's International Resource Exchange. Reproduced by permission of HarperCollins Publishers and the William Morris Agency; Allen Ginsberg: 'A Supermarket in California' from *Collected Poems 1947–1997*, Penguin Modern Classics, 2009 © 1956, Allen Ginsberg, LLC., used by permission of The Wylie Agency (UK) Limited; W.S. Graham: 'The Beast in the Space' from *New Collected Poems*, Faber and Faber, 2004, reprinted by permission of Rosalind Mudaliar, Estate of W.S. Graham; Robert Graves: 'Welsh Incident' from *Collected Poems*, Carcanet, 1995; Lavinia Greenlaw: 'Love from a Foreign City' from *Love from a Foreign City*, Slow Dancer Press, 1992, used by permission of The Wylie Agency (UK) Limited; Thom Gunn: 'Considering the Snail' from *Collected Poems*, Faber and Faber, 1994; Choman Hardi: 'Two Pages' from *Life for Us*, Bloodaxe Books, 2004; Tony Harrison: 'Timer' from *Selected Poems*, Penguin, 1984. Reproduced by permission of the poet; Seamus Heaney: 'St Kevin and the Blackbird' from *Opened Ground: Poems 1966–1996*, Faber and Faber, 2002, and extract from *Beowulf*, Faber and Faber, 1999;

Geoffrey Hill: 'The Kingdom of Offa' (*Mercian Hymns* VII)' from *Mercian Hymns*, Penguin Books, 1992. Copyright © Geoffrey Hill, 1971; Michael Hofmann: 'Marvin Gaye' from *Corona, Corona*, Faber, 1993, reprinted by permission of United Agents; Ted Hughes: 'Wind' from *Collected Poems*, Faber and Faber, 2003; Mick Imlah: 'Maren' from *The Lost Leader*, Faber and Faber, 2008; Kathleen Jamie: 'The Way We Live' from *Mr and Mrs Scotland are Dead: Poems 1980–1994*, Bloodaxe Books, 2002; Linton Kwesi Johnson: 'Sonny's Lettah' from *Selected Poems*, Penguin Books, 2006 (first published as *Mi Revalueshanary Fren*, Penguin Classics, 2002). Copyright © Linton Kwesi Johnson, 2002, 2006; David Jones: 'A, a, a, Domine Deus' from *The Sleeping Lord and Other Fragments*, 1974. Reproduced with the permission of the Trustees of the Estate of David Jones; Anthony Joseph: 'Conductors of His Mystery' from *Bird Head Son*, Salt, 2009 © Anthony Joseph; Patrick Kavanagh: 'Epic' from *Collected Poems*, edited by Antoinette Quinn, Allen Lane, 2004, reprinted by kind permission of the Trustees of the Estate of the late Katherine B. Kavanagh, through the Jonathan Williams Literary Agency; Jackie Kay: 'Dusting the Phone' from *Darling: New and Selected Poems*, Bloodaxe Books, 2007; Mimi Khalvati: 'Rubaiyat' from *In White Ink*, Carcanet, 1991; Philip Larkin: 'Mr Bleaney' from *The Complete Poems*, Faber and Faber, 2012; Denise Levertov: 'To the Snake' from *Selected Poems*, New Directions, 2004, reprinted by permission of Pollinger Limited and New Directions; Alun Lewis: 'Goodbye' from *Alun Lewis: Collected Poems*, ed. Cary Archard, Seren, 2007; Christopher Logue: *Patrocleia* from *War Music*, Faber and Faber, 2001, by kind permission of the Estate of Christopher Logue c/o David Godwin Associates; Michael Longley: 'Wounds' from *An Exploded View* © Michael Longley, 2014. Reprinted by permission of LAW Ltd; Robert Lowell: 'Skunk Hour' from *Collected Poems*, edited by Frank Bidart and David Gewanter, Faber, 2003, reprinted by permission of Farrar, Straus and Giroux; Claude McKay: 'Harlem Shadows', reprinted courtesy of the Literary Estate for the Works of Claude McKay; Louis MacNeice: 'Bagpipe Music' from *Collected*

Poems, Faber and Faber, 2007; Derek Mahon: 'A Disused Shed in Co. Wexford' from *New Collected Poems*, Gallery Press, 2011, by kind permission of the author and The Gallery Press, Loughcrew, Oldcastle, County Meath, Ireland; John Masefield: 'Partridges', by kind permission of the Estate of John Masefield c/o The Society of Authors; Glyn Maxwell: 'The Eater' from *Boys at Twilight: Poems 1990–1995*, Bloodaxe Books, 2000; Elma Mitchell: 'Thoughts after Ruskin' from *People Etcetera: Poems New and Selected*, Peterloo Poets, 1987; Marianne Moore: 'Poetry' from *Complete Poems*, Faber and Faber, 2003, reprinted by permission of Faber and Faber and Farrar, Straus and Giroux; Edwin Morgan: 'Strawberries' from *Collected Poems*, Carcanet, 1990; Andrew Motion: 'The Fish in Australia', by kind permission of the poet; Paul Muldoon: 'Meeting the British' from *New Selected Poems*, Faber and Faber, 1996; Daljit Nagra: 'Look We Have Coming to Dover!' from *Look We Have Coming to Dover!*, Faber and Faber, 2007; Grace Nichols: 'Blackout' from *Sunris*, Virago, 1996. Reproduced with permission of Curtis Brown Group Ltd, London, on behalf of Grace Nichols. Copyright © Grace Nichols, 1996; Sean O'Brien: 'Cousin Coat' from *Cousin Coat: Selected Poems 1976–2001*, Picador, 2003; Frank O'Hara: 'The Day Lady Died' from *Lunch Poems*. Copyright © 1964 by Frank O'Hara. Reprinted by permission of City Lights Books; Alice Oswald: 'Wedding' from *The Thing in the Gap-stone Style*, Faber and Faber, 2007; Don Paterson: 'Walking with Russell' from *Selected Poems*, Faber and Faber, 2013 © Don Paterson. Reproduced by permission of the author c/o Rogers, Coleridge & White Ltd, 20 Powis Mews, London W11 1JN; Sylvia Plath: 'Morning Song' from *Collected Poems*, Faber and Faber, 1981; Jacob Polley: 'Langley Lane' from *The Havocs*, 2012; Peter Porter: 'Your Attention Please' © Peter Porter, 1962. Reproduced by permission of the Estate of Peter Porter c/o Rogers, Coleridge & White Ltd, 20 Powis Mews, London W11 1JN; Craig Raine: 'A Martian Sends a Postcard Home' from *Collected Poems 1978–1999*, Picador, 1999. Reprinted by permission of the author c/o David Godwin Associates; Henry Reed: 'Naming of Parts', reprinted by kind permission of the

Royal Literary Fund; Denise Riley: 'A Misremembered Lyric' from *Selected Poems*, Reality Street, 2000; Michael Symmons Roberts: 'Pelt' from *Corpus*, Jonathan Cape, 2004. Reprinted by permission of The Random House Group; Theodore Roethke: 'My Papa's Waltz' from *The Collected Poems of Theodore Roethke*, Doubleday © Theodore Roethke, reprinted by permission of the publishers; Jacob Sam-La Rose: 'A Life in Dreams', reprinted by permission of the poet; Carol Rumens: E.J. Scovell: 'After Midsummer' from *Collected Poems*, Carcanet, 1988; Jo Shapcott: 'Phrase Book' from *Her Book: Poems 1988–1998*, Faber and Faber, 2006; Owen Sheers: 'Mametz Wood' from *Skirrid Hill*, Seren, 2005 © Owen Sheers, 2005. Reproduced by permission of the author c/o Rogers, Coleridge & White, 20 Powis Mews, London W11 1JN; Edith Sitwell: 'Heart and Mind' from *Collected Poems*, reprinted by permission of Peters, Fraser & Dunlop on behalf of the Estate of Edith Sitwell; Stevie Smith: 'The Galloping Cat' from *Collected Poems and Drawings*, Faber and Faber, 2014; Jean Sprackland: 'The Stopped Train' from *Tilt*, Jonathan Cape, 2007. Reprinted by permission of The Random House Group; Anne Stevenson: 'A Summer Place' from *Poems 1955–2005*, Bloodaxe Books, 2005; Dylan Thomas: 'The force that through the green fuse drives the flower' from *Collected Poems 1934–1953*, Phoenix, 2003, used by permission of David Higham Associates, London, as agents for the Trustees of the copyrights of Dylan Thomas; R.S. Thomas: 'On the Farm' from *Collected Poems*, J.M. Dent, 1993 © R.S Thomas, 1993; Rosemary Tonks: 'Badly Chosen Lover' from *Iliad of Broken Sentences* © Rosemary Tonks, 1967. Reproduced by permission of Sheil Land Associates Ltd; Derek Walcott: 'Sea Canes' from *The Poetry of Derek Walcott 1948–2013*, Faber and Faber, 2014, reprinted by permission of Faber and Faber and Farrar, Straus and Giroux; Anna Wickham: 'Divorce', originally privately published in *Songs of John Oland*, 1911, reprinted in *The Writings of Anna Wickham: Free Woman and Poet*, Virago Press, 1984. Reprinted by permission of the Hepburn family; Kit Wright: 'The Boys Bump-starting the Hearse' from *Hoping It Might Be So: Poems 1974–2000*, Faber and Faber,

2008; Benjamin Zephaniah: 'It's Work' from *Too Black, Too Strong*, Bloodaxe Books, 2001 © Benjamin Zephaniah, reprinted by permission of United Agents (www.unitedagents.co.uk) on behalf of Benjamin Zephaniah.

While every effort has been made to contact copyright holders, the publishers will be happy to correct any error of omission or commission at the earliest opportunity.

Index of First Lines